Reactionary modernism

Reactionary modernism

Technology, culture, and politics in Weimar and the Third Reich

JEFFREY HERF

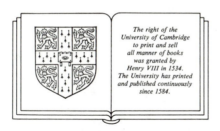

The right of the
University of Cambridge
to print and sell
all manner of books
was granted by
Henry VIII in 1534.
The University has printed
and published continuously
since 1584.

CAMBRIDGE UNIVERSITY PRESS
Cambridge
London   New York   New Rochelle
Melbourne   Sydney

Published by the Press Syndicate of the University of Cambridge
The Pitt Building, Trumpington Street, Cambridge CB2 1RP
32 East 57th Street, New York, NY 10022, USA
10 Stamford Road, Oakleigh, Melbourne 3166, Australia

First published 1984
First paperback edition 1986

Printed in the United States of America

Library of Congress Cataloging in Publication Data
Herf, Jeffrey, 1947–
Reactionary modernism.
Revision of the author's thesis (Brandeis University)
Bibliography: p.
1. Germany – History – 1918–1933. 2. Germany – Intellec-
tual life – 20th century. 3. Enlightment – Influence.
I. Title
DD238.H45   1984   943.086   84 – 3227
ISBN 0 521 26566 5 hard covers
ISBN 0 521 33833 6 paperback

To my parents

Contents

Preface	*page*	ix
1.	The paradox of reactionary modernism	1
2.	The conservative revolution in Weimar	18
3.	Oswald Spengler: bourgeois antinomies, reactionary reconciliations	49
4.	Ernst Jünger's magical realism	70
5.	Technology and three mandarin thinkers	109
6.	Werner Sombart: technology and the Jewish question	130
7.	Engineers as ideologues	152
8.	Reactionary modernism in the Third Reich	189
9.	Conclusion	217
	Bibliographical essay	237
	Index	245

Preface

With this study of the paradoxical and truncated manner in which the German Right incorporated the Enlightenment, I wish to accentuate the positive contributions the Enlightenment has made to modern life. Germany's scientific and technological advances occurred without the benefit of a vital tradition of political liberalism. Nevertheless, many observers concluded that Hitler's evil had its origins in an excess of reason, a view that lies behind much of contemporary cultural pessimism. But Enlightenment reason meant more and other than the means–ends rationality of bureaucratic terror. It is not the Enlightenment but its inadequate and partial incorporation into German society that should be condemned – and understood.

This study is also meant as a reminder that ideas matter, and more specifically, that simplistic explanations of the causes and consequences of technological change can have and have had dangerous political consequences. During a period in which the Western democracies are facing the challenges of the third industrial revolution of computers and telecommunications, a study of the German response to the second industrial revolution has some contemporary significance. Today many intellectuals in West Germany and the West generally are less enthusiastic about the prospects offered by technological changes than the reactionary modernists were. But the mistrust of reason and the inclination to endow technology with qualities it does not possess, while remaining largely ignorant of its inherent technical features, continues to bedevil relations between technology and the soul.

As I worked on this book I could not help noticing the similarity between reactionary modernism and the technologically and financially well-endowed fanaticisms of the Third World. During the 1960s, it became fashionable to decry the application of the European experience to the non-Western world. Unique as the West is, contemporary events in the Third World suggest that, as Ralf Dahrendorf pointed out almost twenty years ago, Germany remains the first new nation, showing their future to the less developed. As long as nationalism remains a potent force, something like reactionary modernism will continue to confront us. The prospects for a better world will not be aided by an illiberal alliance between Western intellectuals who have lost faith in the Enlightenment, and those of the developing nations who mistakenly equate modernity with technology alone.

This book is a study of a cultural tradition and its impact on politics, two dimensions of historical and social analysis that I believe have been too often separated in the social sciences of late. Despite the bluster of recent advocates of "structural" analysis, the evidence returns us to the view that political ideas and cultural traditions are not of lesser significance than structures of classes or states. Any serious student of National Socialism must look upon the social scientific disregard of meaning and intentionality in politics as nothing short of a repetition of the illusions of the Weimar Republic that Hitler exploited so effectively.

When I began this study, I hoped it would demonstrate the usefulness of central categories taken from the Frankfurt school's critical theory of society in explaining historical and political developments. In writing the book, however, I became convinced that the theory that launched the investigation was deeply flawed. Theodor Adorno and Max Horkheimer's idea of the dialectic of enlightenment, as well as Herbert Marcuse's views on technology and society, offered a wealth of insights and questions without which my interpretation of reactionary modernism would not have come into being. The controversy surrounding Marcuse's views on technology and society was an important starting point of this book. Ironically a good deal of whatever insight this interpretive essay contains grows from wrestling with ideas I no longer find convincing. Whether or not I have seen further by standing on the shoulders of these figures is up to the reader to decide. But my debt to the critical theorists remains significant.

I have received support, criticism, and inspiration from many people in the course of this study. This book first took shape as a dissertation in the Department of Sociology at Brandeis University. Kurt Wolff served as the thesis director, offering warm support, critical commentary, and encouragement for a study of the relation between culture, society, and politics. Egon Bittner, who also supervised the dissertation, asked penetrating questions concerning the role of technology in modern societies that forced a better focusing of the issues.

Paul Breines, also a member of the dissertation committee, contributed his considerable insight into cultural radicalism in Central Europe, as well as friendship and support for many years. Carmen Sirianni made probing comments on the dissertation that were useful as I expanded it to encompass the later years of the Third Reich.

George Mosse introduced me to the study of modern European history, culture, and society, offered encouragement, wisdom, and friendship for many years, and commented on the earlier manuscript. The questions raised by his studies of the origins of Nazi ideology provided one of the crucial starting points of this work. Anson Rabinbach commented on the manuscript, inspired parts of it through his own work on National Socialism, social theory, and modern European social and cultural history, and discussed the major issues of the book at length over a period of many years. I am grateful for his enduring friendship and support that have helped to make this book possible.

I would like to acknowledge the financial support of the German Academic Exchange Service for my dissertation research in Frankfurt am Main in 1978–9. At the University of Frankfurt, Iring Fetscher, Ansgar Hillach, and Eike Hennig were most helpful in suggesting connections between discussions in social theory in West Germany today, and the issues raised in this book. Moishe Postone, studying in Frankfurt while I was doing research there, contributed valuable suggestions concerning the origins of anti-Semitism. Although they may take issue with my conclusions, their stimulating company was typical of Frankfurt's lively intellectual community. Alphonse Sollner, now at the Otto Suhr Institute in West Berlin, gladly shared his insights into the Frankfurt school's analysis of National Socialism.

While working on this book I had the benefit of another intellectual community, that of Harvard University. I was fortunate that David Landes, whose own work on technology and society in modern Europe is a starting point for many studies, was serving as chairman of the Committee on Degrees in Social Studies. His support, interest, and wisdom were generously offered. Assisting Daniel Bell in his course on technology and society was the beginning of an extended opportunity to benefit from his thinking on the connection between technological change and social and cultural trends.

Stanley Hoffmann, director of the Center for European Studies, has created an atmosphere conducive to interdisciplinary scholarship. Many conversations with my colleagues there and in Social Studies have helped to clarify arguments: Bill Buxton, Eric Goldhagen, Harvey Goldmann, Stephen Holmes, Richard Hunt, Stephen Kalberg, Ken

Keulman, Charles Maier, Harvey Rishikoff, Michael Smith, Judith Eisenberg Vichniac, and Jeff Weintraub were particularly helpful. Thanks are also due to my students, especially Daniel Goldhagen, who patiently listened to descriptions of "those bizarre engineers" and offered most helpful criticisms. Allan Silver, of Columbia University's Department of Sociology, contributed his insights into social theory, and engineers and politics in comparative perspective.

Classes and then friendship with Professor Hans Gerth, of the Sociology Department of the University of Wisconsin and later, briefly at the University of Frankfurt, were one of the starting points of my interest in social theory and the paradoxes of modern German society. His untimely death only several months after he received me in Frankfurt with his customary graciousness is the source of a particular sadness. If this book succeeds in blending history with the analysis of society, politics, and culture, it will do so in part because of Hans Gerth's belief that this is how sociology ought to be done.

All the people who participated through their friendship and support deserve more than a brief mention: Seyla Ben-Habib, Jessica Benjamin, Stephanie Engel, Art Goldhammer, David Held, Andy Markovits, Thomas McCarthy, Jerry Muller, Larry Simon, Dave Slaney, Peggy Somers, Charles Sowerwine, John Wechter, and Fred van Gelder.

Finally my wife, Sonya Michel, shared in this book from its very beginnings, giving it careful and honest appraisals based on her own incisive understanding of social history and cultural politics in America. Her companionship, intelligence, fine criticism, and warm humor have contributed immeasurably to this book and its author's life. Nadja Simone arrived in time to enliven and bring added joy to the completion of this project. A special thanks is due to my parents, Ernst Herf and Jane Vlier, whose support and understanding have been unflagging. To them this book is dedicated.

1

The paradox of reactionary
modernism

There is no such thing as modernity in general. There are only national societies, each of which becomes modern in its own fashion.
This study examines a cultural paradox of German modernity, namely,
the embrace of modern technology by German thinkers who rejected
Enlightenment reason. Dichotomies – tradition or modernity, progress or reaction, community or society, rationalization or charisma –
predominate in sociological theories of the development of European
modernity. When applied to modern German history, such dichotomies suggest that German nationalism, and subsequently National
Socialism, was primarily motivated by rejections of modernity – the
political values of the French Revolution and the economic and social
realities created by the Industrial Revolution. Romantic Germany, we
are told, rejected scientistic modernity. Had the pastoral vision van-
quished technological advance, German modernity would not have
led to the German catastrophe. In this study of a cultural tradition I
have called reactionary modernism, I am advocating a more nuanced
view of German ideology in the Weimar Republic and the Third
Reich.

My basic point is the following: Before and after the Nazi seizure
of power, an important current within conservative and subsequently
Nazi ideology was a reconciliation between the antimodernist, romantic, and irrationalist ideas present in German nationalism and the
most obvious manifestation of means–ends rationality, that is, modern
technology. Reactionary modernism is an ideal typical construct. The
thinkers I am calling reactionary modernists never described themselves in precisely these terms. But this tradition consisted of a coherent and meaningful set of metaphors, familiar words, and
emotionally laden expressions that had the effect of converting technology from a component of alien, Western *Zivilisation* into an organic
part of German *Kultur*. They combined political reaction with tech-

nological advance. Where German conservatives had spoken of technology *or* culture, the reactionary modernists taught the German Right to speak of technology *and* culture. Reactionary modernism was not primarily a pragmatic or tactical reorientation, which is not to deny that it transformed military-industrial necessities into national virtues. Rather, it incorporated modern technology into the cultural system of modern German nationalism, without diminishing the latter's romantic and antirational aspects. The reactionary modernists were nationalists who turned the romantic anticapitalism of the German Right away from backward-looking pastoralism, pointing instead to the outlines of a beautiful new order replacing the formless chaos due to capitalism in a united, technologically advanced nation. In so doing, they contributed to the persistence of Nazi ideology throughout the Hitler regime. They called for a revolution from the Right that would restore the primacy of politics and the state over economics and the market, and thereby restore the ties between romanticism and rearmament in Germany.

Though I call them reactionary modernists, these thinkers viewed themselves as cultural revolutionaries seeking to consign materialism to the past. In their view, materialism and technology were by no means identical. Thomas Mann captured the essence of reactionary modernism when he wrote that "the really characteristic and dangerous aspect of National Socialism was its mixture of robust modernity and an affirmative stance toward progress combined with dreams of the past: a highly technological romanticism."[1] This book presents what Mann grasped as the interpenetration of German *Innerlichkeit* (inwardness) and modern technology.

The German reconciliation of technology and unreason began in German technical universities around the turn of the century, was first advocated by the nontechnical intellectuals in Weimar's conservative revolution, found a home in the Nazi party in the 1920s and among the propagandists of the Hitler regime in the 1930s, and became a contributing factor in the triumph of totalitarian ideology up to 1945. The bearers of this tradition were numerous professors of engineering as well as contributors to journals published by the na-

Thomas Mann, "Deutschland und die Deutschen," in *Thomas Mann: Essays*, Band 2, *Politik*, ed. Herman Kunzke (Frankfurt, 1977), p. 294. For a critique of dichotomous theories of the development of "industrial society," see Anthony Giddens, "Classical Social Theory and the Origins of Modern Sociology," *American Journal of Sociology* 81 (1976), pp. 703–29. Also see John Norr's essay, "German Social Theory and the Hidden Face of Technology," *European Journal of Sociology* XV (1974), pp. 312–36.

tional engineering associations. In Weimar's conservative revolution the irrationalist embrace of technology was advocated by Hans Freyer, Ernest Jünger, Carl Schmitt, Werner Sombart, and Oswald Spengler, with Martin Heidegger adding a more ambivalent voice to the reactionary modernist chorus. Within the Nazi party, Gottfried Feder's theories of the threat of Jewish finance to German productivity were eventually supplemented by a more subtle diction of romanticism and modern technics under the direction of Joseph Goebbels and Fritz Todt, the administrator of the construction of the *Autobahnen* and Hitler's first armaments minister. Throughout, the reactionary modernists contributed to the coexistence of political irrationalism alongside rearmament and industrial rationalization. By the end of the war, for example, the SS research station in Peenemünde developing V-1 and V-2 rockets was engaged in a desperate search for a weapon that would miraculously turn the tide of the now obviously lost war.

It is not paradoxical to reject technology as well as Enlightenment reason or to embrace technology while celebrating reason. These pairings are the customary outcomes of choosing between scientism and pastoralism. But it is paradoxical to reject the Enlightenment and embrace technology at the same time, as did the reactionary modernists in Germany. Their claim was that Germany could be *both* technologically advanced *and* true to its soul. The whole anti-Western legacy of German nationalism suggested that such a reconciliation between soul and technology was out of the question, for nothing could be more at odds with German culture. But the reactionary modernists recognized that antitechnological views were formulas for national impotence. The state could not be simultaneously strong and technologically backward. The reactionary modernists insisted that the *Kulturnation* could be both powerful and true to its soul. As Joseph Goebbels repeatedly insisted, this was to be the century of *stählernde Romantik*, steellike romanticism.

A fundamental point to be made about National Socialism is that Hitler's ideology was the decisive political fact of the Nazi regime up to the catastrophic end. Very few of Hitler's conservative allies and left-wing opponents expected this would be the case. Some argued that Hitler was a cynical opportunist who would abandon principle for the sake of power. Others simply could not accept the idea that anyone or any large number of people would take such a contemptible blend of irrationality and inhumanity seriously. And still others, at the time and since, argued that National Socialism was fundamentally a complete rejection of the modern world and its values. As such, its ideological dynamism would be broken apart in the course of actually governing and administering the most advanced industrial society in Europe. Why this did not happen has been the focus of a scholarly debate ever since.[2]

In this book, I am bringing interpretive sociology to bear on this problem. As Max Weber put it, sociology is an interpretive endeavor because it can offer causal explanations of social action only to the degree to which such analyses are simultaneously adequate on the level of meaning. Hence, in order to contribute to a causal explanation of the primacy of politics and ideology in Nazi Germany, I have focused on motives, meanings, intentions, and symbolism and have depicted an ideal typical world view I am calling reactionary modernism. In the last decade, a split has opened up between analysts of politics and analysts of meaning and intentionality. On the one hand, militant structuralists have told us that human intentions count for little in the larger scheme determined by classes, states, and the international system. On the other hand, equally militant phenomenologists have abandoned the field of political and historical analysis. This split expresses itself in a linguistic barbarism: "macro-" versus "micro-" sociology. Of late, the militants seem to be a bit less bellicose, and the idea of paying attention to what people actually think and believe has become respectable again. This has nothing to do with social science going "soft" in the head but rather with Weber's point that explanation of social and political events requires careful examination of the meaning and intentionality of actors in a particular historical and social context. In this sense his works on the emergence of the modern state, bureaucracy, or the spirit of capitalism from the psychological anxieties fostered by the Protestant sects are "structural" analyses. This project is elusive and difficult for it calls for examination of the links between socioeconomic structure, cultural trends, and politics. This is, or ought to be, one of the sociologist's main tasks, and it is one of my aims to proceed along these lines in this study. In the remainder of this chapter, I will situate this work in past efforts to grapple with National Socialism and modernity and will define the terms of discussion.

Interpreters of National Socialism have placed the cultural and political revolt against modernity at the center of discussions of Nazi ideology. Georg Lukács called Germany the "classic nation of irra-

---

[2] For an overview of the current debate, see Karl Dietrich Bracher, "The Role of Hitler: The Problem of Underestimation," pp. 211–25, and Hans Mommsen, "National Socialism – Continuity and Change," pp. 179–210, both in *Fascism: A Reader's Guide*, ed. Walter Laqueur (Berkeley, 1976).

4

tionalism." Helmut Plessner's view of the "belated nation," George Mosse's studies of *"völkisch* ideology," Karl Mannheim's work on "conservative thought," and Fritz Stern's analysis of "the politics of cultural despair" all stressed the connection between right-wing ideology and protest against the Enlightenment, modern science, liberalism, the market, Marxism, and the Jews. Talcott Parsons argued that "at least one critically important aspect of the National Socialist movement" was "a mobilization of the extremely deep-seated romantic tendencies of German society in the service of a violently aggressive political movement, incorporating a 'fundamentalist' revolt against the whole tendency of the rationalization of the Western world."[3] Henry J. Turner has recently summarized the analysis presented by modernization theorists. National Socialism, he writes, was the product of a "crisis of modernization." Ideologically it stood for "utopian antimodernism ... an extreme revolt against the modern industrial world and an attempt to recapture a distant mythic past." National Socialist antimodernism contrasted with Italian fascism, with its Futurist fascination with speed and the beauty of machines.[4]

Germany's path to modernity lay behind the intensity of its antimodernist revolt. Compared with England and France, industrialization was late, quick, and thorough. Economic units were large and state intervention extensive. Most important, capitalist industrializa-

---

[3] Georg Lukács, *Die Zerstörung der Vernunft* (Darmstadt, 1962); Helmut Plessner, *Die verspätete Nation* (Frankfurt, 1974); George Mosse, *The Crisis of German Ideology* (New York, 1964); Karl Mannheim, "Conservative Thought," in *From Karl Mannheim*, ed. Kurt Wolff (New York, 1971), p. 132; Fritz Stern, *The Politics of Cultural Despair* (New York, 1961); Talcott Parsons, "Democracy and Social Structure in Pre-Nazi Germany," in *Essays in Sociological Theory* (New York, 1964), p. 123. Also see his "Some Sociological Aspects of Fascist Movements," pp. 124–41 in the same volume. Fritz Ringer documented antimodernist views among German university professors in the humanities and social sciences in *The Decline of the German Mandarins* (Cambridge, Mass., 1969).

[4] Henry J. Turner, "Fascism and Modernization," in *Reappraisals of Fascism* (New York, 1975), pp. 117–39. James Gregor, who focuses on Italy, interprets fascism as an industrializing and modernizing movement, as well as a developmental dictatorship. See James Gregor, "Fascism and Modernization: Some Addenda," *World Politics* 26 (1974), pp. 382–4; *Interpretations of Fascism* (Morristown, N.J., 1974); and *The Fascist Persuasion in Radical Politics* (Princeton, N.J., 1974). On the shared antiindustrialism of the far Left and far Right in Weimar see Helga Grebing, *Linksradikalismus gleich Rechtsradikalismus: Eine falsche Gleichung* (Stuttgart, 1969), esp. ch. 3, "Antiindustrie gesellschaftliche Kultur-, Zivilisations-, und Kapitalismuskritik," pp. 37–50; Rene Konig, "Zur Soziologie der Zwanziger Jahre: oder Ein Epilogue zu zwei Revolutionen, die niemals stattgefunden haben, und was daraus für unsere Gëgenrat resultiert," in *Die Zeit ohne Eigenschaften: Eine Bilanz der Zwanziger Jahre*, ed. Leonard Rheinisch (Stuttgart, 1961), pp. 82–118; Claus Offe, "Technik und Eindimensionalität: Eine Version der Technokratie-these?" in *Antworten auf Herbert Marcuse*, ed. Jürgen Habermas (Frankfurt, 1968), pp. 73–88.

tion took place without a successful bourgeois revolution. The bourgeoisie, political liberalism, and the Enlightenment remained weak.[5] Whereas the concept of the state in England and France was associated with democracy and equality, in Germany it remained authoritarian and illiberal.[6] In Ralf Dahrendorf's words, the "explosive potential of recent German social development" lay in the "encounter and combination" of rapid industrialization and the "inherited structures of the dynastic state of Prussia," an encounter that left little space for political and economic liberalism.[7] German nationalism was largely a countermovement expressing longings for a simpler, preindustrial life. The *Volk* needed to be protected from the corrupting influences of Western *Zivilisation*.

How then did German nationalism, and subsequently National Socialism, become reconciled to modern technology? Barrington Moore, Jr., drew the reasonable conclusion that "the basic limitation" of this "Catonist" rural imagery lay in its uncompromising hostility to industrialism as a result of which it would develop into rural nostalgia.[8] Dahrendorf and David Schoenbaum further developed the idea that Nazi ideology was incompatible with industrial society. Dahrendorf argued that despite their antimodernist ideology, the demands of totalitarian power made the Nazis radical innovators. The "strong push to modernity" was National Socialism's decisive feature resulting in a striking conflict between Nazi ideology and practice. The "veil of ideology should not deceive us," for the gap between ideology and practice was so striking that "one is almost tempted to believe that the ideology was simply an effort to mislead people deliberately."[9] Along similar lines, Schoenbaum described National Socialism as a "double revolution," that is, an ideological war against bourgeois and industrial society waged with bourgeois and industrial means. In his view, the conflict between the antiindustrial outlook of the Nazi ideologues and the modernizing practice of the Nazi regime was resolved through an "inevitable rapprochement" between the Nazi mass movement and the state and industrial elites the movement had promised to destroy. In Schoenbaum's view, the Nazis made their peace with modern tech-

---

[5] On Germany's illiberal path to modernity, see Ralf Dahrendorf, *Society and Democracy in Germany* (New York, 1966).

[6] Karl Dietrich Bracher, *The German Dictatorship*, trans. Jean Steinberg (New York, 1970).

[7] Dahrendorf, *Society and Democracy in Germany*, p. 45.

[8] Barrington Moore, Jr., *The Social Origins of Dictatorship and Democracy* (Boston, 1966), esp. pp. 484–508. Thorstein Veblen made a similar argument in his classic work, *Imperial Germany and the Industrial Revolution* (Ann Arbor, Mich., 1966).

[9] Dahrendorf, *Society and Democracy in Germany*, pp. 381–6.

nology because it was needed to carry out their antimodernist politics, but not because they could discern any intrinsic value in it.[10]

Dahrendorf's and Schoenbaum's views recall Hermann Rauschning's analysis of Hitlerism as a "revolution of nihilism" guided by an utterly cynical, opportunistic set of rationalizations passing themselves off as a world view.[11] The problem is that in too many very important instances, Hitler's practice coincided with his ideology. If ideology and practice were so at odds, how do we account for their terrifying unity during the war and the Holocaust? The thesis of a "double revolution" suggests ideological cynicism where ideological consistency and belief existed. The "strong push to modernity" or at least to certain aspects of modern society existed, but not at the expense of Nazi ideology. Both Dahrendorf and Schoenbaum underestimated the degree to which a selective embrace of modernity – especially modern technology – had already taken place within German nationalism both before and after the Nazi seizure of power in 1933.

The main problem with this approach has been its neglect of the modern aspects of Nazi ideology. Marxists have had little difficulty in this regard because they have examined the Hitler regime as one variant of fascism that, in turn, was a form of capitalism. At times, such analyses suggest that Hitler was merely a tool of the capitalists or that Nazi ideology actually declined in importance after the seizure of power.[12] And at their best, such as Franze Neumann's classic *Behemoth*, they employ a utilitarian concept of class and ideology that rules out the possibility that the Hitler regime could act against the interests of German capital – as indeed it did when it pursued racial utopia and genocide above all else.[13] The route is different, but the

---

[10] David Schoenbaum, *Hitler's Social Revolution* (New York, 1967), p. 276.

[11] Hermann Rauschning, *The Revolution of Nihilism* (London, 1939). For a critique of this view and a presentation of Hitler's ideas as a coherent world view, see Eberhard Jäckel, *Hitler's World View: A Blueprint for Power*, trans. Herbert Arnold (Middletown, Conn., 1972).

[12] As in Nicos Poulantzas, *Fascism and Dictatorship: The Third International and the Problem of Fascism* (London, 1974). Also see Jane Caplan, "Theories of Fascism: Nicos Poulantzas as Historian," *History Workshop Journal* (1977), pp. 83–100; and Anson Rabinbach, "Poulantzas and the Problem of Fascism," *New German Critique* (Spring 1976), pp. 157–70.

[13] Franz Neumann, *Behemoth: The Structure and Practice of National Socialism* (New York, 1944). Neumann wrote that "the internal political value of anti-Semitism will ... never allow a complete extermination of the Jews. The foe cannot and must not disappear; he must always be held in readiness as a scapegoat for all the evils originating in the socio-political system" (p. 125). Erich Goldhagen points out that the murder of the Jews was "the most striking refutation of the thesis that the National Socialists were disbelieving and cynical manipulators of anti-Semitism," in "Weltan-

7

conclusion the same for Marxists and modernization theorists: Whether it was due to the antimodernist nature of the ideology or the overwhelming power of class interests, both suggest that Nazi ideology could not explain the actions of the Hitler regime. They are thus at a loss to explain the triumph of ideology in the Third Reich.[14]

During the 1930s, discussion of the synthesis of technics and unreason in German ideology took place among the critical theorists of the Frankfurt school, as well as in the work of the romantic Marxist, Ernst Bloch. Walter Benjamin's essays on the Weimar Right initiated a discussion of fascism and aesthetics that continues up to the present.[15] Bloch's analysis of *Ungleichzeitigkeit*, roughly "noncontempor-

schauung und Endlösung," *Vierteljahresheft für Zeitgeschichte* (October 1976), pp. 379–405. Also see Andreas Hillgruber, *Hitlers Strategie: Politik und Kriegführung, 1940–1941* (Frankfurt, 1965) and "Die 'Endlösung' und das deutsche Ostimperium als Kernstück des rassenideologischen Programms des Nationalsozialismus," *Vierteljahresheft für Zeitgeschichte* (April 1972), pp. 133–53. Klaus Hildebrand in *The Foreign Policy of the Third Reich* (Berkeley, 1973) clearly distinguishes the points of common ground between Hitler and the traditional conservative elites as well as their points of divergence when Nazi racial ideology replaced "rational power politics" (pp. 106–7). On Marxist analyses of fascism and the avoidance of the Jewish catastrophe in postwar West Germany see Lucy Dawidowicz, *The Holocaust and the Historians* (Cambridge, Mass., 1981); Jeffrey Herf, "The 'Holocaust' Reception in West Germany: Right, Center and Left," *New German Critique* 19 (Winter 1980), pp. 30–52; Moishe Postone, "Anti-Semitism and National Socialism: Notes on the German Reaction to 'Holocaust,' " *New German Critique* 19 (Winter 1980), pp. 97–115; and Anson Rabinbach, "Anti-Semitism Reconsidered: Reply to Piccone and Berman," *New German Critique* 21 (Fall 1980), pp. 129–41.

[14] Critics of the analysis of totalitarianism deny that National Socialism was a monolithic system of domination. For example, Hans Mommsen and Martin Broszat argue that nazism was a "polycracy" of conflicting authorities, which made possible the ascendancy of radicalized SS fanatics. See Broszat's *Der Staat Hitlers* (Munich, 1969), and Mommsen, "Continuity and Change in the Third Reich." The critics have destroyed a straw man. In *The Origins of Totalitarianism* (Cleveland, 1958), Hannah Arendt wrote that the absence of clear hierarchies, the multiplication of offices, and confusion of bureaucratic responsibilities were crucial to totalitarianism in power because the resultant insecurity and fear enhanced the power of the leadership and served to preserve the dynamic of a "movement-state." See "The So-called Totalitarian State," pp. 392–419.

[15] See his discussion of Ernst Jünger and other right-wing thinkers in "Theorien des deutschen Faschismus," in *Walter Benjamin: Gesammelte Schriften*, vol. 3 (Frankfurt, 1977), pp. 238–50; trans. by Jerold Wikoff as "Theories of German Fascism," *New German Critique* 17 (Spring 1979), pp. 120–8. See also *Links hätte noch alles sich zu enträtseln. Walter Benjamin im Kontext*, ed. Walter Burkhardt (Frankfurt, 1978), esp. Ansgar Hillach, "Die Ästhetisierung des politischen Lebens: Walter Benjamins faschismus theoretischer Ansatz – eine Rekonstruktion," pp. 126–67; George Mosse, *The Nationalization of the Masses* (New York, 1970). Rainer Stollman gives an overview of recent West German work in "Faschistische Politik als Gesamtkunstwerk: Tendenzen der Ästhetisierung des politischen Leben im Nationalsozialistischen 'Bewegung,' " in *Die deutsche Literatur im Dritten Reich*, ed. Horst Denkler and Karl Prumm (Stuttgart, 1976), pp. 83–101. Translated as "Fascist Politics as a Total Work of Art," in *New German Critique* 14 (Spring 1978), pp. 41–60.

aneity," drew attention to the fusion of German romanticism with a
cult of technics in the journals of German engineers.[16] Max Horkheimer argued that National Socialism organized a "revolt of nature"
against modern capitalism and industrialism, which eschewed antitechnological themes.[17]

More than any other modern social theorists, Horkheimer and
Theodor Adorno placed the interwining of myth and rationalization
at the center of attention in their classic work, *Dialectic of Enlightenment*.
They opened their book with the now well-known assertion that the
"fully enlightened world" radiated "disaster triumphant."[18] If this was
the case, understanding the relation between nazism and modernity
was crucial. Part of their argument merely repeated standard Marxist
views: "Bourgeois anti-Semitism has a specific economic reason: the
concealment of domination in production."[19] Right-wing anticapitalists identified the Jews with the "unproductive" circulation sphere of
banking, finance, and commerce and praised the sphere of production
and technology as an integral part of the nation. German anticapitalism was anti-Semitic but not antitechnological. But it was a second,
and more sweeping, analysis of the Enlightenment that made Horkheimer and Adorno's work truly distinctive. They argued that the
German disaster was the outcome of a link between reason, myth, and
domination implicit in Enlightenment thought since Kant and Hegel.
The Enlightenment's true face of calculation and domination was
evident in de Sade's highly organized tortures and orgies. In Germany
the Jews suffered from being identified with both abstract rationality
and with backwardness and reluctance to conform to national community.[20] National Socialism telescoped in a particular place and time
the awful potentialities of the Western domination of nature.

[16] Ernst Bloch, *Erbschaft dieser Zeit* (Frankfurt, 1962), and "Technik und Geistererscheinungen," in *Verfremdungen I* (Frankfurt, 1962), pp. 177–85.
[17] In Max Horkheimer, *The Eclipse of Reason* (New York, 1974). Horkheimer also discussed the link between irrationalism and technology in "Zum Rationalismusstreit in
der gegenwärtigen Philosophie," *Kritische Theorie der Gesellschaft*, Band I (Frankfurt,
1968), pp. 123–4.
[18] Max Horkheimer and Theodor Adorno, *Dialectic of Enlightenment* (New York, 1972),
p. 3.
[19] Ibid., p. 173. Herbert Marcuse also discussed the right-wing anticapitalist rhetorical
assault on *Händlertum* or the merchant in "The Struggle Against Liberalism in the
Totalitarian View of the State," *Negations*, trans. Jeremy Shapiro (Boston, 1968), pp.
3–42.
[20] Horkheimer and Adorno, *Dialectic of Enlightenment*, pp. 168–208. On Horkheimer's
sociology of religion and his analysis of anti-Semitism, see Julius Carlebach, *Karl Marx
and the Radical Critique of Judaism* (London, 1978), pp. 234–67; Martin Jay, "The Jews
and the Frankfurt School: Critical Theory's Analysis of Anti-Semitism," *New German
Critique* (Winter 1980), pp. 137–49; and Anson Rabinbach, "Anti-Semitism
Reconsidered."

Horkheimer and Adorno were right to point out that reason and myth were intertwined in the German dictatorship. No doubt, the cultural paradoxes of reactionary modernism were less perplexing for these dialectical thinkers than for those more accustomed to dichotomous modes of thought. But if their perceptions were accurate, their theory of the Enlightenment and their view of modern German history were woefully mistaken.[21] What proved so disastrous for Germany was the separation of the Enlightenment from German nationalism. German society remained partially – never "fully" – enlightened. Horkheimer and Adorno's analysis overlooked this national context and generalized Germany's miseries into dilemmas of modernity per se. Consequently they blamed the Enlightenment for what was really the result of its weakness. Although technology exerted a fascination for fascist intellectuals all over Europe, it was only in Germany that it became part of the national identity. The unique combination of industrial development and a weak liberal tradition was the social background for reactionary modernism. The thesis of the dialectic of enlightenment obscured this historical uniqueness. As a "critical theory," it is strangely apologetic in regard to modern Germany history. It is one of the ironies of modern social theory that the critical theorists, who thought they were defending the unique against the general, contributed to obscuring the uniqueness of Germany's illiberal path toward modernity.

This said, it is better to have been perceptive for the wrong reasons than to have neglected an important problem altogether. It would be less than generous of me not to acknowledge the role concepts such as reification, the aestheticization of politics, and the dialectic of enlightenment have had in directing my attention to the existence of a reactionary modernist tradition in Germany. Although some of the literature on National Socialism inspired by the critical theorists suffers from sloganeering about fascism and capitalism, some very fine reconsiderations of the interaction of modernist and antimodernist currents in National Socialism have also appeared. Karl-Heinz Bohrer's study of Ernst Jünger, Anson Rabinbach's work on Albert Speer's Bureau of the Beauty of Labor, Klaus Theweleit's massive compilation of the unconscious fantasy life of members of the *Freikorps*, Timothy Mason's and Eike Hennig's work on the uses of antimodernist rhetoric in the rationalization of German industry in the 1930s, and Karl-

---

[21] See Ringer, *Decline of the German Mandarins*; Jürgen Habermas, "The Entwinement of Myth and Modernity: Re-reading *Dialectic of Enlightenment*," *New German Critique* (Spring/Summer 1982), pp. 13–30.

The paradox of reactionary modernism

Heinz Ludwig's superbly researched study of engineers and politics before and during the Third Reich all present evidence that right-wing and then Nazi ideology was far more intertwined with modern technology than earlier work suggested.[22] Recent work has also modified our view of the relation between anti-Semitism and antimodernism. Moishe Postone has attempted to explain why anti-Semitism attributes such enormous power to the Jews – they were supposed to be the source of both international finance capitalism and international communism. He turns to Marx's analysis of commodity fetishism to interpret anti-Semitism as a specifically modern form of anticapitalist ideology, despite its atavistic vocabulary.[23] Although some of this new literature suffers from blaming capitalism for the peculiarities of modern German history, it has contributed to a reconsideration of the larger problems of nazism and modernity. I am building on these and other reconsiderations of the problem of modernity and National Socialism while rejecting the implication that German modernity was only one example of a generalized sickness inherent in modern industrial societies.

It is time to clarify terms. I have called the tradition under examination a *reactionary* modernist one to emphasize that it was a tradition of the political Right. A figure such as Oswald Spengler straddled the border between traditional Prussian conservatives – the industrialists, Junkers, military, and civil service – and the postwar conservative revolutionaries. Both were illiberal and authoritarian but the latter reached into the lower middle class to create a mass movement. Like the *völkisch* ideologues of the nineteenth century, the conservative revolutionaries sought a cultural–political revolution that would re-

---

[22] Karl-Heinz Bohrer, *Die Ästhetik des Schreckens: Die pessimistische Romantik und Ernst Jüngers Frühwerk* (Munich, 1978); Anson Rabinbach, "The Aesthetics of Production in the Third Reich," in *International Fascism*, ed. George Mosse (Beverly Hills, Calif., 1979), pp. 189–222; Klaus Theweleit, *Männerphantasien*, 2 vols. (Frankfurt, 1978); Timothy Mason, "Zur Enstehung des Gesetzes zur Ordnung der nationalen Arbeit, vom 20 Januar 1934: Ein Versuch über das Verhältnis 'archaischer' und 'moderner' Momente in der neuesten deutschen Geschichte," in *Industrielles System und politische Entwicklung in der Weimarer Republik*, ed. Hans Mommsen, Dieter Petzina, and Bernd Weisbrod (Düsseldorf, 1974), pp. 323–51; Eike Hennig, *Bürgerliche Gesellschaft und Faschismus in Deutschland: Ein Forschungsbericht* (Frankfurt, 1977); and Karl-Heinz Ludwig, *Technik und Ingenieure im Dritten Reich* (Königstein, TS./Düsseldorf, 1979).

[23] Moishe Postone, "Anti-Semitism and National Socialism: Notes on the German Reaction to 'Holocaust,' " Postone's point of departure is the idea that "the specific characteristics of the power attributed to the Jews by modern anti-Semitism – abstractness, intangibility, universality, mobility – are all characteristics of the value dimension of the social form analyzed by Marx," (p. 108). He interprets Auschwitz as the end point of fetishized anticapitalism in Germany. Postone suggests paradoxes in National Socialist views of technology similar to those I am describing.

11

vitalize the nation. They were reactionaries in that they opposed the principles of 1789 yet found in nationalism a third force "beyond" capitalism and Marxism. Along with Hitler, they were cultural revolutionaries seeking to restore instinct and to reverse degeneration due to an excess of civilization. Like fascist intellectuals all over postwar Europe, the reactionary modernists in Germany viewed communism as merely the obverse of bourgeois materialism, a soulless world's mirror image.[24]

The reactionary modernists were *modernists* in two ways. First, and most obviously, they were technological modernizers; that is, they wanted Germany to be more rather than less industrialized, to have more rather than fewer radios, trains, highways, cars, and planes. They viewed themselves as liberators of technology's slumbering powers, which were being repressed and misused by a capitalist economy linked to parliamentary democracy. Second, they articulated themes associated with the modernist vanguard: Jünger and Gottfried Benn in Germany, Gide and Malraux in France, Marinetti in Italy, Yeats, Pound, and Wyndham Lewis in England. Modernism was not a movement exclusively of the political Left or Right. Its central legend was of the free creative spirit at war with the bourgeoisie who refuses to accept any limits and who advocates what Daniel Bell has called the "megalomania of self-infinitization," the impulse to reach "beyond: beyond morality, tragedy, culture." From Nietzsche to Jünger and then Goebbels, the modernist credo was the triumph of spirit and will over reason and the subsequent fusion of this will to an aesthetic mode. If aesthetic experience alone justifies life, morality is suspended and desire has no limits.[25] Modernism exalted the new and attacked traditions, including normative traditions. As aesthetic standards replaced moral norms, modernism indulged a fascination for horror and violence as a welcome relief to bourgeois boredom and decadence. Modernism also celebrated the self. When modernists turned to politics, they sought engagement, commitment, and authenticity, experiences the Fascists and Nazis promised to provide.[26] When the

[24] On fascism as a cultural revolution, see George Mosse, "Fascism and the Intellectuals," in *The Nature of Fascism*, ed. S. J. Woolf (New York, 1969), pp. 205–25; and Joachim Fest, *Hitler*, trans Richard Winston and Clara Winston (New York, 1974), pp. 104–6.

[25] Daniel Bell, *The Cultural Contradictions of Capitalism* (New York, 1976), pp. 49–52; Jürgen Habermas, "Modernity vs. Post-modernity," *New German Critique* 22 (Winter 1981), pp. 3–14.

[26] See Karl-Heinz Bohrer, *Die Ästhetik des Schreckens*; J. P. Stern, *Hitler: The Führer and the People* (Berkeley, 1975), an excellent study of Hitler's language, in particular of his appeals to the authentic self; and Theodor Adorno, *The Jargon of Authenticity*, trans. Knut Tarnowski and Frederic Will (Evanston, Ill., 1973).

reactionary modernists discussed trains as embodiments of the will to power or saw the racial soul expressed in the *Autobahnen*, they were popularizing what had been the preserve of a cultural vanguard.

The reactionary modernists were *irrationalists*. They simply despised reason and denigrated its role in political and social affairs. Their rejection of reason went far beyond the thoughtful criticisms of positivism in philosophy and social science for which German sociology has become famous. Although Adorno and Horkheimer dissected what they took to be reason's inner tensions, they still looked to it as a court of last resort. But the reactionary modernists spoke what Adorno labeled the "jargon of authenticity" in which certain absolutes such as blood, race, and soul were placed beyond rational justification. In their view reason itself was *lebensfeindlich*, or "hostile to life."[27]

Defenders of nineteenth-century German romanticism have made a simple but important point[28]: There was no straight line between romanticism and nazism. Further, even in Germany the romantic tradition was not exclusively right-wing or antitechnological. On the contrary, romanticism touched all segments of the intellectual and political spectrum in Germany in Weimar from Lukács and Bloch on the far left, through Mann and Max Weber in the center, to Jünger and his conservative revolutionary comrades. Furthermore, as the Hungarian literary critic and sociologist, Ferenc Feher, has put it, World War I was a turning point for romantic anticapitalism among the literary intellectuals, after which right-wing romanticism expressed growing hostility to what had been considered typical romantic themes such as the critique of dehumanization at the hands of the machine. Michael Lowy and Feher attribute the predominance of "romantic anticapitalism" in Germany to the conflict between humanist culture and capitalist exchange relations. Bell points to a "disjunction of realms" between a culture focused on the self and a social-economic system based on efficiency to account for the cultural re-

---

[27] On the role of *Lebensphilosophie* and the meaning of irrationalism in the conservative revolution see Kurt Sontheimer, *Antidemokratisches Denken in der Weimarer Republik* (Munich, 1968); Georg Lukács, *Die Zerstörung der Vernunft*; and Helmut Plessner, *Die verspätete Nation*.

[28] For example, Jacques Barzun, *Classic, Romantic and Modern* (Chicago, 1934), Meyer Abrams, *Natural Supernaturalism* (New York, 1973), and Alvin Gouldner, "Romanticism and Classicism: Deep Structures in Social Science," in *For Sociology* (Middlesex, England, 1973), pp. 323–66, all stress the romantic contribution to twentieth-century liberal and socialist humanism. Gouldner's thesis is that nineteenth-century German romanticism decisively influenced early twentieth-century social theory – Max Weber, Georg Simmel, Lukács, and the Frankfurt school.

13

bellion of intellectuals.[29] The cultural contradictions of capitalism exist in capitalist societies generally, and they were particularly sharp in post-World War I Germany.

Granted that German romanticism was a highly ambiguous tradition, it would do violence to the facts to declare its political innocence. The darker aspects of romanticism appeared in reactionary modernism. Political romanticism in Germany represented the following: First, it was contemptuous of politics as the give-and-take of interest groups or parliamentary conflict. Hence, in Max Weber's words, it fostered a politics of absolute ethics rather than a politics of responsibility. Political romantics entered politics to save their souls, find a new identity, or establish the authenticity of their commitment, or to reestablish a lost *Gemeinschaft* rather than to engage in the difficult and frustrating business of balancing means and ends. Political romanticism was particularly damaging for the Weimar Republic, for it encouraged the far Right and far Left while convincing the Center that politics was not a worthy enterprise for intellectuals, and that individual development took precedence over responsibility to a community of law and obligation.[30]

Second, German romanticism was primarily a part of the illiberal, authoritarian concept of the German state. There were left-wing romantics who criticized Marxist scientism, but they remained on the political margins of the socialist and communist movements.[31] In comparison, the romantics of the Right stood in the mainstream of German nationalism. When they celebrated emotion, passion, action, and

---

[29] For Bell's analysis of the disjunction of realms see *The Cultural Contradictions of Capitalism*, and *The Coming Crisis of Post-Industrial Society* (New York, 1973). Lowy's analysis appears in his study of Lukács, *Pour une Sociologie des Intellectuelles Revolutionnaries* (Paris, 1976). In his very perceptive study of the impact of World War I on Paul Ernst and Georg Lukács, Ferenc Feher interprets the war as "the turning point of romantic anticapitalism" after which the romantics of the nationalist Right had to distance themselves from common prewar romantic themes, e.g. attacks on positivism or technology. See Ferenc Feher, "Am Scheideweg des romantischen Antikapitalismus . . . ," in *Die Seele und das Leben: Studien zum frühen Lukács*, ed. Agnes Heller (Frankfurt, 1972). Paul Breines has stressed the romantic contribution to the young Lukács. See "Marxism, Romanticism and the Case of George Lukács: Notes on Some Recent Sources and Situations," *Studies in Romanticism* (Fall 1977), pp. 473–89; and Andrew Arato and Paul Breines, *The Young Lukacs and the Origins of Western Marxism* (New York, 1979). On the connection between Lukács's search for community and the lure of dictatorship see Lee Congdon's fine study, *The Young Lukács* (Chapel Hill, N.C., 1983).

[30] See Kurt Sontheimer, *Antidemokratisches Denken*; Gordon Craig, *Germany: 1866–1945* (New York, 1980), pp. 469–97; and his *The Germans* (New York, 1982), pp. 190–212; and Walter Laqueur, *Weimar: A Cultural History, 1918–1933* (New York, 1974).

[31] See Breines, "Marxism and Romanticism."

community and criticized "soulless" reason, they turned to the state as an alternative to political liberalism and capitalist society.

The *völkisch* ideologists within the romantic tradition placed particular emphasis on a longing for a preindustrial past, but it would be misleading to try to define German romanticism as primarily a backward-looking movement. More important was the accentuation of individual subjectivity combined with a sense of being subjected to fate and destiny beyond one's control. Romanticism encouraged a preoccupation with a world of hidden powerful forces beyond or beneath the world of appearances. This was a tradition with apocalyptic visions in which a total transformation of a degenerate *Zivilisation* would occur through sudden and violent change. The *Kulturnation* would emerge through a purifying process of death and transfiguration.[32] After World War I, Ernst Jünger and Carl Schmitt prided themselves on their differences with nineteenth-century romanticism. But their enthusisam for the *Fronterlebnis* (front experience) and their belief that the slaughter was bringing forth a new man was an old romantic vision in a modern context.

Romanticism took different forms in different national contexts but everywhere it was part of modernity. At its center stood the celebration of the self.[33] In France and England, it partook of democratic and egalitarian traditions to a far greater degree than in Germany, where it combated such claims. No one understood this better than Thomas Mann. Commenting on the "melancholy history of German *Innerlichkeit*," he said that the "romantic counterrevolution against the Enlightenment" had made decisive contributions to Weimar's "old-new world of revolutionary reaction" as well as to National Socialism. Speaking of Hitler's Germany, he wrote that "there are not two Germanies, a good and an evil one, but only one, which through the cunning of the devil turned the best to the service of evil."[34] National Socialism reconciled *Innerlichkeit* and modern technology. The reactionary modernists were German ideologists who selected from their own national traditions those elements that made these cultural reconciliations possible.

As I said earlier, this book brings together concerns that are too often kept separate: culture and meaning, and history and politics. In my view, this is a realistic approach; that is, it helps explain the

---

[32] See Craig, *The Germans*; Bohrer, *Die Ästhetik des Schreckens* on the fascination with death and violence among the political romantics.
[33] See Barzun, *Classic, Romantic and Modern*; Lionel Trilling, *Sincerity and Authenticity* (Cambridge, Mass., 1969); and J. P. Stern, *Hitler*.
[34] Mann, "Deutschland und die Deutschen," pp. 297–8.

unfolding of events. Contrast it with Franz Neumann's perfectly typical expectations in 1942 that "a most profound conflict" would develop between the "magic character" of Nazi propaganda and the "rational" processes of modern industry. Neumann believed that this conflict would lead German engineers to be among the first to see that Nazi ideology was pure "bunk." He also believed that engineers would comprise "the most serious break in the regime" because as practitioners of "the most rational vocation" they would oppose the misuse of technology by "totalitarian monopoly capitalism."[35] In fact, with few exceptions, the practitioners of the most rational vocation did not break with the German dictatorship, and many came to share its world view. The reactionary modernist tradition contributed to these allegiances and ideological affinities.

In tracing this tradition, I will be paying close attention to what Clifford Geertz has called the "autonomous process of symbolic formulation," that is, how "ideologies transform sentiment into significance and make it socially available." Ideologists do this with symbolism, metaphor, and analogy. If they do their job well, they can bring discordant meanings – *Technik* and *Kultur*, for example – into a unified framework that renders otherwise incomprehensible social conditions meaningful and makes political action within those settings possible.[36]

The accomplishment of the reactionary modernists was considerable. In the country of romantic counterrevolution against the Enlightenment, they succeeded in incorporating technology *into* the symbolism and language of *Kultur* – community, blood, will, self, form, productivity, and finally race – by taking it *out of* the realm of *Zivilisation* – reason, intellect, internationalism, materialism, and finance. The integration of technology into the world view of German nationalism provided a cultural matrix that seemed to restore order into what these thinkers viewed as a chaotic postwar reality.[37] What began as an indigenous tradition of German engineers and right-wing literati ended in the slogans administered by the Nazis. By reconciling technology and *Innerlichkeit*, reactionary modernists contributed to the nazification of German engineering, and to the primacy of Nazi ide-

---

[35] Neumann, *Behemoth*, pp. 471–2.
[36] Clifford Geertz, *The Interpretation of Cultures* (New York, 1973), pp. 211, 220. On politics and language also see Kenneth Burke, *The Philosophy of Literary Form* (Baton Rouge, La., 1941), esp. his analysis of Hitler's rhetoric, pp. 164–89; and his *A Rhetoric of Motives* (Berkeley, 1950).
[37] Joachim Schumacher, *Die Angst vor dem Chaos* (Paris, 1937; reprint, Frankfurt, 1972).

16

ology and politics over technical rationality and means–ends calculation of the national interest up to the end of the Hitler regime. They were contributors to the unity – rather than the separation – of totalitarian ideology and political practice in the German dictatorship.

2

The conservative revolution in Weimar

World War I was a source of hope for those German cultural pessimists who believed in the possibility of a radical reversal of the process of degeneration they felt was threatening the nation's body and soul. Their message was not primarily that the world was godforsaken but that it could be redeemed and the deterioration halted and reversed. These hopes put the nationalists of the postwar era at odds with antiindustrial themes in German nationalism. A limited incorporation of technology into nationalist imagery and language had occurred in the late nineteenth century, but mainly on the part of engineers.

The novelty in the postwar discussions of technology and culture in Germany was that for the first time the nontechnical intellectuals were trying to integrate technology into nationalist language. Like the rest of National Socialism – and European fascism – these nationalist ideas took on a tougher tone as a result of the *Fronterlebnis* of World War I, incubated in the hothouse cultural controversies of the postwar years, and came to political fruition in Nazi propaganda. The confrontation between *Technik und Kultur* did not begin in the Weimar Republic. The major technological advances of the first and second industrial revolutions based on steam, electricity, and chemistry had been introduced to Germany in the nineteenth century, and the jargon of authenticity, German romanticism, the apolitical tradition, and mistrust of the Enlightenment also accompanied the rise of the Prussian Reich.

Yet although the confrontation between technology and culture did not begin in Weimar, it certainly came to a head in those years. It even had a name of its own, *die Streit um die Technik*, the debate about technology.[1] Hundreds of books, lectures, and essays emerged from both the technical universities and nontechnical intellectuals from all

[1] Friedrich Dessauer, *Die Streit um die Technik* (Frankfurt, 1958).

18

points along the political spectrum dealing with the relation between Germany's soul and modern technology. The confrontation between technological advance and the traditions of German nationalism was sharper in Weimar than at any time before or since in modern German history, as well as in any other place in Europe after World War I. The battle over *Technik und Kultur* took place against a background of military defeat, failed revolutions, successful counterrevolution, a divided Left, an embittered and resentful Right, and Germany's famous illiberalism, which could not withstand the challenges of the political extremes. Weimar culture was the crucible in which the cultural synthesis I am calling reactionary modernism was both forged and given a new, harder edge that would eventually bring it into line with the cultural revolution Hitler promised. The story of the rise and collapse of the Weimar Republic has been told often and well. The following will remind the reader of the events that set the background for the reactionary modernist upsurge in the postwar period.

The history of the Weimar Republic is customarily divided into three periods. The first begins in November 1918 with the defeat in World War I followed by the imposition of the Versailles treaty, revolutionary upheavals from the Left, civil war and counterrevolutionary armed response from the Right, ultimately fatal divisions between the reformist and revolutionary Left, foreign occupation of the Ruhr, and the inflation of 1923. The workers' revolts did not succeed in shaking the social and political power of the Junkers, industrialists, army, and state bureaucracy – the pillars of the prewar Prussian coalition – and inflation embittered the middle class and weakened the strength of the republic's strongest defenders in the trade unions and in the Social Democratic party (SPD). A formally republican, democratic political experiment began in the midst of the authoritarian legacies of German industrialization.

The second period, usually called the stabilization phase, began with the fiscal stabilization of 1924, which brought hyperinflation to an end, warded off, at least for a time, the challenges of the far Right and far Left, and inaugurated a period of expanded investment and rationalization in industry. It was during this period of relative prosperity and political stability that Americanization, Fordism, and class harmony based on corporatist arrangements fostering expanded productivity reached their zenith. But the underlying gap between Weimar's formal republican and democratic political institutions and Germany's still unsurmounted illiberal social, economic, and ideological legacies surfaced again from 1929 to 1933 when the depression proved too much for the German political system to handle. In this last period, unemployment and the political extremes grew, the center parties shrank, the lower middle class was attracted to the Nazis, the Communists continued to attack the Social Democrats as "social fascists," the right-wing intellectuals dreamed of smashing the republic, and finally the conservatives turned to Hitler to perform the last rites.[2]

Weimar was a republic without republicans for a number of reasons. First, from the beginning the right-wing intellectuals and political parties attacked it as the symbol of national humiliation and military defeat. The Right rejected parliamentary democracy as simply un-German and called for authoritarian rule to crush the Left, abrogate the provisions of the Versailles treaty, and expose the slanders of the "November criminals" of 1918 who had implicitly accepted German responsibility for the war. Hitler was able effectively to exploit the gulf between army and republic and to present destruction of parliament and the trade unions as an act of national redemption, political emancipation, economic recovery, and technological advance. It is no wonder that the right-wing intellectuals referred to the policy of destroying the republic as the rebirth and breakthrough of the nation.[3]

A second reason for calling Weimar a republic without republicans has to do with the disappointments of the Left. Because Weimar was an effort to establish political democracy on conservative social foundations, the Social Democrats found themselves turning to the Right to crush the threat of revolution from the Left. This only deepened the split between Social Democrats and Communists that had opened wide during the war, thereby weakening the Left while reinforcing the nationalist Right.[4] As Charles Maier has recently put it, the dilemma of the political centrists, such as Stresemann, or the Social Democrats was that "the government must choose to contain social tension on conservative terms or not contain it at all." It proved impossible to oppose the army, big industry, Junkers, the paramilitary right-wing groups, and anti-Semites and still overcome inflation and

---

[2] On the history of the Weimar Republic see Karl Dietrich Bracher, *Die Auflösung der Weimarer Republik: Eine Studie zum Problem des Machtverfalls in der Demokratie*, 2d ed., (Stuttgart, 1957); and *The German Dictatorship* trans. Jean Steinberg (New York, 1970), pp. 124–227; Gordon Craig, *Germany: 1866–1945* (New York, 1980), pp. 396–568; Peter Gay, *Weimar Culture: The Outsider as Insider* (New York, 1968); and Walter Laqueur, *Weimar: A Cultural History, 1918–1933* (New York, 1974).

[3] Ernst Jünger's essay collection *Krieg und Krieger* (Berlin, 1930) was representative of these views. Joachim Fest's discussion of "the great dread" in *Hitler*, trans. Richard Winston and Clara Winston (New York, 1974), contains insightful comments on the spirit of rebirth and cultural revolution on the German Right.

[4] On this see Craig, *Germany*, pp. 396–433.

avoid economic collapse and territorial fragmentation without breaking with prolabor forces that were most sympathetic to Weimar's political institutions. Hence, those whose social interests were defended
by the republic detested its political institutions, and those who might
have been more sympathetic to its political institutions were embittered because they had not achieved the social gains they hoped for.[5]

Within the German Right after World War I, there were a number
of writers who argued for a nationalist ideology more in keeping with
modern times and less restricted by traditional Prussian conservatism.
Known collectively as the "conservative revolution," they were vehe-
ment opponents of the Weimar Republic, identifying it with the lost
war, Versailles, the inflation of 1923, the Jews, cosmopolitan mass culture, and political liberalism.[6] They envisaged a new reich of enormous strength and unity, rejected the view that political action should
be guided by rational criteria, and idealized violence for its own sake.
They denounced what they believed were the boredom and complacency of bourgeois life and searched for renewal in an energizing
"barbarism." Gordon Craig has aptly characterized them as "the intellectual advance guard of the rightist revolution that was to be ef-
fected in 1933," which, although contemptuous of National Socialism
and Hitler, "did much to pave his road to power."[7] Both within and
outside the engineering profession, advocates of the conservative revolution were also important contributors to the reactionary modernist
tradition. This is a cultural paradox, for common sense would suggest

[5] Charles Maier, *Recasting Bourgeois Europe: Stabilization in France, Germany and Italy in the Decade After World War I* (Princeton, N.J., 1975), pp. 385–6; and David Abraham, *The Collapse of the Weimar Republic* (Princeton, N.J., 1981).

[6] The Austrian poet Hugo von Hoffmannstahl was the first to use the term "conserv-ative revolution" in his *Das Schriftum als geistiger Raum der Nation* (Munich, 1927). He spoke of the many Germans who sought "not freedom but communal bonds." Cited in Fritz Stern, *The Politics of Cultural Despair* (New York, 1961), p. 27. Also see Her-mann Rauschning, *The Conservative Revolution* (New York, 1941).

[7] Craig, *Germany*, pp. 486–7. The literature on the conservative revolution is extensive. Also see Bracher, *The German Dictatorship*, pp. 142–43; Wolfgang Hock, *Deutscher Antikapitalismus* (Frankfurt, 1960); Heide Gerstenberger, *Der revolutionäre Konserva-tismus* (Berlin, 1969); Klemens von Klemperer, *Germany's New Conservatism* (Princeton, N.J., 1957); Herman Lebovics, *Social Conservatism and the Middle Classes in Germany* (Princeton, N.J., 1969); Armin Mohler, *Die konservative Revolution in Deutschland, 1918–1932*, 2d ed. (Darmstadt, 1972); George Mosse, "The Corporate State and the Con-servative Revolution," in his *Germans and Jews: The Right, the Left and the Search for a "Third Force" in Pre-Nazi Germany* (New York, 1970), pp. 116–43; Karl Prumm, *Die Literatur des soldatischen Nationalismus der 20er Jahre: 1918–1933*, 2 vols. (Kronberg, 1974); Otto-Ernst Schüddekopf, *Linke Leute von Rechts: National-bolschewismus in Deutschland: 1918–1933* (Frankfurt 1973); Kurt Sontheimer, *Antidemokratisches Denken in der Weimarer Republik*, (Munich, 1968); Fritz Stern, *The Politics of Cultural Despair*; and Walter Struve, *Elites Against Democracy* (Princeton, N.J., 1973).

that partisans of irrationalism and nihilism would detest modern technology as a manifestation of rationality and faith in historical progress. In this chapter, I will discuss the themes, personalities, social and generational bases, and distinctively German dimensions of Weimar's conservative revolution in order to throw this paradox into sharper focus.

The social basis of the conservative revolution was the middle class, broadly defined. The German *Mittelstand* encompassed small- and middle-sized farmers, artisans and shopkeepers, white-collar workers in big industry and civil service, and the professional middle class – lawyers, doctors, professors, higher civil servants, and engineers.[8] These diverse groups were bound together by common reactions to the rapid development of industrial capitalism in Germany. Anxious and afraid of large capital, on the one hand, and the organized working class on the other, they viewed the nation as a redemptive unity.[9] Right-wing nationalist spokesmen claimed that the nation-state alone was above narrow class interests. The German middle class turned enthusiastically to the promise of a "primacy of politics" above egoistic self-interest, one motivated by national "idealism" rather than liberal, Marxist, Jewish, French, or English "materialism," or cosmopolitanism. Heirs to an illiberal tradition to begin with, those whose savings had been wiped out in the inflation of 1923 and who faced bankruptcy and unemployment in the depression, responded favorably to Hitler's promise to the "little man" that the years of "chaos" were coming to an end.[10]

The German *Mittelstand* was an intermediate class in a temporal as well as social sense, a feature Ernst Bloch has described as its *Ungleichzeitigkeit*, its mixture of modern, capitalist and industrial experience alongside traditional, precapitalist, and preindustrial life.[11] The *Mittelstand* lived in the cities and worked in modern industry, but the memories of small-town life and less rationalized forms of production were still vivid in the Germany of the 1920s. Bloch's analysis of German middle-class consciousness was unusual because it qualified an exclusive focus on the antimodernism of the middle classes and pointed attention to their selective embrace of modernity. But most important,

[8] Arno Mayer, *Dynamics of Counterrevolution in Europe, 1870–1956* (New York, 1971), p. 66.

[9] Lebovics, *Social Conservatism*, pp. 4–11. Also see Emil Lederer's classic account, *Die Privatangestellten in der modernen Wirtschaftsordnung* (Tübingen, 1912).

[10] See Bracher, *Die Auflösung der Weimarer Republik*, pp. 152–3; Mayer, *Dynamics of Counterrevolution*; Lebovics, *Social Conservatism*.

[11] Ernst Bloch, *Erbschaft dieser Zeit* (Frankfurt, 1962), pp. 104–26.

Bloch's analysis took issue with the rationalist bias of Marxist orthodoxy. He suggested that the appeal of nazism lay less in traditional
antimodernism than in the promise of cultural and emotional redemption through embracing aspects of the modern world in ac-
cordance with German national traditions. Hence the spokesmen of
the Right would have to be understood in a more differentiated way.
They, not the liberals, Social Democrats, or Marxists, were the real
revolutionaries. They were the ones who did not promise more of the
same *Entseelung* (desouling) but a renewal of the soul in a modern
setting.[12] Sociological juxtapositions of tradition and modernity or
progress and reaction fail to capture the paradoxes of *Ungleichzeitigkeit*. It is in literature, in particular in Thomas Mann's *Doctor Faustus*,
that we find an adequate sociological description of the conservative
revolution as an "old-new world of revolutionary reaction."

In addition to sharing membership in the German middle class, the
conservative revolutionaries were generational cohorts. Although some
contributors, such as Oswald Spengler (1880–1936) and Moeller van
den Bruck (1876–1925), matured before the war, the conservative
revolution as a social and cultural movement was a product of the lost
war and its consequences.[13] Karl Mannheim's claims relating shared
generational experience to shared political outlooks are vividly confirmed by the conservative revolution. Mannheim focused on the late
teens and early twenties in the formation of individual political consciousness. The leading figures of both the conservative revolution
and of National Socialism were born between 1885 and 1895. Their
formative years, in a Mannheimian sense, took place during the Great
War.[14] The war taught them a contempt for bourgeois society, accustomed them to violence, and gave them a sense of community for
which they afterward yearned.[15] Hannah Arendt once wrote of the

[12] Ibid. Joachim Fest also explains how "fascism served the craving of the period for
a general upheaval more effectively than its antagonists," *Hitler*, p. 105. Also see
Ernst Bloch, "Die Angst des Ingenieur," and "Technik und Geistererscheinungen,"
in *Verfremdungen I* (Franfurt, 1962). Anson Rabinbach provides a useful introduction
to Bloch's contribution in "Ernst Bloch's Heritage of Our Times and the Theory of
Fascism," *New German Critique* 11 (1977), pp. 5–21.
[13] Armin Mohler, *Die konservative Revolution in Deutschland* contains a great deal of
biographical information on participants in the conservative revolution.
[14] See Mohler, *Die konservative Revolution in Deutschland*. Also see Karl Mannheim, "The
Problem of Generations," in *Essays in The Sociology of Culture* (New York, 1952), pp.
276–332. Also see Robert Wohl, *The Generation of 1914* (Cambridge, Mass., 1979).
Wohl applies Mannheim's sociology of generations to right-wing intellectuals in post-
World War I England, France, Germany, Spain, and Italy.
[15] A good example was Alfred Bäumler's *Männerbund und Wissenschaft* (Berlin, 1934).
On Baumler and National Socialism, see Lukács, *Die Zerstörung der Vernunft*, Band
III, *Irrationalismus und Imperialismus* (Darmstadt, 1962), pp. 204–6.

"lost treasure(s) of the revolutionary tradition" as fleeting moments of community and political discussion (the American committees of correspondence, the Russian and European post-World War I soviets and workers' councils, the Hungarian revolution of 1956 were some examples) when the abstract ideal of the good society assumed actual historical reality. The Right, no less than the Left, has had its lost treasures. In Weimar, the masculine community of the trenches, recreated in paramilitary groups such as the *Freikorps*, provided the reactionary tradition with its concrete utopia, vision of a good society, and lost treasure.[16]

As we noted earlier, the war was a turning point for romantic anticapitalism. It was after the war that the conservative revolutionaries associated irrationalism, protest against the Enlightenment, and a romantic cult of violence with a cult of technics. Particularly among the nontechnical intellectuals, the war stimulated the development of reactionary modernist ideas. Ernst Jünger expressed a widely held right-wing view when he connected technology with the wartime *Gemeinschaft* rather than the fragmented, postwar *Gesellschaft*. When the right-wing literati idealized the lost communities of the past, they looked back to the modern battlefield and the trenches, not the preindustrial landscape. The *Kriegserlebnis* (war experience) presented postwar reaction with a fully up-to-date masculine alternative to bourgeois society, one preferable to the effeminate and escapist fantasies of previous generations of less daring conservatives.

The conservative revolution took place in and around universities, political clubs, and little magazines. These institutions constituted its public sphere.[17] In this atmosphere of right-wing sectarianism, the

---

[16] Hannah Arendt, "The Revolutionary Tradition and Its Lost Treasure," in *On Revolution* (New York, 1965), pp. 217–85. On the political and ideological importance of World War I for National Socialism also see Timothy Mason, *Sozialpolitik im Dritten Reich: Arbeiterklasse und Volksgemeinschaft* (Opladen, 1978); and "Die Erbschaft der Novemberrevolution für den National Sozialismus," in *Sozialpolitik im Dritten Reich*, pp. 15–41; reprinted as "The Legacy of 1918 for National Socialism," in *German Democracy and the Triumph of Hitler*, ed. Anthony Nicholls and Erich Mathias (London, 1971).

[17] On the concept of the public sphere, see Jürgen Habermas *Strukturwandel der Öffentlichkeit* 3 (Neuwied, 1974). Habermas attributes a normative dimension to the public sphere: It stands for the liberal idea of public discussion of different viewpoints. Here I am using the term in a strictly descriptive sense to refer to a forum in which politics is discussed without all points of view necessarily being represented. Along these lines, West German critics have spoken of a "fascist" or "proletarian" public sphere, uses which are really contradictions in terms. See the Berlin journal of cultural politics, *Ästhetik und Kommunikation* 26 (1976) on "faschistische Öffentlichkeit"; Eberhard Knodler-Bunte, "Fascism as a Depoliticized Mass Movement," *New German Critique* 11 (Spring 1977), pp. 39–48.

charisma of the *Kriegserlebnis* was sustained by an ongoing cultural-political opposition to the republic. From 1918 to 1933, the German Right comprised over 550 political clubs and 530 journals.[18] Some lasted weeks or months; others, such as *Die Tat*, (The Deed), with a readership of 30,000 or *Die Standarte*, the journal of war veterans, with a circulation of 110,000, continued throughout the entire life of the republic.[19] By the time books by Jünger or Spengler came to the attention of a broader reading public, they had been discussed and refined within this narrower but by no means small right-wing public sphere. It served as a linguistic and political incubator of ideology, offering authors financial support and sympathetic readers.

Some of the more important postwar right-wing journals were the following: *Das Gewissen* (The Conscience) was connected to the June Club, a meeting place for ex-soldiers, conservative literati (especially Moeller van den Bruck), and industrialists. It was published from 1919 to 1927 and had a circulation of 10,000 at its height. Its major themes were attacks on Weimar liberalism and appeals for renewed nationalist spirit and rearmament.[20] From 1929 to 1933, *Die Tat* was the most widely read journal on the right. Its central figures were Hans Zehrer and Ferdinand Fried, both of whom had been participants in the prewar youth movement. *Die Tat* advocated a middle-class anticapitalism directed against the "materialism" of both capital and organized labor and favored authoritarian state intervention that was supposed to free the state from the fetters of parliamentary delay.[21]

Die Standarte was the most influential of the journals espousing the views of the "front" generation. Other magazines included *Deutsches Volkstum* (German Qualities of the People), *Ja und Nein* (Yes and No), *Arminius: Kampfschrift für deutsche Nationalisten* (Arminius: Battle Writings for German Nationalists), *Die Kommenden* (The Coming), *Die Standarte: Beiträge zur geistigen Vertiefung des Frontgedankens* (The Standard: Contributions to the Spiritual Deepening of the Ideas of the Front) *Standarte: Wochenschrift des Neuen Nationalismus* (Standard: Weekly Journal of the New Nationalism), *Der Vormarsch* (The Advance), and *Widerstand: Zeitschrift für nationalrevolutionäre Politik* (Resistance: Mag-

---

[18] Mohler, *Die konservative Revolution*, pp. 539–54.
[19] Sontheimer, *Antidemokratisches Denken*, p. 33.
[20] Klemperer, *Germany's New Conservatism* (Princeton, N.J., 1957); Fritz Stern, *The Politics of Cultural Despair*, pp. 279–93.
[21] Kurt Sontheimer, "Der Tatkreis," and *Antidemokratisches Denken*. On the economic views of the group around *Die Tat*, see Hock, *Deutscher Antikapitalismus*.

azine for National Revolutionary Politics).[22] One of the ironies of Hitler's seizure of power was that this plethora of little journals and political clubs, which did so much to aid his coming to power, was abolished when the Nazis made good on their promise to establish totalitarian control over German politics.

Fritz Stern has described the conservative revolution as "an ideological attack on modernity, on the complex of ideas and institutions that characterize our liberal, secular and industrial civilization."[23] There is no doubt that the conservative revolutionaries were hostile to liberalism and Enlightenment rationality, but the totality of their views toward modern technology was more differentiated than those offered by the figures Stern examined – Lagarde, Langbehn, and van den Bruck. Common sense and the dichotomous nature of both Marxist and modernization theories imply that advocates of "thinking with the blood" would reject complex technologies. But such was not the case. To appreciate the paradoxical nature of reactionary modernism as a cultural system, it is important to review some of the traditions of the German Right that suggest a complete incompatibility with modern technology.

The conservative revolutionaries were heirs to European irrationalist traditions, traditions that took on a particularly intense coloration in Germany due to the politicization of *Legensphilosophie*, the philosophy of life. Weimar's right-wing intellectuals claimed to be in touch with "life" or "experience" and thereby to be endowed with a political position beyond any rational justification.[24] To conservative revolu-

---

[22] See Karl Prumm, *Die Literatur des soldatischen Nationalismus der 20er Jahre: 1918–1933*, 2 vols. (Kronberg, 1974); and "Das Erbe der Front: Der antidemokratische Kriegsroman der Weimarer Republik und seine nationalsozialistischer Fortsetzung," in *Die deutsche Literatur im Dritten Reich*, ed. Horst Denkler and Karl Prumm (Stuttgart, 1976), pp. 138–64. Prumm's work is important for analysis of the mixture of irrationalist and modernist currents in National Socialist ideology. For a complete bibliography of Ernst Jünger's journalism in the Weimar years, see Hans Peter des Coudres, *Bibliographie der Werke Ernst Jünger* (Stuttgart, 1970), pp. 50–6. Prumm offers the most extensive analysis of these writings in *Die Literatur*. Also see Gerhard Loose, *Ernst Jünger: Gestalt und Werk* (Frankfurt, 1957); and Hans-Peter Schwarz, *Die konservative Anarchist: Politik und Zeitkritik Ernst Jüngers* (Freiburg, 1962).

[23] Stern, *The Politics of Cultural Despair*, p. 7.

[24] Georg Lukács stressed the importance of *Lebensphilosophie* in *Die Zerstörung der Vernunft*, Band III, *Irrationalismus und Imperialismus*. This volume includes Lukács's often not very subtle analysis of the background to National Socialism in German philosophy – Nietzsche, Dilthey, Simmel, Spengler, Scheler, Heidegger, Jaspers, Klages, Jünger, Bäumler, Boehm, Krieck, and Rosenberg. Lukács did not distinguish between Nietzsche's works and the use made of those works by the Nazis, nor was he fair to critics of positivism – Simmel above all – when he accused them of contributing to the "irrationalist" climate that was conducive to nazism. Adorno viewed the work as evidence of "the destruction of Lukács' own reason" and a reflection of the cultural

tionaries, no accusation was more damaging than to describe an idea or institution – positivism, liberalism, Marxism, science, parliament, reason – as *lebensfeindlich* (hostile to life). They, of course, viewed themselves as representatives of all that was vital, cosmic, elementary, passionate, willful, and organic, of the intuitive and living rather than of the rational and dead.[25]

German romanticism's contribution to the conservative revolution was decisive. The right-wing intellectuals were political romantics insofar as they advocated what Max Weber called the ethic of ultimate ends rather than an ethic of responsibility. There was much in the German romantic tradition and its modern Nietzschean variants that denigrated the role of reason in politics and/or saw in politics above all opportunities for self-realization, authentic experience, or new identities, conceptions of politics that National Socialism also advocated.[26] The rebirth of the nation would also mean the renewal of personal identity. This existentialist stress on the self replaced more prosaic conceptions of politics as a balancing of means and ends with a thirst for action and engagement for their own sake. If nationalist politics would dissolve all personal problems into a great collective political transformation, then force and violence were certainly justified in bringing about national rebirth. Many of the conservative revolutionaries were contemptuous of Hitler and the Nazis, but they could not deny that their own romantic thirst for action and commitment for their own sake was also part of his appeal and his program. As Carl Schmitt put it at the time, "Everything romantic stands in the service of other, unromantic energies."[27] Consistent with their political irresponsibility and romanticism, the conservative revolu-

repression of the Stalin era. But Adorno himself agreed with Lukács that *Lebensphilosophie* was prominent in the right-wing assault on reason. See his *Jargon of Authenticity*, trans. Kurt Tarnowski and Frederic Will (Evanston, Ill., 1973). Although *Lebensphilosophie* was not an exclusively right-wing subjectivism, it was one of those German traditions that contained a fund of metaphors that entered into right-wing ideology. If Nietzsche, for example, was misinterpreted, the misinterpretation was remarkably consistent. On this see J. P. Stern, *Hitler: The Führer and the People* (Berkeley, 1975), pp. 43–77; and Ernst Nolte, *Three Faces of Fascism*, trans. Leila Vennewitz (New York, 1966), pp. 441–6. Jürgen Habermas warns against rejecting criticisms of positivism too quickly in his review of Fritz Ringer's *The Decline of the German Mandarins*, "Die deutschen Mandarine," in *Philosophisch-politische Profile* (Frankfurt, 1973), pp. 239–51; David Bathrick and Paul Breines in "Marx oder Nietzsche: Anmerkungen zur Krise des Marxismus," in *Karl Marx und Friedrich Nietzsche*, ed. Reinhold Grimm and Jost Hermand (Königstein, 1978), pp. 119–35, discuss the left-wing Nietzschean critique of Marxist scientism.

[25] See Sontheimer, *Antidemokratisches Denken*, pp. 56–61, on "vulgar *Lebensphilosophie*."
[26] J. P. Stern, *Hitler*; and Adorno, *The Jargon of Authenticity*.
[27] Carl Schmitt, *Politische Romantik* (Munich, 1919), p. 162.

tionaries did not bother to ask what the consequences of destroying Weimar's democracy would be.

Friedrich Georg Jünger (Ernst's brother) expressed a widespread conservative revolutionary view when he wrote in his *Der Aufmarsch des Nationalismus* (1926) that rationality was synonymous with weakness, decadence, and lack of communal feeling characteristic of those intellectuals who "betray the blood with the intellect." He favorably compared the "community of blood" (*Blutgemeinschaft*) to the "community of mind" (*Geistgemeinschaft*), adding that a "community of blood does not [need to] justify itself: it lives, it is there without the necessity of intellectual justification." The conservative revolutionaries identified Germany with the *Blutgemeinschaft* while relegating the people, ideas, and institutions they despised – England, France, democracy, parliament, Weimar, economic and political liberalism, Marxian socialism, and often enough the Jews – to the *Geistgemeinschaft*. In Jünger's representative view, the purpose of politics was to make possible the realization of the *Blutgemeinschaft* over the rationalized and soulless *Geistgemeinschaft*.[28]

Jünger's juxtaposition of mind and blood presents an important paradoxical feature of the conservative revolution: This was a case study in the antiintellectualism of the intellectuals. They attacked abstraction and the intellect while celebrating intuition, the self, and immediacy. They would have rejected the label "intellectual," with its French, left-wing, cosmopolitan, and Jewish connotations. In Nazi parlance, the term was an expression of contempt and ridicule. If life or blood was the central force in politics, it was pointless to engage in critical analysis. Whereas ideology was necessary, intellectuals were not, because everyone had feelings and could thus be his own ideologist. The conservative revolutionaries wrote in a profoundly antiintellectual atmosphere of Junkers, generals, and the emerging Nazi party. Like fascist intellectuals elsewhere in Europe, their self-contempt was the other side of a fascination for violence, action – and technology.

Despite their hostile attitude toward intellectuals, the conservative revolutionaries were intellectuals. That is, they were viewed and they viewed themselves as a cultural elite with a special responsibility and ability to work with traditions, ideas, symbols, and meanings in an effort to make sense of their times. They used some traditions unchanged while altering others in a manner Raymond Williams has referred to as the "work of selective tradition" to underscore active

---

[28] Friedrich Georg Jünger, *Der Aufmarsch des Nationalismus*, p. 21, cited by Sontheimer, *Antidemokratisches Denken*, p. 56.

reworking of received traditions and symbolism to deal with new and potentially unsettling situations and events.[29] We have already touched on some of the German traditions on which the conservative revolutionaries drew, namely, romanticism, *völkisch* ideology, the existentialist language of the self and authenticity, a widespread acceptance of social Darwinism, *Lebensphilosophie*, Wagnerian visions of apocalypse and transformation, Nietzsche's amoral celebration of aesthetics, and a general antipathy to Enlightenment thought and morality.[30] Although it is true that elements of all of these traditions could be found throughout Europe in the first third of the century, nowhere else did they constitute such an important part of national identity as in the *Kulturnation*.

The accomplishment of the reactionary modernists within the conservative revolution was to demonstrate that this national cultural protest could serve to celebrate, rather than denounce, mechanization of war and labor. For example, the Nietzschean Left – Martin Buber and Gustav Landauer, to name two – saw the idea of the will to power as a slogan of individual protest against mechanization and positivism; the Nietzschean Right did the opposite.[31] The right-wing intellectuals touched base with the modernist avant-garde insofar as they also advocated an amoral aestheticism "beyond good and evil" that could juxtapose war and technics to civilian decadence.[32] Ernst Jünger, for example, celebrated the will over "lifeless" rationality by pointing to its presence in a non- and antibourgeois "hardness" evident in the "battle" against nature waged with technological devices. Jünger, one of the most self-conscious of the reactionary modernists, wrote that Nietzsche had no room for the machine "in his Renaissance landscape. But he taught us that life is not only a struggle for daily existence but a struggle for higher and deeper goals. Our task is to apply this doctrine to the machine."[33] The West German critic Karl-Heinz Boh-

[29] Raymond Williams, *Marxism and Literature* (New York, 1977), pp. 122–3. Also see Edward Shils on the relationship between the traditions of the intellectual elites and modern politics in *The Intellectuals and the Powers, and Other Essays* (Chicago, 1972).
[30] See Fest, *Hitler*, pp. 36–57; J. P. Stern, *Hitler*, pp. 43–9. On Wagner, see Jacques Barzun, *Marx, Darwin, and Wagner* (New York, 1958), pp. 231–339.
[31] Bathrick and Breines, "Marx oder Nietzsche."
[32] On this see Karl-Heinz Bohrer, *Die Ästhetik des Schreckens: Die Pessimistische Romantik und Ernst Jüngers Frühwerk* (Munich, 1978), esp. pp. 13–64, which includes his discussion of the separation between aesthetics and morality in the European avant-garde from 1890 to 1930; and Ansgar Hillach, "Die Ästhetisierung des politischen Lebens," in *Walter Benjamin in Kontext*, ed. Walter Burkhardt (Frankfurt, 1978), pp. 127–67.
[33] Ernst Jünger, "Die Maschine," *Standarte* 15 (1925), p. 2. Also cited by Loose, *Gestalt und Werk*, p. 364.

rer, in a recent study of Ernst Jünger, has underscored the contributions of European theorists of decadence such as Wilde and Baudelaire in this effort. By elevating the idea of beauty over normative standards, linking this concept of beauty to an elitist notion of the will, and finally interpreting technology as the embodiment of will and beauty, Weimar's right-wing intellectuals contributed to an irrationalist and nihilist embrace of technology.[34]

Spengler offered another variant of the selective use of the Nietzschean legacy. He focused on Nietzsche's attack on Christian "slave morality" to support a Social Darwinist defense of inequality. Spengler equated the good with power and the bad with powerlessness. Faced with what they described as bourgeois decadence, Spengler and his fellow conservative revolutionaries appealed for the revival of a masculine elite, a "beast of prey" (*Raubtier*) whose will had not yet been tamed by the feminizing impact of Christian and bourgeois morality.[35] The Weimar right-wing intellectuals presented war, militarism, and nationalism as the breeding ground for a new, postdecadent, antibourgeois man. Nietzsche had provided these thinkers with an antibourgeois language as well as the pathos of a heroic struggle against convention. They transformed his message of the late nineteenth century into an effective element of the politics of youth in Weimar.

Although reactionary modernism was a variant of German romanticism, it entailed subtle yet important shifts in the meanings attributed to romantic words and symbols. For example, when Carl Schmitt and Ernst Jünger referred to romanticism, they referred to the idea of will and decision, rather than to antiindustrial imagery. Both Schmitt and Jünger were critics of what they saw as romanticism's passive and effeminate aspects. They argued that political romanticism was the product of the war, rather than of pastoral poetry.[36] Although the reactionary modernists used terms such as *Gemeinschaft* or *Innerlichkeit*, they redefined these legacies of romanticism in ways that elude the dichotomies of tradition *or* modernity, and progress *or* reaction.

But the paradox of rejecting reason and embracing technology did not elude all social and cultural observers. One of the first to understand that the German feeling for nature was making its peace with the industrialized landscape was Walter Benjamin. Given the impor-

---

[34] Bohrer, *Die Ästhetik des Schreckens*.

[35] Oswald Spengler, *Der Untergang des Abendlandes*, Band II (Munich, 1923; reprint, 1972), p. 981. Spengler presented the idea of man as a *Raubtier* or beast of prey in *Der Mensch und die Technik* (Munich, 1931; reprint, 1971), pp. 10–17.

[36] See Schmitt, *Politische Romantik*. Jünger's critique is found throughout *Der Arbeiter* (Hamburg, 1932; reprint, Stuttgart, 1962).

tance that sociological investigation has attached to the process of the rationalization of society (indeed, sociology as a discipline began as reflection on this process in Europe), Benjamin's fragmentary but suggestive comments on the aestheticization of political life and technology among Weimar's right-wing intellectuals deserve attention from sociologists reflecting on the nature of modernity.[37]

Benjamin's views on fascist aesthetics first appeared in his 1930 review of Ernst Jünger's essay collection in praise of the front experience (*Fronterlebnis*) entitled *Krieg und Krieger* (War and the Warrior).[38] Right-wing intellectuals, Benjamin wrote, were drawn to fascism partly because they hoped it would lead to a resolution of a cultural crisis in bourgeois society. Fascism in Europe and National Socialism in Germany promised creativity, beauty, aesthetic form, and the spiritual unity of the nation in place of materialism, positivism, and formless, soulless, and chaotic liberalism. The soul would be able to express itself in the political imagery and symbolism of the nation rather than in divisive social classes and compromising parliaments.[39] Benjamin argued that this program of aesthetic rejuvenation and "overcoming" cultural decadence served the more mundane interests of German militarism and imperialism.

Benjamin's essays on technology and the Right were attempts to dissolve reification, that is, the perception that technology possessed, in Georg Lukács's terms, "a phantom objectivity," an automony so strictly rational and all-embracing as to conceal every trace of its fundamental nature: the relation between people.[40] Lukács's theory of reification as developed in *History and Class Consciousness* was a cornerstone of Benjamin's ideas on the aesthetics of technology in the

---

[37] In *The Nationalization of the Masses* (New York, 1970), George Mosse writes: "Against the problem of industrialization, German nationalism defined itself as truly creative; the artistic became political" (p. 4). Also see Mosse's essay, "Fascism and the Intellectuals," in *The Nature of Fascism*, ed. S. J. Woolf (New York, 1969), pp. 205–25. "The shift from 'aesthetic politics' to the national state as the repository of aesthetic rejuvenation distinguished the fascist intellectuals from antifascist intellectuals whose world view, in other respects, was closer to such fascist idealism" (p. 208).

[38] Walter Benjamin, "Theorien de deutschen Faschismus,' in *Walter Benjamin: Gesammelte Schriften*, vol. 3 (Frankfurt, 1977), pp. 238–50.

[39] Ernst Robert Curtius made this point in *Maurice Barres und die geistigen Grundlagen des französischen Nationalismus* (Bonn, 1921): "Barres's world of the soul conceals an inner logic evident in the fact that his political will is dominated by the same law that rules his relationship to art." In both, Barres wanted to express his soul and will.

[40] Georg Lukács, *History and Class Consciousness* (Cambridge, Mass., 1971), p. 83. On the concept of reification in the Frankfurt school, see Russell Jacoby, "Towards a Critique of Automatic Marxism: The Politics of Philosophy from Lukács to the Frankfurt School," *Telos* 10 (Winter, 1971), pp. 119–46; and his *The Dialectics of Defeat* (New York, 1982).

German Right. The reactionary modernists we will be examining saw in the machine various categories taken from aesthetics and philosophy, but none taken from society or social relations. Benjamin, like Lukács, rejected the attempts of Soviet Marxists, such as Bukharin, to separate technology from social relations and view it as an autonomous force.[41] But like all of Benjamin's work, his insights are situated between an unrepentant Marxist orthodoxy and his own, less systematic but more perceptive, interpretations. At times, his work echoes standard Marxist, Leninist, and Luxemburgian arguments. At other times, he seemed to accept the idea that technology did indeed possess its own dynamic, spilling over the bounds of civilian production and pushing forward in the service of the search for markets and imperialist war.[42]

Benjamin's special contribution lay in his understanding that for Germany's right-wing intellectuals, the "liberation" of technology from Weimar's social and political restrictions was synonymous with recovery of the German soul. Whatever this program may have meant for German industry, for the right-wing intellectuals it meant resolution of a cultural crisis. The idea that economic advance could overcome a cultural crisis was new, at least for Germany's nontechnical intellectuals. It seemed to Benjamin that the less important the individual on the industrialized battlefield became, the more the right-wing enthusiasts of technology stressed his presence. Benjamin thought Jünger and his colleagues turned war into a cultic object, an eternal power that transforms the soul, and that in so doing they were engaging in "nothing other than an uninhibited translation of the principles of art for art's sake to war itself."[43] In the language of battle, the Right abandoned its enmity to technology. At times, Benjamin wrote of fascism in general and compared the Germans to the French and Italians. But he also noticed that Weimar's right wing saw World War I as the culmination of German idealism. This was the meaning of

---

[41] Georg Lukács, "N(ikoloai) Bukharin: Historical Materialism," in *Georg Lukács: Political Writings, 1919–1929* (London, 1972), pp. 134–42.

[42] See Walter Benjamin, "The Work of Art in the Age of Mechanical Reproduction," in *Illuminations* (New York, 1968), p. 244, for Benjamin's analysis along these lines. In "Theorien des deutschen Faschismus," Benjamin spoke of imperialistic war as a "slave revolt of technology" against the discrepancy between the means of production and their "inadequate realization in the process of production." Ansgar Hillach in "Die Äthetisierung des politischen Lebens" draws out these aspects of Benjamin's work.

[43] Benjamin, "Theories of German Fascism," *New German Critique* 17 (Spring 1979), p. 125.

the praise for submission as "heroic surrender" and the stoic bearing present in their postwar writings.

Benjamin referred to "a new theory of war" in the postwar Right whose real purpose was a compensatory one, that is, to transform the actual humiliating defeat in the war into a victory of form and beauty. The beautiful form of the soldier emerging purged and intact from the hell of the trenches turned mass destruction into a redemptive experience. War is the crucible from which a new collective subject of history develops. To make war the subject of aesthetic considerations obscured the political and social interests and purposes that had brought the war about. At times, Benjamin's analysis sounded like so many other general indictments of European fascism, but the specifically German dimension was never completely lost, as the following passage indicates. Here he insists that Jünger's descriptions of the landscape of the battlefield were a perversion, not the logical culmination of German romanticism and idealism:

With as much bitterness as possible, it must be said that the German feeling of nature has had an undreamt-of upsurge in the face of this "landscape of total mobilization ... " Technology wanted to recreate German Idealism's heroic features with ribbons of fire and approach trenches. *It went astray.* For what it took to be the heroic features were those of Hippocrates, the features of death ... To elevate war into a metaphysical abstraction as the new nationalism does, is nothing other than an effort to use technology to solve the mystery of nature as German Idealism understood it in a mystical way instead of illuminating and using nature's secrets via the rational organization of society ... In the parallelogram of forces formed by nature and the nation, war is the diagonal [emphasis added].[44]

The idea of a dialectic of progress, of advances in society taking place through repression of individuals, has been a central theme in modern social theory evident in Hegel, Marx, Durkheim, Weber, and Freud. Benjamin's particular contribution to theoretical reflection on the dialectic of progress is to have understood that cultural and political revolt against the rationalization of society in Germany took the form of a cult of technics rather than backward-looking pastoralism. After World War II, Max Horkheimer developed this idea in his analysis of National Socialism as a "revolt of nature." Horkeimer claimed that nazism combined strict organization and bureaucratic rationalization with cultural revolt. In "modern fascism," he wrote, "rationality now exploits nature by incorporating into its own system the rebellious potentialities of nature."[45] It was Benjamin's analysis of

---

[44] Ibid., p. 127.
[45] Max Horkheimer, *The Eclipse of Reason*, p. 127.

the right-wing ideological reflection on World War I that first indicated that Germany's rebellion against the Enlightenment would incorporate technical advance. This insight, rather than Benjamin's own literary speculations on the relation between technology and society (which tended to attribute to technology the same phantom objectivity that Lukacs criticized in Bukharin's Marxism), was Benjamin's major contribution. Put in other terms, Benjamin understood that technical and industrial modernization did not necessarily imply modernization in a broader political, social, and cultural sense.

Benjamin was also one of the first to note that certain concepts of beauty were connected to *Lebensphilosophie*. In "The Work of Art in the Age of Mechanical Reproduction," he wrote that "fascism sees its salvation in giving [the] masses not their rights but instead a chance to express themselves."[46] Five years earlier, in his essay on Jünger, he had observed that the right-wing intellectuals had transferred the idea of expression from the language of *Lebensphilosophie* to the interpretation of historical events. For Weimar's right-wing nationalists, the violence of the battlefields, the efficiency and power of tanks and ships, and the explosions of grenades were the external expression of inner impulses toward "life." Rather than offer political, economic, or social analyses of events, they could be explained away as being merely the expression of some deep, mysterious, eternal, and irresistible force, some *Ding an sich* immune to rational description. If this were the case, the distinction between history and nature would also be blurred, as it became in Jünger's description of the war as a "storm of steel."

In disputes that originated in the conflicts of the 1960s, a number of critics of the Frankfurt school have argued that the origins of the critical theorists' views on technology lay in the anticivilizational mood of the Weimar right-wing intellectuals. In my view, this analysis is mistaken. Far from indicating a convergence with the views of technology on the German Right, Benjamin's essays were efforts to pierce what Marcuse later called the "technological veil," that is, the idea that technology is an autonomous entity that obeys "imperatives" unrelated to social relations.[47] Grounded in Lukács's theory of reification, Benjamin's insights pointed to some of Marcuse's and Horkheimer's subsequent discussion of technological rationality. His ideas developed from his criticisms of the postwar cult of technology on the Right. The evidence does not support the claim that his interpretation con-

---

[46] Walter Benjamin, "The Work of Art . . .," p. 243.
[47] Herbert Marcuse, *One Dimensional Man* (Boston, 1964), p. 32.

verged with the conservative revolution. As I suggested in the previous chapter, the problem with Benjamin's and Horkeimer's analyses was rather that when they were insightful it was for the wrong reasons. Too often they presented the particularities of modern German history as characteristics of modern society in general. Keeping this in mind allows us to save their valuable insights without accepting their generalizations about the state of the modern world. We will now return to the conservative revolution to delineate its major themes and underscore its distinctively German nature.

The combination of received tradition and active refashioning of these traditions produced an ideology that was distinctively German, notwithstanding some commonalities with fascist ideology as it developed elsewhere in Europe. The following were its common themes.

First, the conservative revolutionaries were nationalists who believed that the virtues of the German *Volk* were superior to the destructive influences of Western capitalism and liberalism on the one hand, and Marxist socialism on the other. This gave their writings an overwhelmingly antimodernist thrust. They defended *völkisch Kultur* against cosmopolitan *Zivilisation*. The former was rooted in the people. The latter was soulless, external, artificial. Modernism was difficult to define, but its tangible symbols of *Entseelung* were everywhere. Berlin was a loveless metropolis of left-wing intellectuals, pornography, and mass consumption. Jewish speculators were creating giant corporate bureaucracies and displacing small businesses and German craftsmen and engineers.

The core juxtaposition of their nationalism was that of *Kultur* and *Zivilisation*. On one side stood the *Volk* as a community of blood, race, and cultural tradition. On the other side was the menace of *Amerikanismus*, liberalism, commerce, materialism, parliament and political parties, and the Weimar Republic. Nationalism served as a secular religion that promised an alternative to a world suffering from an excess of capitalist and communist rationalization. German nationalists elevated Germany's geographical position between East and West into a cultural-political identity as well. The *Kulturnation* would escape the dilemmas of an increasingly soulless modernity.[48]

Second, the prominent advocates of the new nationalism after the war – Spengler, Moeller van den Bruck, Schmitt, and Ernst and Friedrich Jünger – did not place anti-Semitism at the center of their *Weltanschauung*. Rather, they believed that German superiority lay in historical traditions and ideas rather than in biology. But anti-Semi-

[48] Sontheimer, *Antidemokratisches Denken*, p. 244–78.

tism was not absent from the conservative revolution. Some believed that the process of cultural decay and moral disintegration in Weimar was by no means accidental; it was a part of a concerted and planned conspiracy by world Jewry to undermine everything that was healthy in Germany so that the country could never again recover and rise to greatness. Although the Nazis' rhetoric about the "world enemy" found few converts among them, they often associated the Jews with the spirit of commercial abstraction, which they attacked as incompatible with a united nation. As Ernst Jünger put it, the ideal of form and beauty inherent in the *Volk* excluded the Jewish *Gestalt* from Germany as clearly as oil was distinct from water.[49]

Third, they were advocates of *Gemeinschaft* as something inherently good and unified in contrast to a divided and fragmented *Gesellschaft*. Further, the idea of *Gemeinschaft*, and later that of the *Volksgemeinschaft*, had pronounced authoritarian implications. It both proclaimed the existence of social harmony without addressing actual social conflicts and established a moral and ethical basis for individual sacrifice and surrender to existing political powers. Hence the conservative revolutionary notion of the *Volksgemeinschaft* was an attack on both the liberal idea of individual rights and socialist assertions that class divisions and inequalities stood in the path of genuine community.[50]

Fourth, the conservative revolution called for a "primacy of politics," that is, a reassertion of an expansion in foreign policy and repression against the trade unions at home. National idealism was to triumph over the selfish interests of the unions and the materialist philosophy of the left-wing parties. Hans Freyer's "revolution from the Right" combined anticapitalist and nationalist themes. Where the far Left sought to end the domination of the economy over social life through communist revolution, those of the far Right pursued a similar goal through the expansion of the state over society. The primacy of politics blurred the distinction between war and politics, and placed cultural protest in the service of a technologically advanced and powerful

[49] Ernst Jünger, "Nationalismus und Nationalismus," *Die Kommenden* 4 (1929), pp. 481–2. On anti-Semitism and German nationalism, see George Mosse, *The Crisis of German Ideology* (New York, 1964).
[50] Sontheimer, *Antidemokratisches Denken*, pp. 250–1. On the incorporation of the idea of *Gemeinschaft* into the rationalization measures undertaken by the Nazi regime, see Mason, "Zur Enstehung des Gesetzes zur Ordnung der nationalen Arbeit," in *Industrielles System und politische Entwicklung in der Weimarer Republik*, ed. Mommsen, Petzina, and Weisbrod (Düsseldorf, 1974).

state.[51] The explicit implications of the primacy of politics in the conservative revolution were totalitarian. From now on there were to be no limits to ideological politics. The utilitarian and humanistic considerations of nineteenth-century liberalism were to be abandoned in order to establish a state of constant dynamism and movement.[52]

Finally, the conservative revolution articulated the idea of a German or national socialism. The idea of a national socialism was ingenious. It reformulated a potentially threatening idea, socialism, to suit indigenous German traditions. Moeller van den Bruck, the single most important figure of the conservative revolution, wrote in his most significant work, *Das Dritte Reich*, that German socialism began where Marxism ended, and that "the task of German socialism in the context of the cultural history of humanity was to dissolve all traces of liberalism [remaining in the idea of socialism]." He also contrasted the "young peoples" of the "East" – Germany and Russia – with those of the capitalist and materialist "West."[53] Some figures in the conservative revolution, such as the "national Bolsheviks" around Ernst Niekisch, interpreted van den Bruck's alliance of the "young peoples" as a call for a German-Russian alliance rooted in a shared antiliberalism and resentment of the Western democracies.[54] But Spengler (and later Heidegger) expressed a more common view, namely, that Germany as the nation "in the middle" ought to pursue a "third way" between the capitalist West and communist East. Socialism, Spengler argued, must be made compatible with the antiliberal, authoritarian traditions of German nationalism.[55]

The idea of national socialism was all the more powerful for the generation that lived through the war because it was an idea that many believed had been realized in the trenches. The West German political scientist, Kurt Sontheimer, has pointed out that National

---

[51] George Mosse, "Fascism and the Intellectuals" and *Masses and Man: Nationalist and Fascist Perceptions of Reality* (New York, 1980), develops the idea of fascism as a cultural revolutionary movement that appealed to intellectuals seeking spiritual values in a materialistic, bourgeois age.

[52] See Hannah Arendt, *The Origins of Totalitarianism*, (Cleveland, 1958).

[53] Moeller van den Bruck, *Das Dritte Reich* (Berlin, 1923), p. 68. Also see Fritz Stern, *The Politics of Cultural Despair*, pp. 310–20 for a discussion of this work. Van den Bruck's comments on the young people were in *Das Recht der jungen Volker* (Munich, 1919).

[54] See Schüddekopf, *Linke Leute von Rechts: National-bolschewismus in Deutschland* (Frankfurt, 1973); and John Norr, "German Social Theory and the Hidden Face of Technology," *European Journal of Sociology* XV (1974), pp. 312–36, for comments on Niekisch's friendship with Jünger.

[55] Oswald Spengler, *Preusentum und Sozialismus* (Munich, 1920).

Socialism united the two most powerful ideological impulses of the epoch and "anticipated the synthesis the age had yet to complete." The socialist parties were not nationalist, and the bourgeois parties were not socialist. "Here, however, appeared to be a party [the Nazis] that represented both things at the same time, the party of the German future."[56] To a political generation that believed that national socialism had been realized, however briefly, in the very recent past, the Nazis presented themselves as the party of the German future. They promised to make the national unity of August 1914 a permanent condition.[57] The war experience of the recent, not the distant, past had become the concrete utopia of the Right, a lost treasure that this reactionary tradition was intent on recapturing.

Not all of the conservative revolutionaries were reactionary modernists. Considerable antagonism to technology persisted in the Weimar Right. For example, Moeller van den Bruck did not exempt technology from his general indictment of Enlightenment rationality. His "third reich" beyond capitalist and communist materialism was to provide the answers to questions such as "what to do with our masses ... and how to save human nature from the machine."[58] Spengler's *The Decline of the West* had an ambiguous impact. It is a major document of reactionary modernism and also contains enough references to the "devilish" nature of the machine or the "enslavement of man by his creation" to please the antitechnological mood.[59] Spengler was sufficiently worried that his book might encourage the revolt of youth against technology that he wrote *Man and Technics* to establish his protechnological credentials. Many of the cultural politicans of the engineering profession repeatedly criticized him for fostering hostility, even if unintentionally, to technical advance.[60]

There was no ambiguity whatsoever in the antitechnological views

---

[56] Sontheimer, *Antidemokratisches Denken*, p. 278.
[57] Here is how Robert Ley, director of the German Labor Front in the Third Reich, described the significance of World War I: "The German revolution began in the August days of 1914 ... The people were reunited in the trenches in the East and West. The grenades and mines did not ask whether one was high- or low-born, if one was rich or poor, or what religion or social group one belonged to. Rather this was a great, powerful example of the meaning and spirit of community." *Durchbruch der sozialen Ehre* (Munich, 1935), cited in Timothy Mason, *Sozialpolitik im Dritten Reich*, p. 26.
[58] Moeller van den Bruck, *Das Recht der Jungen Volker*, p. 115.
[59] Spengler is still viewed by some as an antitechnological critic. See Gerd Hortleder, *Das Gesellschaftsbild des Ingenieurs: Zum politischen Verhalten der Technischen Intelligenz in Deutschland* (Frankfurt, 1970), p. 86.
[60] Carl Weihe, the editor of *Technik und Kultur*, a journal for graduates of the technical universities, repeatedly criticized Spengler's views on technology. See chap. 7.

of adherents of the conservative revolution such as the philosopher Ludwig Klages, the poet Paul Ernst, and the journalist Ernst Niekisch. Klages's three-volume work, *Der Geist als Widersacher der Seele* (The Mind as the Antagonist of the Soul), published from 1929 to 1931, was the most elaborate attack on scientific and technological rationality to emerge from the conservative revolution.[61] Its main theme was this: Human history consists in the growing domination of *Geist* (mind) over soul, of consciousness over dream and fantasy, of concepts and logic over imagery and myth. This all-powerful, disenchanting *Geist* characterizes Christianity, Marxism, liberalism, and modern science and technology. In Klages's view, the abstractions of science and technology are really new myths that seek to foster the illusion that they are synonymous with natural phenomena themselves. He wrote that "the machine . . . can destroy life but never create it," and he believed that conceptual grasp of the physical universe led to a "death of reality."[62] This juxtaposition of abstraction, rationality, technics, and death with immediacy, intuition, feelings, nature, and life has the kind of consistency one would expect from an irrationalist position. In his *Der Zusammenbruch des deutschen Idealismus* (The Collapse of German Idealism), Paul Ernst presented a comparable consistency. Criticizing the impact of the division of labor on individuals, he wrote, "Whoever uses machines, receives a machine heart."[63]

Though they were in a minority, there were right-wing intellectuals who had survived the war and now hated technology. Ernst Niekisch, for example, wrote the following in an essay entitled "Menschenfresser Technik" (Man-eating Technology):

Technology is the rape of nature. It brushes nature aside. It amounts to cunningly tricking nature out of the free disposal of one piece of land after another. When technology triumphs, nature is violated and desolated. Technology murders life by striking down, step by step, the limits established by nature. It devours men and all that is human. It is heated with bodies. Blood is its cooling lubricant. Consequently, war in this technological era is a murderous slaughter . . . The antilife [*lebensfeindlich*], demonic quality of technology manifests itself most horribly in modern war. In war, technology's productive capacity is so up-do-date that on the hour it is able to annihilate everything organic, whatever it may be – suddenly, totally and precisely.[64]

---

[61] Ludwig Klages, *Der Geist als Widersacher der Seele* (reprint, Bonn, 1969). On Klages's contributions to the conservative revolution, see Hillach, "Ästhetisierung des politischen Lebens"; Horkheimer, "Zum Rationalismusstreit"; and Lukács, *Die Zerstörung der Vernunft*, Band III, pp. 195–9.
[62] Klages, *Der Geist als Widersacher der Seele*, p. 695.
[63] Paul Ernst, *Der Zusammenbruch des deutschen Idealismus* (Munich, 1918), p. 451.
[64] Ernst Niekisch, "Menschenfresser Technik," *Widerstand* 6 (1931), p. 110. Cited by Karl Prumm, *Die Literatur des soldatischen Nationalismus*, Band 1, p. 376.

Like the ideas of van den Bruck, Klages, and Ernst, Niekisch's thinking possesses the virtue of internal consistency: If technology "murders life," then the defense of life calls for opposition to technology. In this view, technology belongs in the realm of *Zivilisation* rather than *Kultur*. Despite its logical coherence, however, such a cultural system was hardly suited for German nationalism in an age of technological warfare. The accomplishment of the reactionary modernists within the conservative revolution was to have made a virtue out of the necessity of embracing technics by shifting technology out of the sphere of *Zivilisation* and into that of *Kultur*. By so doing, they could embrace technology without adopting a rationalist world view in politics and culture. The resulting cult of technics went far beyond pragmatic resignation to a necessary evil. It possessed the same emotional fervor present in the antitechnological mood that spread across the Weimar political spectrum.

Among Weimar's cultural currents, reactionary modernism was unique in combining irrationalism with enthusiasm for technology. Expressionists generally attacked technology and bourgeois philistinism from the left. Dramatists such as Ernst Toller and Georg Kaiser saw technology as a source of dehumanization. Although they also called for cultural as well as political revolution, the synthesis of unreason and modern technology was beyond them. A non- or less industrialized Germany would have suited them.[65]

The architects, artists, designers, and engineers in the Bauhaus tried to demonstrate that Enlightenment reason was indeed fully compatible with a fruitful interaction of art and technology. Walter Gropius, the leading spirit of the Bauhaus, saw no conflict between cosmopolitanism, social democratic values, and reason, on the one hand, and beauty on the other. Given a sufficient measure of reason and passion, Gropius saw no reason why technology should pose a threat to mankind. The Bauhaus embraced technology as part of modernity in a broader sense.[66]

---

[65] Helmut Lethens, *Neue Sachlichkeit: Studien zur Literatur des Weissen Sozialismus* (Stuttgart, 1970), p. 64. This book contains much useful material on the German response to Americanism and technology. Lethens's thesis is that *Neue Sachlichkeit* was the dominant current of Weimar culture and that this fetishization of industrial rationalization culminated in nazism. Drawing on the Frankfurt theorists, he stresses the continuity of a technocratic liberalism and fascism. But his own evidence suggests that the Nazis' primacy of politics was hardly so exclusively technocratic. Lethens's book suffers from a common trait of West German Marxist analyses of "fascism": It subsumes German traditions under the more general (and less painful?) rubric of capitalism.

[66] Gay, *Weimar Culture*, pp. 98–101.

Other forms of accepting technology in Weimar lacked the Bauhaus's sense of proportion. *Neue Sachlichkeit* or the New Objectivity signaled a more sober, disillusioned, resigned, and cynical mood in literature and reportage during the stabilization phase of the Republic. Writers on the Left, such as Erich Kastner and Alexander Doblin, distanced themselves from expressionist hostility to technology.[67] It was also in this period that technocratic visions found support among liberals eager to use technological advances to increase productivity and attenuate social conflicts. As Charles Maier has pointed out, the German response to Fordism bore similiarities to strategies of bourgeois defense in France and Italy.[68] Indeed, in Germany, Henry Ford was not only the apostle of assembly-line techniques and scientific management but also of what Gottfried Feder called "creative" or productive capital as opposed to Jewish finance.

Those unhappy with productivist visions of the future could hardly look to the Communist Party for an alternative view. The German Communist Party exuded Leninist enthusiasm for capitalist technology. "Forward through the trusts and beyond to socialism" was the view of one leading theorist, who also went so far as to call Henry Ford a revolutionary "no less revolutionary than capitalism itself."[69] The Communists and Social Democrats distanced themselves from the antiindustrialism of the cultural radicals in favor of Marx's teleology of the progressive unfolding of the productive forces that would eliminate feudal residues, enlarge the proletariat, and lead to socialism or communism. Some suggested that the left-wing parties had succumbed to capitalist ideology. Bela Belasz denounced *Neue Sachlichkeit* as the "*Lebensgefühl* (life feeling) of trust capital, ... the aesthetics of the assembly line," whereas Ernst Bloch called it "the doctor at capitalism's deathbed" whose "hatred of utopia" (*Utopiefeindschaft*) served the rehabilitation of capital after the postwar years of revolution and counterrevolution. Bloch argued that German Marxism was so committed to capitalist development that it left the field of cultural revolution and appeals to myth and emotion to the Right.[70] For example, although the left-wing cultural critic Siegfried Kracauer described the American chorus line as a welcome sign of the disen-

[67] Ibid., pp. 120–2; Craig, *Germany*, pp. 484–5.
[68] Charles S. Maier, "Between Taylorism and Technocracy: European Ideologies and the Vision of Productivity in the 1920s," *Journal of Contemporary History* 5 (1970), pp. 27–51.
[69] Jakob Walcher, *Ford oder Marx*, p. 51, cited in Lethens, *Neue Sachlichkeit*, p. 82.
[70] Bela Belasz, "Sachlichkeit und Sozialismus," in *Die Weltbuhne* 14 (1928), p. 917, cited in Lethens, *Neue Sachlichkeit*, p. 32.

chantment of society that could only help to dissolve German *völkisch* mysticism, the right-wing intellectuals from *Die Tat* were disgusted and horrified by it. In their view, *Amerikanismus* – mass production and consumption, Taylorism, rationalization of industry – was a plague threatening the German soul. Those conservatives such as the industrial psychologist Fritz Giese, who praised the chorus line as the disciplining of previously wild and chaotic instincts, were in a minority.[71] *Die Tat's* synthesis of nationalism, anti-Americanism, and middle-class anticapitalist rhetoric was a more widespread cultural complex.

In short, with the exception of the reactionary modernists, those who rejected the Enlightenment and its legacy rejected technology, whereas those who defended the Enlightenment accepted the need for technical development. In the following chapters I will discuss in greater detail the contributions of the following five thinkers: Hans Freyer, Ernst Jünger, Carl Schmitt, Werner Sombart, and Oswald Spengler. I will also discuss Martin Heidegger's works on technology, which share in some but by no means all of the reconciliations of technics and unreason favored by these other authors.

Ernst Jünger (b. 1895) was the most important and prolific contributor to reactionary modernism in the conservative revolution. A much-decorated soldier, during the Weimar years Jünger produced about ten books and over a hundred essays on war, death, heroism, nationalism, sacrifice, and technology. Among these were two commercial successes, *In Stahlgewittern* (The Storm of Steel, 1920) and *Der Arbeiter* (The Worker, 1932).[72] The titles of two works he published between these, *Der Kampf als inneres Erlebnis* (The Battle as an Inner Experience, 1922) and *Feuer und Blut* (Fire and Blood, 1925), suggest the vitalist fascination for war and technics that makes him so im-

---

[71] See Fritz Giese, *Girlkultur: Vergleiche zwischen amerikanische und europäischen Rhythmus und Lebensgefühl* (Munich, 1925).

[72] Ernst Jünger, *In Stahlgewittern* (Berlin, 1920; reprint, Stuttgart, 1960); and *Der Arbeiter* (Hamburg, 1932; reprint, Stuttgart, 1960). The two West German studies that discuss Jünger's modernism are Bohrer, *Die Ästhetik des Schreckens*, and Prumm, *Die Literatur des soldatischen Nationalismus*. Other useful secondary works on Jünger are Klaus-Frieder Bastian, *Das Politische bei Ernst Jünger: Nonkonformismus und Kompromiss der Innerlichkeit* (Freiburg, 1962); Christian Graf von Krockow, *Die Entscheidung: Eine Untersuchung über Ernst Jünger, Carl Schmitt, Martin Heidegger* (Stuttgart, 1958); Gerhard Loose, *Ernst Jünger: Gestalt und Werk*; Hans-Peter Schwarz, *Die konservative Anarchist*; J. P. Stern, *Ernst Jünger: A Writer of Our Time* (Cambridge, 1953); and Struve, *Elites Against Democracy*. *In Stahlgewittern* was one of the most popular books of its time; *Der Arbeiter* was a best seller in 1932. See *Elites Against Democracy*, p. 377, on Jünger's literary success.

portant for this study. He published his political essays in *Arminius*, *Die Standarte*, and *Vormarsch*. Although he never joined the Nazi party and retreated from politics after 1933, his work before then helped create a climate favorable to National Socialism.[73]

Like Jünger, Oswald Spengler (1880–1936) was rooted in right-wing political clubs and journals, not the university. Although usually thought of as Weimar's leading advocate of cultural pessimism, Spengler shared in the reactionary modernist synthesis. Whereas some observers, at the time and since, have interpreted *Der Untergang des Abendlandes* (The Decline of the West, 1918–1922) and *Der Mensch und die Technik* (Man and Technics, 1931) as antitechnological tracts, I will discuss them as documents that associated technology with beauty, will, and productivity, thereby placing it in the realm of German *Kultur* rather than Western *Zivilisation*.[74]

There are many who consider Martin Heidegger (1889–1976) the most important German philosopher of the twentieth century, whereas others think he did almost irreparable damage to the German language in the service of philosophical obscurantism. In either case his was a major voice raised against the dangers of technology. Less well known is his friendship with Ernst Jünger and the similarities between their views on technology.[75] I will consider Heidegger's essays on technology and politics taken from the 1930s. Although his enthusiasm for technical advance did not match that of the other members of the conservative revolution under consideration, neither was he an ardent Luddite. His hope that Germany would be the country to achieve a fusion of technology and soul places his work at this time firmly within the reactionary modernist current of German nationalism. Heidegger made a tenuous peace with both nazism and tech-

---

[73] Ernst Jünger, *Der Kampf als inneres Erlebnis* (Berlin, 1922); and *Feuer und Blut* (Magdeburg, 1926; reprint, Stuttgart, 1960). On the parallels between Jünger's view of technology and Hitler's vision of totalitarian movement, see Wolfgang Sauer, *Die Nationalsozialistische Machtergreifung: Die Mobilmachung der Gewalt* (Frankfurt, 1974), pp. 165–74. Sauer focuses on Jünger's desire to "set aside the barrier between war and revolution and to fuse both into a single all-encompassing process of embattled dynamism." On Jünger's relationship to nazism, see Prumm, *Die Literatur*, Band 2, pp. 385–400.

[74] On Spengler's role in the conservative revolution see Klemperer, *Germany's New Conservatism*; Mohler, *Die konservative Revolution*; and Struve, *Elites Against Democracy*. For a view of Spengler as an antagonist of technology, see Hortleder, *Das Gesellschaftsbild des Ingenieurs*.

[75] On the similarities in Jünger's and Heidegger's views, see Norr, "German Social Theory and the Hidden Face of Technology."

nology, whatever his postwar retrospectives on technological dehumanization may have been.[76]

Hans Freyer (1887–1969) exerted a powerful influence on German sociology and philosophy from the 1920s through the 1960s. His most important popular contribution to the conservative revolution was *Revolution von Rechts* (Revolution from the Right, 1931), in which he praised the virtues of the *Volk* and attacked industrial society. However, in this work, in several philosophical essays of this period, and in his *Soziologie als Wirklichkeitswissenschaft* (Sociology as a Science of Reality, 1931), a continuous theme in Freyer's work was the reification, its separation from social relationships, not the rejection, of technology.[77]

Carl Schmitt (b. 1888) was the most widely read and respected political scientist of his day, a position due to his literary talent and to his praise of power and conflict as values in themselves. In 1932, as Germany moved into the protracted constitutional crisis that resulted in Hitler's accession, Schmitt argued in his book-length essay, *Der Begriff des Politischen* (The Concept of the Political), that the actual situation creates its own legality, that emergencies obviate normative law, and that he is sovereign who makes the decision regulating the emergency situation. In the spring of 1933, he joined the Nazi party in the belief that Hitler and National Socialism were the realization of this theory of decisionism, according to which political action was a value in itself regardless of the normative justifications attached to it.[78] His contributions to reactionary modernism may be found in two

---

[76] Ibid. Also see Winifred Franzen, *Von der Existenzialontologie zur Seinsgeschichte: Eine Untersuchung über die Entwicklung der Philosophie Martin Heideggers* (Meisenheim am Glan, 1975); and George Steiner, *Martin Heidegger* (London, 1978).

[77] Hans Freyer, *Revolution von Rechts* (Jena, 1931); and "Zur Philosophie der Technik," *Blätter für deutsche Philosophie* 3 (1927–8), pp. 192–201. On Freyer in the conservative revolution see René König, "Zur Soziologie der Zwanziger Jahre," in *Die Zeit ohne Eigenschaften: Eine Bilanz der Zwanziger Jahre*, ed. L. Rheinisch (Stuttgart, 1961, pp. 82–118; and George Mosse, "The Corporate State and the Conservative Revolution." On Freyer's contributions to Weimar sociology, see Herbert Marcuse, "Zur Auseinandersetzung mit Hans Freyers Soziologie als Wirklichkeitswissenschaft," in *Herbert Marcuse: Schriften I*, (Frankfurt, 1978) pp. 488–508. On Freyer's importance for discussions of technology in postwar West Germany, see Otto Ulrich, *Technik und Herrschaft* (Frankfurt, 1977).

[78] On Schmitt and National Socialism, see Joseph Bendersky, "The Expendable *Kronjurist*: Carl Schmitt and National Socialism, 1933–1936," *Journal of Contemporary History* 14 (1979), pp. 309–28; Neumann, *Behemoth*; and Sontheimer, *Antidemokratisches Denken*. On Schmitt's political theory, see Christian Graf von Krockow, *Die Entscheidung: Eine Untersuchung über Ernst Jünger, Carl Schmitt, Martin Heidegger*; Herbert Marcuse, "The Struggle Against Liberalism in the Totalitarian View of the State," in *Negations*, trans. Jeremy Shapiro (Boston, 1968), pp. 3–42; Franz Neumann, "The Change in

works: *Der Begriff des Politischen* (The Concept of the Political, 1932), and *Politische Romantik* (Political Romanticism, 1919).[79] A student of Max Weber, Schmitt believed that the authoritarian state, when combined with advanced technology could restore political dynamism in a bureaucratized society. Along with Ernst Jünger, he argued that political romanticism demanded a break from what he viewed as the passivity and escapism of nineteenth-century German romanticism.[80]

Werner Sombart (1865–1941) was the most important representative of German sociology to influence the conservative revolution as well as the reactionary modernist tradition. Along with Max Weber, he edited one of the major journals of German social science, *Die Archiv für Sozialwissenschaft und Sozialpolitik*.[81] During the Weimar years he extended his influence into the conservative revolution through popularization of his scholarly work in *Die Tat*.[82] Although Sombart was an enthusiastic supporter of the German war effort (see his *Händler und Helden*, Traders and Heroes, 1915), World War I was not the formative influence on his thinking. His main contribution to reactionary modernism preceded the war. *Die Juden und das Wirtschaftsleben* (The Jews and Economic Life, 1911) was an interpretation of the origins of capitalism in Europe that translated social-historical categories into religious and psychological archetypes.[83] Sombart identified the Jews with market rationality and commercial greed and the Germans with productive labor and technology. The result was to shift cultural protest against capitalism and the market away from antitechnological resentments and onto liberalism, Marxism, and the Jews. His *Deutscher Sozialismus* (German Socialism, 1934) was an explosive mixture of sympathy for National Socialism, enthusiasm for

the Function of Natural Law," pp. 22–68, and "Notes on the Theory of Dictatorship," pp. 233–56, in *The Democratic and Authoritarian State* (New York, 1966).
[79] Carl Schmitt, *Der Begriff des Politischen* (Munich, 1932); *Politische Romantik* (Munich-Leipzig, 1919). See also Schmitt's *Der Hüter der Verfassung* (Tübingen, 1931); and *Die Geistesgeschichtlichen Lage des heutigen Parlamentarismus*, 2d ed. (Munich-Leipzig, 1926); *Die Diktatur* (Munich, 1921); *Politische Theologie* (Munich, 1922).
[80] See Schmitt's *Politische Romantik*.
[81] On Sombart's importance for the Weimar Right, see Lebovics, *Social Conservatism*, pp. 49–78.
[82] Ferdinand Fried, an editor of *Die Tat*, was the most active popularizer of Sombart's ideas. See his *Das Ende des Kapitalismus* (Jena, 1931); Hock, *Deutscher Antikapitalismus*; and Klaus Fritsche, *Politische Romantik und Gegenrevolution. Fluchtwege in der bürgerlichen Gesellschaft: Das Beispiel des "Tat"- Kreises* (Frankfurt, 1976). On Sombart's influence in German social science, see Arthur Mitzman, *Sociology and Estrangement* (New York, 1973), pp. 135–264.
[83] Werner Sombart, *Die Juden und das Wirtschaftsleben* (Leipzig, 1911).

"German technology," and disgust with the supposedly bygone liberal-materialist-Jewish era.[84]

In this chapter, I have situated the conservative revolution in Weimar's social, cultural, and political climate to underscore the paradox of the embrace of technology by nontechnical intellectuals who were the inheritors of irrationalist and romantic traditions. Like their contemporaries in the political Center and Left, the reactionary modernists were romantic anticapitalists in juxtaposing *Kultur* and *Zivilisation*. Unlike these other critics of positivism, however, the political romantics of the Right separated the idea of *Kultur* from the humanistic dimensions of the, albeit comparatively weak, German Enlightenment. Instead they equated *Kultur* with suprahistorical first principles – life, blood, race, struggle, will, sacrifice – which required no rational justification. The reactionary modernists were no less hostile to reason than their comrades who detested the machine as a threat to the German soul. Their accomplishment was to articulate a set of cultural symbols for the nontechnical intellectuals in which technology became an expression of that soul, and thus of German *Kultur*. It is no wonder that their reconciliation of technics and unreason strikes us as paradoxical. For if they broke with the hostility to technology that had characterized aspects of German nationalism for a century, they continued its century-old revolt against Enlightenment rationality. Here lay the great appeal of this illiberal and selective view of German modernization.

Two final issues deserve comment: the relation of the reactionary modernists to Hitler and to the irrationalist enthusiasm for technology among fascist intellectuals in Italy, France, and England. Because they either never joined the Nazi party (Jünger, Freyer, Sombart, Spengler) or joined for only a short time (Heidegger, Schmitt), some interpreters have stressed the gap between their views and those of National Socialism. But the commonalities outweighed the differences. Whether they liked it or not, Hitler tried to carry out the cultural revolution they sought. It may seem odd to describe Hitler as a cultural revolutionary but both his roots and his intentions point in this direction. He shared with the reactionary modernists an ideology of the will drawn from Nietzsche and Schopenhauer, a view of politics as an aesthetic accomplishment, a Social Darwinist view of politics as struggle, irrationalism, and anti-Semitism, and a sense that Germany was

---

[84] Werner Sombart, *Deutscher Sozialismus* (Berlin, 1934). On Sombart and National Socialism, see Werner Krause, *Werner Sombarts Weg vom Kathedersozialismus zum Faschismus* (East Berlin, 1962).

sinking into a state of hopeless degeneration. The promise of Hitler's totalitarian politics was to reverse this process by attacking the main source of the disease, the Jews. His genius lay partly in convincing his followers that he was going to carry out a cultural revolution and break the drive toward the disenchantment of the world brought about by liberalism and Marxism without pulling Germany back into preindustrial impotence. Like the reactionary modernists, he was contemptuous of *völkisch* pastoralism, advocating instead what Goebbels called "steellike romanticism." But unlike them, Hitler was an actor committed to pursuing the implications of ideas to their logical or illogical conclusions – war and mass murder. Against Hitler, the advocates of the *Blutgemeinschaft* were without alternative ideals. Though not a prolific writer on the subject, Hitler was the most important practitioner of the reactionary modernist tradition, the one who built the highways and then started the war that was to unify technology and the German soul.[85]

Finally, what distinguished the German reconciliations of technics and unreason from those common among fascist intellectuals in postwar Europe? In Italy, France, and England, the avant-garde associated technology with a new antibourgeois vitalism, masculine violence and eros, and the will to power; a new aesthetics, and creativity rather than commercial parasitism; and a full life lived to the emotional limit that contrasted with bourgeois decadence and boredom. Marinetti and the futurists in Italy, Wyndham Lewis and Ezra Pound in England, Sorel, Drieu la Rochelle, and Maurras in France were all drawn to right-wing politics partly out of their views on technology.

To be sure, there were similarities between the modernist vanguard in Germany, especially Jünger, and right-wing modernism in Europe generally.[86] Some observers have interpreted these parallels as lending support to Adorno and Horkheimer's thesis of the dialectic of enlightenment according to which enlightenment rationality contains within itself a return to myth regardless of national histories and traditions. In my view, however, the urge to compare has obscured German uniqueness. Nowhere else in Europe did technological mod-

---

[85] This view of Hitler draws on Bracher, "The Role of Hitler"; Fest, *Hitler*; Jäckel, *Hitler's World View: A Blueprint for Power*, trans. H. Arnold (Middletown, Conn., 1972); Mosse, *The Crisis of German Ideology*; and J. P. Stern, *Hitler*.

[86] On the parallels between Jünger and the avant-garde generally see Bohrer, *Die Ästhetik des Schreckens*, pp. 13–159. Also see Miriam Hansen, *Ezra Pounds frühe Poetik und Kulturkritik zwischen Aufklärung und Avantgarde* (Stuttgart, 1979); and Frederic Jameson, *Fables of Aggression, Wyndham Lewis: The Fascist as Modernist* (Berkeley, 1979); Helmut Kreuzer, *Die Boheme: Analyse und Dokumentation der intellektuellen Subkultur vom. 19 Jahrhundert bis zur Gegenwart* (Stuttgart, 1971).

ernity and romantic protest clash with such force as in Germany. Nowhere else had industrialization developed so quickly in the absence of a successful bourgeois revolution. And nowhere else was protest against the Enlightenment a constitutive element in the formation of national identity as it had been in Germany from the early nineteenth century up through Weimar. Although Italian, French, and British intellectuals presented similar themes, none of these societies witnessed anything comparable to the *Streit um die Technik* that filled the political clubs of the literati and the lecture halls of the technical universities in Weimar. Nor did they produce a cultural tradition spanning three-quarters of a century.

The reason for the depth and pervasiveness of the reactionary modernist tradition in Germany had less to do with capitalism or modernity in general than with the form they took in Germany. The conservative revolution must be understood in light of the German problem in general, that is, the weakness of democracy and the liberal principle in a society that became highly industrialized very quickly. Neither anti-Western resentments nor technological proficiency were monopolies of the Germans. But nowhere else did the two coexist in such thorough forms. This is why reactionary modernism became part of German nationalism while elsewhere in Europe it remained one of the fads and fashions of the avant-garde. It was the weakness of the Enlightenment in Germany, not its strength, that encouraged the confusions concerning technology I have called reactionary modernism. And it was also Germany's unique (at that time) path to modernity that made possible the ultimate political impact of reactionary modernist ideology. Having presented the background, it is now time to turn to the evidence, beginning with an ambivalent but central figure of the reactionary modernist tradition, Oswald Spengler.

3

Oswald Spengler: bourgeois antinomies, reactionary reconciliations

Both the title and the contents of Oswald Spengler's most famous work, *The Decline of the West*, mark him as one of the major exponents of the anticivilizational mood of cultural criticism in the Weimar Republic. It is replete with the familiar catalogue of antimodernism, but it also presents a theme that has received less attention, namely, the reconciliation of romantic and irrationalist sentiments with enthusiasm for technical advance. Spengler's close personal ties to German industrialists and to the conservative revolutionaries in the June Club nurtured his ambiguous synthesis of technics and irrationalism that later afforded engineers a central role in the new elite whose task it was to rescue Germany from the liberalism of the Weimar Republic.[1] To be sure, Spengler juxtaposed German *Kultur* and Western *Zivilisation*, but unlike Klages or Moeller van den Bruck, he sought to reconcile *Kultur* with twentieth-century German nationalism. In 1918 he wrote to a friend: "Truly our future lies on the one hand in Prussian conservatism *after it has been cleansed of all feudal-agrarian narrowness* and on the other hand in the working people after they have freed themselves from the anarchist-radical masses." (emphasis added).[2] He hoped that *The Decline of the West* would encourage the young generation to turn toward technology and politics instead of poetry and philosophy.[3] In a number of essays and books, Spengler created an

[1] On Spengler's connections to German industrialists, see Walter Spengler: Caesar and Croesus," in *Elites Against Democracy* (Princeton, N.J., 1973), pp. 232–73. Spengler considered using less pessimistic titles, such as the "completion" rather than the "decline" of the West, but the loss of the war suggested the gloomier term.
[2] Letter of December 27, 1918, to Hans Klores in *Briefe 1913–1936*, ed. Anton M. Koktanek and Manfred Schroter (Munich, 1963), p. 115. Cited in Struve, pp. 236–7.
[3] Oswald Spengler, *Der Untergang des Abendlandes*, Band I (Munich, 1923; reprint, 1977).

uneasy truce between right-wing romanticism and modern politics by celebrating modern technology with a language and symbolism adaptable to nationalist mass politics. Behind the smooth, lean surfaces of modern technical artifacts, Spengler saw at work the dark, elemental, demonic forces that had been the focus of so much previous (antiindustrial) romanticism in Germany. The expressionist Left and resigned Center restated the old dichotomies of *Kultur* versus *Zivilisation*. What distinguished Spengler and like-minded conservative revolutionaries was their belief that this cultural crisis could be "overcome" through nationalist mobilization.

In *Preussentum und Sozialismus* (Prussian Virtues and Socialism), published in 1919, Spengler's self-appointed task was "liberating German socialism from Marx," as well as demonstrating that "old-Prussian spirit and socialist values," which are now diametrically opposed, can be shown to be "one and the same thing."[4] His reformulation of the idea of socialism amounted to shifting it from a world of *Zivilisation* associated with the West, England, and the Jews, into a German world of *Kultur*. The form of this simple procedure was identical to that of the incorporation of technology into the rhetoric of the postwar Right.

Spengler's attack on Marx illustrates the metamorphosis of philosophical-political categories into nationalist ones: Marx was a "good materialist but a bad psychologist" who mistakenly attributed to the proletariat the "Prussian" concept of socialism, and to the bourgeoisie the "English" idea of capitalism. Marx's concept of class struggle, Spengler thought, was a mistaken transference of a racial and national contradiction between the German and the English "spirit" onto the conflict between social classes within these societies. Marx's deficiencies in psychological insight were typical of nineteenth-century English materialism, so it was hardly surprising that Marxists tended to hold labor in "contempt."[5] But it was not only Manchester liberalism that stood in the way of soulful profundities. Marx's Jewishness contributed as well. Spengler regarded Marxism as a legacy of the materialism and positivism of the nineteenth century and thus lacking in the subjective and psychological dimensions of life. Marxism was the "capitalism" of the working class. Spengler, on the other hand, viewed himself as a man of the twentieth century, a fully modern man, one who understood "the feeling that life dominates reason, ... that knowledge of men is more important than abstract and general ideas." Prussian qualities refer to fate, instinct, and the organic, whereas

[4] Oswald Spengler, *Preussentum und Sozialismus* (Munich, 1919), p. 4.
[5] Ibid., p. 73.

Marxism is the rationalist, unromantic countertype. Rejection of rationalism, rather than its defense, is truly modern.[6]

If Marxism was the opposite of Prussian virtues, England and France were the countertypes of Germany. Neither country had a proper understanding of power: In France, power "belongs to no one," because of French instincts of anarchy and egalitarianism, whereas in England, power is dispersed among individuals on the competitive market. In Prussia, "power belongs to the whole. The individual serves this whole. The totality is sovereign."[7] Socialist virtues are German virtues – loyalty, discipline, selfless denial, and sacrifice, placing the good of the national *Gemeinschaft* over that of the individual.[8] These qualities are manifest in the civil service, the officer corps, and in the movement of the working class under Bebel and Lasalle's leadership. Spengler did not conceal his admiration for the militaristic aspects of the "battalions" of German workers who displayed "decisiveness, discipline, and the courage to die" for ideals not measurable in material demands. Yet he denounced the revolution of 1918–19 as "the most senseless act of German history," one led by "literary scum."[9] Prussian virtues and socialism stand united against the "inner England, against the *Weltanschauung* (Marxist and liberal rationalism) which permeates our whole life as a people, paralyzes it, and takes away its soul."[10]

There is another formula that contributes to Spengler's version of a national socialism, namely, Nietzsche's notion of the will to power. "Socialism," Spengler wrote, "means power, power, and yet again power."[11] Here Spengler's political romanticism is apparent. Power ought not to serve mundane material interests but rather the more elevated realms of duty, mission, and sacrifice. Spengler's Prussian socialism aims at a "dictatorship of organization" motivated by political ideals that will replace the "dictatorship of money" and plunder that is ruining Germany.[12] In other words, the state, not the proletariat, will be the historical subject of this German anticapitalism of the Right. *Preussentum und Sozialismus* identified socialism with Prussia and cap-

---

[6] Ibid., p. 74.
[7] Ibid., pp. 14–15.
[8] Ibid., p. 31.
[9] Ibid., p. 10.
[10] Ibid., p. 97.
[11] Ibid., p. 98. The complete quote is: "Become men! We don't need any more ideologues, no more speeches about cultivation, and world bourgeoisie and the spiritual mission of the Germans. We need hardness. We need a more fearless skepticism: we need a class of socialist master characters [*Herrennaturen*]. Once again: socialism means power, power, and yet again power."
[12] Ibid., p. 65.

italism with England. Here the conservative revolution continued the cultural politics of World War I. Opposition to capitalism and German nationalism went hand in hand, for Germany was, by definition, anticapitalist. The idea of a Prussian or national socialism brought with it a set of symbols and metaphors that gave voice to a protest against the rationalization of society without calling class and property relations into question at all. This shift of domestic crisis onto the field of nationalistic conflict was a characteristic feature of German anticapitalism.

Preussentum und Sozialismus also presented the philosophical basis of Spengler's denunciation of liberalism and Marxism. It lay in *Lebensphilosophie*. "Life," he wrote, was the "first and last thing," freed from any program or system. It displayed a "profound order" that could only be "observed and felt," yet not explained or ruled by reason.[13] Socialism championed this idea of "life" and thereby was in tune with a more widespread German revolt against the Enlightenment. Now socialism was separated from the "anarchist-radical masses." This was only a first step in cleansing Prussian conservatism of all its "feudal-agrarian narrowness." In *Der Untergang des Abendlandes*, Spengler took further steps, also grounded in *Lebensphilosophie* and Nietzsche's will to power, to reconcile German nationalism and romanticism with modern technology.

Spengler's dubious judgments on the causes of the rise and decline of civilizations are important for the mood of impending disaster and possible salvation they exude, rather than for any serious insights into the past they might provide. Spengler's reconstruction is based on what he called a "morphological" perspective, an essentially romantic intuition that external artifacts – political and cultural institutions, architectural forms, economic organizations – are the outer images of something internal and hidden: the soul or "life." History consists of successive externalizations of these elementary life forces in outer forms. Theodor Adorno wrote of this procedure that "real history is ideologically transfigured into a history of the soul in order to bring what is antithetical and rebellious in man, consciousness, all the more completely under the sway of blind necessity."[14] We need not agree

---

[13] Ibid., p. 81. See Lukács, *Die Zerstörung der Vernunft*, Band II (Darmstadt, 1962), pp. 138–52. Despite his scattershot attack on liberal and left-wing critics of positivism in Germany, Lukacs's analysis offers insight into the reorientation of nationalist ideology. See also Hillach, "Die Asthetisierung des politischen Lebens," in *Walter Benjamin im Kontext*, ed. Walter Burkhardt (Frankfurt, 1978), pp. 127–67, on *Lebensphilosophie* in the aesthetics of technology.

[14] Theodor Adorno, "Spengler After the Decline," in *Prisms*, trans. Samuel Weber and Shierry Weber (London, 1967), p. 69.

with Adorno that this was Spengler's intention to accept the conclusion that the Spenglerian melodrama had such an effect on its readers. The power of Spengler's metaphors lay in their ability to present phenomena of contemporary history as the externalized forms and symbols of the beautiful German soul. At the very least, this procedure obscured the social and political forces at work, and contributed to acceptance, if not celebration, of "blind necessity."

In volume one of *Der Untergang des Abendlandes*, subtitled *Gestalt und Wirklichkeit* (Form and Reality), Spengler defines and distinguishes two explanatory principles: *Gestalt* and law.[15] Law is the principle appropriate to the "exact, deadening procedures of modern physics. The idea of *Gestalt*, on the other hand, operates in the realm of moving and becoming."[16] The former seeks a "systematic" grasp of natural laws and causal relations in the natural and social world; the latter aims at a "morphology" of the "organic," of history and "destiny." Spengler describes this latter form of explanation as "physiognomic."[17] The systematic mode has reached a high point in the West and is now declining. The future belongs to physiognomic explanations. Spengler's historical morphology is itself a harbinger of the future, a map of world cultures from the standpoint of supposedly ascendant mythic principles.

These contrasting ways of perceiving the world are not equally valid, in Spengler's view. The distinction between "*Gestalt* and law, image and concept, symbol and formula," is one between "life and death, creation and destruction." Conceptual understanding measures, divides, and thus "kills" the object it comprehends, whereas intuition fills the perceived object with soul and feeling. Spengler's sympathies clearly lie with *Gestalt*, intuition, symbolism, and image, the immediate and concrete, as opposed to law, system, concepts, the mediated and abstract. For Spengler and the right-wing intellectuals of Weimar, this unbridgeable chasm of reason and feeling was a matter of cultural life and death. If historical phenomena – states, economies, battles, art, science, religion, mathematics – are "an expression of a soul, . . . the final and highest certainty" of Spengler's work is that "everything transitory is only an image" of forces accessible to the powers of intuition alone rather than to the apparatus of abstraction.[18]

[15] Spengler, *Der Untergang des Abendlandes*, Band I, pp. 130–1. On the forward-looking aspects of the idea of *Gestalt* in Nazi racial ideology, see Lukács, *Die Zerstörung der Vernunft*, Band I, pp. 148–9.
[16] Spengler, *Der Untergang des Abendlandes*, Band I, p. 135.
[17] Ibid., p. 137.
[18] Ibid., pp. 136–7.

Here we come across an interesting paradox in Spengler's view of modern science and technology. As Fritz Ringer pointed out in his study of German university professors, the German "mandarins" attacked science and technology as embodiments of the positivist spirit threatening German *Kultur*.[19] Spengler, on the other hand, saw the forces of intuition and will at work in the rise of Western science and technology. Further, scientific theory that grasps the invisible processes of the natural world possesses the same cultic and mythic aspects as religion.[20] In Spengler's view, modern Western science was an extension of the Greek idea of *Gestalt* and space. It expressed a "Faustian world feeling," a drive to expand into the natural spaces of the earth, to overcome resistance and formlessness. In so doing it drew from a religious impulse to lend form to a previously formless world. But once science and technology appear as outcomes of a primal Faustian drive, it is merely "scientific prejudice" that asserts that only primitive peoples create myth and images of God and that in modern culture the power to form myths is lost. On the contrary, the soul fills the world with forms in modern no less than in primitive times. Myth creation occurs at the dawn of all great cultures and is the sign of a soul awakening.[21] Spengler clearly implies that Germany's soul stands at such a turning point. The key words here are creation, myth, form, soul, and power of form creation (*Schöpfung, Mythos, Gestalt, Seelentum, Gestaltungskraft*). They provide a way of speaking about the rationalization of German industry and disenchantment of modern thought as if these represented processes of renewed myth and reenchantment.[22] They also blur the distinctions between religious, aesthetic, and political language. The "power of form creation," for example, is a phrase that evokes artistic, religious, and political efforts to impose order on a chaotic world. Myth and form are objects of aesthetic beauty. Their presence promises a beautiful and orderly world of *Gestalten* or forms. The politically explosive aspect of Spengler's version of romanticism and *Lebensphilosophie* did not lie in a restatement

[19] Fritz Ringer, *The Decline of the German Mandarins* (Cambridge, Mass., 1969), pp. 253–304.
[20] Spengler, *Der Untergang des Abendlandes*, Band I, p. 507.
[21] Ibid., pp. 512–13.
[22] While Spengler was writing this, Max Weber wrote that "the fate of our times is characterized by rationalization and intellectualization and, above all, by the 'disenchantment of the world.'" See "Science as a Vocation," in *From Max Weber*, ed. Hans Gerth and C. Wright Mills (New York, 1964), p. 155. On technological advance and the reenchantment of society, see Ernst Bloch's essay, "Technik und Geistererscheinungen," in *Verfremdungen I* (Frankfurt, 1962). There Bloch noticed that modern technology had not precluded a "new middle ages" in Germany, complete with "transcendent demons," spooks, and spirits.

54

of the dichotomies of *Kultur* and *Zivilisation*. These dichotomies had become the common coin of cultural pessimism.[23] Rather, his originality lay in combining a panorama of the past with a view of myth and symbol that suggested the possibility of a new age of aestheticized politics dawning in the future. Further, to view modern technical advances through the prisms of such symbolism transformed the profane facts of everyday life into the sacred and transcendental.[24]

In volume two of *Der Untergang des Abendlandes*, Spengler looks at the modern world as one of distinct "form worlds" – politics, the city, economics, and technology, each of which is an externalization of far older qualities residing in the soul. Such a view is typical of the selective acceptance and rejection of capitalist modernity evident in the writings of the right-wing nationalists in Weimar. The brooding pessimism, the sense of crisis and impending transformation, the chorus of cultural despair, all this has turned attention away from the Spenglerian embrace of technology. Yet throughout one comes upon stark juxtapositions of abstraction and concreteness in which technology lands in the German world of creative, productive domination over nature that faces the alien world of parasitic, unproductive, cosmopolitan finance. Spengler rejected political liberalism and endorsed technical rationality linked to the willful self that knew no limits to its own celebration.[25]

The particular contrast of production and parasitism appears in the contrast of the city and the country. The farmhouse is a symbol of rootedness, of "property in the holiest sense," whereas the feudal aristocracy represents the force of "blood and tradition." Both exist in the realm of soul, feeling, and intuition. The city, on the other hand, is the world of spirit (*Geist*), that is, of intellect and abstraction. It is the locus of history, politics, art, religion, science, and in modern times, of "the bourgeoisie, the stratum of *Geist*." Most important, the

[23] On the importance of the idea of chaos in right-wing and Nazi ideology in Weimar, see Joachim Schumacher, *Die Angst vor dem Chaos* (Paris, 1937; reprint, Frankfurt, 1972). Schumacher traced a shift in the meaning of the term. When applied to German political and economic expansion, it was viewed as "productive." In the later years of the republic, the right-wing intellectuals depicted chaos as a negative specter. In their view, the will to power had to bring order and ward off *Angst* caused by the terrors of society and nature. Also see Hillach, "Die Aesthetisierung des politischen Lebens," p. 140. Hillach argues that the myths, forms, and symbols Spengler creates point to a nihilistic "overcoming" of decadence.
[24] For a study that draws on Durkheim's insights into myth, see Klaus Vondung, *Magie und Manipulation: Ideologischer Kult und politische Religion des Nationalsozialismus* (Göttingen, 1971).
[25] Bell, *The Cultural Contradictions of Capitalism* (New York, 1976), pp. 49–52.

city replaces the "primordial value of the land" with a "concept of money separated from goods." In place of the premarket notions of exchange rooted in the rural economy, the city introduces "money thinking" (*Gelddenken*). "The city does not only mean *Geist*, but money as well."[26]

Money, not the machine, advances the rationalization of the world. It subjects the circulation of commodities and individuals to its own imperatives, just as the earth and nature had previously subjected the peasant to their rhythms. "But the earth is something real and natural; money is something abstract and artificial, a mere category such as virtue" in Enlightenment thought.[27] Without roots in human essence, money threatens to establish a dictatorship of impersonal formlessness over the structured and personal world of the aristocracy, the "embodiment of blood and race, a being (that is) in as completed form as is conceivable."[28] The historical precursor of the modern intelligentsia, the countertype of the aristocracy and peasantry, was the priesthood. Swamped in abstractions as it was, Spengler refers to it as a "nonrace . . . independent from the land, free, timeless, ahistorical being."[29] Although Spengler could protest that he and his fellow conservative revolutionaries were attacking the bourgeoisie, it is indisputable that he and they were intellectuals. This antiintellectualism of the intellectuals was only one of the paradoxes of his ambiguous modernism. Intellectuals in a feudal-industrial society would have to learn to think with the blood, as the Nazis later would put it.

Agrarian aristocracy, Prussian militarism, and the traditional values of patriarchy and family find expression in Spengler's categories and symbols. All of these precapitalist institutions resist the intrusion of exchange relations. The mother holding her child to her breast is "the great symbol of cosmic life; the man, weapon in hand, is the other great symbol of the will toward permanence."[30] Both the private sphere of the family and the public sphere of war stand in opposition to money, for it erodes all fixed and enduring social relations. Whereas money is a destructive, life-denying force, "war is the creator of all

---

[26] Spengler, *Der Untergang des Abendlandes*, Band II, pp. 660–1, and 669–70.
[27] Ibid., p. 671. Alfred Sohn-Rethel offers a Marxist analysis of the connection between Enlightenment thought and commodity exchange in *Warenform und Denkform* (Frankfurt, 1978).
[28] Spengler, *Der Untergang des Abendlandes*, Band, II, p. 973.
[29] Ibid.
[30] Ibid., p. 1,006.

great things."[31] The military and the family are institutions untouched by the cash nexus. For the German anticapitalists of the Right such as Spengler, they were oases of form, permanence, and beauty. But it was war, not the family, that was truly creative. The intellectuals of the postwar Right responded to the antimilitarism of the Left by celebrating the most important artwork to emerge from the trenches – the "new man."

Spengler might have taken Hölderlin's saying, Where the danger is greatest, there emerges hope for a saving force, as the motto of *Der Untergang des Abendlandes*. To be sure, its two repetitive volumes are filled with the standard antimodernist complaints. But it does not end on a note of despair and resignation. It is a call to action, the manifesto of a flawed modernism. Politics, blood, and tradition must rise up to defeat the power of *Geist* and *Geld*. Democracy and liberalism, about which Spengler wrote not a single favorable word, brought with them the "triumph of money" over the deeper forces of blood and instinct. The purpose of politics was clear: reverse this state of chaos and decadence, of pointless elections, superfluous and self-interested parties, paralyzed parliaments. Politics demanded leadership built on a "flowing being" (*strommende Dasein*), a "life energy" that is "blind and cosmic, ... longs for prestige and power," is racially bound to the soil, and borne by an elite of "higher men" who make "great decisions" in the face of uncertain "destiny."[32] The aristocracy, not the bourgeoisie, is the archetypal political class, for it understands the centrality of war and struggle to politics. Politics, not economics, is the decisive force in the battle of blood and tradition against mind and money. This conception of political leadership was Spengler's alternative to liberal rationalism and materialism. It was indicative of the failure of German liberalism that Max Weber warned would be the legacy of Imperial Germany's weak parliamentary traditions. Spengler's conception of politics was precisely the kind of salvation of souls that Weber had insisted ought to have nothing to do with politics as a vocation.

Spengler was not interested in economic reforms but rather in end-

---

[31] Ibid., p. 1,007. War's "creative" contributions were a common theme among the conservative revolutionaries. For example, in his *Der Genius des Krieges und der deutsche Krieg* (1915), Max Scheler wrote that "the true roots of all war lie in the fact that all of life itself ... possesses a tendency to expansion, growth, development. ... Everything dead and mechanical only wants to survive ... while life grows or declines" (p. 42).

[32] Spengler, *Der Untergang des Abendlandes*, Band II, pp. 1,002 and 1,108–9.

ing the influence of the economy on social life and culture. The economy, he wrote, debases the soul and saps the "energy of the race." It corrupts individuals by arousing in them an "appetite for an ugly, common, wholly unmetaphysical kind of fear for one's life." Economic life destroys "the higher form world of culture," replacing it with unfettered struggle for mere survival.[33] It is politics that demands idealism, sacrifice. Culture finds its true expression in war, the real and most radical alternative to bourgeois culture and society. Ironically, mass destruction appears as the opposite of the "naked struggle for existence" of the civilian economy. Here, in war-as-politics, is the *Kultur* that supplants the stifling, secure boredom of bourgeois *Zivilisation*. But unlike some of his colleagues, such as Klages and Moeller van den Bruck, Spengler pointed to the need for "unconditional domination of the most modern means; the danger of an aristocracy is to become conservative in the matter of means." Just as Bach and Mozart mastered the "musical instruments" of their time, so modern politics requires a similar mastery of the instruments of war.[34] The battle of *Kultur* against *Zivilisation* cannot be won by German Luddites spouting the clichés of *völkisch* ideology. Preservation of "blood and tradition" requires the most modern technological resources. In short, Spengler's target was not the machine, but money.

This rejection of "feudal-agrarian narrowness" modernized deep-seated romantic and irrationalist traditions, but it did not eliminate them. The conservative revolution's attack on the cash nexus pointed to a "battle to the end between the leading powers of a dictatorial money economy arrayed against the purely political will toward order of the new Caesars."[35] From this battle a renewed primacy of politics over the economy would emerge. War and nationalism linked Germany's romantic and irrationalist traditions to a faulty and reactionary form of modernism, an appeal for political dictators to end the sway of economic liberalism over social life. The soul that lives in the modern economy was, in Spengler's view, that of Manchester liberalism, it was Germany's "inner England." In the attacks on commerce and pleas for a primacy of politics over economics, one senses a compensatory function of cultural criticism in Weimar Germany. The war against England and France that ended in defeat on the battlefield could be continued and won on the terrain of cultural criticism.

Of course, even Spengler recognized that some kind of economic

[33] Ibid., p. 1,148.
[34] Ibid., pp. 1,118–19.
[35] Ibid., p. 1,144.

activity was indispensable for social life. As one would expect, his criticism of economic activity was restricted to its "parasitic" dimensions. The peasantry cultivating the German soil was "creative" rather than exploitative. Its economic activity did not break the confines of religion and local custom. Urban economic activity, however, is a "mediating" activity that amounts to a "refined parasitism [that is] completely unproductive and thus alien to the land." Technology is part of the productive sphere. It shapes, works over, and transforms the natural world. It is the blacksmith and his "creative utilization" of nature that anticipate Germany's machine-tool industry.[36]

But if the blacksmith performed a crucial economic role, the urban merchant or middleman did not. The latter lacked "an inner bond with the land." It is through him "that goods turn into commodities, [that] exchange becomes commerce" and "money thinking" replaces thinking in terms of goods and human needs.[37] Hence it should come as no surprise that urban merchants do not often come from the "firmly self-contained life of the countryside," but rather are strangers such as the "Jews, ... Byzantians, Persians, Armenians in the Gothic West."[38] The beauty of rural landscapes, so important for the peasantry, means nothing to these rootless strangers. The city dweller sees quantitatively. His gaze transforms the qualitatively unique dimensions of the natural world into dimensions measurable in "abstract money value." It is this human type – the merchant and middleman – not social processes such as industrialization or capitalism that threatens to eliminate a particular German identity and particularity.

Furthermore, and most important, Spengler claims that "the merchant has become the master rather than the tool of economic life." Speculation and profit seeking, aided by corrosive intellectualism, are supplanting the power of producers and consumers. The third force of circulation dominates the processes of supply and demand and "elevates mediation to a monopoly and then into the major aspect of economic life."[39] Thinking in money terms rather than capitalist social relations is the force behind commodification of social life. "Money is above all the form of spiritual energy in which the will to domination, the political, social, technical, and intellectual formative powers and the yearning for a new life of grand style are concentrated." In fact,

[36] Ibid., pp. 1,158–9.
[37] Ibid., p. 1,162.
[38] Ibid., pp. 1,161–62. On Spengler's view of the Jews, see Alex Bein, "Die Judenfrage in der Literatur des modernen Antisemitismus als Vorbereitung zur Endlösung," *Leo Baeck Institute Bulletin*, no. 21 (1963), pp. 4–51.
[39] Spengler, *Der Untergang des Abendlandes*, Band II, p. 1,165.

Zivilisation is the level of social development at which point the values of tradition and personality lose their independent validity and must be recast in commercial terms in order to be realized.[40] What is economic history but a "desperate struggle" between tradition, soul, and race, on the one hand, and the spirit of money on the other? The latter possesses a Faustian drive to incorporate the whole of social life into the web of its abstractions.

Two points stand out. First, the circulation sphere is said to have already achieved predominance over industry and agriculture. Second, this victory is the product of a particular type of person, the merchant, who, Spengler complains, is parasitic and unproductive. We are dealing here with documents of reification. Social processes, in this case, circulation, are said to emanate from individual types, here the merchant. "Anticapitalism" or "anti-money thinking" legitimates nationalist, and subsequently racial, programs that seek to do away with the individuals who are the bearers of capitalism, that is, "capitalist man" or "the Jew." Marx, in his analysis of commodity fetishism, argued that in capitalism the social relations between human beings appeared to be social relations between things. Spengler takes this process of reification one step further: The social aspect of relations between human beings disappears and they appear instead as emanations of different human souls. Then the revolt against abstraction takes on sinister, that is, racial, proportions. But in its German form this revolt was by no means necessarily an effort to stifle or hinder technological advances.

In the final chapter of *Der Untergang des Abendlandes*, Spengler wrote that "the machine is the devil," a statement that at first appears to confirm his standing as a cultural Luddite.[41] Yet on second thought, such attributions of an independent will and autonomy to technology served to ensure a pact with this devil. The Spenglerian version of the Faust legend was an important aspect of his reconciliation of irrationalist and romantic traditions with the products of the first and second industrial revolutions in Germany. His argument was as follows: Modern Western technology possesses a particular *Geist*. Unlike Greek and Roman technology, it is neither of modest proportions nor content with merely copying the natural world. Instead, it is a "Faus-

---

[40] Ibid., p. 1,167.
[41] Ibid., p. 1,187. For a discussion of Spengler as a representative of antidemocratic and antitechnological thinking, see Hortleder, *Das Gesellschaftsbild des Ingenieurs: Zum politischen Verhalten der techischen Intelligenz in Deutschland* (Frankfurt, 1970), pp. 86–7.

tian technology," one that displays a "will to power over nature."[42] Faustian technology signifies a turning point in the relationship between human beings and nature. Man shifts from passive observation and perception to active transformation and direction of the material world. The Faustian person's will exudes a "primordial violence" that is channeled into the "steel energy of his practical consideration." Western man's soul is that of the discoverer who uncovers and unleashes nature's hidden powers. The origin of technical innovation is ultimately religious, that is, the urge to reveal the mysteries of God's universe.

However, this limitless striving against nature's boundaries creates a technological world that threatens to dominate the human will that created it. This theme, namely, that of the reversal of means and ends and the loss of human control over history, had been a common one in German social thought since Hegel elaborated the notion of the cunning of history. In Spengler's time, it found expression in the works of Max Weber, Georg Lukács, and Georg Simmel. But even in their speculations on the tragedy of culture, they shared the basic assumption that the direction of modernity was toward disenchantment and rationalization of the world. With Spengler, the technological world appears not at all as a disenchanted or demystified one. The tyranny of technical *Geist* by no means signifies the "dethronement of God" or the emergence of human omniscience. Divine causality has not been handed over to human beings because the machine has now taken on a life of its own.[43] Technology becomes "ascetic, mystical, esoteric, . . . even more spiritual." Driven to dominate nature by the Faustian soul, which permits no return to primitivism or pastoral reconciliation with nature, Western man also cannot escape the frenzied and seemingly ineluctable will of an apparently autonomous technology.[44]

This tyrannical technology, however, possesses a "magic soul." Therefore any attempts to overcome the current cultural crisis must include groups with affinities to this magic. The peasantry and merchants are ruled out. So are the Jews, whose talents as entrepreneurs do not cultivate the technical *Geist*, and the Russians, "who look with

[42] The claim about the particular *Geist* of Western technology appears throughout the first volume of *Der Untergang des Abendlandes*. The third section of Spengler's chapter on the machine in volume two is: "Faustian technology: the will to power over nature."
[43] Ibid., p. 1,190.
[44] Langdon Winner discusses the idea of "autonomous technology" in twentieth-century political theory in his *Autonomous Technology: Technics-out-of-control as a theme in Political Thought* (Cambridge, Mass., 1977).

fear and hatred at this tyranny of wheels, cables and rails" and dream of a "wholly new world, in which nothing of this devil's technique remains."[45] The entrepreneur and industrial proletarian are products of and slaves to technology. Thus it is up to the engineer, "the erudite priest of the machine," to provide guidance and leadership in the midst of Weimar's cultural and political crisis. There is a danger that these "100,000 talented, well-schooled heads who will master and advance technology" could succumb to the influence of metaphysics and mysticism that is taking the place of rationalism, or be "overpowered by a growing sense of [technology's] Satanic quality."[46] Spengler's defense of technology rests on pointing not to its rational properties but to its essentially irrational and romantic "metaphysics and mysticism."

Although the engineers are able to grasp these irrational and romantic dimensions of technology, those tainted with the commercial spirit cannot. *Der Untergang des Abendlandes* concluded with a warning against the power of money, not the power of the machine. "High finance," the banks, the stock exchange, and "money thinking" threaten industry and technical thinking. The battle between industry and finance in Weimar is only a modern form of the "primordial struggle between productive and creative versus plundering" economics, between the forces of industry and agriculture that are "rooted in the soil" and those of finance that are "wholly free and intangible." It is a desperate struggle by technical thinking for its freedom from thinking in money.[47] This fateful struggle is ultimately one waged between "money and blood."

Blood's victory over money ushers in a new "Caesarism," an authoritarian state that will "break the dictatorship of money and its political weapon, democracy. The sword triumphs over money, the will to mastery once again subdues the will to plunder."[48] "Socialism," understood as a national political community that transcends all class conflicts, will replace "capitalism," understood as self-seeking liberal individualism. "Money can be overcome and mastered only by blood." "Life" triumphs over lifelessness. Here the category of "life" is interchangeable with "race" or the "triumph of the will to power," but never with the "victory of truth, discoveries or money."[49] Abstract truth and morality are insignificant in the face of the appeals of the

[45] Spengler, *Der Untergang des Abendlandes*, Band II, p. 1,190.
[46] Ibid., p. 1,191.
[47] Ibid., p. 1,192.
[48] Ibid., p. 1,193.
[49] Ibid., p. 1,194.

immediacy and concreteness of this "life." This celebration of the right of the stronger, of a racially tinged Social Darwinism, appears as the resolution of a cultural crisis brought on by a supposed excess of abstraction and intellect.

Although *Der Untergang des Abendlandes* contains the full catalogue of cultural despair, its message is not one of resignation or nostalgia. Rather it places technology at the center of a nationalist revolt against political liberalism and rootless international finance. Spengler equated capitalism with the predominance of circulation and money, whereas socialism meant a program of technological advance carried out by the national community of blood. The book was filled with both despair and hope. The hope lay in refuting the antitechnological mood of postwar Germany, by relieving technology of the burden of anti-capitalist resentments, while freeing those resentments of their antiindustrial components. This new German anticapitalism would fit well into a nationalist resurgence. The German soul would be at home on the farm, on the battlefield, and in the factory. Spengler viewed social processes as emanations of national and racial souls and thus offered a seemingly plausible "philosophical" foundation for locating the alien world of abstract finance and commerce in the alien body and soul of the Jews.

Spengler was neither a Nazi nor closely tied to Italian or French fascist currents. But, as we indicated in Chapter 2, the conservative revolution in Germany was an important source of many of the ideas of National Socialism. One important parallel lay in the perception of political life through aesthetic categories. For example, the term *Gesalt* applies to both aesthetics and productivity. The medieval merchant and modern international banker lack the "power of form creation" (*Gestaltungskraft*) displayed by the peasant, factory worker, engineer, soldier, and artist. These latter figures perform the labor of creative production and destruction, thereby placing new *Gestalten* into the world. War's creativity lies in its aesthetic creations, that is, in the new forms of battle and death it brings forth. The sphere of circulation by contrast is artless. It dissolves all fixed and stable forms in favor of growing chaos and formlessness. By characterizing production as the creation of a world of beautiful and stable forms, Spengler presented labor as an act of cultural redemption, one that wards off the specter of a world without form. His aesthetics of production and destruction point to a "productive chaos" of political authoritarianism and technical advance that would eliminate the unproductive chaos of liberal capitalism.[50] Many German engineers and

[50] See Schumacher, *Die Angst vor dem Chaos.*

businessmen were unhappy over Spengler's gloomier ruminations concerning the machine's "Satanic" nature. Especially during the period of the rationalization of big German industry in the mid-1920s, they stressed the promise of technology in leading to the possible overcoming of class conflicts through corporatively organized increases in production. But these practical and technocratic visions were accompanied by one of the peculiarly German features of the European response to the second industrial revolution, namely, the degree to which practical men of affairs were also drawn to this romantic synthesis of aesthetics and productivism.[51]

In 1931, Spengler, now famous as the advocate of cultural pessimism, published a small book entitled *Der Mensch und die Technik* (Man and Technology). In it he repeated familiar themes and sought to dispel the idea that he was hostile to technology. He expressed disappointment that many readers of *Der Untergang des Abendlandes* had become lost in its maze of historical detail and could not understand his intentions. His point had been that culture was primary and that religion, politics, art, and technology could be understood only in its light.[52] This was the purpose of *Der Mensch und die Technik*. It was a response to the antitechnological sentiments fostered by the youth movements, the expressionists, and weary humanist intellectuals that Spengler thought constituted a distinct cultural threat to the kind of nationalist revival for which he yearned.

At the outset, Spengler rejects what he describes as idealist and materialist views of technology. Idealist humanism is contemptuous of all matters concerning technology because it mistakenly views it as being outside and/or beneath the realm of culture. Materialism, on the other hand, is an English import borne by liberalism and Marxism that has nothing whatsoever to say about the cultural significance of technology. "If the former lacked a sense of reality, the latter, to a disturbing degree, lacked a sense of depth."[53] Unlike the "philistines of progress" such as Mill and Bentham, who defend technology by pointing to its utilitarian aspects, Spengler characteristically stresses its ties to the soul.

The idea that really lies behind the new chemical and electrical revolutions is primordial, not at all specifically modern. Life is strug-

---

[51] On Albert Speer's Office of the Beauty of Labor in the Third Reich, see Rabinbach, "The Aesthetics of Production in the Third Reich," in *International Fascism*, ed. George Mosse (Beverly Hills, Calif., 1979). On the aesthetics of technology in Nazi propaganda see chap. 9.
[52] Oswald Spengler, *Der Mensch und Die Technik* (Munich 1931). Foreword.
[53] Ibid., p. 3.

gle. "Technology is the tactic of the whole of life, the inner form of the methods of struggle."[54] It is certainly not a subsystem of the economy, politics, or war. On the contrary, all of these phenomena are "sides of an acting, struggling life infused with soul" that creates a direct line from the primitive struggle for survival to the procedures of modern inventors and engineers.[55] As before, Spengler enlists Schopenhauer, Darwin, and Nietzsche to describe the permanent element in technology, "the will to power – cruel, pitiless, merciless struggle."[56] Through technics, human beings evolve from "plant eaters" to "beasts of prey" and in so doing free themselves from the "constraints of the species." He describes technological development as a heroic ascent, a creative emancipation of the species from its natural limits. Tools and weapons create a more artificial world; they also expand human freedom. Such claims in themselves are not particularly remarkable, even if unexpected from one of the grand spokesmen of cultural pessimism. What is important is the way Spengler reconciles technical advances and German traditions at war with the Enlightenment.

In Adorno's terms, Spengler lent to the social division of labor the qualities of "a second nature"; that is, he presented human results as the outcome of extrahuman, hence unalterable, forces.[57] Adorno's criticism followed on Lukács's theory of reification and was intended to apply to Max Weber's theory of rationalization. Spengler went considerably beyond Weber in arguing that particular groups were uniquely well suited to serve as elites. In *Der Untergang des Abendlandes*, he had written that in politics and economics there are "subjects and objects of control, groups who arrange, decide, organize, and invent, and others whose business it is to carry out orders."[58] In *Der Mensch und die Technik*, he again distinguished between the "labor of leadership" and the "labor of execution," calling the distinction between the two the "fundamental technical form of all human life."[59] The dichotomy between the few who rule and the many who obey is a

---

[54] Ibid.
[55] Ibid., p. 6.
[56] Ibid., p. 9.
[57] Adorno discusses second nature in *Negative Dialectics*, trans. E. B. Ashton (New York, 1973), esp. pp. 351–8. "The traditional antithesis of nature and history is both true and false – true insofar as it expresses what happened to the natural element; false insofar as, by means of conceptual reconstruction, it apologetically repeats the concealment of history's natural growth by itself" (p. 358). See also Russell Jacoby, *The Dialectics of Defeat* (New York, 1981).
[58] Spengler, *Der Untergang des Abendlandes*, Band II, p. 1,159.
[59] Spengler, *Der Mensch und die Technik*, p. 35.

simple fact of nature. Human beings are subordinated to the natural imperatives of authoritarian organization and become "enslaved" by culture. The "beast of prey" becomes a "domestic animal." The Faustian impulse drives the civilizing process forward, yet leads to a technological web that weakens that impulse.[60] Spengler recommends stoicism and heroic submission to fate, to technology's supposedly immutable imperatives. In the years to come, some readers would take Spengler to task for presenting a picture of gloomy determinism, a right-wing version of Weber's iron cage, whereas others responded to his seemingly contradictory appeals to take up and advance the Faustian drive.

What was unmistakable was Spengler's desire to view contemporary problems through the prism of myths and symbols only dimly connected to them. The advantage of such archetypal constructs lay in their ability to present complex, ambiguous realities in the form of stark, simple, clear alternatives. This was evident in Spengler's contempt for intellectuals. He wrote, for example, that "nobles, soldiers, and adventurers live in a world of facts," and "priests, scholars and philosophers live in a world of truths." The first group thinks about destiny, the second about causality. One wants to place *Geist* in the service of a "strong life"; the other wants to place life in the service of *Geist*. "Nowhere has this contradiction assumed a more unreconcilable form than in Faustian culture, where, for the last time, the proud blood of the beast of prey revolts against the tyranny of pure thinking."[61] One of the mistakes of nineteenth-century materialism was to have placed technology in the world of thought rather than blood. The engineer's and inventor's passion had nothing to do with utilitarianism. Only the "materialistic religion" of the "philistines of progress of modern times from Lamettrie to Lenin" failed to grasp this basic truth.[62] Yet again, Spengler celebrates a virile antiintellectualism and forges links between technology and feudal images of nobles, soldiers, and adventurers. The metaphors are feudal *and* industrial, antibourgeois *and* militarist, illiberal *and* oriented to a technological future.

Yet Spengler remained ambivalent in his views on technology's role in the twentieth-century battle between spirit and blood. Technology had become a symbol of artifice, of a life separated from nature and the soil, of the "devastation of the soul."[63] It now moves with the force

[60] Ibid., pp. 39–40.
[61] Ibid., p. 45.
[62] Ibid., p. 49.
[63] Ibid., p. 50.

of destiny and inner necessity to "completion." The Spenglerian image is one of a tragedy reaching its climax. The "creation rises up against the creator." Just as man once rose up against nature, so today the machine "revolts against Nordic man. The master of the world has become slave to the machine. It forces him, us, and all human beings without exception, whether or not we are aware of it or desire it, in the direction of its path."[64] Now Spengler presents us with the familiar indictments of cultural pessimism. Technology's path leads away from its vitalist origins. As it becomes more dependent on mathematics and science, it becomes "more esoteric." The natural world is "poisoned" by an artificial one. "Civilization itself has become a machine." We look at waterfalls and see only potential electric power. The machine represents merely a "soulful-intellectual" ideal, not a vital one.[65]

Yet just as it appears that Spengler will join the antitechnological chorus, he turns to attack these laments as symptoms of, rather than solutions to, Germany's cultural crisis. Faustian thinking is satiated with technology. A "pacifism" in the battle against nature spreads. The youth turn to simple forms of life closer to nature and away from big cities, engineering, and similar "soulless" places and activities. The finest minds turn away from the natural sciences to pure speculation and Eastern philosophy. "The flight of born leaders in the face of the machine begins." This flight is not only a threat to the nation, but also a "betrayal of technology" (*Verrat an die Technik*).[66]

It was common in the German literature on technology and culture to refer to a European cultural crisis. Spengler's *Der Mensch und die Technik* was typical. Only Europe, he claimed, had the cultural resources to develop the machine. The nonwhite world regards technology from a purely utilitarian perspective, that is, as a weapon in the battle against "Faustian civilization." It has no "inner need" to develop technology comparable to that of European Faustian man's. If the Faustian spirit dies, the machine technology of the West would also be forgotten, a victim of spiritual decadence and erosion from within, and political attack from without. Spengler's not very satisfying answer to such a grim future is a "short life full of deeds and fame rather than a long one without content," and an appeal to the old Prussian virtues of "remaining at a lost position, without hope, without rescue. Only dreamers believe there is a way out. Optimism is cowardice."[67] Such stoicism was still too mired in cultural pessimism to

[64] Ibid., p. 52.
[65] Ibid., p. 55.
[66] Ibid., pp. 57–9.
[67] Ibid., p. 61.

satisfy those members of the conservative revolution, such as Ernst
Jünger, who had been through the war. They looked for more hopeful
visions to emerge from the horror of the trenches.

The Nazis as well took Spengler to task for his excessive gloominess
and distaste for mass movements, which is not to say that he did not
help their coming to power by joining in the chorus of abuse heaped
on the fragile republican institutions of Weimar. Spengler's incorporation of technology into a German cultural revolt against the Enlightenment pointed beyond his gloomy conclusions. His political essays
contributed to a nationalist appropriation of the ideas of socialism
and revolution. By linking technology to the romantic and irrationalist
traditions, to will, struggle, *Gestalt*, soul, destiny, and blood, he helped
to shift the technology from the realm of *Zivilisation* to that of *Kultur*.
His depiction of the Faustian man created a vivid image suggesting
instinctual bonds between embattled patriarchy and masculine will on
the one hand, and technology, on the other. Arrayed against them
was an effeminate and treasonous pacifism willing to abandon the
struggle against nature and the anticolonial awakening outside Europe.[68] A link between German *Innerlichkeit* and romanticism and
technical modernization was essential if Europe was to withstand such
challenges.

Just as Hegel's critics disagreed that the world spirit reached its end
point in the Prussian state of the early nineteenth century, so Spengler's younger colleagues in the conservative revolution saw no reason
to assume that the Faustian will embodied in modern technology had
reached a state of exhaustion. Ernst Jünger, in particular, rejected
the remnants of conservative ambivalence toward and distance from
industrialism and technology without succumbing either to cowardice
or materialism. First in the trenches of World War I, then in Mussolini's claims to authoritarian efficiency and in the Russian five-year
plans, Jünger saw the possibility that "processes of a high soulful plane
can be imputed to the whole apparatus of civilization."[69] The masculine *Gemeinschaft* of the trenches had created leaders who would
embrace technology rather than escape from it. The impact of the
Great War did much to eradicate right-wing ambivalence to technol-

[68] On this theme see two recent West German studies: Klaus Theweleit, *Männerphantasien*, 2 vols. (Frankfurt, 1978–9); and Hans Mayer, *Aussenseiter* (Frankfurt, 1977),
esp. the discussion of Otto Weininger's pastische of antibourgeois *Kulturkritik*, cult
of masculine *Gemeinschaft*, anti-Semitism, and rage against women, pp. 118–26.
[69] Ernst Jünger, "Totem," *Arminius* 8 (1927), p. 70. On the impact of the war on young
intellectuals in England, France, Germany, Italy, and Spain, see Robert Wohl, *The
Generation of 1914* (Cambridge, Mass., 1979); and Paul Fussell's very important work
The Great War and Modern Memory (New York, 1975).

ogy in the generation of 1914. Although Spengler's stoicism could leave some room for doubt concerning the possibility of the survival of Faustian man in the modern technological world, the same could not be said for Jünger's unmitigated enthusiasm for the beautiful and destructive capacities of steam, chemistry, and electricity.

4

Ernst Jünger's magical realism

"Ours is the first generation to begin to reconcile itself with the machine and to see in it not only the useful but the beautiful as well."[1] With unmatched literary flare, Ernst Jünger sought to reorient attitudes toward technology among the right-wing intellectuals of the Weimar Republic. His works are free of the ambivalences that still plagued Spengler. Rather, they exude a sense of explosive discovery, of a revolutionary breakthrough beyond bourgeois society. More than any of the leading conservative revolutionaries, Jünger drew on the *Fronterlebnis* (front experience) of World War I to reconcile political reaction and modern technology. During the Weimar Republic, his essays and political writings were prolific to say the least. Five books, over 100 essays, three collections of photographs, and an edited collection of essays on the war experience testify to the energy Jünger devoted to recalling the lost treasure of the postwar German Right, the armed community of men in the trenches, and to generalizing this charismatic experience into a political utopia applicable to the postwar industrial order. Jünger appealed to the returned veterans unable or unwilling to adjust to civilian life and to those too young to compare his mythic descriptions of the war with their own memories. The *Fronterlebnis* was, to use Ernst Bloch's term, his *concrete utopia*, one that prefigured a community uncorrupted by capitalist exchange relations. Jünger's contempt for the market was no less intense than that of left-wing communists such as Lukács. But where the romantics of the Left found their images of the good society in the central European worker's councils that sprang up after the war or in the new Soviet regime

[1] Ernst Jünger, *Feuer und Blut: Ein kleiner Ausschnitt aus dem grossen Schlacht* (Berlin, 1929; reprint, Stuttgart, 1960), p. 81.

70

in Russia, right-wing romantics such as Jünger saw their forward-looking *Gemeinschaft* in the war.[2]

There are a number of levels on which Jünger's contributions to reactionary modernist ideology can be explained. He was a member of the generation that lived through the Great War, the generation that produced the entire Nazi leadership.[3] He was an ideal typical aesthete of the Right and, like other members of the European avant-garde, was drawn to technology because he believed it could help aestheticize politics and thus resolve a crisis of cultural decadence and decline.[4] As a political romantic, he constantly claimed to discern hidden, magical, yet real forces at work behind surface appearances. He thus reified technology, that is, separated it from any apparent connection to social relationships.[5] Klaus Theweleit, in a psychological study of the men of the Free Corps (*Freikorps*), has connected Jünger's views to what he calls the "fascist unconscious."[6] Theweleit turns to psychoanalytic theory to account for certain prevalent themes in the essays and diaries of several members of the *Freikorps* – repressed sexuality, alternating appeals for order and release, hatred for democracy, women, Jews, and leftists, hypernationalism and militarism, celebration of an image of the new man, a "steel form" or the "con-

---

[2] Georg Lukács's path from romantic anticapitalism to communism was marked by these hopes. See Lowy, *Pour une Sociologie des Intellectuelles Revolutionnaires*, (Paris, 1976), pp. 107–70; and Arato and Breines, *The Young Lukács and the Origins of Western Marxism* (New York, 1979), pp. 61–74.

[3] See Robert Wohl, *The Generation of 1914*, (Cambridge, Mass., 1979).

[4] See Bohrer, *Die Ästhetik des Schreckens: Die Pessimistische Romantik und Ernst Jüngers Frühwerk* (Munich, 1978); and Hillach, "Die Ästhetisierung des politischen Lebens," in *Linke hatte noch alles sich zu enträtseln. Walter Benjamin in Kontext*, ed. Walter Burkhardt (Frankfurt, 1978).

[5] See Kurt Lenk, "Das tragische Bewusstsein in der deutschen Soziologie," *Kölner Zeitschrift für Soziologie und Sozialpsychologie* 16 (1964); and Lowy, *Pour une Sociologie* . . . , pp. 25–78.

[6] Klaus Theweleit, *Männerphantasien*, 2 vols. (Frankfurt, 1978–9). On the history of the *Freikorps*, see Robert G. L. Waite, *Vanguard of Nazism: The Free Corps Movement in Postwar Germany, 1918–1923* (Cambridge, Mass., 1952). Theweleit draws on the "object relations" school of psychoanalysis to focus on the impact of mother–son relations on the "fascist unconscious." His ideal typical "marital man" wards off the terror of engulfment by the mother through rigid defenses against experiencing the body as a source of pleasure, and through identity formation in authoritarian political groups. These men projected onto the proletariat or the Jews the sexuality and tenderness they found unacceptable in themselves. The form and clarity of Fascist rallies were a welcome contrast to a "feminine" absence of form. Theweleit's arguments parallel those of feminist theorists. See Jessica Benjamin, "The End of Internalization: Adorno's Social Psychology," *Telos* 32 (Summer 1977), pp. 42–64; Nancy Chodorow, *The Reproduction of Mothering* (Berkeley, 1978); and Herbert Marcuse, "Marxismus und Feminismus," in *Zeit Messungen* (Frankfurt, 1975), pp. 9–20.

servative utopia of the totally mechanized body."[7] War and right-wing politics promised decisiveness, clear boundaries, and masculine community with an opportunity for instinctual release. Technology also combined control and explosiveness in ways that pointed to a new man beyond the sentimentality of "the old man."[8] Jünger's writings of the 1920s repeatedly contrast the lifeless and mechanized human body with the animated and self-moving instrument of human will that is modern technology. Whatever unconscious motivations may have fed this cult, it manifested a consciousness that sought cultural renewal and intoxication through technical advances.

Jünger's two most famous books were *In Stahlgewittern* (Storm of Steel, 1920) and *Der Arbeiter* (The Worker, 1932).[9] The first presented a spectacularly aestheticized version of life in the trenches; the second placed the new man, the worker-soldier, at the center of an elaborate vision of a future totalitarian order mobilized for industrial production and destruction. Unlike the pacifist and expressionist novels and plays of the early 1920s such as Remarque's *All Quiet on the Western Front* or Toller's *Gas*, Jünger's *Stahlgewittern* celebrated the *Fronterlebnis* as a welcome and long overdue release from the stifling security of prewar Wilhelmian middle class. Jünger remembered the war as an exciting and romantic contact with sudden danger, death, masculine energy, and exotic and elemental forces that reminded him of his prewar travels to Africa. He celebrated a heroic ideal of soldiers immune to the fear of death and the horror of killing, and bemoaned the eclipse of a gallant "nobility" by the mechanized *Materialschlacht* (battle of material).[10] Although he did not lay particular emphasis on technology in this work, he described the war as a conflict of natural forces, something that would be typical of the reified depictions of human action that surfaced again and again in his subsequent works on technology. An artillery barrage was a "storm of iron" (*Eisenhagel*), an exploding shell a "hurricane of fire" (*Feuerorkan*). An airplane dropping bombs was like a "vulture" (*Aasvogel*) circling over enemy troops who were, in turn, a "swarm of bees" (*Bienenschwarm*). Houses

---

[7] Theweleit, *Männer phantasien*, vol. 2, p. 188.

[8] Ibid., vol. 2, p. 186. Freud discussed technical advance in relation to sublimation of sexual energies in *Civilization and Its Discontents*, trans. James Strachey (New York, 1962). Herbert Marcuse developed the views Freud expressed in *Eros and Civilization* (Boston, 1955), where Freud wrote that "the diversion of primary destructiveness from the ego to the external world feeds technological progress" (p. 52).

[9] Ernst Jünger, *In Stahlgewittern* (Stuttgart, 1960), and *Der Arbeiter*. See J. P. Stern, *Ernst Jünger: A Writer of Our Time* (Cambridge, England, 1953), for an excellent discussion of Jünger's "new style of assent to death and to total warfare" (p. 10).

[10] Jünger, *In Stahlgewittern*, p. 100.

were destroyed, walls and roofs collapsed, "as if by the power of magic." During an offensive in 1918, Jünger wrote, "I watched the slaughter ... as if I was in the loge of a theatre."[11] At the time, these metaphors were vivid and served to make the historical appear as a result of nature as well as to describe unprecedented forms of technological warfare in the vocabulary of a preindustrial landscape. They communicate a stunned sense of wonder that elevates spectatorial surrender to the war experienced as "fate" into a "heroic" posture.

In *Der Kampf als inneres Erlebnis* (Battle as an Inner Experience) and *Feuer und Blut* (Fire and Blood), published in 1922 and 1926, respectively, Jünger wedded this heroic posture to a celebration of technology.[12] He portrayed the war as the crucible of his generation. Those who had lived through it felt distant from both prewar conservatism and Weimar's social democracy. The war, Jünger wrote, was "the *father* of all things ... (and) ... our father as well" (emphasis added). "It hammered, chiseled and hardened us into what we are ... As long as life's oscillating wheel rotates inside us, this war will remain the axle around which it hums."[13] Reification is embedded in these sentences. The relation between human subjects and external objects is reversed; the war is anthropomorphized into a "father" endowed with subjectivity. It "hammers, chisels and hardens" the body of the front generation, thereby creating the new man. For Jünger, the war did not portend the decline of the West. Rather it presaged cultural renewal. Intellectual refinement, "the tender cult of the brain, collapsed in a rattling rebirth of barbarism. Other gods have been raised to the throne of the day: power, Faust, and manly courage."[14] This rebirth of barbarism unleashes primal passions stifled by civilian life. The most modern yet "blind" technological warfare exists alongside the *Ur* or "primordial relation" of one soldier facing another.[15] Jünger welcomed the war as a relief from the restrictions placed on the "will to battle" of a bored and boring middle class obsessed by a need for security. And, like Sorel, he welcomed action as a relief from the intellect's restrictions.

Jünger's use of the categories of *Lebensphilosophie* lend a peculiarly grotesque quality to his celebration of war. The sources of war are

[11] Ibid., p. 126. Repeated references to magic in connection with technology led Ernst Bloch to comment on "the spook which lives on in spite of the streams of electric current," in "Technik und Geistererscheinungen," *Verfremdungen I* (Frankfurt, 1961), pp. 177–85.
[12] Ernst Jünger, *Der Kampf als inneres Erlebnis* (Berlin, 1922; reprint, Stuttgart, 1960).
[13] Ibid., p. 13.
[14] Ibid., p. 38.
[15] Ibid., p. 33.

73

not to be found in national conflicts of interest but in suprahistorical terms such as "life" or "blood." Jünger's bizarre combinations of intellect and nihilism are evident in statements such as "to live means to kill,"[16] or "the true sources of war come from deep in our breast and everything horrible that now flows over the world is only a mirror image of the human soul manifesting itself in events."[17] His program of rebirth and renewal was a specifically masculine one. "Oh, the baptism of fire! The air was so laden with an overflowing manliness that every breath was intoxicating. One could cry without knowing why. Oh hearts of men that could feel this!"[18] Jünger describes this masculine rite with religious and sexual metaphors that suggest a Durkheimian community-forming ritual:

Once again: the ecstasy. The condition of the holy man, of great poets and of great love is also granted to those of great courage. The enthusiasm of manliness bursts beyond itself to such an extent that the blood boils as it surges through the veins and glows as it foams through the heart ... It is an intoxication beyond all intoxication, an unleashing that breaks all bonds. It is a frenzy without caution and limits, comparable only to the forces of nature. There [in combat] the individual is like a raging storm, the tossing sea and the roaring thunder. He has melted into everything. He rests at the dark door of death like a bullet that has reached its goal. And the purple waves dash over him. For a long time he has no awareness of transition. It is as if a wave slipped back into the flowing sea.[19]

What Freud called the "oceanic feeling, a feeling of a indissoluble bond of being one with the external world as a whole,"[20] which he found in religious mysticism and in the rapture of love, is apparent in this description of war as well. Drawn out from his isolation, the individual soldier finds himself in the natural maelstrom of combat where he discovers new bonds and opportunities for instinctual release. He is at once powerful "like a raging storm," yet subject to the "waves that engulf him." As in so much of his writing, Jünger places

[16] Ibid., p. 45.
[17] Ibid., pp. 46–7.
[18] Ibid., p. 22.
[19] Ibid., p. 57.
[20] Sigmund Freud, *Civilization and Its Discontents*, p. 11. Freud's analysis of the separation of sensuality and tenderness in men – "where such men love they have no desire and where they desire they cannot love – sheds light on the psychic life of the members of the *Freikorps* in Theweleit's study. See "Contributions to the Psychology of Love: The Most Prevalent Form of Degradation in Erotic Life" (1912), in *Sigmund Freud: Collected Papers*, vol. IV (London, 1971), pp. 203–16. Theweleit's discussion of the juxtaposition of the imagery of the white nurse to the red or proletarian woman presents some examples of such degradation in erotic life. See Theweleit, *Männerphantasien*, vol. 1, pp. 141–28.

these romantic themes of death and transformation in a modern context.

Jünger wrote not only about the individual at war but also about the wartime community of men. The existence of this community expanded the war's transformative powers; the "small conflicts" of this "special community" did not challenge this basic fact. The soldiers share a "great destiny, ride the same wave, are for once together as an organism in the face of the hostile outside world, encompass a higher mission."[21] The individual soldier who "melts into everything," who, by so doing, finds a symbiotic bond to a masculine community, also affirms the clear boundaries between himself and others. He becomes a new man with a "granite face, a voice that rattles order" with the precision of a machine gun, a body that is "smooth, lined, lean, ... with chiseled features, eyes hardened under a thousand horrors."[22] War as a ritual of rebirth and transfiguration produces men like "steel forms" racing through battlefields in tanks or flying over them in planes. Here emerged the "new man, the storm pioneer, the elite of central Europe. A wholly new race, intelligent, strong and full of will. What emerges here in battle, ... tomorrow will be the axis around which life will revolve faster and faster."[23]

The image of the "steel form" as the "axis around which life will revolve" became a central theme in Jünger's work. It brought together the masculine community, aesthetic clarity and form, and a utopian vision of a body so mechanized and tough that it was beyond pain. For Jünger the slaughter and death had not been in vain and those pacifists who said it was lacked any appreciation for its "deeper" significance. The war had done no less than burn away the excess of bourgeois and feminine refinements, revealing a utopian and anticipatory image of a new man. The masculine community of the trenches and the resulting image of the new man served as lost treasures of the postwar reactionary tradition. The Marxists claimed that alienation in production when pushed to its limits would lead to revolution; Jünger argued that suffering and death would lead to a new era. His vision of man made whole again suggested no transcendence of the division of labor or mechanization. But it did promise that in dialectical fashion, the war would be the source of a new world. Here was the modernist cult of the new in its fascist variant:

---

[21] Jünger, *Kampf als inneres Erlebnis*, p. 89.
[22] Ibid., p. 57.
[23] Ibid., p. 76.

The glowing dusk of a sinking era is at the same time a dawn, by arming us for new, harder fighting. . . . The war is not the end but rather the emergence of violence. It is the forge in which the world will be hammered into new limits and new communities. New forms filled with blood and power will be packed with a hard fist. The war is a great school and the new man will be taken from our race.[24]

The soldiers become "day laborers of death" constructing a new world on the ruins of prewar culture and society. "The battle is not only a process of destruction, but also a masculine form of creation."[25] The redemptive role of the war experience must be stressed here. Despite the fact that the war and millions of lives were lost, Jünger seeks to salvage a cultural – and subsequently political – victory from the ashes of military disaster. The masculine *Gemeinschaft* was the actually existing alternative to an "effeminate" and "sinking era." This tendency to neglect the relations between means and ends in politics, to seek through politics salvation of souls, authenticity, and self-realization rather than more mundane purposes, placed Jünger in the romantic and apolitical traditions that Max Weber warned should remain distant from politics. But in the wake of Germany's defeat, Jünger's cultural compensations were more appealing to many than Weber's gloomy, brooding, most unmagical realism.

Jünger bitterly opposed pacifist sentiment in postwar Germany and advocated the intrinsic merits of action, decision, existential commitment, and violence as the means toward genuine self-realization. Once he admitted that

perhaps we are sacrificing ourselves for something inessential. But no one can take away our worth. What is essential is not what we fight for but how we fight. The quality of fighting, the engagement of the person, even if it be for the most insignificant idea, counts for more than brooding over good and evil.[26]

Although such celebrations of sacrifice for its own sake were not uncommon among the conservative revolutionaries, Jünger was distinctive in linking this jargon of authenticity to technology. For him it was the instrument of nihilist engagement. His writing is filled with passages that strive to present technology as something obeying "laws of the blood" or the needs of the human body, rather than merely the laws of physics. He presented war as a deliverance, as an intoxication, a tremendous release of energy "comparable only to eros."[27]

[24] Ibid., p. 77.
[25] Ibid., pp. 33, 53–4.
[26] Ibid, pp. 53–4.
[27] Ibid., p. 19.

This unleashed energy transformed the battlefield from a "gigantic, dead mechanism" that "spreads an icy, impersonal wave of destruction over the earth," into the external manifestation of an unseen "Caesaristic will" that

endlessly brings forth magnificent and merciless *spectacles*. Only a few are granted the opportunity to sink in to this sublime purposelessness, *as one would sink into an work of art*, or into the starry heavens. Whoever felt only the denial, only his own suffering and not the affirmation, the higher movement in this war, lived through the war as a slave. He did not have an inner but only an outer experience of the war [emphasis added].[28]

The very purposelessness of the spectacle of destruction, its quality as something done for its own sake alone, these features of war are what Jünger celebrated in his language of will and beauty. For this "inner experience" of the war, wholly divorced from the questions of war aims or of the relation between sacrifices and political ends, meant a deliverance from middle-class society, from individual isolation, and from the emotions of pity and compassion. It meant an active assertion of self at the same time that it fostered an actual surrender to forces beyond one's control.

Just at those points in his works where Jünger's descriptions of the power of the spectacle threaten to dampen his celebration of the will, he finds a collective subject to restore both culture and conservative revolutionary politics:

Today we are writing poetry out of steel and struggle for power in battles in which events mesh together with the precision of machines. In these battles on land, on water, and in the air there lay a beauty that we are able to anticipate. There the hot will of the blood restrains and then expresses itself through the dominance of technical wonder works of power.[29]

There are several important aspects of Jüngerian symbolism evident in this passage. First, it is typical of the presentation of aesthetic as normative judgments and the accompanying "definition of the beautiful in an ever more normative, absolute sense, . . . its hypostasization into a metaphysical dimension," which Bohrer and other critics have viewed as a central feature of the German and European wide revolt against bourgeois "decadence" since Nietzsche. Here Jünger deserves to be placed alongside Ezra Pound, Wyndham Lewis, Marinetti, Celine, and D'Annunzio as the right wing of the modernist avant-garde that was drawn to fascism.[30] Second, the passage is indicative of the

[28] Ibid., pp. 107–8.
[29] Ibid., p. 107.
[30] Bohrer, *Die Ästhetik des Schreckens*, p. 61.

right-wing politicization of the categories taken from *Lebensphilosophie*, especially the cult of the will. Third, the juxtaposition of the "hot will of the blood" and "technical wonder-works of power" suggests an instinctual cathexis onto the machine, a phenomenon discussed both by Theweleit and Herbert Marcuse in his analyses of aggression in advanced industrial societies. But whether we view this and similar passages primarily as examples of fascist aestheticism, the entry of the irrational in politics, or finally as a virulent return of the repressed of unconscious fantasy, one thing is clear: It fuses romantic celebration of will and violence with modern technology. Jünger's "poetry of steel" reconciles beauty to the world of precision technology and military power, while distinguishing this masculine aesthetic from what it views as a contemptible, feminine, pacifist sensibility. It suggests that the masculine aesthetic is fully modern. Although he was fully at home in the German romantic tradition, Jünger took pains to differentiate his romanticism from a softer, supposedly less modern variety.

Jünger's appeals to the will comprise an ironic complement to his essentially passive and spectatorial stance toward the instrumentalization of human beings, and even toward death. Some of Jünger's more perceptive critics have noticed this parallel between a celebration of total calculation and functionality with its apparent opposite, adventure and dynamism. Christian Graf von Krockow, for example, has written that Jünger discovered "pure adventure in the heart of functionality."[31] A reified consciousness and unconscious fantasy complement one another. "Heroic" acceptance of the storm of steel accompanies the capacity to regard one's own body as a machine beyond pleasure, pain, and emotion. Jünger represents a new kind of political romanticism, one that links technology to the primordial forces of the will and thus rescues this "dead mechanism" from the attacks of the antitechnological currents of German romanticism. Rather than apologize for or deny the reality of the subordination of war and labor to industrial rationalization, Jünger as the "heroic realist" welcomed such a process, promising deliverance from the features of bourgeois society he most detested: reason and feeling.

Jünger continued to develop this symbiosis of irrationalism and technics in two book-length essays of the mid-1920s, *Das Wäldchen 125* and *Feuer und Blut*. The generation of the trenches was one that

---

[31] Christian Graf von Krockow, *Die Entscheidung: Eine Untersuchung über Ernst Jünger, Carl Schmitt, Martin Heidegger* (Stuttgart, 1960), p. 86. On the connection between positivism and decisionism in social theory, see Jürgen Habermas's essay "Dogmatism, Reason, and Decision: On Theory and Practice in Our Scientific Civilization," in *Theory and Practice* (Boston, 1973), pp. 253–82.

"builds machines and for whom machines are not dead iron but rather an organ of power, which it dominates with cold reason and blood. It gives the world a new face."[32] It had borne with dignity the "storm of material" and looked forward to seeing its will find "expression" in material objects.[33] Unlike the antibourgeois youth of prewar Germany, the front generation

begins to reconcile itself with the machine and to see in it not only the useful but the beautiful as well. This reconciliation is an important first step out of a grey, frightful world of utilitarianism, out of the Manchester landscape in which coal dust covers over all values.[34]

It is a reconciliation of machine and the body that is exemplified in the relation between the soldier and the technology of war:

We have to transfer what lies inside us onto the machine. That includes the distance and ice-cold mind that transforms the moving lightning stroke of blood into a conscious and logical performance. What would these iron weapons that were directed against the universe be if our nerves had not been intertwined with them and if our blood didn't flow around every axle.[35]

Transferring "what lies inside us" onto technology not only creates a man–machine symbiosis. It is also an improvement on the body because, unlike the body, the machine is capable of attaining the utopian stage of flawless functioning. But if, as Jünger insists, our nerves are in fact intertwined with technology, the conservative suspicion of and hostility toward this aspect of modernity must be set aside. I quote Jünger's plea at length:

Yes, the machine is beautiful. It must be beautiful for him who loves life in all life's fullness and power. The machine must also be incorporated into what Nietzsche (*who, in his renaissance landscape, still had no place for the machine*) meant when he attacked Darwinism. Nietzsche insisted that life is not only a merciless struggle for survival but also possesses a will to higher and deeper goals. The machine cannot only be a means of production, serving to satisfy our paltry material necessities. Rather, it ought to bestow on us higher and deeper satisfactions. . . . The artistic individual, who suddenly sees in technics the totality [*Ganzheit*] instead of a functional assembly of iron parts and thus grasps a strategy that seeks to break off from the path of the production by seeing that totality and that strategy in war, this artistic individual is as involved in finding the solution, that is, finding the deeper and more elevated satisfactions in the machine, as the engineer or the socialist is! [emphasis added][36]

[32] Ernst Jünger, *Das Wäldchen 125: Eine Chronik aus den Grabenkampfen 1918* (Berlin, 1925), p. 19.
[33] Ernst Jünger, *Feuer und Blut*, p. 37.
[34] Ibid., p. 81.
[35] Ibid., p. 84.
[36] Ibid., p. 81.

Where Nietzsche's cultural critique still pointed to a preindustrial landscape, Jünger sees no conflict between technology and "a will to higher and deeper goals." As the preceding passages make clear, these goals are not the utilitarian ones of expanded production and/or release from burdensome physical labor, but the "deeper satisfactions" accessible to the aesthete, the philosopher of life and the will, and the soldier. An amoral aestheticism of technological form rather than the pastoral landscapes of *völkisch* kitsch was the end point of Jünger's antimaterialism. The armed male community of the trenches was his utopian alternative to "lifeless" industrial society. He was the first of Germany's right-wing literary intellectuals to separate the idea of *Gemeinschaft* from the slightest hint of preindustrial nostalgia.

A year after Hitler came to power, one Nazi commentator pointed with gratitude to Jünger's contribution to the education of German youth.

> German youth owe a debt above all to Ernst Jünger for the fact that technology is no longer a problem for them. They have made his beautiful confessions to technics born from fire and blood their own. They live in harmony with it. They require no more ideologies in order to "overcome" technology. Rather they grasp it as the arm of the idea. This was something new for us, this incorporation of matter into the meaning of events. Jünger has liberated us from a nightmare.[37]

The "nightmare," of course, was the hostility to technology, industrialization, and urbanism that was the legacy of *völkisch* antimodernism, the cultural despair of a Moeller van den Bruck, or the gloomy pessimism of a world-weary Spengler. In his political essays, Jünger attacked those archaic elements of German conservative ideology that stood against a cultural reconciliation of "nationalism and modern life." Jünger believed that postwar "revolutionary nationalism" had to fight a two-front battle against both liberalism and traditional conservatism. The former was removed from the "elementary" and "deeper" aspects of life that surfaced in the war. The latter was a hopelessly antiquated variant of nationalism in a technological era.[38] Jünger rejected these antiurban, antitechnological ideas and tried to

---

[37] Wolf Dieter Mueller, *Ernst Jünger: Ein Leben im Umbruch der Zeit* (Berlin, 1934), p. 42. Cited by Prumm, *Die Literatur des Soldatischen Nationalismus der 20er Jahre: 1918–1933*, 2 vols. (Krönberg, 1974), vol. 2, p. 375. Jünger's influence is apparent in E. Gunther Grundel's *Die Sendung der jungen Generation* (The Mission of the Young Generation) (Munich, 1932), which combined themes from the youth movements, the front experience, anti-Semitism, and a stylization of the worker-soldier overcoming the nervous bourgeois.

[38] Jünger develops this theme in "Zum Jahreswechsel," in *Vormarsch* I (1927–28), pp. 79–80.

demonstrate that *Lebensphilosophie*, aestheticism, and irrationalism did not require them. From 1925 to 1933, the high point of his political-literary engagement, Jünger published over 130 essays in the little magazines of the far Right.[39] In the following pages, I will draw out the main themes and recurrent metaphors of this corpus.

Jünger's political outlook was both antiparliamentary and antidemocratic as well as irrationalist and romantic. He was contemptuous of "the masses" and celebrated a myth of a charismatic elite, a community born of the trenches that prefigured a more extensive national authoritarian community. In his view, the "experience" of the war ought to take precedence over intellectualistic haggling over political programs and ideologies.[40] His essays juxtaposed the cult of wartime community, filled with death and danger, and the prosaic, civilian humdrum of Weimar. Jünger praised both the "living energy" and willingness to sacrifice that he thought was evident in the Nazi party (though he never joined), and the "positive and warlike will to power" of the Communists.[41] However, he abstained from personal involvement in parties or formal political organizations because he thought they served primarily to routinize the charismatic community born of the *Fronterlebnis*. Political programs and specified goals were less important than "movement and living force"[42] and the degree to which intellect and abstraction were subordinated to "blood" and the "will."[43]

No other figure of the Weimar Right did more than Jünger to nurture what I have called the lost treasure of the reactionary modernist tradition, that is, the *Fronterlebnis*. In his view, the purpose of politics was to make the *Fronterlebnis* permanent. This focus on experience and community as the purpose of politics is certainly at one with political romanticism as I have defined it. But this was a political romanticism that did not imply backward-looking or pastoral visions. Libidinal bonds within a community of men at arms were not, he believed, at all incompatible with "modern life." In Weberian terms,

---

[39] For a complete bibliography of Jünger's political essays see Hans Peter des Coudres, *Bibliographie der Werke Ernst Jünger* (Stuttgart, 1970), pp. 50–6. The most thorough secondary analysis is found in Prumm, *Die Literatur*, vol. 2, pp. 337–400.

[40] See Ernst Jünger, "Die zwei Tyrannen," *Arminius* 8 (1927), p. 3.

[41] "Die Geburt des Nationalismus aus dem Krieg" (The Birth of Nationalism in the War), *Deutsches Volkstum* 11 (1929), pp. 576–82.

[42] "Das Ziel entscheidet" (The Goal Decides), *Arminius* 8 (1927), pp. 4–6.

[43] "Das Blut und Intellekt" (Blood and Intellect), *Die Standarte: Beiträge zur Vertiefung des Frontgedankens* (14, 1925), p. 2. Juxtaposition of blood and mind was one of Jünger's recurrent themes: See "Der Frontsoldat und die innere Politik" (The Front Soldier and Inner Politics), *Die Standarte* (13, 1925), p. 2; "Das Blut" and "Der Wille" in *Standarte: Wochenschrift des neuen Nationalismus* (5, 6, 1926), pp. 104–7, and 126–30.

Jünger's cultural politics were intended both to prevent the routinization of charismatic masculine community of the trenches and to assert the superiority of a politics of absolute ethics over an ethic of responsibility. Although these essays were written during the period in which rationalization of German industry accompanied a flowering of corporatist utopias in overcoming class conflicts through expanded productivity,[44] the Jüngerian vision was not a technocratic one. He did not see in technology a leveler of ideological politics. On the contrary, he constantly stressed its supposedly non- and irrational impulses.[45]

In 1927, Jünger published an essay entitled "Nationalismus und modernes Leben" (Nationalism and Modern Life), in which he developed the notion that was at the heart of his perceptions of technology: "magical realism."[46] He claimed that modern life, which at one point appeared to be heading toward utter chaos and formlessness, was instead witnessing the emergence of a new symbolic dimension. At first glance, "this life between machines and combustible fuels" could be described as "sober and without soul" (*unbeseelt*). Labor and leisure were being subjected to massification and mechanization. Yet the more geometrical and precise the forms of modern life become, the more

the natural reaches through the plaster layers of the modern cities and fills the operation of machines and cleaned-up marionettes with a deeper life, one superior to the purposeful life and whose essence cannot be grasped with mathematics [emphasis added].[47]

The "outer form" of modern life displays the precision of a mosquito net that coexists with "small parts" that perform "wild, irregular and apparently senseless movement." An unnamed "higher order, . . . the mathematic or the organic," reveals an "intoxication in the highest degree" behind the facade of efficient sobriety.[48] The traffic of a modern city, the crisscrossing of endless forms, leaves Jünger with a

---

[44] See Prumm, *Die Literatur*, vol. 1. On the rationalization movement see Robert Brady, *The Rationalization Movement in German Industry* (Berkeley, 1933); and Charles Maier, *Recasting Bourgeois Europe: Stabilization in France, Germany and Italy in the Decade after World War I* (Princeton, N.J., 1975), and "Between Taylorism and Technocracy: European Ideologies and the Vision of Industrial Productivity in the 1920s," *Journal of Contemporary History* 5 (1970), pp. 27–51. On the rationalization movement and *Neue Sachlichkeit* see Lethens, *Neue Sachlickeit: Studien zur Literatur des weissens Socialismus* (Stuttgart, 1970).

[45] Prumm, *Die Literatur*, vol. I.

[46] Ernst Jünger, "Nationalismus und modernes Leben," *Arminius* 8 (1927), pp. 4–6.

[47] Ibid., p. 4.

[48] Ibid.

sense of "numbness" and does not appear so different from a "swarm of mosquitoes." The rational character of modern commerce and transportation

is the expression of a powerful life, which strikes like a flame out of the earth and scorches its unconscious bearers, . . . It is an eternal meaning in a particular space and particular time. In our space and in our time.[49]

Jünger wrote that literature in this space and time demanded a "double vision" or "magical realism" that understands that "everything transitory is only a mirror," which separates the surface and mechanical from the deep "moving power" beneath it.

It is the view which manifests itself in our time in those images of magical realism in whose spaces every line of the outer world is recorded with the precision of a mathematical formula, and whose coldness, although in a fashion that is both inexplicable and transparent, illuminates and warms a magical background.[50]

Jünger's magical realism found clearest expression in his descriptions of the war. Here were seemingly endless "syntheses" of fire and blood, precision and passion, rationality and magic, outer form and hidden will. The following description of a sinking battleship, for example, clearly presents Jünger's nihilist fascination with technology:

But haven't we, who of course are not materialists, but instead label ourselves realists, already felt the experience of mathematical precision and magical background during the war. Didn't phenomena such as the modern battleship arouse the same impression in us. *This embodiment of an icy will*, all coal and steel, oil, explosives and electricity, manned by specialized positions from admiral to boiler heater, the image of the latest precision mechanics, served by workers and directors, functional in the highest degree, composed of millions of objects – this whole apparatus is sacrificed in seconds for the sake of things which one does not know but rather in which one can only take on faith. It goes down burning, shot to pieces, sinking with flags flying, perishing forever, in moments in which destiny itself appears to intoxicate the blood amid the cries of the dying, sacrificed in a sea most distant from one's fatherland, which perhaps will belong to history tomorrow, but perishing amid a "hurrah" that must shake every individual wherever he may stand, to the core of his heart, because in this cry the whole tension between two worlds is illuminated as by a moving lightning bolt – yes, isn't all this taken together not the image of a contradiction which has captured every one of us between its poles from the last office girl to the very last factory worker? [emphasis added].[51]

[49] Ibid., p. 5.
[50] Ibid.
[51] Ibid., pp. 5–6.

When viewed through the spectacles of Jünger's magical realism, the battleship emerges as the objectification of tremendous energy and technical potential. Human beings enter as part of the functioning machinery that is utterly reified; that is, it appears to have its own autonomous laws separate from human consciousness and organization, but it is not soulless or inhuman. The battleship's functional rationality provides evidence of a Prussian "icy will" rather than any particular social or historical structures. Precision, exactitude, subordination of the individual to his specialized task, as well as unthinking sacrifice, represent both technology's icy will and the lost treasure of the conservative revolution's notion of community. Literally and figuratively, the battleship represents an iron necessity that Jünger welcomes.

The effect of Jünger's descriptions is to redeem sacrifices, to encourage submission to destiny, and, ironically, to prevent the victory of a lifeless machine by presenting the immensity of its destructive capacities. Technology, sacrifice, and destiny are bound together in his mind. It is technology that provides the material for great modern spectacles of sacrifice and martyrdom in which antinomies of reason and unreason are miraculously overcome. The dying affirm their own destruction. Jünger, like Spengler and the rest of the technological romantics in Germany, endlessly proclaimed that this or that dichotomy or antinomy had been overcome in these unities of blood and technology. War served as the stage on which the central dichotomies of German modernity, *Kultur* versus *Zivilisation* or *Gemeinschaft* versus *Gesellschaft*, were reconciled. Jünger's outlook had none of those remnants of tragic consciousness, or resignation to inevitable rationalization that Spengler had not completely expunged from his works. Rather he advocated a "heroic" affirmation of passivity in the face of the "contradiction that has captured every one of us between its poles." Jünger tried to recapture the dramatic moment of the sinking battleship in descriptions of street scenes in the modern city.

In the big city, between automobiles and electric signs, in political mass meetings, in the motorized tempo of work and leisure, in the middle of the bustle of the modern Babylon, it is necessary to stand like a person from another world, with the deep astonishment of which only children are usually capable and say: All of this has its meaning, a deep meaning, which I felt also in myself.[52]

Jünger never really clarifies what this deep meaning could be, presumably because to explain it would rob it of its depth. But what is

[52] Ibid., p. 6.

clear is that Jünger ennobles passivity, raises a contemplative, spectatorial view of events into a heroic cult, and turns aggression against
the German middle class into acceptance of supposedly immutable
technological imperatives. This is Jünger's answer to a society he viewed
as decadent and drowning in materialism. In Hegelian terms, he celebrates the heroic subject and in so doing offers an apology for submission and conformism of the individual. For the astonished urbanite,
the battleship and urban traffic are parts of a "second nature," one
no less mysterious than the natural landscape was for the German
romantics of the early nineteenth century.

The war of the trenches and its technological accoutrements reduced the importance of the individual soldier. Even Jünger's magical
realism could not obscure the obvious: Heroic virtues and technical
advance stood in an ambivalent relationship to one another. The will
was only so powerful when arrayed against the machine gun and the
tank. How could elitist politics withstand such a formidable challenge?
Jünger turned his attention to aviation as an arena in which a military
aristocracy could coexist with technical advances. The "flyer" represented an "age of transition, . . . the new man, the man of the twentieth
century." Flying was more than a triumph of science and functional
rationality; it was "the living expression of a powerful life force" that
contradicted pessimistic prophesies about "the decline of the race."
It signifies "far more than the merely technical. Its soaring flights stake
out the districts of a *cultic* world" (emphasis added). It is indispensable
for the fulfillment of Germany's national destiny and must be unleashed from the restrictions on German rearmament imposed by the
Versailles Treaty.[53] Here again, Jünger places the language of will
and the soul in the service of German nationalism.

Jünger's romance of aviation was not uniquely German, nor did it
represent a break with prewar conservatism. The issue had simply
not yet presented itself. But Jünger's views on urbanism were a direct
challenge to *völkisch* antimodernism. In a 1926 essay, "*Grosstadt und
Land*" (Metropolis and Countryside), he was unrestrained in his enthusiasm for big cities.[54] This was a novelty for a German right-wing
intellectual. Juxtapositions of a rooted and healthy landscape to root-

[53] On the erosion of romantic heroes due to the slaughter at the front, see Paul Fussells's
discussion of British postwar literature in *The Great War and Modern Memory* (New
York, 1975). Advertisements for flying lessons appeared regularly in journals such as
Der Vormarsch. Jünger celebrated the airplane pilot in "Der Flieger" (The Flyer), *Der
Tag* 15 (1928). See also Ernst Jünger, "Nation und Luftfahrt," *Vormarsch* (1, 1927/
8), pp. 314–17.
[54] Ernst Jünger, "Grosstadt und Land," *Deutsches Volkstum* 8 (1926), pp. 577–81.

less cosmopolitanism were standard elements of right-wing antimodernist ideology. Jünger countered that this "faith in the land is the faith of a declining existence that, without realizing it, has inwardly relinquished power. It is the symbol of the national crisis of our time.[55] In the first half of the nineteenth century, appeals to the land may have had a revolutionary force; today (in Weimar, that is), "other powers, . . . another spirit" must be called into the service of the nation. Nothing will be accomplished by propagandizing "old Fritz with all the means of modern advertising." The ideas of "blood, tradition . . . and race" are "metaphysical" rather than "primarily biological" ideas. If the nation is to have a future, a "new nationalism" will have to grasp the "spirit [*Geist*] of the large city."[56]

The country and the nation . . . must come to terms with the following necessity: We must penetrate and enter into the power of the metropolis, into the *forces of our time — the machine, the masses, and the worker.* For it is in them that the potential energy so crucial for tomorrow's national spectacle resides. All of the people of Europe are at work to use these powers. We will try to put aside the objections of a *misguided romanticism which views the machine as in conflict with Kultur.* The machine and *Americanism* are two different things. If our era does possess a culture, it will be through the use of machines alone that it will be in a position to either expand or defend its living space [*Lebensraum*]. It is often said that the masses represent the decline of personality. But it is precisely these masses who will produce a decisive and unrestricted type of leader, one who will have far fewer restrictions on his actions than even the sovereign of the absolute monarchy did [emphasis added].[57]

These masses, including the proletariat, would no longer be led in the direction of internationalism, pacifism, and Marxist socialism. Rather, they can be won over to the "new nationalism," once it realizes that at its center is a "big-city feeling" (*grosstadtisches Gefühl*). The most modern *Geist*, Jünger wrote, made its first and definitive appearance in the self-sacrifice of the front soldiers in the Great War. It was a *Geist* that did not exist in the sleepy countryside. The city and the front soldier incorporated a "metaphysical will," whether or not "we," that is, the German Right, realized this fact.

The city is the brain through which the fundamental will of our time thinks, the arms with which it creates and strikes, and the mediating consciousness through which the finite comprehends what the infinite has to say to it. *Let us throw ourselves into this era, which possesses its hidden beauties and its characteristic and fascinating powers as every other age, and we will wholly become what we are. This is a better service to the nation than that offered by a romanticism of a distant*

[55] Ibid., p. 578.
[56] Ibid., p. 579.
[57] Ibid., pp. 579–80.

place and a past time, one which is not equal to the tasks that stand before us [emphasis added].[58]

The romanticism of a distant time and place, as it appeared among the *völkisch* ideologues and in the youth movement, had contrasted whole, unalienated individuals wandering through the German (later Aryan) landscape with the anomie of the modern city. Jünger himself had traveled through North Africa before the war, seeking the vitalism that he felt was lacking in Europe. He was not rejecting romanticism, only one of its favorite themes. In place of pastoral escape, he promised his readers that the battlefield and the metropolis could fulfull the romantic yearnings of antibourgeois youth.

It was Jünger's selectivity that distinguished his response to modernity; in particular, his differentiation of Americanism from technology was important in integrating technics into a nationalist resurgence. For the conservative revolutionaries, Americanism meant commercialism, mass culture, Taylorism, and liberalism. Jünger proposed to incorporate the machine and even the metropolis into German *Kultur*, rather than to reject both as products of alien forces. Above all, it was his aesthetic and philosophical prisms that allowed him to fashion such a vision.

In 1927, Jünger published an essay entitled "Fortschritt, Freiheit und Notwendigkeit" (Progress, Freedom and Necessity).[59] It appeared in several different small journals circulating in conservative revolutionary circles. In it, Jünger explicitly set out to demonstrate that acceptance of technological modernity did not entail the embrace of a more all-encompassing view of the modern world that would include liberalism, Marxism, rationalism, or individual liberty. It is a remarkable document of reactionary modernist sentiment because it catalogues the eclipse of individuality at the hands of technology – and accepts the process. "In our technical era," he wrote, "the individual appears to be ever more dependent, unfree and endangered," torn from older bonds and perhaps facing extinction. "The process of the dissolution of form in favor of movement" whittles down the individual personality in the urban mass. At the same time, however, it is "possessed with the speed of electric current" and breaks down the capacities of individuals to sustain their identity. The more technical the world becomes, the more tasks are subject to the movement of machines, the more the individual will is suppressed. "The nature of these bonds is, of course, not a personal one, and thus they are less

[58] Ibid., p. 581.
[59] Jünger, "Fortschritt, Freiheit und Notwendigkeit," *Arminius* 8 (1926), pp. 8–10.

visible than those of the feudal era. Hence they are even more absolute than the absolute monarchies."[60] Every advance of reason and progress brings with it a "new attack on freedom." Rather than criticize this process, Jünger assimilates it into the rhetoric of heroic submission and sacrifice.

The technical world does not exist for itself. Rather it is the *expression of inner processes and transformations*. And the machines are not only directed against nature but against us as well. We depend on these *steel translations of our blood and our brains,* just as the actor depends on his act. This explains the full force of the compulsion under which we are standing. No power is in a position to offer the stars to us other than we, ourselves. If it is not our intention, so it is certainly our innermost will to sacrifice our freedom, to give up our existence as individuals and to melt into a large life circle, in which the individual has as little self-sufficiency as a cell which must die when separated from the body [emphasis added].[61]

Surrender to this condition, which he describes as an "anonymous slavery," expresses "our innermost will." Jünger places the language of will and authenticity in the service of their apparent opposites: objectification and reification. This language of "inner processes and transformations" seals technology off from society and history. Rather than reject technology or accept its apparent ideological counterparts, liberalism and Marxism, Jünger opts for the heroic sacrifice of individual freedom.

Jünger's ode to sacrifice bears comparison with what has been called the "tragic vision" of German social theory.[62] To be sure, Jünger was not a social theorist, but his writings addressed problems raised in the work of such contemporaries as Max and Alfred Weber, Werner Sombart, Georg Simmel, and Georg Lukács. In Simmel's words, the "tragedy of culture" was an inescapable result of the objectification of subjective intention and labor in the external world. *Geist* was powerless to slow down or transform the process of rationalization of social life and culture. If one were schematically to divide German social theory of this period into a Right, Left, and Center, the resulting picture would look something like this. Weber and Simmel stood for the Center, advocating tragic resignation while defending remnants of individual autonomy. The Left would be represented by Lukács and Ernst Bloch, who believed that tragic consciousness was itself a product of reification produced by capitalist commodity relations. They argued that tragic consciousness would be overcome, *aufgehoben,*

---

[60] Ibid., p. 8.
[61] Ibid.
[62] Lowy, *Pour une Sociologie* . . . , pp. 77–8.

by proletarian revolution that would destroy the capitalist origins of reified consciousness.[63]

Jünger is representative of those right-wing intellectuals who also believed "overcoming" tragic consciousness was a possibility. Unlike the romantic Marxists, the cultural revolution Jünger advocated endowed the eclipse of individuality with a halo of heroism. Reactionary modernists agreed with exponents of the "tragic vision" that suprahistorical forces lay behind external appearances of modern culture and that these forces were the genuinely decisive ones. They also agreed that individuals were powerless to change or oppose these forces. Where they differed was in justifying acceptance of these supposedly omnipotent forces. In this regard, Jünger's discourse of will, nature, and sacrifice is important, for it comprises a collection of metaphors and symbols that urge acquiescence to one's own powerlessness.

There was another important difference between the romantics of the far Right and far Left. Lukács and Bloch remained fringe phenomena in the history of modern communism, which rejected them, or at least the romantic aspects of their work, as out of step with Marxist claims to scientific truth. But the fascist and later the Nazi intellectuals who attacked reason were wholly at one with mainstream cultural politics of the fascist and National Socialist movements in general. In this sense, the right-wing romantics were speaking the same language as that of the fascist mass movements, something that left-wing intellectuals could rarely claim.

Either directly or indirectly, nationalist intellectuals, be they on the right or the left, must integrate the needs of the nation-state with their commitments to a vision of national identity. Jünger was no exception. His rejection of liberalism and Marxism was partly due to a belief that, as materialist traditions, they were alien to a true German nationalism.[64] "Nationalism," he wrote, "is the first attempt to take a brutal look straight at a brutal reality."[65] German nationalism had to reject both antitechnological escapism and liberal internationalism. Nationalism was a "very modern act" because it recognized the ne-

---

[63] Lukács's view of proletarian revolution as the resolution to otherwise unresolvable antinomies of bourgeois thought appears in his essay, "Reification and the Consciousness of the Proletariat," in *History and Class Consciousness*, trans. Rodney Livinstone (Cambridge, Mass., 1971), pp. 83–222.

[64] Mosse has interpreted such rejections of both bourgeois and Marxist materialism as the intellectuals' "search for a third force in pre-Nazi Germany." See his *Germans and Jews: The Right, the Left and the Search for a "Third Force" in Pre-Nazi Germany* (New York, 1970).

[65] Jünger, "Fortschritt, Freiheit und Notwendigkeit," p. 9.

cessity of modern technology as well as the obsolescence of humanistic culture.[66] Marxism and liberalism aimed merely for a "community of spirit" (*Geistgemeinschaft*), whereas German nationalism sought a "community of blood" (*Blutgemeinschaft*).[67] Wage increases would not abolish wage slavery nor could capitalism or communism grasp or reward the "inner meaning of labor." Only nationalism could do that. Nationalism would offer workers what historical materialism never could, namely, the promise of "once again placing life under the sway of great ideas and thereby *winning a victory of the soul over the machine.*"[68] Thereby it would break away from Marx's "mechanistic, rationalistic and materialist" currents in favor of the "deeper, ... organic" aspects of labor that cannot be subsumed under commodity relationships.[69] Jünger connected this victory to resurgent nationalism.

Labor is an expression of national life and the worker is one of the parts of the nation. *Every effort to rob the worker of his living bonds by placing him under the empty concepts like "humanity" or an international community of interest is high treason of the blood by the intellect.* The meaning of labor does not lie in profit making or wage earning but in creating for the nation the fullness of values that it needs for its unfolding. Thus labor has within it a value directed outward that is at the same time of a warlike nature. Every hand gripped on a machine suggests a shot will be fired, every completed work day is like a marching day of an individual in an army unit, ... Labor is a moral deed, not a mechanical performance that can be measured with the Taylor system or in money. What is more important to the worker than wage increases is the feeling of dignity of creative individuals, a feeling that has been lost in the Marxist-capitalist world [emphasis added].[70]

War and the nation will transform labor into a moral deed. Jünger advocates the familiar third way "beyond" both capitalism and communism. It is not the actual labor process that robs labor of its deeper meanings, but liberal and Marxist interpretations of that process. For Jünger and his fellow conservative revolutionaries, a spiritual and

---

[66] Ernst Jünger, "Der unsichtbare Kern" (The InvisibleCore), *Vormarsch* (2, 1929), pp. 329–31.

[67] Ernst Jünger, "Unsere Kampfstellung" (Our Battle Position), *Arminius* 8 (1927), p. 8.

[68] Ernst Jünger, "Schliesst Euch Zusammen" (Unite), *Standarte* 1 (1925), pp. 224–5.

[69] Ernst Jünger, "Revolution um Karl Marx" (Revolution according to Karl Marx), *Widerstand: Zeitschrift für nationalrevolutionäre Politik* (Resistance: Magazine for national revolutionary politics) (4, 1929), pp. 144–60. On Jünger's criticisms of Marxism and his attitudes toward the Soviet Union, see Schüddekopf, *Linke Leute von Rechts: National-bolschewismus in Deutschland: 1918–1933* (Frankfurt, 1972); and Norr, "German Social Theory and the Hidden Face of Technology," *European Journal of Sociology* XV (1974), pp. 312–36. Norr argues that Soviet industrialization was behind Jünger's image of total mobilization. In fact, Jünger saw the five-year plans as the realization of the total mobilization he confronted for the first time during the war.

[70] Jünger, "Unsere Kampfstellung," p. 8.

cultural revolution by the Right that leaves existing property relations intact will do more to break the spell of commodities than would a socialization of the means of production by the Left. In place of the utopia of workers' councils or revolutionary parties, Jünger found his refuge from the world of exchange value in war and the idealism of the trenches.

Part of the appeal of Marxism for the intellectuals lay in its claim to be able to see a new society emerging within the conflicts of the existing order. In a 1929 essay entitled "Untergang oder neue Ordnung?" (Decline or New Order?), [71] Jünger made a similar claim for right-wing analysis. The new order was not a hopeless utopia; it was prefigured in war and labor, both of which pointed toward a post-bourgeois industrial society. Jünger glimpsed three bases of this new order: first, a "new principle or new lawfulness ... which guarantees the unity of the emergent order"; second, a "new man ... who brings this principle to realization"; and third, "new and superior forms ... in which the activity of this new type of person finds expression."[72] Labor was the new principle. In contrast to labor in the nineteenth century, labor now had a "precise quality" evident in the uniform movements of the body and machine in disparate areas of life: sports, transportation, traffic, and war on the sea and in the air.[73] The new man is a stylized image of the worker. Jünger's idea of the worker refers less to a political or economic category than it does to the bearer of a new "life feeling." It refers to Prussian, not Marxist, socialist traditions and celebrates the virtues of "discipline, order, subordination, leadership, obedience and military service."[74] The specifics of this new order remained vague, though Jünger thought both Italian fascism and the industrializing Soviet Union offered glimpses of what it would look like when completed. Here some of Jünger's work bears the marks of national bolshevism, a strange ideological mix of Prussian and Russian traditions. What Jünger found attractive in the Soviet Union was the regulation and militarization of labor by the state. He even wrote an essay praising Trotsky's proposals concerning the militarization of labor. In his view, if Germany were to break free from the restrictions on armament stipulated by the Versailles treaty, it would have to adopt a similar kind of statism.[75]

---

[71] Ernst Jünger, "Untergang oder neue Ordnung?" *Deutsches Volkstum* 15 (1929), pp. 413–19.
[72] Ibid., p. 415.
[73] Ibid., pp. 416–17.
[74] Ibid., p. 418.
[75] Ibid., pp. 418–19.

Whenever Jünger described this new order, he stressed the contrast between its supposed clarity and precision and the manifest "chaos" and confusion of Weimar. The front soldier, for example, represents "technical precision" and a "will to form" utterly different from "literature's general vagueness and unclarity" (*Verschwommenheit*).[76] The soldier was "the symbol of the modern worker and fighter" who combined "a minimum of ideology with a maximum of performance" and whose mission it was "to cast that which is German into a new *Gestalt*."[77] Jünger's *Gestalt* of the worker-soldier was one of the most enduring of reactionary modernist symbols. It presented a vivid, easily understandable blend of cultural tradition and technical modernism, one that became a common theme in the propaganda of the Hitler regime.

Jünger used the term *totale Mobilmachung* or total mobilization to describe the functioning of a society that had really grasped the meaning of the war. In a 1930 essay with that title, he expanded his descriptions of the war into more comprehensive views on the connection between technology and society. The essay, which first appeared in a collection, *Krieg und Krieger* (War and Warrior), which Jünger edited,[78] merits close attention, not only because it contains ideas that Jünger developed further in *Der Arbeiter*, but also because it was this essay that first led Walter Benjamin to write about the aestheticization of politics among the intellectuals of the Right.

The notion that World War I was a natural catastrophe stands at

[76] Ernst Jünger, "Der Wille zur Gestalt" (The Will to Form), *Widerstand* (4, 1929), p. 249. Jünger refers to a "Copernican" revolution in conservative thought (p. 247) after which backward-looking tendencies are abandoned.
[77] Jünger, "Die Geburt des Nationalismus aus dem Krieg," p. 478.
[78] Ernst Jünger, "Die totale Mobilmachung," in *Werke*, Band 5, *Essays I* (Stuttgart, 1960–5), pp. 125–47. *Krieg und Krieger* was representative of the nationalism of the returning soldiers. Friedrich Georg Jünger's essay, "Krieg und Krieger" (pp. 53–67), extolled the masculine origins of both war and technology while denigrating democracy's "feminine instincts" (p. 65). Albrecht Erich Gunther, in "Die Intelligenz und der Krieg" (The Intellectuals and the War) (pp. 71–100), attacked mistrust of science and technology by the humanistic intellectuals and bemoaned the lack of prestige of engineers and scientists in the country of *Bildung* (cultivation). Gunther further claimed that *Kultur* and *Zivilisation* had been reconciled in the war. The U-boat captain combined "intellectual mastery of technology with primordial soldierly qualities" (p. 88), whereas the left-wing intellectuals had no alternative to the existing "plutocratic society" but more of the "anonymous powers of economic and technical rationalization" (p. 99). But the war had been an option to the world of "functionaries." It was a creative deed that "bound primal immediacy to the most advanced rationality" (p. 100). It had created a group of armed men who "would be able to transform the decayed soil of civilization into fertile earth once again" (p. 100). On the identification of the Left with capitalist rationalization, see Bloch, *Erbschaft dieser Zeit* (Frankfurt, 1962); Fest, *Hitler*, trans. Richard Winston and Clara Winston (New York, 1974); and Arno Mayer, *Dynamics of Counterrevolution*, (New York, 1971).

the center of the essay. Jünger referred to the war as a "captivating spectacle" that recalled a volcano spewing forth lava and fire. The battlefield was a crater-marked "landscape" on which the most "unmediated struggle for life and death" pushes all historical and political considerations aside. Although the war does possess timeless aspects, Jünger distinguished "the last war, the greatest and powerful event of this era"[79] from previous ones. The "original feature of this great catastrophe" lay in the fact that "in it the genius of war permeated the spirit of progress."[80] The war destroyed the belief that scientific and technical progress would usher in an era of peace. On the contrary, Jünger claimed, the "actual significance of progress was something different, more secret" than what was implied by the "mask of reason."[81] The really distinguishing feature of the twentieth century, in Jünger's eyes, was the process of total mobilization of social and technological resources by the state. The nineteenth century, by way of contrast, had still been an era of limited war, of firm distinctions between soldiers and civilians, and of "partial mobilization," a partiality that corresponded to "the essence of monarchy." The era of partial mobilization imposed limits on the extent to which technology would be placed in the service of armament and of popular mobilization in wartime.[82]

The specifically modern significance of World War I was, as Jünger put it, "the growing transformation of life into energy"[83] and of "war into a gigantic labor process." New kinds of armies, armies of transportation, supply, armaments, "the army of labor in general" developed alongside the battlefield armies.

Perhaps the beginning of an age of labor is most strikingly indicated in this absolute mobilization of potential energy which transformed the warring industrial states into the volcanic forges ... It is the task of total mobilization to develop such a mass of energy. Total mobilization is an act through which, as a result of a singular grasp of the control panel, the great current of the

---

[79] Jünger, "Die totale Mobilmachung," p. 125.
[80] Ibid., pp. 125–6.
[81] Ibid., pp. 126–7.
[82] Ibid., pp. 126–9.
[83] Ibid., p. 129. J. P. Stern, in his *Ernst Jünger*, calls the idea of total mobilization, "Jünger's most distinct intellectual achievement" (p. 11). He summarizes it as follows: "It describes a self-moved activity, bearing its aim and purpose within itself, and there is in his [Jünger's] view no other. What nature meant to earlier ages, machines mean to ours. Technical perfection is not progress but an elementary fact. Any scale of values which disregards it, or fails to account for it positively, is as decadent and false as any earlier system would have been had it rejected nature" (p. 43–4). See also Stern's analysis of Jünger's "embattled style" (pp. 17–42).

energy of war will be transmitted throughout the far-flung and multicircuited network of modern life.[84]

Total mobilization first made its appearance during the war. But it continued in what Jünger believed was a worldwide trend toward state-directed mobilization in which individual freedom would be sacrificed to the demands of authoritarian planning. In welcoming this trend, Jünger believed that different currents of energy were coalescing into one powerful torrent. The era of total mobilization would bring about an "unleashing" (*Entfesselung*) of a nevertheless disciplined life.

It was with "feelings of horror combined with pleasure" that Jünger described the "physics and metaphysics" of the modern technological world in which "there is not an atom that is not at work" in "this frenzied, raging process." The reader looking for specific economic and political proposals concerning the relation between state and economy, instead, would come across statements such as the following:

Total mobilization is less something that is completed than something that completes itself. In war and peace it is the expression of the mysterious and compelling claim that subjects us to this life in the era of masses and machines. So it is that every individual life develops ever more clearly into the life of a worker and the wars of the worker follow those of the knights, kings, and the bourgeoisie.[85]

As we have said before, Jünger radically separated technology from society, making it instead "the expression" of a "mysterious and compelling claim." Mundane questions are left unasked. How does this process "complete itself"? What is so mysterious about the relationships between the decisions of nation-states and their economics and technological mobilization for war? Is all of society really being transformed into the singular image of the worker? Are there no countertrends? But Jünger's statements did not rely for their effect on empirical verification but rather on their affinity to a familiar apolitical tradition in Germany in which it was common to ignore such details and focus on allegedly more fundamental cultural processes.

There is a sadomasochistic, spectatorial aspect to all of Jünger's strange broodings on the war. Pleasure and horror are inseparable in statements such as, "The monotony of this spectacle ... suggests the operation of a turbine filled with blood."[86] Although the pain and suffering the body must endure in modern warfare arouse horror, the

[84] Jünger, "Die totale Mobilmachung," p. 130.
[85] Ibid., p. 32.
[86] Ibid., p. 120.

national readiness for mobilization touches a "life nerve" that takes
pleasure in the "purposelessness" of a process that has a "cultic nature."[87] It is this very lack of purpose, this separation from an utilitarian calculus, that makes total mobilization a source of pleasure for
Jünger. Walter Benjamin put it well: Jünger transforms the thesis of
art for art's sake into that of production for the sake of production
and destruction for the sake of destruction. War is its own end.

For all this, the idea of total mobilization had a practical aspect as
well. Jünger believed that Germany had lost the war because its economic and technological mobilization had been insufficient, partial
rather than total.[88] His cultural politics aimed at removing the barriers
to total mobilization created by conservative hostility to the Enlightenment. He lamented that the Germans had not been able either to
place the modern "spirit of the age" in the service of nationalism or
to surmount remnants of antiindustrial sentiment. Total mobilization
would solve this problem by combining the vocabulary of will and
dynamism with technical advances. Germany had a special mission
among the industrialized nations to demonstrate that technology and
culture, modern means and traditional values, were not necessarily
in conflict. Technology in the service of a "German war"[89] would foster
the "victory of the soul over the machine."

[87] Ibid., p. 134. On German nationalism and later Nazi ideology as secular religions,
see George Mosse, *The Nationalization of the Masses* (New York, 1975); and Klaus
Vondung, *Magie und Manipulation: Ideologischer Kult und politische Religion des Nationalsozialismus* (Göttingen, 1971).

[88] Jünger, "Die totale Mobilmachung," p. 136.

[89] The expression "German war" comes from George Lukács's unfinished wartime
essay, "Die deutsche Intellektuellen und der Krieg," *Text und Kritik* 39/40 (October
1973). Also see Arato and Breines, *The Young Lukács and the Origins of Western Marxism*,
"The German War and the Russian Idea" (New York, 1979), pp. 61–74; and Feher,
"Am Scheideweg des romantischen Antikapitalismus," in *Die Seele und das Leben:
Studien Eum frühen Lukács* (Frankfurt, 1972), for discussions of Lukács's rejection of
the right-wing celebration of the war as a long-sought-after *Gemeinschaft*. Like Jünger,
Lukács focused on the mechanization of warfare. Unlike Jünger, he saw it as another
step in the capitalist rationalization of society: "As the contemporary economy has
replaced the independent, individual worker by the machine and by organized groups
of workers, leading to the disappearance of the value of work for the personality,
so, too, contemporary war juxtaposes not men but machines and servants of machines.
From these servants one will demand more performance than from earlier warriors;
this will be possible only through the subordination of personality to performance
in all essentials. The result of the war will be on the one hand a further development
of the capitalist economy, on the other, the emergence of a socialism of officials"; in
Paul Ernst und Georg Lukács: Dokumente einer Freundschaft, ed. Karl August Kutzbach
(Emsdetten, 1974), p. 151. Letter dated April 15, 1919. Cited and translated by Arato
and Breines, *The Young Lukács*, p. 61. Although he later became a staunch defender
of the Weimar Republic, during World War I Thomas Mann subsumed German
militarism and nationalism under the rubric of *Kultur*. The war presented an aesthetic

Jünger was an intellectual of the far Right, but not a defender of bourgeois society and culture. He believed that bourgeois legality, that is, restrictions on the powers of the authoritarian state created by the existence of political parties and parliament, must be abolished in order to liberate technological advance. In 1930, Jünger wrote an essay on technology and military strategy in the Great War that suggested that this talk of liberating technology was partly a metaphor for the actual stalemate caused by increased firepower and limited mobility in the war of attrition. In *Feuer und Bewegung* (Fire and Movement), he commented on the domination of expanding firepower over lagging forms of movement that had turned the war into a stalemate. The result was that the balance of forces had shifted from the offense to the defense. The relationship between firepower and movement had gone through three stages. In the first, the old forms of movement failed to achieve victory. In the second, firepower assumed an absolute domination over movement. Finally, efforts were made to restore movement once again, this time with new technical methods.[90] The machine rendered the horse and foot soldier obsolete. German will, French élan, and English reserve and courage were all paralyzed in the face of expanded firepower. Traditional military strategy had to recede before the stalemate of industrialized armies in what was appropriately called the *Materialschlacht* (battle of material). Jünger took note of the obvious: hand grenades, mines, artillery, and machine guns expanded firepower at the same time that they reduced the offensive capability of the cavalry. A new means of moving forward had emerged in aerial war. It was no surprise that many former cavalry officers had moved over to the air forces. Now the "urge toward movement" used more modern, up-to-date forms.[91] On the ground, however, the war remained stalled, conducted as it was with the "primitive energies" of men and horses. In 1918, the war of movement in the air and at sea was still too primitive to change fundamentally the nature of large battles on land.

It was the tank that would accomplish that. Jünger saw in the introduction of this "machine for the production of movement" a decisive moment in the history of war. The tank was the "expression of a new epoch of the spirit" because it rescued the infantry from be-

---

synthesis, an "interweaving of enthusiasm and order" in which the "German soul" triumphed over bourgeois rationalism. It was a "sublimation of the demonic"; in "Gedanken im Krieg" (1914), in *Thomas Mann: Essays*, vol. 2, *Politik*, ed. Herman Kunzke (Frankfurt, 1977), pp. 23–37.

[90] Ernst Jünger, *Feuer und Bewegung, Werke*, Band 1, pp. 113–14.
[91] Ibid., p. 116.

coming an appendage to artillery – or at least it held out that promise. World War I still contained a "fragmentary character" because it destroyed older forms of warfare but had not yet created a wholly new image of war. Jünger wrote that the war thereby served as a mirror for an era in which "the spirit that stands behind technology may be able to destroy old bonds but has not yet left the experimental stages in construction of a new order."[92] If the war was a microcosm of conflicting archaic and modern tendencies, Jünger's sympathies were clear: He urged the development of aviation and tank warfare to break the stalemate of the war of attrition. Restoration of a dynamic of fire and movement demanded both right-wing politics and technical advance. Through the fog of Jünger's prose, the combination of tanks and planes that made up Hitler's *Blitzkrieg* is dimly visible.

Military strategists want their armies to be well equipped. Their technological modernism responds to obvious practical necessities. Those who fail to keep up are defeated. But Jünger's embrace of technology went beyond the purely practical. A cultural modernist and a member of the literary avant-garde, he shared modernism's tendency to separate aesthetics and morality, and to aestheticize violence as a component of cultural rebellion. Jünger once wrote that the "inclination" for war, or for love, was a "matter of taste" that had "nothing to do with morality."[93] That he took this notion seriously was evident in a 1929 essay collection, *Abenteurliche Herz* (Adventurous Heart), and in several collections of essays and photographs published from 1930 to 1933,[94] in which he offers "magical realism" as the key to penetrating to the "deeper and necessary" laws at work behind surface appearances of logic and rationality.[95] Along with a modernist amoral aestheticism, Jünger transfers the pleasure and horror he first experienced in the *Materialschlacht* to the postwar urban and industrial landscape.

The shadow of the war hung over his descriptions of technology, which he saw as both threatening and beautiful. The cities were becoming "simpler, ... deeper, ... more civilized, ... that is, more

[92] Ibid., pp. 120–1.

[93] Ernst Jünger, "Die Abruster" (The advocate of disarmament), *Arminius* 8 (1927), p. 6.

[94] Ernst Jünger, *Abenteurliche Herz* (Berlin, 1929), Jünger's photo collections were *Das Antlitz des Weltkrieges: Fronterlebnisse deutscher Soldaten* (The Face of the World War: Front Experiences of German Soldiers) (Berlin, 1930); *Der gefährliche Augenblick* (The Dangerous Moment) (Berlin, 1931); and *Die veränderte Welt* (The Transformed World) (Breslau, 1933). *Die veränderte Welt* is a photographic presentation of the ideas in Jünger's *Der Arbeiter*.

[95] Jünger, *Abenteurliche Herz*, p. 86. Also see Prumm, *Die Literatur*, vol. 1, pp. 279–85.

barbaric, ... once again possessed by nature."[96] He sensed a "series of colorful explosions" in the functioning of engines whose beauty and danger shatter the security of the German middle class.[97] The apparently uneventful operations of a machine shop contain a "cold fury that is never satiated, ... a very modern feeling that ... anticipates the fascination of a more dangerous game" still searching for appropriate symbolic representation. This mechanical fury smashes "visions of the landscapes of the old style, of smugness and uprightness."[98] Its exotic and dangerous residues can be found in everyday life. A machine ship has a "heroic image." The "whistling buzz of steel in the air" is "lulling and exciting."[99] Street noise has about it a "most threatening" quality.[100] A street cafe can "arouse a devilish impression," whereas the ringing of an alarm clock recalls "catastrophe."[101] Neon signs, a modern bar, an American film, are "all slices of a powerful devilish rebellion, whose spectacle fills the individual with raging lust as well as crushing anxiety."[102] The individual stands in astonishment in the face of this technological spectacle "in which everything moves softly likes a mysterious fog or like a miraculous process."[103] Jünger was afraid of a great many things.

He found in photography a technical device that helped him preserve these assorted dangerous moments.[104] In 1931, Jünger published an essay on danger, "Über die Gefahr," whose theme was the "growing penetration of the dangerous" into everyday life, a trend he saw as one of the specifically modern aspects of German society. One no longer had to go to war to be terrified. Danger was a relief, an antipode of security, boredom, and reason. The war had provided one, if fleeting, respite from a supposedly stifling security. But technological advance built into fast cars and airplanes offered another. A "new and different return to nature," in which men become "at the same time more civilized and more barbaric," places individuals in industrial societies in touch with "the elementary once again."[105] What,

---

[96] Ibid.
[97] Ibid., p. 96.
[98] Ibid., pp. 153–4.
[99] Ibid., p. 223.
[100] Ibid., p. 109.
[101] Ibid., p. 168.
[102] Ibid., p. 89.
[103] Ibid.
[104] See Bohrer, *Die Ästhetik des Schreckens*, "Der gefährliche Augenblick," pp. 325–35, for an excellent discussion of Jünger's incorporation of photography into the dangerous realms that offered relief from bourgeois respectability.
[105] Ernst Jünger, "Über die Gefahr," *Widerstand* (3, 1931), p. 67.

then, is the camera but a "register of the moment in which danger appears?" With unparalleled clarity, it produces images of "mathematical demonism" that depict man's "new relation to danger."[106] Jünger titled one of his essay collections *The Dangerous Moment (Der gefährliche Augenblick)* and filled it with photos of ships sinking, cars colliding, airplanes crashing, earthquakes, and street demonstrations. The book might make the reader decide that leaving the house in the morning was a risky affair. If he should muster the courage to cross the street, the text would also confuse him as to the distinctions between natural and man-made disasters. The photographs also created distance from human suffering, while transforming that suffering into a series of "beautiful" forms.

Walter Benjamin's concept of the shocks of modern culture is helpful in analyzing the "aesthetics of horror" in Jünger's view on photography and danger.[107] Benjamin elaborated Freud's idea that protection against external stimuli is as important in the prevention of anxiety as the perception of these stimuli to begin with. Such stimuli pose the threat of shocks to the psychic system. The more readily consciousness registers them, the less likely they are to have a traumatic effect. Psychoanalytic therapy is one way of lessening these shocks by expanding the scope of consciousness over the unconscious. Another method of reducing the impact of cultural shocks is to locate the stimulus in question at a particular point in time and in consciousness, albeit at the cost of losing the fullness and depth of the experience. This, in Bohrer's view, is precisely what Jünger's interest in photography is designed to do. It is a mechanism of defense against the anxiety caused by the shocks of modern culture, and of social and technological change. When Jünger graphically describes a sinking battleship or artillery barrages with an air of detachment and distance, he assigns these incidents to a precise point in time, at the cost of the integrity of the content of the experience. His literary style and photographic reproductions ward off potentially traumatic shocks of fear and horror by freezing them at the level of conscious perception before their full emotional impact is felt. Heroic realism is, then, the aesthete's means of coping with the shocks of the war and modern

---

[106] Ibid.
[107] Bohrer, *Die Ästhetik des Schreckens*, pp. 190–200. Bohrer takes off from Walter Benjamin's statement that "the threat from these energies is one of shocks. The more readily consciousness registers them the less likely they are to have a traumatic effect"; in "On Some Motifs in Baudelaire," *Illuminations* (New York, 1968), p. 163.

technology through denial of terror. For Jünger, photography was the most modern method for accomplishing this task.[108]

Despite his own claims to have lived through the battle as an inner experience, Jünger's aesthetics guaranteed that he would be immune from any genuine emotional confrontation with the past. Photography appealed to Jünger because it was a mechanical eye completely severed from the heart. Jünger's heroic realism also sought to foster the illusion that this cool and distanced observer was immune to the horrors he presented.[109]

In 1933, Jünger published two books that synthesized his world view. The first was another collection of photographs, *Die veränderte Welt* (The Transformed World).[110] It presented in pictures the ideas that were elaborated in repetitive prose in Jünger's most well known work, *Der Arbeiter*, also published in 1933. The central message of the pictures and captions of *Die veränderte Welt* was that a new, technically advanced, worldwide authoritarianism had developed. Workers' parades in Moscow appear alongside a meeting of Hitler's stormtroopers, both indicative of a new "voluntary uniformity." Soldiers in uniform are on the opposite page from workers wearing uniformlike work clothes. Women are shown working at machines. Sports figures breaking records and measurements timing the reactions of automobile drivers signify the expanding quantification of life. Cosmetics, mannequins, loudspeakers, New York skyscrapers, advertising, mass political rallies and slogans, church services being filmed, tank formations, geometrically planned cities, Soviet poster art of workers, Nazi election placards, lines of motorcycles, labor heroes and "saboteurs" in Russia, airplanes, and hydroelectric dams form a montage of authoritarian vitality. Tremendous energies are being unleashed all over Europe, in the Soviet Union, and in the United States.

The message to the German readership was clear: Germany too had to gather its political will, overcome its disunity, and forge ahead with technological advances and military rearmament if it was to sustain itself in this ever more threatening environment. Jünger was a friend of Ernst Niekisch, an exponent of a variety of German nationalism known as national bolshevism. Niekisch saw Stalin's Russia as a model form of Prussian authoritarianism, one that Germany

[108] Robert Jay Lifton has suggested a related process he calls "psychic numbing," an emotional distancing from past horrors, which transforms guilt over having survived into mythic romanticization of catastrophe. See his *The Broken Connection* (New York, 1977).
[109] See Susan Sontag, *On Photography* (New York, 1978), p. 168.
[110] Ernst Jünger, *Die veränderte Welt*.

would do well to ally with and emulate. Here the worker and soldier had already been united. But Jünger's *Die veränderte Welt* is less a plea for sympathetic emulation than a general warning to the Germans: We face formidable potential foes to the East, but also to the West. In order to survive, we too must overcome liberal barriers to unleashing the powers of this century of explosive energy. If Germany does not do so, it will perish. Jünger's aesthetic modernism in regard to technology reinforced his pragmatic argument that the limits on technological advance had to be overcome.

These short essays and photo collections suggested the themes Jünger developed in his best known and most important work on the relationship between technology and society, *Der Arbeiter*, a remarkable anticipation of Hitler's dictatorship.[111] Unlike his previous essays and books, *Der Arbeiter* achieved a degree of commercial success beyond the right-wing circles and became a best-selling book in early 1933. Jünger defined technology as the "mobilization of the world through the *Gestalt* of the worker."[112] This cryptic and endlessly repeated sentence, like the work from which it was taken, derives its power from the emotive and visual power of its metaphors – technology, mobilization, *Gestalt*, worker, and so on – rather than from any insight into the technology–society relationship it might offer. At the time, Ernst Bloch was one of the few Marxists to have understood that the political success of right-wing ideology was due not to a superior analysis of society, but rather to an ability and willingness to appeal to the emotions, something that socialist and communist appeals eschewed. Together with Spengler's works, *Der Arbeiter* played a key role in bringing reactionary modernist mythology into a public discourse broader than that constituted by the readership of small right-wing journals such as *Arminius* or *Vormarsch*.

The central symbol of *Der Arbeiter* is that of *Gestalt* or form. *Gestalt* refers to the external appearances of objects – buildings, tanks, planes, etc. – and people – workers, soldiers, and the bourgeois. Although grasping the *Gestalt* of a phenomenon means doing no more than clearly depicting its surface appearance, Jünger wrote that "in the *Gestalt* lies the whole, which encompasses more than the sum of its parts ... In politics everything depends on bringing *Gestalten* rather than concepts or ideas ... into the conflict."[113] Specific individuals are

---

[111] Ernst Jünger, *Der Arbeiter: Herrschaft und Gestalt* (The Worker: Domination and Form) (Berlin, 1932; reprint, *Ernst Jünger Werke*, Band 6, *Essays II* [Stuttgart, 1962], pp. 9–329). All references are to the Stuttgart edition.
[112] Jünger, *Der Arbeiter*, pp. 12–13.
[113] Ibid., pp. 38–9.

only the medium through which an underlying "will toward form" (*Wille zur Gestaltung*)[114] finds external expression. Viewing the present through the mythic prism of *Gestalt* rules out historical perspective, for forms have no history. "Developmental history is ... not the history of forms."[115] What conflicts Jünger does see in society take place between archetypes, not actual individuals or groups.

The central conflict in *Der Arbeiter* is between the form of the bourgeois and that of the worker. Jünger's message was that bourgeois society and the bourgeois individual were obsolete. He spoke of the bourgeois era in the past tense as having been one of "false authority" (*Scheinherrschaft*).[116] The *Bürger* as a type strove for security above all else and tried to seal off life from the "instrusion of the elementary."[117] This he did by suppressing the reality of danger in the world with the illusion that progress would be attained through the exercise of reason and by the predominance of the market economy over the interests of the state.[118] Not only was faith in reason and progress a relic of the bourgeois nineteenth century, according to Jünger. Such complacency must also bear a "war guilt," or more precisely, responsibility for the German defeat in the war, because it prevented the total mobilization that would have been necessary to win. Vitalist, antiintellectual, and nationalist impulses strengthened by the war were far more modern than nineteenth-century traditions. Jünger convicted the bourgeois of "high treason of mind against life ... The best answer ... is the high treason of mind against *Geist*. It is one of the high and cruel pleasures of our time to participate in this blasting operation."[119] It is bourgeois and liberal culture that is alien to the nation.

What was distinctive about Jünger's attack on the bourgeois, certainly what distinguished it from Marxist anticapitalism, was his understanding of the *Gestalt* of the worker as a fully modern alternative. The worker is the "immediate successor to the rational-virtuous individual" because, unlike the bourgeois type, he does have a "relationship to elementary powers."[120] Further, he is fully at home in the traditions of Prussian socialism. "Domination and service are one and the same. The age of the third estate has never recognized the won-

[114] Ibid., p. 231.
[115] Ibid., p. 89.
[116] Ibid., p. 17.
[117] Ibid., p. 54.
[118] Ibid., p. 57.
[119] Ibid., p. 48.
[120] Ibid., p. 23.

derful power of this unity because the all too cheap and human pleasures appeared so desirable."[121] The worker rejects bourgeois
materialism in favor of authoritarian asceticism. "Our belief is that
the rise of the worker is synonymous with a new ascent of Germany."[122]
The coming predominance of the worker means the end of the "dictatorship of economic thinking" over social life in favor of a "higher
law of struggle."[123]

The right-wing intellectuals in Weimar insisted that they knew how
to end the domination of the economy over society. Jünger's language
of war and the will lifted labor out of a materialistic context. In war,
the soldier's virtue consists in his readiness for unthinking sacrifice.
Like part of a machine, "his virtue lies in his replaceability"[124] within
the minute division of labor in war. Jünger's cult of labor, then, is not
parallel to the productivism of the Soviet Union. Rather it stems from
the affinities he saw between peacetime labor and military obedience
practiced by the "day laborers of death." In both war and labor, he
celebrates the decline of a complex, differentiated bourgeois individual and the ascent of a clear, sharply defined type.

Every stance that has a real connection to power … *regards the individual as
a means, not an end*, as the bearer of power as well as freedom. *The individual
develops his highest power, develops domination in general where he is in a position
of service*. It is the secret of a genuine discourse of command that it makes
demands, not promises. *The deepest happiness of man lies in the fact that he will
be sacrificed* and the highest art of command consists in the capacity to present
goals that are worthy of sacrifice [emphasis added].[125]

Criticisms of dehumanization at the hands of technology were common coin in Weimar culture. What is distinctive about Ernst Jünger
is that he seems to welcome the process by which human beings are
instrumentalized. It is as if Weber had looked with pleasure on the
prospect of an "iron cage." Jünger's was not a conventional defense
of the status quo, denying its more authoritarian features. His language is ahistorical, but the clear implication of his rhetoric is to
encourage submission to actually existing social relationships. But he
rarely, if ever, presents phenomena as social. Take, for example, his
description of labor. It is "the tempo of the fist, of thoughts, of the
heart, of life in day and night, science, love, art, belief, cult, war, …
the oscillation of atoms and the force that moves the stars and the

[121] Ibid., p. 20.
[122] Ibid., pp. 30–1.
[123] Ibid., p. 34.
[124] Ibid., p. 162.
[125] Ibid., p. 81.

solar system.""[126] At every point, Jünger countered a Marxist analysis
with one supposedly more in tune with German tradition. Thus, the
workers are bearers of a "richer, deeper and more fruitful world,"
not because they revolt against economic exploitation, but because
their own daily activity puts them into close proximity to "the force
that moves the stars and the solar system.""[127] Whatever this force was,
it was not the labor theory of value or the internal contradictions of
the capitalist economy. Later we will see that when German engineers
wrote about technology, they often referred to the *Vergeistung*, roughly
and inadequately translated as "spiritualization," of labor. Although
Jünger did not use that exact term, his references to the forces that
move the stars and solar system were an example of such *Vergeistung*.

As in his previous essays, Jünger referred to the war and the front
experience as the decisive event that had transformed a previously
backward-looking youth movement. One thinks of Durkheim's references to the emergence of the sacred in collective gatherings when
reading Jünger's nostalgia for the war. The pastoralism of the prewar
protest gave way to a discovery of the "elementary" in the "here and
now.""[128] The decisive leap from romantic protest to action had become
manly and healthy. The days when protest took the form of effeminate escape into the preindustrial mists were thankfully over. Now
it was time to realize that the "false return to nature" must give way
to the recognition that

technology and nature are not opposites ... There is no exit, no turning to the
side or going backward. On the contrary, the fury and speed of the processes
in which we are not enmeshed must be increased. Behind the dynamic excesses
of the era an unmoved center remains hidden [emphasis added].[129]

All contradictions and antinomies, even that between technology and
nature, could be resolved by returning to the *Fronterlebnis*. Weber
sighed that we must learn to live with the unavoidable. Lukacs claimed
the tragedy of culture would give way under the impact of revolutionary dialectics.[130] Jünger left society unchanged. It was symbolism
he was interested in, a symbolism that would serve to modernize the
romantic anticapitalism and antipositivism of the Right.

We have already noted that Jünger saw the *Gestalt* of the worker
while sitting in the trenches. But in his descriptions of both, one looks

[126] Ibid., p. 74.
[127] Ibid., p. 36.
[128] Ibid., pp. 61–2.
[129] Ibid., pp. 213–14.
[130] See James Schmidt's very fine unpublished dissertation, "From Tragedy to Dialectics:
On the Theoretical Significance of Lukacs' Path from Simmel to Marx" (MIT, 1974).

in vain for discrete individuals. Instead there are uniform types: Their faces are "metallic ... galvinized. The gaze is silent and fixed. It is the face of a race that represents the individual not as a person or individual but rather as a type." This face is the result of an "amazing identity of processes" in the sphere of production and the battlefield, of an overlapping of the "war front and the labor front ... The soldier's uniform appears ever more clearly to be a special case of a labor uniform," whereas the uniforms of labor appear more militarized.[131]

Technology, as an essential component of the Jüngerian mythic construct of the worker-soldier *Gestalt*, is the centerpiece of a utopian vision of a postbourgeois, advanced industrial dictatorship. Bourgeois politics and parliamentary discussion are chaotic and formless, especially when compared to the "greater cleanliness and definition of ... technical will toward form [*technischen Gestaltungswillens*]." Politics must turn away from compromise and obscurity and model itself on the clarity evident in technology. A new "landscape" at once "more dangerous, colder and more glowing," is evident and politics must follow suit.[132] But in order to pursue this new politics, the cultural baggage of the Enlightenment must be thrown out because it cannot grasp this "martial side of technology's Janus face."[133] Total mobilization of technology demands abolition of this obstacle. Jünger's symbolism of the worker-soldier presents an image of modernity that is neither liberal nor Marxist but purely technological. There can be no doubt that Jünger was a technological determinist in the extreme and believed that use of technology brings with it "a very particular style of life, which extends to the great and little things of life."[134] Far from being a neutral force, technology was inherently in conflict with democracy. Authoritarian technology required an authoritarian state. And the political elite of this state ought to be the worker-soldiers who first understood that "the motor is not the master but the symbol of our time, the image of a power for which explosiveness and precision do not constitute a contradiction."[135]

---

[131] Jünger, *Der Arbeiter*, pp. 119, 110, 121, 133.
[132] Ibid., p. 183. The noun *Gestaltung*, roughly translated as "process of form creation," fuses the ideas of will and beauty. It was common in the literature of engineers in this period, as in *Gestaltungsfreude*, "joy in form creation," or *Gestaltungsarbeit*, "labor of form creation."
[133] *Der Arbeiter*, pp. 171–2.
[134] Ibid., p. 175.
[135] Ibid., p. 42. See Marcuse's analysis of heroic realism in "The Struggle Against Liberalism in the Totalitarian View of the State," in *Negations*, trans. Jeremy Shapiro (Boston, 1968).

Jünger was a myth maker, not a social analyst. He made no effort to explain why there was a connection between technology and social domination. He simply asserted it to be the case. The "total technical sphere" makes "total domination possible," whereas only those who are truly dominant really control technology.[136] Although the logic of the argument passes the reader by, the ubiquitousness of the word "total," closely followed by "domination" and "technology," fosters acceptance of the unexamined clichés that were at the base of Jünger's myths. For example, he simply assumed that there existed a "perfection of technology" that produced an aesthetic form and clarity as technology's end point, a trend that was supposedly at work beneath the "anarchic surface."[137] Or he asserted that technology and domination were linked because "every technical means contains a secret or open military quality."[138]

We are examining these statements not for their insight into modern technology, but for their significance as the constituents of a particular cultural system. Whether or not it was his intention, the effect of Jünger's visions of total mobilization and the transformation of "life into energy" was to associate political and social domination with the most elevated symbols of German cultural traditions – beauty, will, and form. Who could deny that phrases such as transforming life into energy did indeed capture something of the quality of dramatic advances associated with the second industrial revolution? In focusing on technology as he did, Jünger and the other reactionary modernists proved themselves as "progressive," if not more so, than the left-wing intellectuals. But where the Left linked the advance of technology to the Enlightenment, the reactionary modernists such as Jünger found the beauty of technics precisely in its attack on the greatest achievement of the Enlightenment, namely, the autonomous individual. The force of technology lay in the suprahistorical mysteries of the will to power, and its contribution to a forward-looking political utopia lay in the creation of distinct, clear forms in an age of chaos, anxiety, and confusion. In his metaphors, Jünger blended the feudal imagery of service and sacrifice with a modernist celebration of efficiency and vitalism.

Although his ideas overlapped in many ways with those of National Socialism, Jünger never joined the Nazi party, and he abandoned

---

[136] *Der Arbeiter*, p. 191.
[137] Ibid., p. 183.
[138] Ibid., p. 201.

politics after 1933.[139] He was too much the elitist to accept an actual
mass movement that received many of his own ideas, and too much
implicated in those ideas ever to openly criticize the Hitler regime, as
an examination of his 1934 essay, "On Pain" (*Über den Schmerz*), makes
clear.[140] One of the features that distinguished the twentieth from the
nineteenth century, he claimed, was not the amount of severity of
pain inflicted on people, but rather people's "relationship to pain." The
nineteenth century had been a world of sentimentality, one that sought
to avoid pain and to seek security and comfort. In contrast to that
pacific, bourgeois era, the twentieth century was "heroic and cultic."
Workers now cared more for discipline and pain in war and in labor
than for the mere material gains sought by the socialist workers' movements. Because this sentimental world had sought to avoid pain at all
costs, it had not learned to "treat the body as an object."[141]

The modern world was different. In the epochal shift from the age
of the bourgeois individual to the *Gestalt* of the worker-soldier, Jünger
claimed that the sphere of sensitivity and feeling shrinks. The worker-
soldier, stoically accepts pain as a sacrifice demanded by "heroic realism." Nowhere is this political and cultural shift more obvious than
in the comparison of two faces, that of the Prussian soldier with that
of the bourgeois individual. Whereas the latter is "nervous, moving,
changing, open to the most varied of influences and suggestion," the
"disciplined face," of the former is "determined ... has a firm focus,
and is unambiguous, objective and rigid."[142] This new and harder face
is only one example of the impact of technology on modern life.
"Technology is our uniform."[143] Those who wear this uniform, the
modern worker and soldier, have a "second and colder consciousness"
that has the "capacity to view itself as an object" and is therefore able
to place the body beyond pain and pleasure.[144]

The technical advances associated with the second industrial revolution enhance this ability to see the human body as a thing. Jünger

[139] Hermann Rauschning, the Nazi party leader who subsequently opposed nazism (see
his *The Revolution of Nihilism* [New York, 1939] and *The Conservative Revolution* [New
York, 1941]), reports that Hitler gave his assent to Goebbels's efforts to recruit
Jünger into the Nazi party. The attempt was unsuccessful, as Jünger thought the
Nazis far too plebeian. See Hermann Rauschning, *Hitler Speaks* (London, 1939), p.
36; and Norr, "German Social Theory and the Hidden Face of Technology," p.
320.
[140] Ernst Jünger, "Über den Schmerz," in *Blätter und Stein* (Hamburg, 1934; reprint,
Ernst Jünger: Werke, Band 6, pp.. 151–98).
[141] Ibid., pp. 164–5.
[142] Ibid., p. 171.
[143] Ibid., p. 180.
[144] Ibid., p. 187.

describes the camera as an eye without feeling, one that commits an "act of aggression" in the taking of a photograph.[145] Modern sports, "psychotechnology" in the workplace, and anesthesia in surgical practice either accustom the body to or free it from pain, while viewing it above all as an object of performance.[146] In this new era, Jünger worried that cultural legitimation was lacking. He was not alone in surmising that a purely technocratic order would undermine its own cultural foundations. The "new relation to pain" he described and advocated in "Über den Schmerz" offered a starting point. In this new "instrumental era," acceptance of the objectified body inured to pain was a precondition for viewing the state as an object of cultic veneration rather than a prosaic instrument for the implementation of political programs. It was also necessary to understand the "ethos" of technology that lay hidden beneath its instrumentalist surface.[147]

For Ernst Jünger, the conservative utopia of the mechanized body and rearmament of the nation were two sides of the same process. Carl Schmitt and Hans Freyer asserted that the primacy of politics was an alternative to, and an extension of, a postbourgeois instrumental era. Like Jünger, their ideological offensive against bourgeois rationalism served the cause of technical advance. But before we turn to them, Martin Heidegger's elusive views on technology merit comment. Heidegger was personally close to Jünger, read and was impressed by *Der Arbeiter*, and took up "the question concerning technology" several times in the 1930s and after. If Heidegger's writings on technology lack the unqualified enthusiasm for technology one finds in Jünger, they do communicate a sense of Germany's special mission to save the world from the soulless East and West. We would be straining the phrase beyond its limits to label Heidegger a reactionary modernist. But it would be fair to say that his Nazi sympathies in the 1930s had a great deal to do with his views on technology, some of which bore striking resemblance to those of the advocate of "magical realism."

[145] Ibid., pp. 188–90.
[146] Ibid., pp. 192–5.
[147] Ibid., p. 197.

5

Technology and three mandarin thinkers

Fascination with technology was not limited to right-wing thinkers outside the universities. During the Weimar Republic and into the first years of the dictatorship, three of Germany's most prominent mandarin professors, Martin Heidegger, Carl Schmitt, and Hans Freyer, devoted considerable effort to the issue of technology and its challenge to German society and culture. Of the three, Heidegger was least drawn to any aspect of modern technological society, though for a brief time both he and Schmitt were ardent advocates of National Socialism. Although Freyer was less drawn to active and public support for the Nazis, his philosophical and sociological essays of the period were striking examples of reactionary modernist reconciliations.

The case of Martin Heidegger is an interesting chapter in the history of German reactions to the second industrial revolution, but it is not a chapter in the history of the reactionary modernist tradition. Heidegger wrote several essays in the 1930s on "the question concerning technology," and there is no doubt that his views on the subject were important in his initial attraction to National Socialism. Further, like the intellectuals of the Right whose enthusiasm for technology knew no limits, Heidegger believed that the Germans had a special mission to combine *Technik* and *Kultur.* For a while he thought that the Nazis would fulfill this special mission. When he concluded instead that Hitlerism would continue the long-term process of Western domination over "being," he retreated from politics and fell into disfavor with the Nazis. His fundamental distaste for modern technology became obvious. In short, Heidegger throws an interesting light on the reactionary modernists because he was not able or willing to reconcile his version of antimodernist protest with modern technology. Before turning to his views on technology, I will briefly recount the well-known facts concerning his relationship to nazism, as well as the connection between his thought and his politics in the early 1930s.

In the ten months from April 1933 until February 1934 when he was rector of the University of Freiburg, Heidegger delivered a number of lectures and speeches that openly and enthusiastically supported Hitler and National Socialism. Some have justified Heidegger's decision to accept this position as his attempt to prevent the total politicization of the university by the Nazis. Others have seen his decision as confirmation of the affinities between his thought and that of National Socialism. However, it became clear to Heidegger by February 1934 that upholding the autonomy of the university was an illusion, and he handed in his resignation.[1]

The speeches, essays, and lectures Heidegger delivered in these ten months speak for themselves: Heidegger was an ardent exponent of Nazi ideology and of its corresponding political practice as it was then defined. The titles communicate some of the flavor of the time: "The Self-Affirmation of the German University" ("Die Selbstbehauptung der deutschen Universität"), "Labor Service and the University" ("Arbeitsdienst und Universität"), "German Students" ("Deutscher Studenten"), "German Men and Women" ("Deutscher Männer und Frauen"), "German Teachers and Comrades! German Members of the Volk!" ("Deutscher Lehrer und Kameraden! Deutsche Volksgenossen und Volksgenossinnen!"), "The Call to Labor Service" ("Der Ruf zum Arbeitsdienst"), "National Socialist Scientific Training" ("Nationalsozialistische Wissenschulung"), "Why Are We Staying in the Provinces?" ("Warum bleiben wir in der Provinz?").[2]

His inaugural address as rector did little to rise above the slogans of the day. The Germans were the chosen people, filled with "the forces of earth and blood," attuned to leadership and obedience. Students should consider themselves loyal members of the *Volksgemeinschaft*, committed to the "honor and destiny of the nation" and

---

[1] On the connection between Heidegger's "existential ontology" and National Socialist ideology, and on his activities as rector of Freiburg University, see the excellent study by Winfred Franzen, *Von der Existenzialontologie zur Seinsgeschichte: Eine Untersuchung über die Entwicklung der Philosophie Martin Heideggers* (Meisenheim am Glan, 1975), esp. pp. 67–101; also see Theodor Adorno, *The Jargon of Authenticity*, trans. Kurt Tarnowski and Frederic Will (Evanston, Ill., 1973); Beda Alleman, "Martin Heidegger und die Politik," *Merkur* XXI (1967), pp. 962–76; Jean Pierre Faye, "Heidegger et la 'revolution,' " *Mediations* 3 (1961), pp. 151–9; "Attaques nazies contre Heidegger," *Mediations* 5 (1962), pp. 137–54; "A propos de Heidegger: La lecture et l'énonce," *Critique* 237 (1967), pp. 288–95; François Fedier, "Trois attaques contre Heidegger (über Schneeberger, Huhnerfeld, Adorno IV), *Critique* 234 (1966), pp. 883–904; "A propos de Heidegger: Une lecture denoncée," *Critique* 242 (1967), pp. 672–86; and George Steiner, *Martin Heidegger* (London, 1979).

[2] See Franzen's discussion in *Von der Existenzialontologie zur Seinsgeschichte*, pp. 77–90. The documents are reprinted in Guido Schneeberger, *Nachlese zu Heidegger. Dokumente zu seinem Leben und Denken* (Bern, 1962).

to the "spiritual mission of the German people." They must do their part in labor service, military service, and knowledge service (*Wissensdienst*).[3] A half year after his inaugural address, Heidegger wrote that the "National Socialist revolution" would bring with it the "complete transformation of our German being" (*Dasein*). He told his students that ideas were not their guides. "The *Führer* himself and only the *Führer* is the contemporary and future German reality and its law."[4] Before elections to the Reichstag in November 1934, Heidegger wrote that there is "only one will for the realization of the being of the state. It is the *Führer* who has awakened this will in the whole *Volk* and brought it together into a single decision. No one can stay away on the day this will is manifested."[5]

These are revolting passages, and doubly so when they come from the man many consider to be Germany's most important philosopher of the century. The controversy concerning the relation between Heidegger's thought and his sympathy for nazism has raged since he made these statements. What did the author of *Sein und Zeit* and student of the eminent Jewish phenomenologist, Edmund Husserl, have to do with the demagogic university rector in Freiburg in 1933–4? Was this merely an aberration, or was it an outgrowth of Heidegger's existential ontology of being and existence? There is much to be said for the argument that Heidegger's Nazi sympathies and his existential ontology were closely related. The language of being, existence, and anxiety until death was in the mainstream of the apolitical traditions of German letters. Total withdrawal from politics was a means of self-preservation. The human dilemma was rooted in suprahistorical existential conditions. A turn inward among the elite few who could escape the vulgarity of inauthentic existence was the message of *Sein und Zeit*. The public sphere and democratic politics had no contribution to make to the realization of authenticity. Democracy was a sympton of decay. Where, then, could the isolated and anxious individual turn for solace? A movement promising national renewal under an authoritarian leader was an obvious alternative.

Heidegger repeated the antimodernist message but presented no political alternative. He did not advocate biological racism or German nationalism as answers, but his attack on modern science and ration-

[3] Martin Heidegger, *Die Selbstbehauptung der deutschen Universität* (Breslau, 1933), pp. 13, 15–16.
[4] Martin Heidegger, "Deutsche Studenten (November 3, 1933), in Schneeberger, *Nachlese zu Heidegger*, p. 135.
[5] Martin Heidegger, "Deutsche Männer und Frauen" (November 10, 1933), in Schneeberger, *Nachlese zu Heidegger*, p. 135.

ality left no philosophical grounds on which the irrationalist ideologies of the Right could be resisted. On a far more philosophically elaborate – and abstruse – plane, *Sein und Zeit* presented a view of the individual subject not so different from that of Jünger or Spengler. Heidegger himself did not find the journey from the depths of the most extreme alienation, isolation, and anxiety to the comforts of the new reintegrated *Volksgemeinschaft* particularly long or tortuous. *Sein und Zeit* did not inevitably lead to the inaugural address, but Heidegger's nazism was latent in it. His radical subjectivism, emotionalism, and antimodernist lament over the isolated and angst-filled individual could find a way out through identification with a national collective subject. The leap from individual isolation of rootedness to the being of this new subject entailed a radical and resolute decision. When Heidegger was able to connect the destiny of the Germans with that of "being" in general, his path to Hitlerism was cleared.

Heidegger's philosophy, when viewed in this light, is a plea for a politics of cultural revolution. Politics was worthless unless it addressed these inner dilemmas. National Socialism represented the revolt of the German *Volk* to regain its threatened being. If, as Heidegger suggested, Western culture had been moving away from its great beginnings of the Greeks, National Socialism represented the return to the essence of being, a return that could only take place once the internal and external dangers to the German *Volk* had become evident.[6] Heidegger hoped that National Socialism would solve several thousand years of historical riddles. The German *Volk* became the means whereby being would be saved from further devastation by soulless, Western progress. One of Heidegger's interpreters put it well when he wrote that for Heidegger, "Philosophy is for Hitler because Hitler stands on the side of Being."[7]

Heidegger's public statements lend support to this interpretation. The crisis of being now demanded heroic decisions. Being was now in "extreme distress" and danger. Only the "strong and unbroken" would be able to lead the *Volk* to the "secret of its new future." The crisis demanded decisiveness (*Entschlossenheit*).[8] Without leaving the existential categories of *Sein und Zeit*, Heidegger entered politics by

---

[6] Martin Heidegger, *Platons Lehre von der Wahrheit. Mit einem Brief über den Humanismus*, 2d ed. (Bern, 1954), p. 13.

[7] Paul Huhnerfeld, *In Sachen Heidegger: Versuch über ein deutsches Genie* (Hamburg, 1959), p. 98.

[8] Martin Heidegger, *Die Selbstbehauptung der deutschen Universität*, pp. 10, 13; "Deutsche Studenten," p. 136; "Deutscher Männer und Frauen," p. 129; cited by Franzen, *Von der Existenzialongtologie zur Seinsgeschichte*, p. 83.

identifying individual authenticity with the German people and the inauthentic public sphere with world opinion. The national *Gemeinschaft* could fulfill the demands of inwardness in a way that isolated subjectivity could not. Radical subjectivism and collectivism complemented one another. "Hitler," he said, "had awakened the will to a full being of the state [*Dasein des Staates*] in the whole of the *Volk* and had brought this will together into a single decision."[9] It is clear that Heidegger shared much with those intellectuals such as Jünger who had weakened democratic institutions and welcomed the emergence of the new dictatorship.

Studies of intellectuals in politics have often pointed out that the appeal of totalitarian movements and governments lies partly in the promise of integration into the social whole. This is an important point, because the Nazis were so virulently opposed to the life of the mind. In *Mein Kampf*, Hitler had attacked intellectuals as *Volksfremd*, alien to the people. In his essay on National Socialist educational principles, Heidegger argued that the old distinctions between mental and manual labor had been overcome. The miner's labor, he wrote, was no less spiritual than the teacher's.[10] Not only could intellectuals be at one with the masses; labor was to be spiritualized and hence incorporated into the intellectual's vision of the nation. If Heidegger's turn to Nazi sympathies was philosophically inspired, it must be said that even in his own terms, his views amounted to a grotesque misunderstanding of National Socialism. He resigned as rector of Freiburg University in February 1934 and retreated from public life, disillusioned that National Socialism had not fulfilled his hopes for German *Dasein*. What was the cause of Heidegger's disillusionment? His 1935 essay, "Einführung in die Metaphysik" (Introduction to Metaphysics), offers some clues.

As before, Heidegger viewed Western philosophy and history as a long process of decay set in motion by the Greek initiation of an active, dominating stance toward nature. *Dasein* was at a crisis point in Germany. "Our *Volk* feels it is in the middle of a sharp pincer movement between America and Russia. We are the people with the most neighbors, thus the most endangered people. But we are also the most metaphysical people."[11] The promise of National Socialism had been to save German being from this pincer movement, and in Heidegger's view it had betrayed this promise. In 1935 he wrote, "Today what is

[9] Heidegger, "Deutsche Männer und Frauen," p. 146.
[10] Martin Heidegger, "Nationalsozialistische Wissenschulung" (February 1, 1934) in Schneeberger, *Nachlese zu Heidegger*, p. 198.
[11] Martin Heidegger, *Einführung in die Metaphysik*, 3d. ed. (Tübingen, 1966), p. 29.

offered as the complete philosophy of National Socialism does not have the slightest thing to do with the inner truth and greatness of this movement. This inner truth and greatness refers to the *confrontation of planetary technology with modern man*" (emphasis added).[12] Unfortunately the actually existing National Socialist regime had not brought this deeper meaning into existence. Even Hitler had not grasped it. Heidegger was intent on distinguishing the mere appearances of National Socialism from its essence. And this essence was to push the decay of being to its apogee, at which point a crisis of such proportions would explode that the "forgetting of being" (*Seinsvergessenheit*) due to technical advances would be somehow overcome. By 1935, Heidegger believed that prosaic reality fell far short of this scenario. Two thousand years of the forgetting of being and of technical advances continued. Hitler was not pointing the way back to true being. From Heidegger's metaphysical standpoint, the Americans and the Russians were identical. Both fostered a "wild and endless race of unleashed technology and rootless organization of average individuals."[13] The extent of spiritual decay in the West and East was simply beyond repair. Only the nation in the middle stood a chance of developing a new historical, spiritual force and by so doing could prevent Europe from being destroyed. Heidegger's meaning was evident: Recovery of true being meant halting technological development. Nazism clearly was not pursuing an antitechnological program; hence Heidegger insisted that it had deviated from the path of true German being. For Heidegger, unlike the reactionary modernists, the choice still had to be made *between* the German soul and modern technology. The two remained irreconcilable. Nazism had been perverted by technology. The revolution from the Right had been betrayed.

He presented these views in four essays written during the 1930s: "Einführung in die Metaphysik" (Introduction to Metaphysics, 1935); "Kunstwerk Vertrag" (Essay on Art, 1935); "Die Zeit des Weltbildes" (The Time of the World Image, 1938); and "Überwindung der Metaphysik" (Overcoming Metaphysics, 1936).[14] His postwar claims to have "never been against technology" are clearly belied by these essays. They repeat the standard antitechnological lament of individuals overwhelmed by an autonomous, self-steering force. Heidegger was

[12] Ibid., p. 29.
[13] Ibid., p. 28.
[14] See Steiner, *Martin Heidegger*; and Martin Heidegger, *Einführung in die Metaphysik* (1935); "Kunstwerk Vertrag"; "Die Zeit des Weltbildes"; and "Überwindung der Metaphysik."

clearly most at home in field and forest. His was the pastoral nostalgia that Jünger and Spengler found so threatening to the national revival.

Whatever its ideological appeals to irrationalism, National Socialism was, from Heidegger's viewpoint, a force that fostered further rationalization. Heidegger differed from the reactionary modernists in his rejection of technology, but he shared their view that it was an autonomous force with a will of its own.[15] Like them, he assumed that it made sense to speculate on the essence, spirit, or soul of technology, rather than to examine the social context in which technical innovations occurred as well as the political responses to such innovation. Certainly his speculations on Western philosophy and modern technology did as little to clarify the relationships between technology and society as did Jünger's celebrations of the worker-soldier. And his references to the mission of the "nation in the middle" presented the military constellation of World War II in philosophical jargon. However, Heidegger was not able to resolve contradictory desires. On the one hand, he appealed to the nation in the middle to save the world from the soulless technology of the Russians and Americans. On the other hand, he rejected the technical advances needed for Germany to perform that cultural mission. It was precisely this contradiction the reactionary modernists believed they had resolved. Whatever merits Heidegger may or may not have had as a philosopher, and whatever contributions he made to fostering a cultural climate conducive to the rise of nazism, he was of little or no use to the Nazis when it came to the problem of reconciling the German soul with nazism in power. Heidegger opted for the simple life in Freiburg instead of the more complex antinomies of Hitler's Berlin. His failure – or refusal – to come to terms with technology throws the accomplishment of the reactionary modernists into sharper focus.

Carl Schmitt was one of the leading political theorists of his day and certainly the most important critic of liberal political theory in the conservative revolution. He was also a close friend of Jünger's in the early 1930s.[16] As we mentioned in Chapter 2, he was a member

[15] John Norr's contention that the Frankfurt school took its views on technology from Heidegger, in "German Social Theory and the Hidden Face of Technology" (*European Journal of Sociology* XV [1974], pp. 312–36), is questionable on two grounds. First, Heidegger became a prime object of the criticial theorists' discussions of reification. Second, despite their pessimism, the Frankfurt theorists retained the view that transformations in social relations, however unlikely, combined with a new attitude toward nature, would make possible a new and/or better technology. This view is clear in Herbert Marcuse's essay, "Some Implications of Modern Technology," *Studies in Philosophy and Social Science* IX (1941), pp. 414–39.
[16] Norr, "Hidden Face of Technology," p. 313.

of the Nazi party and provided theoretical justification for Hitler's seizure of dictatorial power. His three contributions to reactionary modernism were a critique and incorporation of political romanticism, an attack on liberalism grounded in his theory of "decisionism," and an attack on processes of social rationalization that attempted to separate technology from an age of "neutralization and depoliticization."[17] These contributions appeared in the period from 1919 to 1932 and nourished his support of Hitler's regime after 1933.

In 1919, Schmitt published *Politische Romantik* (Political Romanticism), an analysis and critique of nineteenth-century German political theory that focused on Adam Müller, the Schlegel brothers, Schelling, and Novalis.[18] He argued that political romanticism was defined by two features. First, the political romantics had looked to the past – the Middle Ages or ancient Greece – as the locus of the "fantastic, wonderful and mysterious" that judges, negates, and points to a way out of and beyond "concrete, contemporary reality."[19] Second, and more important, political romanticism celebrated a *self* of infinite possibilities in the face of the restrictions of the given reality. It did so, however, in a way that produced at most "projections" or mere "appearances," rather than any actual changes in the political and historical world.[20] Schmitt called this cult of the historically impotent self, "occasionalism." Occasionalism referred to Novalis's or Müller's view that the objective, external world existed to offer occasions for the exercise of individual subjectivity. Such a view, he continued, produced the illusion of "subjectivistic autarky" of the self over an external world that itself was changed not at all.[21]

Although the romantic poets and philosophers attacked the commercial bourgeoisie, Schmitt pointed out that it was precisely this

[17] See Bendersky, "The Expendable *Kronjurist*: Carl Schmitt and National Socialism, 1933–36", *Journal of Contemporary History* 14 (1979), pp. 309–28; Carl Schmitt, *Politische Romantik* (Munich, 1919); *Der Begriff des Politischen* (Leipzig, 1932); and "Das Zeitalter der Neutralisierungen und Entpolitisierungen" (The Age of Neutralization and Depoliticization), in *Der Begriff des Politischen*, pp. 66–81.

[18] Schmitt, *Politische Romantik*. Other figures he discussed were Burke, de Maistre, and Bonald. On Adam Müller's importance for German conservatism, see Mannheim, "Conservative Thought," in *From Karl Mannheim*, ed. Kurt Wolff (New York, 1971).

[19] Schmitt, *Politische Romantik*, p. 65. On the romantic use of precapitalist imagery to criticize capitalism see Gouldner, "Romanticism and Classicism: Deep Structures in Social Science," in *For Sociology* (Harmondsworth, 1973); E. P. Thompson, "The Moral Economy of the Eighteenth Century Crowd," *Past and Present* 59 (1971), pp. 76–136; Christopher Hill, *The World Turned Upside Down* (New York, 1972); and Paul Breines, "Marxism, Romanticism, and the Case of George Lukács: Notes on Some Recent Sources and Situations," *Studies in Romanticism* (Fall 1977), pp. 473–89.

[20] Schmitt,, *Politische Romantic*, p. 74.

[21] Ibid., p. 90.

"settled bourgeois order" that was the "external precondition" for the romantics' "undisturbed preoccupation" with the self. "Romanticism," he wrote, "is psychologically and historically a product of bourgeois security."[22] The romantic tradition in politics had been an escapist one, not only or primarily backward into the past, but inward into the self. In Schmitt's words, "The romantic doesn't want to *do* anything. He only wants to experience and then to form his experience."[23] Hence, whether romantic rhetoric was reactionary or revolutionary, its "occasionalist" essence ensured that it would have no impact on politics.[24]

Where political romanticism did find an outlet for self-expression, Schmitt lamented that it did so in "romantic aestheticism," which he described as an "irresponsible subjectivism" posing as "aristocratic individualism."[25] In their artistic productions, the romantics claimed to bypass "normal causal connections" for "creative power" and to fuse (especially in music) mathematical precision and unfathomable passion.[26] In Schmitt's view, this substitution of aesthetics for politics signified an "unmanly passivity" and an "amoral helplessness" instead of political action and responsibility. "Politics," he wrote, "is as alien to them as morals or logic. . . . Where political activity begins, political romanticism ends."[27]

Although Schmitt rejected political romanticism because of what he saw as its passivity and impulse to escape from politics into the self, he embraced what he called the "romantic politician" as an actor who demonstrates that the self finds its realization not in "lyrical descriptions of experience" but in politics, itself considered a work of art.[28] The romantic politician (Cervantes's Don Quixote was an early model of one whose battles were "fantastically senseless, but were . . . struggles in which he was exposed to personal danger") embodied the values of Schmitt's decisionist doctrine.[29] In his perspective, the value of politics lies above all in the opportunity it affords for existential

---

[22] Ibid., p. 91.
[23] Ibid., p. 100.
[24] Ibid., p. 142–3. Further, romantic rhetoric could describe the same institutions in utterly opposed ways. The state could be a "dead, artificial machine to which the living forces of noble privilege must not be sacrificed."
[25] Ibid., p. 112–14.
[26] Ibid., p. 104. Thomas Mann's *Doctor Faustus* illuminates this synthesis of passion and the irrational with order and mathematical precision in music.
[27] Schmitt, *Politische Romantik*, pp. 143, 162.
[28] Ibid., p. 143. See Martin Jürgens, "Der Staat als Kunstwerk: Bemerkungen zur Ästhetisierung der Politik," *Kursbuch* (20, 1970), pp. 19–39.
[29] Schmitt, *Politische Romantik*, p. 146.

decisions in favor of values, regardless of what those values may be.[30] Like the "political romantics," Schmitt placed the self at the center of his concerns. Unlike them, however, he claimed that self-realization was possible only through the exercise of will and decision on the part of the political actor.

Schmitt believed that political romanticism as well as the "endless" talk of liberal parliamentarism were characteristic of both feminine passivity and lack of aesthetic form. Romantic politicians (such as Mussolini) brought clear and decisive deeds into politics and thereby made it beautiful. As with Spengler and Jünger, a masculine cult of action and will permeates Schmitt's protest against the rationalization of political conflict and is meant to distinguish this cult from nineteenth-century German romanticism, which it viewed as effeminate and hence passive and apolitical. Schmitt wrote that "everything romantic stands in the service of other, unromantic energies. The lofty talk about 'definition' and 'decision' evolves into a serviceable accompaniment of alien powers and alien decisions."[31] One of those alien powers was technology. Schmitt's celebration of the romantic politician served to place an activist cult of the self in the service of further technological advances. Here again, the work of selective tradition draws on some elements of tradition in order to embrace some elements of modernity.

I have already noted that Schmitt's theory of decisionism reduced all political relationships to that of friend and enemy, and divorced all political decisions from any normative foundation other than that of affirmation of the self. Schmitt's hope was thereby to save politics from being engulfed by the overarching trends of "neutralization and depoliticization" that, he feared, would replace politics with administration.[32] (In this quest, Schmitt was indeed a right-wing Weberian, though Weber would have rejected Schmitt's political theory as an example of politics based on an ethics of conviction rather than an ethic of responsibility.) In *Der Begriff des Politischen*, Schmitt attacked political and economic liberalism from a decisionist standpoint. Lib-

---

[30] On Schmitt's "decisionism" see Krockow, *Die Entscheidung: Eine Untersuchung über Ernst Jünger, Carl Schmitt, Martin Heidegger* (Stuttgart, 1958); and Franz Neumann, "Notes on the Theory of Dictatorship," in *The Democratic and Authoritarian State* (New York, 1966), pp. 233–56.

[31] Schmitt, *Politische Romantik*, p. 28.

[32] See Lethens, *Neue Sachlichkeit: Studien zur Literatus des weissen Socialismus* (Stuttgart, 1970), "Sachlichkeit oder 'Primat der Politik': Die Kontrovere zwischen Ernst Robert Curtius und Karl Mannheim (1929)," pp. 13–18. Lethens discusses Schmitt's advocacy of politics over economics as typical of the right-wing intellectuals' efforts to defend a new "transcendence of being" in the face of rationalization processes they associated with the Weimar Republic.

eralism, he wrote, stood for the "negation of the political . . . for mistrust" of politics.[33] Liberal individualism undermined the creation of a militant, national, political community and fostered a "whole system of demilitarized and depoliticized concepts."[34] Worst of all, liberalism eroded the primacy of politics with "ethical pathos and materialist-economic sobriety."[35] It domesticated political struggle by turning it into economic competition, emasculated real intellectual conflicts by making them parliamentary discussions, and sought to submerge the autonomy of the state in a welter of conflicting yet self-interested publics.[36] Whereas liberalism was willing to accord autonomy to art, religion, morals, and, above all, to the economy, it sought to subordinate the state to society and to deny to politics an autonomous existence.[37] Schmitt shared the rather common right-wing view that Marxism was an extension of bourgeois and liberal materialism. It denied the primacy of politics, stressed the centrality of economic conflict, and shared what in Schmitt's view was liberalism's naive faith in both cultural and technological progress. He rejected a linear conception of historical evolution that he imputed to liberalism and Marxism and stressed in its place the coexistence of different historical epochs in German society.[38] Again echoing Weber's thesis of the rationalization of the modern world, Schmitt wrote that the major trend of European history since the sixteenth century was a regrettable "striving toward a neutral sphere" in which struggle and conflict would cease.[39] The liberal attempt to preserve the state as a neutral sphere was merely the modern variant of this older – and futile – effort.[40] Other forces were at work in postwar Germany.

Schmitt's rejection of the idea that technology was a tool in the service of progress and depoliticization played an important role in his general assault on liberalism and Marxism. In his view the belief that technical progress went hand in hand with progress in morality was a relic of "magical thinking," one especially indefensible in the period after the Great War. Beginning with Saint-Simon, he complained, theorists of industrial society had imputed their own liberal teleology to technology, while refusing to see that technology was not

---

[33] Schmitt, *Der Bergriff des Politischen*, p. 56.
[34] Ibid.
[35] Ibid., p. 58.
[36] Ibid.
[37] Ibid., p. 59.
[38] Ibid., p. 61.
[39] Ibid., p. 74.
[40] Ibid., p. 76.

a force for "neutralization" of conflicts. Rather, it was an indispensable aspect of war and political domination.[41]

But at the same time he rejected a positivist's faith in the beneficence of technology, he also distanced himself from the cultural pessimism emanating from the humanistic intellectuals, such as Max Weber and Ernst Troeltsch.[42] Schmitt was aware that many among the humanists equated technological advance with "the domination of spiritlessness over spirit or perhaps an intellectualized but soulless mechanism."[43] According to the pessimists, the soul had been made powerless and helpless because of "neutralization driven to its end point." In Schmitt's view, such voices of gloom demonstrated a lack of faith in the capacity of human beings to place technology in the service of their own ends. Like Spengler and Jünger, Schmitt rejected the view that technology was "dead or soulless." Rather, he saw in it an activist metaphysic.

> The spirit of technology that had led to the mass adulation of an antireligious, this-worldly activism is spirit [*Geist*], perhaps a more evil and satanic spirit, but not to be dismissed as mechanistic and not to be attributed to technology alone. It is perhaps somewhat terrifying, but not itself technical or machine-like. It is the belief in an activistic metaphysic, the belief in the limitless power and domination over nature, even over the human body, in the unlimited recession of natural boundaries, in unlimited possibilities for transforming the naturally constituted existences of men. One can call this fantastic or demonic, but not simply dead, spiritless, mechanized soullessness.[44]

Along with Jünger, Schmitt placed his hopes in a new elite, one prepared to abandon security in order to be in a position to grasp the activist metaphysic ignored by the exponents of cultural pessimism.[45] Far from furthering the trend toward neutralization or eliminating politics in favor of administration, technology would be the handmaiden of a political renewal directed against these trends.

Technology's *Geist* was not identical with the positivism or romanticism (assuming that for romanticism we use Schmitt's definition of a hostility to technology deriving from an "unmanly" deficit of will). But this spirit did harmonize with an ethic of will, battle, and struggle. Schmitt's concept of the political favored domination over human beings and nature enhanced by technology, and opposed parliamen-

[41] Ibid., p. 78.
[42] For Troeltsch's views see *Spektator-Briefe: Aufsätze über die deutsche Revolution und die Weltpolitik, 1918–1922* (Tübingen, 1925); and Max Weber, "Politics as a Vocation," and "Science as a Vocation," in *From Max Weber*, ed. Hans Gerth and C. Wright Mills (New York, 1964), pp. 77–156.
[43] Schmitt, *Der Begriff des Politischen*, p. 78.
[44] Ibid., pp. 79–80.
[45] Ibid., p. 80.

tary discussion. Like Lukács, he too sought to end the domination of
the economy over politics, but instead of communist revolution, he
argued in favor of subordinating the economy to the demands of the
nationalist, authoritarian state. For Schmitt, the *Geist* of technology,
once separated from liberal and Marxist notions of progress and rationality, possessed an elective affinity to authoritarian politics. Walter
Benjamin's view that Jünger's postwar writings represented a perverted German idealism and romanticism applies to Schmitt as well. The
language of the will and struggle evident in the work of the reactionary
modernists was, as Schmitt himself made clear, incompatible with
German romanticism of the nineteenth century. It was instead, as
Jünger would have put it, fully modern and up-to-date, and no longer
mired in the obsolete sentimentalism of the bourgeois nineteenth
century. The language of right-wing vitalism did not reject technology
but sought the liberation of its suffocating *Geist* from the fetters of
the political and social relations of the Weimar Republic. Hans Freyer
referred to such a program as a "revolution from the Right."

Like Schmitt, Hans Freyer bridged the worlds of the conservative
revolution and the German university. He made his mark as a sociologist and philosopher. His *Revolution von Rechts* was one of the most
well known tracts of the conservative revolution. Freyer added a dimension to reactionary modernism absent in Jünger and Spengler
and rather feeble even in Schmitt. He was able to work through the
antinomies posed by German social theory and philosophy and argued
convincingly that these antinomies could only be resolved by a revolution from the Right rather than the Left. He lent to reactionary
modernism the tone of a social theory that was irrationalist yet fully
modern.[46] From 1921 through the first years of the Third Reich, he
made three major contributions to the reactionary modernist legacy:
First, he interpreted and selectively incorporated nineteenth-century
German idealism and romanticism;[47] second, he placed the theme of
"technology and culture" in the context of discussions of social theory
concerning the relationship between "objective and subjective culture";[48]

[46] Freyer's major theoretical work was *Soziologie als Wirklichkeitswissenschaft* (Stuttgart,
1930; reprint, Stuttgart, 1964). Herbert Marcuse called it "the most fully developed
scholarly self-evaluation of contemporary sociology," in "Zur Auseinandersetzung
mit Hans Freyers 'Soziologie als Wirklichkeitswissenschaft,' " in *Herbert Marcuse: Schriften
I* (Frankfurt, 1978), pp. 488–508.
[47] Hans Freyer, *Die Bewertung des Wirtschaft im philosophischen Denken des 19. Jahrhunderts*
(The Evaluation of the Economy in the Philosophical Thought of the 19th Century)
(Leipzig, 1921; reprint, Hildesheim, 1966).
[48] Ibid. Also see Freyer's *Theorie des Objektiven Geistes* (Theory of Objective Spirit) (Leipzig and Berlin, 1934)

and third, he combined the political symbolism of the "revolutionary" *Volk* in revolt against "industrial society" with an activistic will attributed to technology.[49] The constant in all of Freyer's writings on technology (as his postwar work also demonstrates) is reification. In a fashion not unlike that which Lukács critized in Bukharin, Freyer described technology as something wholly separate from social relationships.[50] In this, of course, he was a typical exponent of the reactionary modernist tradition.

In his 1921 essay, "Die Bewertung des Wirtschaft im philosophischen Denken des 19. Jahrhunderts" ("The Evaluation of the Economy in the Philosophical Thought of the 19th Century"), Freyer explored the philosophical residues of what he described as the domination of the economy over all other spheres of life.[51] As I have noted in discussing Spengler, Jünger, and Schmitt, when intellectuals, especially politically oriented ones, interpret the past, they engage selective tradition. That is, they choose from previous traditions those ideas that are most useful for their current purposes. The process of selective tradition is evident in Freyer's works as well. He saw the German idealist tradition – Hegel, Fichte, Schiller, and Goethe – as a tradition of protest against the "objectification" of life by "the economy."[52] At the core of of the idealist criticism of nineteenth-century *Zivilisation* was the claim that the economy had "torn the bonds of

[49] See Hans Freyer, "Zur Philosophie der Technik" (On the Philosophy of Technology), *Blätter für deutsche Philosphie* 3 (1927–8), pp. 192–201.
[50] Freyer's postwar works on technology are: *Über das Dominantwerden technischer Kategorien in der Lebenswelt der industriellen Gesellschaft* (On the Emerging Dominance of Technical Categories in the Life World of Industrial Society) (Mainz, 1960); and *Die Technik als Lebensmacht, Denkform und Wissenschaft* (Tehcnology as Life power, Thought form and Science) (Mainz, 1970). On the continuities in the pre- and postwar writings on technology of Jünger, Schmitt, Freyer, and Helmut Schlesky, see Martin Greiffenhagen, "Demokratie und Technokratie," in *Texte zur Technokratiediskussion*, ed. Claus Koch and Dieter Senghass (Frankfurt, 1970), pp. 54–70. For a comparison of Freyer and Marcuse, see Hans-Dieter Bahr, *Kritik der "Politischen Technologie"* (Frankfurt, 1970). Also see Gunter Ropohl, "Zur Technokratiediskussion in der Bundesrepublik Deutschland," in *Technokratie als Ideologie*, ed. Hans Lenk (Stuttgart, 1975), pp. 58–76; and Otto Ulrich, *Technik und Herrschaft* (Frankfurt, 1977), pp. 32–6, for comments on Freyer's views of an autonomous logic in technology. Ulrich also contains material on Schelsky's arguments that technology has replaced political or class forms of domination. It is interesting to contrast this with Schelsky's *Sozialistische Lebenshaltung* (Socialist Attitudes to Life) (Leipzig, 1934), each chapter of which is introduced by a quote from Hitler.
[51] Freyer referred to the "*Verwirtschaftlichung Europas*," which roughly translates means "Europe's transformation in the image of the economy." In focusing on the domination of the economy over social life, Freyer presented a right-wing variant of the romantic anticapitalism evident in the young Lukács.
[52] Freyer, *Die Bewertung des Wirtschaft*, pp. 24–5.

human nature apart," leaving it to waste in a desert of "soulless business."[53] "Overcoming" nineteenth-century materialism meant different things for different thinkers. Hegel turned to politics and the
state, Schiller and Goethe to aesthetics and *Bildung*. Whether they
turned to politics or aesthetics, the idealist philosophers, Freyer argued, sought to defend the autonomous individual in the face of an
economy that reduced him to the status of a means.[54] But they eschewed celebration of *völkisch*, primitive communities. Although they
criticized the consequences of the division of labor and the market,
they essentially praised "work and vocation."[55]

What distinguished the romantic protest against the predominance
of the economy (here Freyer was thinking of Müller and Novalis)
from that of idealism, was, first, a view of human beings in which the
individual was subordinated to the needs of the national economy;[56]
and second, a lack of appreciation for the centrality of labor in any
kind of economy. The "economic ideal" of the romantics, Freyer wrote,
was inadequate "not only for capitalism but for any technically and
organizationally conscious epoch."[57] If the idealists placed too much
value on the individual and not enough on the national community
(as the romantics had), the romantics' antitechnological views doomed
them to irrelevance. Freyer believed that French positivism (especially
as expounded by Comte and Saint-Simon), as well as Marx and Marxism, was worse than irrelevant. Both were uncritical in accepting the
capitalist organization of labor, defended a naive conception of progress, and left little or no room for a cultural sphere that was autonomous from the economy.[58]

But they did pose what Freyer called the problem of "technology
and the soul." This problem was intertwined with the speculations on
the polarity of subject and object that distinguished German philosophy beginning with Kant and Hegel. Freyer described it as the problem of the "formation of objective forms and laws out of . . . subjective-
cultural life" and of the "relation between the creating forces and the
created forms, between subjective and objective spirit."[59] What Simmel
called the tragedy of modern culture, Weber, the reversal of ends and
means, and Lukács, the antinomies of bourgeois thought, Freyer re-

[53] Ibid., p. 26.
[54] Ibid., p. 28.
[55] Freyer, *Die Berwertung des Wirtschaft*, p. 34.
[56] Ibid., p. 52.
[57] Ibid., p. 53.
[58] Ibid., pp. 63–9.
[59] Ibid., p. 132.

formulated as the conflict between technology and the soul.[60] In his view, capitalism and modern technology had become independent of the intentions of those who first created them and had taken on an "independent automatism" obedient not to the human will but to "economic factors ... and the laws of capital ... [which] make both the employer and the worker slaves of the processes of production."[61] The more complex modern technology becomes "the more the apparatus grows into a self-sufficient being and the greater is the danger of a tyranny over human beings." Means turn into ends. Technology escapes human control. That is why its "value" becomes a "burning question of conscience" that concerns the crucial (in Freyer's view) issue of German social theory and philosophy, namely, the relation between subjective and objective culture.[62]

In Freyer's view both Marxism and liberalism "solved the problem of technology and the soul by denying" its existence.[63] Only German idealism and romanticism, by formulating the ideals of *Kultur* and *Bildung*, had never ceased to attack the "mechanization of the world ... into a soulless and degraded age."[64] German conservatism had been a second source of cultural pessimism. It was a tradition spoken in the language of idealism and romanticism to defend the peasantry and aristocracy against the "technical floodtide." These traditions created a dilemma for German nationalism. Nationalists identified technology with the "spirit of Manchester" (the English liberalism of Smith and Ricardo as well as Marx's materialism). Therefore, the "theoretical-philosophical as well as practical-political struggle against technology took place under special conditions" in nineteenth-century Germany.[65] On the one hand, the idea of *Kultur* lent great weight to the antitechnological mood, for technology was equated with English (i.e., foreign) influences. Hence it was hardly surprising that antitechnological sentiments were an integral part of German nationalist traditions and that they fit well within their generally antimodernist tone. But cultural Luddism was hardly compatible with the practical requirements of the nation-state in the era of steam, not to mention the

---

[60] See Georg Simmel, *The Conflict in Modern Culture and Other Essays* (New York, 1968); and Karl Lowith, "Weber's Interpretation of the Bourgeois-Capitalistic World in Terms of the Guiding Principle of 'Rationalization,' " in *Max Weber*, ed. Dennis Wrong (Englewood Cliffs, N.J. 1970), pp. 101–22; and Lukács, *History and Class Consciousness*, trans. Rodney Livingstone (Cambridge, Mass., 1971).

[61] Freyer, *Die Bewertung des Wirtschaft*, pp. 133–34.

[62] Ibid., pp. 134–5.

[63] Ibid., p. 137.

[64] Ibid., pp. 141–2.

[65] Ibid., p. 145.

age of chemistry and electricity. Freyer believed that *the* problem facing German nationalism was how to incorporate technical advance without destroying German *Kultur*.[66]

The German nationalists of the nineteenth-century had failed in their efforts to combine technology and culture. It was left to the generation that had survived World War I to create "culture, not through technology and certainly not against technology but rather culture within technology through the overcoming of capitalist man."[67] Now was the time to break with backward-looking, antitechnological defenses of *Kultur* against commerce and industry. The antipathy of this tradition to "material interests" had become so total that it guaranteed its own political irrelevance. The path from Nietzsche and Jacob Burckhardt, in Freyer's view, led to a complete rejection of the economic and technical world and to visions of complete liberation from its domination. "The new man, who is the hope and goal of this tradition, has overcome not only the capitalist economy, but the sphere of the economy per se." The concept of *Kultur* advocated by German nationalism had been a "pure reaction against the spirit of the nineteenth-century ... and, in the final analysis, a child of this spirit itself."[68] Both rationalistic "socialist utopianism" and German conservatism had attacked capitalist man and aimed at his transcendence. But neither had succeeded in presenting a vision that could incorporate both technology and the soul. The result was that both were ideologically resigned to accept capitalism.[69]

Freyer was not resigned in this manner. He insisted that only the political Right, albeit a transformed and modernized one, could bring technology and the soul together. Nationalism must become a secular religion that would solve the dilemmas left unresolved by both romanticism and positivism. What was necessary was a "strong, structured unity that seizes and encompasses the individual completely ... a new religion" that would replace class and political differences with a new "productive will ... a reawakening of shared constants of willing and believing." Only with such a new nationalist religion could the Germans be led "out of fragmentation and clever materialism of the 19th century and toward a new culture."[70] Economic life would have

---

[66] Ibid., p. 147.
[67] Ibid., p. 148.
[68] Ibid., pp. 153–4.
[69] Ibid., p. 159.
[70] Ibid., pp. 159–60. This is what George Mosse has in mind when he refers to German nationalism as a secular religion in which "the people worship themselves, and the new politics sought to guide and formulate this worship," in *The Nationalization of the Masses* (New York, 1970), p. 2.

to be reintegrated into this new religion. German anticapitalism would no longer be at odds with the requirements of German nationalism. Nationalism must become modern and in so doing it would be a force of cultural redemption leading Germany out of the desert of soulless materialism. In Freyer's postwar reformulation, the very same rhetorical arsenal – "deep forces . . . productive will . . . shared constants of willing and believing" – that had been employed in denunciations of technology would now be placed in the service of technical advance.

In 1928, Freyer again turned to the task of reconciling technology and the soul in an essay entitled "Zur Philosophie der Technik" (On the Philosophy of Technology). On the one hand, he took issue with humanist "cultural philosophers" who saw no cultural value in technology or in the work of engineers, and on the other hand he chided engineers for neglecting to examine how technology "can be linked to the inner fate of a whole culture."[71] He wanted to present a "philosophy of technology" that would reconcile *Kultur* and *Bildung* with *Technik* and *Zivilisation* by demonstrating the previously unrecognized contribution of the latter to the former.[72]

Freyer criticized Simmel as a typical humanist opponent of technology. When Simmel elaborated on the "dialect of means," he viewed the machine as a mere means with no intrinsic value that had unfortunately usurped a value for itself. Simmel's fear was that this supposedly intrinsic dialectic of technical development threatened to produce a "slave revolt of the means against the ends . . . to turn the apparatus into a self-sufficient being . . . The slave – the means – has become the master of its master – man."[73] Freyer focused on Simmel's view of this dialectic of means as the core of cultural pessimism and resignation among the humanistic intellectuals.

Freyer did not accept the initial premise of this argument, namely, that technology was a neutral instrument. Rather technology was itself the result of a particular cultural context and the "armament of a particular will . . . nothing other than the objectification of a path that humanity has chosen."[74] It was "not neutral with regard to values . . . but rather has its own clear value as the embodiment of a historical will."[75] From the Greeks through the Middle Ages in Europe, technology was a projection and mirroring of external and human nature. Within the context of a constant will to transform and dominate na-

---

[71] Freyer, "Zur Philosophie der Technik," p. 192.
[72] Ibid.
[73] Ibid., pp. 196–7.
[74] Ibid., p. 198.
[75] Ibid.

ture, modern technology had, in his view, three distinguishing features: The first was the "principle of the machine," a principle that stood for the extension of technology beyond the limits of organic nature. Rhythmic movements of one sort or another were replaced by rotating motion. Propellers, for example, replace the flapping of bird's wings. Second was the principle of the transformation of energy that had resulted in the conversion of energy latent in nature – wood, coal, gas, the atom – into "planned administration," light, heat, and movement. Third, modern technology was distinguished by its "systematic nature ... the interweaving of individual technical instruments and procedural methods resulting in a flawless network," which then served to enhance the domination of nature.[76] Freyer did not believe that any of these features of modern technology posed a threat to the soul. On the contrary, they built on "the idea of the plasticity of material that has been stirring in the European spirit from its beginning ... and that forms the spiritual foundation of the new technology."[77] Freyer insisted that it was this *Geist* and its accompanying will, and not the capitalist economy, that constituted the real foundation of technology. In Germany, the idealist and romantic traditions had not been able to separate anticapitalism from antipathy to technology. In Freyer's view, once the *precapitalist* philosophical origins of technology were made apparent, German anticapitalism could embrace technics while rejecting bourgeois society, liberalism, and Marxism. The program of "overcoming" capitalist man could now incorporate technology into a new "life totality of the European peoples."[78]

Freyer's most important contribution to the conservative revolution and to the reactionary modernist tradition was *Revolution von Rechts* (Revolution from the Right, 1931). He called for a "revolution of the *Volk* against industrial society," which, however, had rid itself of the antitechnological sentiments identified with German *völkisch* ideology. As he succinctly put it: "Contemporaneity is no longer compromise."[79]

Liberalism and Marxism, not the conservative revolution, had lost revolutionary élan. The revolution from the Right was a new concept of revolution distinct from both bourgeois and proletarian varieties.[80] Marxism had ceased to be a theory of revolutionary transformation and had become a "sober, secular affair" governed by "natural laws"

[76] Ibid., p. 200.
[77] Ibid.
[78] Ibid., p. 201.
[79] Freyer, *Revolution von Rechts* (Jena, 1931), p. 72.
[80] Ibid., p. 18.

of the economy and dispensing with revolutionary "heroism" as "no longer needed." Neither the bourgeoisie nor the working class could claim to represent the whole of society's interests. A new collective subject, one not grounded in the materialistic principles of capitalist or industrial society, was necessary.[81]

Freyer echoed Schmitt's attacks on liberalism and Marxism as nineteenth-century materialistic residues. Like Spengler, he believed that Marxism reproduced the rationalizing tendencies of the age, tendencies that worked to transform hitherto incalculable elements in "the image of the machine."[82] In theory, Marxism reproduced the factorylike existence it claimed to oppose. In practice, the proletariat had dropped its initial revolutionary assault on industrial society and had been tamed into seeking the renewal of the society "from within." The "revolutionary dialectic" of the nineteenth century had come to an end.[83] But Freyer argued that a new revolutionary dialectic and revolutionary subject had emerged. It was the *Volk*, a historical subject not at all defined by class interests. "It is precisely the dismantling of the revolution from the Left that opens the door to the revolution from the Right."[84] Freyer skirted a clear definition of what the *Volk* was, but stressed what it was not, namely, the antagonist (*Gegenspieler*) to industrial society," which seeks to "emancipate the state from its century-long entanglement with social interests," thereby restoring primacy of politics over economics.[85] On the far Left, the program of ending the domination of the economy over society took the form of proletarian revolution. On the far Right, according to Freyer, it took the form of authoritarian statism. The revolution of the *Volk* against industrial society amounted to the "unification" of the *Volk* and the state.[86]

At every point in this argument, protest against "industrial society" sees the state as the alternative to modernity's ills. Like Carl Schmitt, Freyer believed that renewing the primacy of politics would reconcile the *Volk* with technology. Linked to the state, technology would cease to be a servant of commercial interests. Rather it becomes a "broad layer of nature, a vessel of spirit and will, which traverses the country" and contributes to making it into a unified "human world." A strong state demands advanced technology. "Contemporaneity is no longer

[81] Ibid., pp. 10–11, 18.
[82] Ibid., p. 21.
[83] Ibid., pp. 31, 35.
[84] Ibid., p. 37.
[85] Ibid., pp. 55–6.
[86] Ibid., p. 56.

compromise and orientation to the future no longer utopia. Rather they coincide."[87] The revolution from the Right was antipositivist, anti-Marxist, illiberal, and protechnological. The will that Freyer attributed to technical advance preceded and, in his view, would succeed, bourgeois society. *Revolution von Rechts* offered a preview of the Nazis' distinctive synthesis of hostility toward industrial society combined with a fascination for technical advances. It was a synthesis in which antiindustrial rhetoric served both nationalist assertion and technical advance. It is possible to trace antecendents of Schmitt's and Freyer's views in previous German thinkers. But what is more interesting is to note how skillfully they both work through the problems of German philosophy and political theory to deal with the cultural challenge to the *Kulturnation* posed by the second industrial revolution. Heidegger's inability to come to terms with technology throws Schmitt and Freyer's ideological syntheses into even sharper focus.

Although they were all bitter antagonists of the Weimar Republic and must bear some responsibility for fostering the illiberal trends that Hitler thrived on, none of the intellectuals discussed so far devoted much time to the connection between the Jewish question and German reconciliations with modern technology. Werner Sombart's version of German anticapitalism, to which we will turn next, was centrally involved with this problem.

[87] Ibid., pp. 66–7, 72.

6

Werner Sombart: technology and the Jewish question

From *Die Juden und das Wirtschaftsleben* (The Jews and Economic Life, 1911) to *Deutscher Sozialismus* (German Socialism, 1934), Werner Sombart contributed to the reactionary modernist tradition by translating social and historical categories into racial archetypes.[1] Sombart shared the aesthetic and philosophical assumptions that Spengler, Jünger, Schmitt, and Freyer relied on to incorporate technology into German *Kultur*.[2] But more than any of these other leading figures of Weimar's conservative revolution, he translated the rhetoric of anticapitalism and antimodernism, the lament over money, abstraction, economic parasites, and commercial opportunists into both an attack on the "Jewish spirit" and a defense of supposedly primordial German virtues, among which he included productive labor and technical "creation." He reconciled "German socialism" to technical advance by defending what he described as the realm of the concrete and productive against the tentacles of abstraction and unproductive circulation.[3]

Before examining Sombart's views on technology in more detail, it will be useful to introduce the following brief comments on explanations of anti-Semitism in Germany. In particular, I want to comment on Horkheimer and Adorno's analyses in *The Dialectic of Enlightenment*. The least convincing aspect of Horkheimer and Adorno's theory was their assertion that modern anti-Semitism was connected to the tran-

[1] Werner Sombart, *Die Juden und das Wirtschaftsleben* (Leipzig, 1911); *Deutscher Sozialismus* (Berlin, 1934).
[2] Arthur Mitzman makes this point in *Sociology and Estrangement* (New York, 1973), esp. "Sombart's Voluntarism," pp. 168–75.
[3] The contrast with Max Weber's thesis concerning the Protestant ethic and the spirit of capitalism is striking. On the political significance of Weber's and Sombart's interpretation of religion and the rise of capitalism, see Iring Fetscher, "Die industrielle Gesellschaft und die Ideologie der Nationalsozialisten," *Gesellschaft, Staat und Erziehung* (1962), pp. 16–23.

sition from competitive to monopoly capitalism. They argued that power had shifted to the corporations, yet the economic power of the Jews remained in finance. As the circulation sphere declined in power and influence, the attacks on it as the source of Germany's problems grew.[4] "Bourgeois anti-Semitism has a specific economic reason," they wrote, namely, "the concealment of domination in production."[5] According to Horkheimer and Adorno, although the capitalists called themselves productive, "everyone knew the truth." The truth was that this was an ideological mystification obscuring the realities of exploitation in the labor process. Attacks on the merchant, middleman, and banker are "socially necessary pretenses" directed at the circulation sphere to obscure the real source of exploitation.[6] Proudhonian anarchism and German *völkisch* traditions, though differing in many ways, were similiar in redirecting the resentment of peasants, artisans, and later the urban lower middle classes against capitalism into rage at the Jews.[7] By the time they wrote *Dialectic of Enlightenment*, Horkheimer and Adorno had distanced themselves from this restatement of conventional Marxist accounts to incorporate a more Weberian and, in the last years of the war, more pessimistic and more interesting perspective.

This second account was part of their view of the disastrous consequences of the Enlightenment. Anti-Semitism, they claimed, represented a distorted "appeal to idiosyncrasy" in the face of civilizational reason and abstraction. By viewing the Jews as the cause of the destruction of particular, idiosyncratic individuals and their national identity and culture, the anti-Semite turned anticivilizational moods into racism. In Helmut Plessner's phrase, antimodernism in Germany ends in the "hour of authoritarian biology."[8] Rather than conceptualize the origins of social problems, anti-Semitism served to rally nationalist sentiment against conceptual thinking per se. Scientific and technical progress seemed to arouse hatred of the intellect because the conceptualization associated with it always "absorbed the different by the same," thus eclipsing a mimetic world of religious myth and imagery with one in which all experience would be subject to quantification. What was peculiar about modern anti-Semitism was that it

[4] Max Horkheimer, "Die Juden und Europa," in *Autoritärer Staat* (Amsterdam, 1967), pp. 7–39, and Horkheimer and Adorno, *Dialectic of Enlightenment* (New York, 1972), "Elements of Anti-Semitism: Limits of Enlightenment," pp. 168–208.
[5] Horkheimer and Adorno, *Dialectic of Enlightenment*, p. 173.
[6] Ibid., p. 174.
[7] Ibid., pp. 175–6. This is what Sartre had in mind when he described anti-Semitism as a "poor man's snobbery" in *Anti-Semite and Jew* (New York, 1946), p. 36.
[8] Helmut Plessner, *Die verspätete Nation* (Frankfurt, 1974), pp. 148–50.

presented the Jews as *both* the primary agents of this rationalization process *and* the remnants of tabooed elements of life that civilization was trying to repress. The Jews both lagged behind and were too far ahead of civilization. As Horkheimer and Adorno put it, "They are both clever and stupid, similar and dissimilar . . . Because they invented the concept of kosher meat, they are persecuted as swine."[9] The Jews were the demiurge of rationalization as well as representatives of backward remnants, both members of German-Jewish assimilated cosmopolitanism and the East European ghetto. Moishe Postone has recently analyzed these paradoxes in terms taken from Marx. Modern anti-Semitism translated a revolt against commodity fetishism into biological terms. The Jews stood for abstract labor and the Germans for concrete labor. Anticapitalist revolution was thus redefined into its subsequent murderous paths. A powerful German revolution was necessary to destroy the all-pervasive power of the Jews.[10]

These authors' efforts are interesting from our perspective not because they succeed in presenting a general theory of modern anti-Semitism. Such success is, in my view, both impossible and not worth the effort. Rather, their interest lies in grasping German, and subsequently National Socialist, anti-Semitism as possessed of equal parts of modernist and antimodernist components. This is what Horkheimer meant when he described National Socialism as a system of rule that used bureaucratic organization and modern propaganda to organize this "revolt of nature" against abstraction.[11] If the Jews were simultaneously agents of abstract rationality and symbols of backwardness, then attacking them both placed one firmly within the traditions of the national insiders and signified adaptation to the spirit of modern times. Anti-Semites attacked the Jews for being both soul-

---

[9] Horkheimer and Adorno, *Dialectic of Enlightenment*, p. 186.
[10] Postone, "Anti-Semitism and National Socialism: Notes on the German Reaction to 'Holocaust,' " *New German Critique* 21 (Fall 1980), pp. 129–41. He adds that "in this form of fetishized 'anticapitalism,' both blood and the machine are seen as concrete counterprinciples to the abstract. The positive emphasis on 'nature,' on blood, the soil, concrete labor, and *Gemeinschaft*, can easily go hand in hand with a glorification of technology and industrial capital" (pp. 110–11). While appearing to be anachronistic, anti-Semitism was a "new form(s) of thought," which became prevalent with the development of industrial capitalism. "It is precisely this hypostatization of the concrete and the identification of capital with the manifest abstract which renders this ideology so functional for the development of industrial capitalism in crisis," and which helped to bring about Auschwitz as the "German revolution" against abstraction and capitalism, pp. 110–13.
[11] See Horkheimer's analysis of the revolt of nature in *The Eclipse of Reason* (New York, 1974).

less and overintellectualized, and oversexed and money hungry. It was a form of racial hatred that attacked the mind yet did not call industrial advance into question. Instead of attacking machines or the capitalists, anti-Semites dreamed of a world without Jews.[12]

These paradoxical views of the Jews were present in Sombart's theorizing about the development of capitalism in Europe, the problem at the center of his concerns.[13] He rejected Marxism's concerns with classes and social relations, substituting for it a focus on *Geist* to explain the origins of a distinctly modern spirit of enterprise. What was distinctive about modern capitalism, in Sombart's view, was its combination of a spirit of enterprise with rationality, a synthesis that began in Renaissance Italy.[14] He also distinguished capitalist from precapitalist technology. The former was the result of the application of scientific theory to specific problems; the latter was embedded in custom and tradition. In modern technology and modern capitalism, Sombart saw an objectification of scientific rationality as well as of the spirit of enterprise. In fact, Sombart viewed all social phenomena as objectifications of *Geist*. He approved or disapproved of them according to the kind of *Geist* he believed they embodied. *Geist* was both a normative and evaluative concept. Thus he celebrated or denounced technology depending on whether he saw it as the objectification of the spirit of enterprise, on the one hand, or of lifeless bourgeois rationalism, on the other.[15]

In an early essay, "Technik und Kultur" (Technology and Culture, 1911), Sombart claimed that technology was having a disastrous impact on culture and the labor of the skilled craftsman.[16] Even in this fairly conventional sample of cultural despair, Sombart placed the blame for Germany's current problems primarily on the domination of technology by "the economy."[17] The popular entertainment industry, for example, turns out "hard, cold, loveless . . . international"

[12] On this see Norman Cohn, *Warrant for Genocide* (New York, 1967). On Hitler's "utopia" of a Germanic empire comparable to ancient Egypt, Babylon, or Rome, and on the "idealism" of the SS, see Bracher, *The German Dictatorship*, trans. Jean Steinberg (New York, 1970), pp. 407–9, 420–31.

[13] See Talcott Parsons, *The Structure of Social Action*, vol. II (New York, 1968), pp. 495–9.

[14] Ibid., p. 499. Sombart's analysis of the history of capitalism focuses on the economy as a self-enclosed system. For a criticism of his neglect of politics, see Otto Hintze, "Economics and Politics in the Age of Modern Capitalism," in *The Historical Essays of Otto Hintze*, ed. Felix Gilbert (New York, 1975), pp. 424–52.

[15] Ibid.

[16] Werner Sombart, "Technik und Kultur," *Archiv für Sozialwissenschaft und Sozialpolitik* 33 (2, 1912), pp. 305–47.

[17] Ibid., pp. 323–4.

music that does not fit well with the traditions of national folk songs.[18] But the thrust of this essay is wholly antimodernist; no specific exception is made for the machine. One student of Sombart, Arthur Mitzman, has made the interesting point that as his esteem for modern science and mass culture declined, his admiration for the philosophies of the will increased.[19] Sombart divided capitalism into an active and willing component arrayed against a calculating and rationalistic one. In the most interesting and important parts of his work, Sombart fused his voluntarism to his sociological analyses of capitalism. Like Spengler and Jünger, he placed technology in the sphere of an active, Nietzschean will to power. Here again, we see the now familiar anticapitalist rhetoric bereft of pastoralism. Sombart spoke more and more about technology *and* culture rather than technology *or* culture.

Sombart's early works, such as *Sozialismus und soziale Bewegungen im neunzehnten Jahrhundert* (Socialism and Social Movements in the nineteenth Century, 1897), or *Der moderne Kapitalismus* (Modern Capitalism, 1902), communicate an uncompromising critique of the economy and culture of capitalism. He attacked the "Moloch of business" whose "extended talons" reduced individuals to "involuntary gears in the giant works of business dealings." Entrepreneurs have money making as the exclusive goal of their activity, thereby reducing the whole social and natural world to numerical and commercial calculations.[20] Like Simmel, in his view of the tragedy of culture, Sombart bemoans the fate of a will that seeks to dominate nature yet winds up treating individuals as objects of business transactions. What distresses him in particular is the seeming congruity between German national character and a society dominated by a culture of acquisitiveness and competition. In *Die deutsche Volkswirtschaft im neunzehnten Jahrhundert* (The German Economy in the nineteenth century, 1903), he despaired of an apparent German proclivity for specialization and the acceptance of means–ends rationality. The German *Teilmensch* gladly renounced his personality and whole individuality to the "great mechanism" of what Sombart viewed as a dehumanizing division of labor.[21]

[18] Ibid., p. 347. Also see Ringer, *The Decline of the German Mandarins* (Cambridge, Mass., 1969), pp. 261–2.
[19] Mitzman, *Sociology and Estrangement*, pp. 170–4.
[20] Werner Sombart, *Sozialismus und soziale Bewegungen im neunzehnten Jahrhundert* (Bern, 1897); and *Der Moderne Kapitalismus* (Leipzig, 1902), p. 387.
[21] Werner Sombart, *Die deutsche Volkswirtschaft im neunzehnten Jahrhundert* (Berlin, 1903). In Sombart's view the division of labor was so destructive that by 1903 he had lost his earlier faith in the proletariat or the trade union as sources of new community. See Mitzman, *Sociology and Estrangement*, pp. 194–206.

In these early works, Sombart suffers from a double estrangement. Both capitalism and German culture seem to be threatening real *Kultur*. Arthur Mitzman points out that in the decade before the publication of *Die Juden und das Wirtschaftsleben* in 1911, Sombart reexamined the spirit of capitalism in a manner that helped him to overcome his earlier estrangement. Where he once saw the capitalist spirit as above all a destroyer of the German *Gemeinschaft* and harbinger of spiritless mechanization, he was increasingly drawn to a celebration of Nietzschean values. The result was a division of the capitalist spirit into an adventurous, entrepreneurial element, which he identified with the Germans, and a calculating, bourgeois spirit, which he associated with outsiders. The centrality of the will was, in Mitzman's words, "to remain the continuing basis of [Sombart's] life's work."[22] Here again, we see the labor of selective tradition helping to shape the reactionary modernist tradition. In both his analysis of the contribution of the "Jewish spirit" to the development of capitalism, and his wartime polemics against "the spirit of Manchester," Sombart overcame his brief if intense estrangement from the Germans and from aspects of industrial capitalism. Sombart, unlike Jünger, Spengler, Schmitt, and Freyer, reconciled himself to modern capitalism before, rather than after, World War I. The war reinforced his basic views, but did not create them. They refer back to an older anti-Semitic tradition in central Europe that found expression in Sombart's scholarly explanation of the role of the "Jewish spirit" in the development of capitalism in Europe.

In the decade and a half preceding the war, there was a lively debate in German social science concerning the origins of capitalism in Europe, a debate in which *Die Juden und das Wirtschaftsleben* played an important part. But in the following interpretation, I will approach this work as a document of reactionary modernist sentiment rather than as part of this debate. It has not stood up well under the scrutiny of economic historians. In David Landes's words, "It should have been dismissed out of hand as a pseudo-scholarly hoax, a pedantic effort to confer, by the lavish use of polyglot footnote references, an academic respectibility on errant nonsense already current in plain Ger-

---

[22] Mitzman, *Sociology and Estrangement*, pp. 237–8. Sombart praised the "unbounded drive for power, passionate joy in work . . . and pronounced intellectual-vitalist talent" of the capitalist entrepreneur in "Der kapitalistische Unternehmer," *Archiv für Sozialwissenschaft und Sozialpolitik* 29 (1909), pp. 689–758. Sombart believed that both the scholar and entrepreneur brought an aesthetic and willing dimension to a life threatened by economic calculation. See his preface to *Der moderne Kapitalismus*.

man terms."[23] Another recent commentator, Paul Mendes-Flohr, reaches a similar conclusion: *Die Juden und das Wirtschaftsleben* marked a turning point in Sombart's reintegration with the Germans, but despite its scholarly pretensions it is primarily an "ideological exercise, preparatory to the Germanophilia that would distinguish Sombart's later work." By identifying despicable capitalism with the Jews, Sombart could reconcile himself with Germany.[24]

Sombart's version of the development of European capitalism was roughly as follows: The transition from feudalism to capitalism was basically a shift from a Christian *Gemeinschaft* to a Jewish *Gesellschaft*. The Jews served as the agents of the "commercialization of economic life" by introducing the spirit of acquisition and calculation into the medieval community, which had been organized around respect for honest labor and the just price.[25] The precapitalist economy had been a "personal" or "natural" one in which "the category of useful goods defined on *qualitative* criteria still stands in the center of judgment."[26] The urban merchant plays a secondary role compared to that of the activities of peasants and craftsmen. The purpose of all economic activity remains the "creation of useful goods" and has not yet been wholly identified with "pure commodity production."[27] But the Jews had "stormed" into the medieval economy and in contrast to all natural purposes, recognized the primacy of acquisition.[28] The primacy of the economy over politics, culture, religion, and morality had been

---

[23] David Landes, "The Jewish Merchant – Typology and Stereotypology in Germany," *Leo Baeck Institute Yearbook* (1974), p. 22. For further criticism of Sombart, see Julius Carlebach, *Karl Marx and the Radical Critique of Judaism* (London, 1978), pp. 227–34; Toni Oelsner, "The Place of the Jews in Economic History as Viewed by German Scholars," *Leo Baeck Institute Yearbook* (1962), pp. 183–212; and Werner Mosse, "Weber, Sombart and Beyond," *Leo Baeck Institute Yearbook* (1979), pp. 3–15.

[24] Paul R. Mendes-Flohr, "Werner Sombart's 'The Jews and Modern Capitalism': An Analysis of Its Ideological Premises," *Leo Baeck Institute Yearbook* (1976), pp. 87, 92. Mendes-Flohr refers to the "jaundiced and contrived" picture of the Jews that Sombart presents and attributes its respectful reception to the "dangerous pretentiousness of German bourgeois life, and in particular ... to the self-deprecatory posture of German Jewry."

[25] Werner Sombart, *Die Juden und das Wirtschaftsleben*, p. 61. Published in English as *The Jews and Modern Capitalism* (New York, 1951). All citations are to the 1911 German edition. Weber's criticism of Sombart was that by focusing on commerce and acquisitiveness, he neglected the characteristics of modern capitalism.

[26] Ibid., p. 142.
[27] Ibid., p. 148.
[28] Ibid., p. 155.

the special contribution of "the Jewish spirit."[29] Three factors accounted for this unique Jewish contribution to the development of capitalism in Europe: the Jews' social and historical experience in Europe, the nature of Judaism as a religion, and a special Jewish psychology that fostered an "objective inclination" for capitalism.

Sombart stressed four aspects of European Jewish social history that contributed to the origins of modern capitalism. First, the Jews were dispersed in different countries and thus had international contacts.[30] Second, their existence as outsiders forced them to be more attentive to new economic opportunities and to favor economic rationalism over local custom and tradition. In Sombart's view, the Jews, as an alien minority, developed a *Fremdenmoral*, a double standard governing economic activity between Jews and non-Jews. But because Jews did most of their business with non-Jews, this double standard became the norm for transactions among Jews as well.[31] Third, because Jews had been excluded from full citizenship rights, they turned their attention away from politics to economics. Thus they displayed a "certain indifference to the state in which they lived," an indifference that enhanced their role as bearers of a "capitalist *world* economy."[32] Fourth, Jewish wealth made banking and lending possible, activities from which modern capitalism "was born."[33] Money lending dissolves quality in favor of quantity, negotiation over performance, and transforms economic activity into a "purely intellectual" matter.[34] The European Jews represent all that is universal, rootless, international, and *abstract* in contrast to all that is local, rooted, nationalist, and *concrete*. When Sombart juxtaposed abstraction and concrete immediacy in this manner, he provided the anticapitalist rhetoric of the German Right with a living embodiment of the processes of abstraction identified with exchange relations. These relations, in turn, he dissociated from

[29] Ibid., pp. 191–2. On the association of Jews with commerce in anti-Semitic ideology, see Arendt, *The Origins of Totalitarianism* (Cleveland, 1958), pp. 3–88; Mosse, *The Crisis of German Ideology* (New York, 1964), pp. 126–45; and *Towards the Final Solution* (New York, 1978); Peter Pulzer, *The Rise of Political Anti-Semitism in Germany and Austria* (New York, 1964); and J. L. Talmon, *The Unique and the Universal* (New York, 1965).

[30] Sombart, *Die Juden und das Wirtschaftsleben*, pp. 199–204.

[31] Ibid., pp. 205–6.

[32] Ibid., p. 212.

[33] Ibid., p. 222. For criticism of Sombart's empirical claims about Jewish wealth, see Mendes-Flohr, "Werner Sombart's 'The Jews and Modern Capitalism'"; Oelsner, "The Place of the Jews in Economic History"; and Hans Wolfram Gerhard, "Die Wirtschaftlich argumentierende Judenfeindschaft," in *Judenfeindschaft*, ed. Karl Thieme (Frankfurt, 1963), pp. 80–125.

[34] Sombart, *Die Juden und das Wirtschaftsleben*, p. 223.

any hints of class domination or property claims such language might suggest. Postone has aptly termed such rhetorical twists in the anti-Semitic tradition a "biologization" of the social relations of capitalism.[35]

Sombart's argument was also a social psychological one. Developing capitalism represented objectifications of a spirit rooted in Jewish religion and psychology. Judaism was a "work of reason" (*Verstandeswerk*), that is, one lacking in feeling and emotion and thus in conflict with a "natural" or "organic" world. Rationalism and intellectualism were the "fundamental features" of Judaism, as well as of capitalism, and threatened "that which is irrational and mysterious, . . . sensuous, artistic and creative . . . *The Jewish religion knows no mystery*" and was the "only" religion that knew no mystery (emphasis added).[36] It was not Protestant asceticism but Judaism that had been the force behind the rationalization of the modern world. Second, Jewish religion had an elective affinity to the spirit of capitalism because "the whole religious system is basically nothing more than a contract between God and the chosen people."[37] It was this contractual relationship that gave Jewish theology a quantitative view of sin "separated from the qualitative personality."[38] Third, Judaism had contributed to the rationalization of life by replacing "natural instincts" through self-discipline and purposefulness. The "leading idea that dominates Jewish moral theology . . . is that life is a great struggle against hostile powers of human nature" – inner human nature as well as outer nature.[39] It was these aspects of Jewish theology that gave religious sanctions to the spirit of acquisition, calculation, and rationalization of social life that accompanied capitalist development in Europe. Aware of Weber's work on the Protestant ethic and the spirit of capitalism, Sombart wrote: "Puritanism is Judaism."[40]

The Jews also had a distinctive collective psychology. They were highly intellectual, lacking in visual and creative sensibility, and were "born representatives of the liberal world view of the abstract citizen."[41] They always tried to grasp the world "with reason, rather than with cold blood." In Jewish collective psychology, "paper stands against blood. Reason against instinct. Concept against perception. Abstraction against sensuousness."[42] At home in this barren world of surface

[35] Postone, "Anti-Semitism and National Socialism."
[36] Sombart, *Die Juden und das Wirtschaftsleben*, pp. 242–3.
[37] Ibid., pp. 244–5.
[38] Ibid., p. 248.
[39] Ibid., p. 265.
[40] Ibid., p. 293.
[41] Ibid., pp. 313–18.
[42] Ibid., p. 319.

rationalism, the Jews had a seemingly endless restlessness and ability to adjust to different circumstances. It was hardly surprising that they excelled in professions such as journalism, the theatre, and law that rewarded cleverness more readily than unyielding conviction.

The Jewish ethic and Jewish psychology had uncanny parallels to the spirit of capitalism. The abstract nature of capitalist society "represents the exact counterpart to the Jewish spirit." In both capitalism and the Jewish *Geist*, "all qualities are dissolved through purely quantitative exchange value," merchants and salesmen replace "multicolored technical activity," cultural phenomena are stripped of their concreteness, all "earlier multiplicity" is leveled. But

> what is most important is that this process through which the world is stripped of its concrete properties is successful primarily because all social phenomena are coordinated by abstract money. Money places us in the center of the capitalist economy and also ensnares us in everything that comprises the Jewish essence. *Both capitalism and Judaism express their innermost essence in money* [emphasis added].[43]

Such passages are typical of the way Sombart transformed a Marxist theoretical vocabulary – use value, exchange value, and so on – into metaphors of race and nationality. They present the juxtaposition of use value and exchange value that became common within German romantic anticapitalism discussed earlier. Sombart defends particularity and concreteness against universality and abstraction. But where the romantic anticapitalists of the Left, such as Lukács, sought to connect the process of commodity fetishism to capitalist production, Sombart (like Proudhon in nineteenth-century France) first pointed the finger at money and circulation as the source of the abstraction of social relations; second, separated sources of abstraction from the labor process; and third, found an embodiment of the spirit of abstraction in the Jews.[44]

Sombart claimed to reject crude biological explanations for the per-

---

[43] Ibid., p. 329.
[44] Marx made similar points in his criticism of Proudhon. See Karl Marx, *The Poverty of Philosophy* (New York, 1963). Marx criticized Proudhon for assuming the existence of money as a given without inquiring into the social conditions that give rise to a "special agent of exchange," and for separating money from the mode of production (p. 81). In *Capital* and the chapter on money in *Grundrisse: Foundations of the Critique of Political Economy*, trans. Martin Nicolaus (London, 1973), pp. 115–238, Marx seeks to connect abstractions such as money to social relationships. From this perspective Sombart's focus on the power of money and the Jews succumbs to fetishism. Marx himself was not immune. See his very "un-Marxist" assimilation of the Jews and capitalism in the unfortunate essay, "On the Jewish Question," *Karl Marx: Early Writings*, trans. Rodney Livingstone and Gregor Benton (New York, 1975), pp. 211–41.

sistence "over several thousand years" of the affinity between the Jews and capitalism.[45] The source of this supposed persistence was, in his view, to be located in geographical factors. The Jews' "world historical significance" lay in the fact that they were an "Oriental" or desert people who wandered to and then throughout the European, Nordic north, thereby producing the economic-cultural synthesis called modern capitalism. The "nomadic instincts" that the Jews had developed as a desert people but that had then been repressed for centuries surfaced "under the influence of European exile." It was the fate of the Jews to have remained a wandering and desert people. Simply as a result of processes of Darwinian natural selection, character traits associated with rootedness to the soil were repressed in favor of those linked to the nomad or urban merchant.[46]

When the wandering Jews arrived in Europe, they happened upon peoples formed by the wholly contrasting geographical and ecological context formed by "the forest." The forest people were attuned to the mysterious, immediate, dreamlike, and concrete. The Nordic communities of peasants and craftsmen were "living, organic, ... and matured." The brilliant sunlight and clear, moonlit nights of the deserts encouraged abstraction and rationality and discouraged "sense perception and an emotional relation" to inner and outer nature. In the desert, where the shepherd's flock of sheep could grow quickly and be destroyed with equal rapidity by disease or hunger, the idea of unlimited acquisition and production took root as it never could in a settled agricultural community. It was nomadism that first elevated quantity over quality in economic life. Capitalism had been the product of the "endless desert" rather than the rooted forest. The desert–forest metaphor recurs in Sombart's discussions of money and the Jewish essense. Money unites "both factors of the Jewish essence, desert and wandering, Saharism and nomadism." The Jews and money

---

[45] Sombart, *Die Juden und das Wirtschaftsleben*, pp. 384–5. Although Sombart was not a crude biological racist, he did not hesitate to ascribe to the Jews an "anthropological character ... as well as ... a spiritual essence which has remained constant over several thousand years." This rootless, wandering, commercial, and money-lending character was hardly a flattering portrayal. Further, Sombart toyed with the idea that "illumination" into the "race problem" might come from research into the "chemical qualities of the blood," although at the time, he continued, the state of knowledge was inconclusive in the face of arguments by "race theorists" (pp. 350–1). This scholarly and scientific tone was common in much of the anti-Semitic ideology of the period. In a 1912 pamphlet, *Die Zukunft der Juden*, Sombart was less circumspect. The Jews, he claimed, were a foreign element utterly incompatible with German culture. Germans must guard against "bastardization" by curbing Jewish influence in intellectual and cultural life.
[46] Sombart, *Die Juden und das Wirtschaftsleben*, pp. 403, 407–8, 415.

share a number of features: absence of all concreteness, transience, rootlessness, obsession with abstract-quantitative conceptions. It is no surprise that it was the Jews who "unlocked all the secrets which lay hidden in money,... recognized its incredible powers,... became masters of money and, through money,... became masters of the world."[47] Where Max Weber defined modern capitalism by its focus on methodical, rational pursuit of profit, Sombart turned to the more popular equation of capitalism with the market. By identifying capitalism with the domination of money and abstraction per se, and then by identifying these evils with the Jews – who were non- as well as anti-German forces – Sombart reconciled himself to his fellow Germans. Germany was the land of the deep, dark forest of use value. *Die Juden und das Wirtschaftsleben* borrowed frequently from *völkisch* rhetoric about the German landscape threatened by urban rationalism, while conjuring up the familiar anti-Semitic myth of the tremendous power of the Jews. As Horkheimer and Adorno's comments suggested, a work such as *Die Juden und das Wirtschaftsleben* provided a set of metaphors around which big industry and the Junkers could meet on the common ground of rhetorical opposition to the circulation sphere. Whether or not it was his intention, Sombart gave the marriage of iron and rye one of its most eloquent ideological elaborations.

In Sombart's view, two ideas dominated modern capitalism: acquisition and economic rationalization. Economic rationalization, in turn, proceeded in two broad directions. The first was the rational planning of production and the predominance of means–ends rationality over tradition and custom. The second was a more general tendency to reduce all values, both inside and outside the production process, to money values and numerical calculation. The ideal-typical capitalist corresponded to these two trends of rationalization. He combined "two essentially different natures ... into a unity ... Two souls live in the capitalist entrepreneur," the dynamic risk taker and the calculating merchant.[48]

The entrepreneur has "a mission to fulfill." He sacrifices his life for this task and is obsessed with a "need for realization" (*Verwirklichungbedürfnis*) of his inner will within the external world. The merchant (*Händler*), on the other hand, is a man whose sensibility and imagination are focused on the money value of things. For him, "the world is a large market." Paraphrasing Marx, Sombart referred to the entrepreneur as the "constant and the merchant as the variable" element

[47] Ibid., pp. 421–7.
[48] Ibid., pp. 186–9.

141

of the capitalist economy. The entrepreneur's constancy is evident in his capacity to focus his will on a "distant goal" whose attainment constitutes the "foundation of his character." The variable merchant must change his activities from moment to moment and adapt to changing market conditions. The entrepreneur is a "discoverer, inventor, conqueror and organizer" whose personal decisiveness and knowledge of men lead to greater performance. In short, he is a hero of production. On the other hand, the merchant is indifferent to the specific object produced. He is at home in a world of speculation, calculation, and circulation. Finally, a "commercialization of industry" has taken place in the German economy. The power of the banks over industry has grown. The predominance of circulation over production has transformed modern economies into "merchant societies."[49]

Sombart viewed the commercialization of industry in modern capitalism as evidence of the presence of the Jewish *Geist*, just as the creation of credit notes and the stock exchange had indicated its presence in an earlier period of capitalist development.[50] The Jews were more qualified to be merchants than entrepreneurs because their deficiency in a "feeling for the organic and natural" gave them an advantage in postpatriarchal, rationalized modern capitalism.[51] In fact, the fit between Jewish psychology and merchant activity could not have been more perfect.

The merchant lives in numbers, and numbers have always been the element of the Jew ... Provide the sober, careful, exactly calculating man with a strong dose of combinatory fantasy – something with which the Jew is well equipped – and the perfect stock exchange speculator is standing before us in completed form.[52]

It was hardly surprising that the Jews were the "fathers of modern advertising," for this was one of those economic practices designed to "lock the customers in by cheap prices" rather than high quality.[53] The central role played by Jews in the development of the modern

---

[49] Ibid., pp. 189–92, 129–30. Sombart pointed to the *Allgemeine Elektrizität Gesellschaft* (AEG) under the direction of Walter Rathenau as "the most instructive example" of the commercialization of industry. Werner Mosse, in "Weber, Sombart, and Beyond" (*Leo Baeck Institute Yearbook*, 1979), pp. 3–15, writes that anti-Semitic businessmen in Germany referred to the firm as the *Allgemeine Judengesellschaft* (General Jewish Business). Also see James Joll's discussion of Rathenau in *Three Intellectuals in Politics: Blum, Rathenau, Marinetti* (New York, 1965).
[50] Sombart, *Die Juden und das Wirtschaftsleben*, pp. 61, 69, 94.
[51] Ibid., p. 332.
[52] Ibid.
[53] Ibid., pp. 165–6.

department store was yet another indication of their "complete in-difference" to the actual content of economic production. These stores made possible the "crass juxtaposition of articles that belong to the most diverse branches and uses conceivable."[54]

Die Juden und das Wirtschaftsleben presented examples from the German economy to illustrate the parallel juxtaposition of Germans and Jews with production and circulation. Sombart contrasted Krupp and Siemens, "old-style entrepreneurs" who were identified with production of a particular good, with newer, commercialized, and "colorless" capitalists such as Walter Rathenau, who was indifferent to the specific object being produced. Sombart succinctly expressed the juxtaposition as follows: "The Christian ascends to heaven as an engineer, while the Jew does so as a traveling salesman or clerk."[55] The Jews stand for abstract, exchange value in contrast to the concrete use value of the "Christian" economy.

Sombart's transfer of the categories of social theory into categories of race and nationality had profoundly important implications for his view of technology, as the following passage makes clear.

In its essence, capitalism means nothing other than the dissolution of economic processes into two constituent elements: *technology and commerce, and [subsequently] the primacy of commerce over technology*. So, from its beginnings, capitalist industry offered the Jews the opportunity for activity that *was in keeping with their character* [emphasis added].[56]

Passages such as this were typical of Sombart's "German anticapitalism."[57] If capitalism stood for the primacy of commerce over technology, then anticapitalism simply meant the reversal of this relationship by making technology predominant over commerce. Ideologically, this meant that technology ought to be incorporated into a German, Christian universe of use value that battled against an alien, international, Jewish universe of exchange value. Sombart's views on the connection between Jewish *Geist* and the spirit of capitalism provided a foundation for incorporating modern technology into the German soul.

It was in *Die Juden und das Wirtschaftsleben* and *Deutscher Sozialismus*, published in 1934, that Sombart devoted the most effort to the relationship between Germans, Jews, and technology. But between 1911 and 1934, he touched on this theme in several other works. *Der Bour-*

---

[54] Ibid., p. 178.
[55] Ibid., p. 134.
[56] Ibid., p. 132.
[57] See Wolfgang Hock, *Deutscher Antikapitalismus* (Frankfurt, 1960).

geois (1913) declared the Germans innocent of participating in the foundation of capitalism.[58] The peoples and nations of Europe had displayed varying inclinations toward capitalism. The Celts, for example, were "under-inclined" whereas those "over-inclined" to capitalism were the "heroic peoples" (the Romans, Venetians, English, and Germans) and the "trading people" (the Florentines, Scots, and the Jews).[59] In direct contrast to Max Weber, Sombart saw in Catholic "scholasticism" a fundamental cause of the rationalization of life that had contributed to the emergence of capitalism; in Protestantism he saw a source of religiously grounded "indifference" to economic activity.[60] Explaining that his ideas had "undergone little change" since writing *Die Juden und das Wirtschaftsleben*, Sombart again placed the responsibility for the birth of the modern capitalist spirit squarely on the shoulders of the Jews and Judaism.[61]

Händler und Helden (Merchants and Heroes) was a wartime polemic much along the lines of Spengler's *Preussentum und Sozialismus.* Germany was the nation of heroes at war with England, the nation of merchants.[62] In the prewar years, the "merchant spirit" (*Händlergeist*) was identical with the Jewish *Geist*. During the war, Sombart shifted his focus. Now England was the "trading nation" consumed with commercial interests and utterly devoid of any "cultural value."[63] The national euphoria of August 1914 represented the meeting of nationalism and anticapitalism, a synthesis he called "German socialism." He celebrated the outbreak of the war as a victory of German idealism – Goethe, Schiller, Fichte, Hegel, Nietzsche, and Bismarck (!) – over the acquisitive ethos that had threatened to drown prewar Germany in "the oozing flood of commercialism."[64] The metaphors of *Händler und Helden* depicted the war against England as a crusade against the capitalist spirit.

[58] Werner Sombart, *Der Bourgeois* (Leipzig, 1913), trans. as *The Quintessence of Capitalism* by M. Epstein (New York, 1967). The following citations are to this translation. *Händler und Helden* (Merchants and Heroes) (Munich, 1915); *Das Wirtschaftsleben im Zeitalter des Hochkapitalismus* (Munich, 1927). On *Der Bourgeois* see Mitzman, *Sociology and Estrangement*, pp. 243–54. On *Das Wirtschaftsleben* and Sombart's work during the Weimar Republic, see Lebovics, *Social Conservatism and the Middle Classes in Germany* (Princeton, N.J., 1969), pp. 49–78.
[59] Sombart, *The Quintessence of Capitalism*, pp. 201, 214–15.
[60] Ibid., pp. 236–50.
[61] Ibid., p. 265. Sombart again focused on the double standard of the Jews in economic activity and lending money as the basic capitalist activity that dissolves quality into quantity.
[62] Sombart, *Händler und Helden*, p. 14.
[63] Ibid., p. 50.
[64] Ibid., p. 145.

In *Das Wirtschaftsleben im Zeitalter des Hochkapitalismus* (Economic Life in the Era of High Capitalism), Sombart once again translated political and economic categories into national and racial terms when he defined specifically modern capitalism as a German–Jewish synthesis. The "Germanic race" contributed forward-looking drive, Faustian will, perserverance, and tenaciousness, while "the Jewish race" offered "great industriousness, a flair for speculation, strong accounting ability, insight into human nature and a hunger for progress."[65] Sombart's discussion of Germans and Jews allowed for an embrace of capitalism, but it was a selective embrace. The old-style bourgeois differed from the modern businessman in the same way that production for use differed from production for exchange and acquisition.[66] Not surprisingly, Sombart attacked what he called "modern" capitalism because it fostered speculation, "cold reason," and diminishing business ethics, and he defended earlier entrepreneurial virtues that lived on, in his view, in small and middle-sized firms.[67] The entrepreneur, with his "irrationalistic-emotional-voluntaristic instinct for invention, power and economic activity," was modern capitalism's driving force.[68] This driving force was threatened by its division into three distinct personalities: the captain of industry, the merchant or businessman, and the financier.[69] In advanced capitalism, the merchant and financier had defeated the captain of industry and thus threatened to extinguish the entrepreneurial spirit that was the foundation of the whole system. By depicting the growth of monopolistic and oligopolistic capitalism as a result of the growing preponderence of the Jewish aspect of the German–Jewish synthesis called modern capitalism, Sombart's construction had the effect of transforming anticapitalist resentments into anti-Jewish hatred.

Before the war, Sombart's views on technology were ambivalent. In *Der Bourgeois* he described technology as part of the larger complex of modern rationalism that was out to dominate and repress the "natural world with its fullness of life . . . a fullness that has been shattered to pieces."[70] But, along with natural science, Sombart began to view technology as an externalization of the "Germanic-Roman spirit" that contrasted sharply with the speculating Jewish spirit.[71] By incorpo-

---

[65] Sombart, *Das Wirtschaftsleben*, p. 26.
[66] Sombart, *The Quintessence of Capitalism*, pp. 154, 164–6, 170–6.
[67] Ibid., pp. 183–5.
[68] Sombart, *Das Wirtschaftsleben*, pp. 9, 12.
[69] Ibid., pp. 15–16.
[70] Sombart, *The Quintessence of Capitalism*, p. 319.
[71] Ibid., p. 333.

rating technology into German, national traditions he separated it from an alien world of abstraction.

In *Händler und Helden*, Sombart makes his peace with technology. "We need not fear it any more," for now its purpose is clear. The weapons of war have "once again" made clear what "the meaning of technical progress is ... Everything that previously appeared to be senseless has again taken on meaning and significance, since it has derived its worth from a higher, and for us, more elevated, value."[72] The higher and more elevated values to which Sombart referred were those of the nation and the virtues of nationalism – duty, sacrifice, *Gemeinschaft*, honor, courage, authority. Technology regained a cultural meaning in the service of the nation. Like Spengler and Jünger, Sombart viewed the war as a preserve of non- or even anticapitalist action that was outside the network of exchange relations and was therefore capable of giving to technology the meaning it had lost in the commercial world.

In the postwar period, he continued to view technology as the "true child of the revolutionary, European, Faustian spirit."[73] Technology was inseparable from the systematic nature of modern science and thus possessed an "immanent tendency to limitless and almost automatic expansion of technical knowledge."[74] Sombart's analyses of technological issues combined factual accounts of energy sources with more obscure references to emancipation from "the limits of living nature." He continued to speak of the tragedy of the heroic entrepreneur, but added another unsung hero, the self-sacrificing engineer surrounded on all sides by the "meaninglessness of our material culture." Sombart's "most important conclusion" from his discussion of technology was that capitalist profit seeking conflicted with the form of technical advance most favorable for the nation.[75] It soon became clear in his *Deutscher Sozialismus*, published a year after the Nazi seizure of power, that Sombart's anticapitalist rhetoric was not incompatible with either National Socialism or modern technology – or, for that matter, with modern capitalism as well.

The goal Sombart set for himself in *Deutscher Sozialismus* was straightforward. He sought a "unified view of different contemporary social problems from the standpoint of a National Socialist convic-

---

[72] Sombart, *Händler und Helden*, p. 125.
[73] Sombart, *Das Wirtschaftsleben*, p. 78.
[74] Ibid., p. 85.
[75] Ibid., p. 96.

tion."[76] He believed that writers sympathetic to National Socialism had neglected the importance of theory and that it was now time for "responsible scholarship," which often assumes "a certain distance from everyday politics," to contribute to the difficult task of blending nationalism and socialism.[77]

The themes of *Deutscher Sozialismus* were not new. It was an indictment of a mercifully now bygone "economic era."[78] The nineteenth century had been the age of "intellectualization" (*Vergeistung*) and "eclipse of the soul" (*Entseelung*), as was evident in the nature of modern forms of work and leisure.[79] It had been an age of "impersonalization and objectification" (*Versachlichung*), and it was the era of the erosion of individuality in favor of uniform work, clothing, housing, and culture.[80] The cause of this rationalized and soulless era was not hard to find. It was due to the predominance of the economy over all other spheres and values – beauty, strength, goodness, wisdom, artistic talent, birth, family tradition, and race to name only a few.[81] But the most singular feature of the economic era had clearly been the subordination of politics to economics as manifested in the rise of both businessmen and proletarians to the center of political activity. The proletariat did not offer an alternative to a completely degenerate era. On the contrary, it was its "characteristic product . . . Classes and class struggle are true children of the economic era."[82]

Finally things were changing for the better. The "new spirit" of German socialism was "nothing other than the renunciation of the economic era as a whole."[83] Nothing had suffered more from the unholy influence of the economic era than the idea of socialism itself. No theory had done more to damage and pervert this idea than Marxism. Marxism, Sombart claimed, not only mirrored the primacy of economic interests. It actually celebrated the rise of the "soulless"

---

[76] Sombart, *Deutscher Sozialismus*, p. xii. Lebovics stresses that in *Deutscher Sozialismus*, Sombart made his peace with modern industrialism, *Social Conservatism and the Middle Classes*, pp. 76–7. See also Werner Krause, *Werner Sombart's Weg vom Kathedersozialismus zum Faschismus* (East Berlin, 1962) for a discussion of Sombart and the Nazis.

[77] *Deutscher Socialismus*, p. xvi.

[78] Ibid.

[79] Ibid., pp. 17–18. The following was typical of Sombart's analysis: "Every worker is forced to leave his soul in the coatroom upon entering the large, bureaucratized factory" (p. 18).

[80] Ibid., p. 20. Sombart described the "tendency to uniformity" as "the modern form in which the plague appears" (p. 20).

[81] Ibid., p. 21.

[82] Ibid., pp. 24–5.

[83] Ibid., p. 43.

modern factory as a progressive step.[84] A specifically German socialism
would escape the economy's corrupting influence and appeal instead
to a sense of duty, national mission, and activism. Germany had a
special mission to preserve its identity in the face of the "monotony
of the East [the Soviet Union] and the West [England, France and
the United States]."[85]

Students of nationalism often refer to it as a secular religion, a
description that is most appropriate for the vision of cultural redemption presented by Sombart's *Deutscher Sozialismus*. The goal, as
before, was to attain "a condition we call *Kultur* ... and to dissolve
the existing condition we call *Zivilisation*." Reaching this goal would
"lead Germany out of the *desert* of the economic age" (emphasis
added).[86] German socialism aimed at far more than a redistribution
of the utterly discredited blessing of the economic era. Its real goal
was bringing peace to the soul by liberating it from the "exaggerated
intellectualization" of our life.[87] Sombart recalled the metaphor of the
desert and the forest he had used in *Die Juden und das Wirtschaftsleben*.
After a century of wandering in the desert of the economic era, the
German people would return to the complex – not primitive or backward – German forest. "Loving and expert hands" had created this
forest. Here was a return to nature that also appealed to the virtues
of labor. It was a vision that did have room for technology.[88]

Sombart returned to examination of the impact of the Jewish *Geist*
on the German *Volk*. He insisted that he did not accept biologically
grounded racism, but many passages from *Deutscher Sozialismus* were
at the very least ambiguous. Particular "soulful-spiritual forms" may
predominate in a particular race. "With the help of science, we can
never rule out a particular correspondence between body and the

[84] Ibid., pp. 81, 87. Sombart's indictment of Marxism also included its refusal to integrate any of the "sharp criticisms which all great 18th and 19th century thinkers
have made of modern civilization." Marxists, he wrote, only reject capitalist property
but accept modern civilization at its core. On the relation between Marxist scientism
and the resultant elaboration of critiques of positivism outside Marxism, see Breines,
"Marxism, Romanticism and the Case of George Lukacs," *Studies in Romanticism* (Fall
1977), pp. 473–89; Fest, *Hitler*, trans. Richard Winston and Clara Winston (New
York, 1974); and George Lichtheim, *Marxism: An Historical and Critical Study* (New
York, 1964). Sombart's critique of Marxism is most fully developed in *Proletarischer
Sozialismus*, 2 vols. (Jena, 1924). See Lebovics, *Social Conservatism and the Middle Classes*,
pp. 64–6.
[85] Sombart, *Deutscher Sozialismus*, p. 159.
[86] Ibid., pp. 162, 160.
[87] Ibid., p. 165.
[88] Ibid., p. 167.

mind just as we cannot claim such a correspondence to be a necessary one." In Sombart's view, science could not demonstrate that more than one kind of *Geist* could exist in a particular race any more than it could claim that a particular *Geist* could exist in only one race.[89] In other words, the Jewish or Negro *Geist* exists not only in Jews and blacks, but many penetrate the Germans as well. Hence, it was best that only those people whose *Geist* was in accord with the national *Geist* as a whole should live in and be allowed to immigrate to Germany.[90]

Unfortunately, the Jewish *Geist* had already infused all of modern Germany and would continue to exist "even if every last Jew and Jewish family was to be annihilated." It was "sedimented and objectified in a thousand organizations, . . . above all in our economy," even though many banks and the stock exchange were managed by non-Jews.[91] Germany's liberation from the Jewish *Geist* was the primary task facing the German people and German socialism. This task could not be attained through exclusion of Jews from Germany. Rather, it was necessary "to transform the institutional culture so that it no longer serves as a bulwark of Jewish *Geist*."[92] German socialism equaled anticapitalism, which, in turn, meant "struggle against the Jewish spirit," a cultural revolution of the Right that would overthrow the domination of the economy over social life. Although Sombart disclaimed belief in biologically based racism, it stretches credulity to believe that he or his readers would not associate the Jewish *Geist* with the Jewish people.[93]

Deutscher Sozialismus also restated Sombart's views on technology. He called for an authoritarian state that would place politics, that is, noneconomic values, in command of the economy.[94] Then the state would be able to rescue technology from its misuse by profit seekers. Sombart's references to technology still contained residues of ambivalence. There is a great deal here about the heroic domination of nature as well as an equal amount of complaining about dehumanized labor in the modern factory. But the phenomena he singled out for

---

[89] Ibid., p. 191. Although this is not a ringing endorsement of Nazi biological racism, neither is it, in Lebovics's words, a "rejection of the thorough-going racism of the Nazis," *Social Conservatism and the Middle Class*, p. 72. Sombart's work lent academic respectability to popular anti-Semitism.

[90] Ibid., p. 192.

[91] Ibid., p. 195.

[92] Ibid.

[93] See Carlebach, *Karl Marx*.

[94] *Deutscher Sozialismus*, p. 171. Sombart accepted Carl Schmitt's view of politics as "friend–enemy relations" as the basis of existential confrontations beyond calculations of efficiency and the market.

criticism, Taylorism and Fordism, were attributable to capitalist misuse rather than to an immanent technological telos. Unlike Spengler,
Jünger, Freyer, Schmitt, and Heidegger, Sombart rejected any "philosophy of technology" that would impute to it an inherent will to
power. Instead he claimed that technology was "culturally neutral,
morally indifferent," and could be placed in the service of both good
and evil. This was why it was so important that the authoritarian state
rescue technology from its misuse and distortion at the hands of the
capitalists.[95]

Sombart called such a project the "taming of technology," a phrase
he used as the title of a 1937 reprint of part of *Deutscher Sozialismus*,
and vigorously rejected the contentions of his critics that he was an
"enemy of technology."[96] He insisted that he had only criticized the
"deification" of technology that occurs when individuals no longer
question its meaning or significance but rather "canonize it as the
highest and most elevated value." The inventor's caprice must not be
allowed to get out of control. A "technopolitics" must replace laissez-
faire. The state must insure that technology serves the common welfare, thus fulfilling the National Socialist principle that "common good
comes before self-interest."[97] Sombart's work on technology displaced
assorted discontents with modern German society onto the Jews via
an anticapitalism that focused on a sphere of circulation identified
with a pervasive Jewish *Geist*. The series of displacements ends in an
appeal to an authoritarian state, the one major institution of German
society that has been able to resist the blandishments and corruptions
of the economic era.[98]

Finally, Sombart's *Deutscher Sozialismus* continues what was his central contribution to reactionary modernism, that is, the translation of
the language of social theory into the language of race and the transfer
of a highly emotional protest against rationalization into a set of metaphors that contributed to a forward-looking nationalism. His defense

---

[95] Ibid., pp. 249–53, 257–8, 261–2, 264.
[96] Werner Sombart, *Die Zähmung der Technik* (Berlin, 1935). Sombart denied he was a
cultural pessimist, adding that he had hope for the future because views "not at all
different from mine" were represented "in circles of our ruling party" (p. 31).
[97] Ibid., pp. 34–5.
[98] On the shift of social and economic conflicts into demands made on the state see Daniel
Bell, *The Coming of Post-Industrial Society* (New York, 1973); and Jürgen Habermas
Legitimation Crisis (Boston, 1975); Claus Offe, "Political Authority and Class Structure
– An Analysis of Late Capitalistic Societies," *International Journal of Sociology* (Spring,
1972), pp. 72–108. Generalizations about capitalism, middle or late, should be tem-
pered with a reminder of the legacy of state intervention in the economy that was
particularly marked in Germany. On this see Dahrendorf, *Society and Democracy in
Germany* (New York, 1966).

of the concrete, the authentic, and the particular against the abstract, false, and universal was a defense of Germany against Jewish *Geist.* Dichotomies abounded in German cultural politics in this period. Sombart's accomplishment can be summarized as follows:

Jewish Geist	*German technology*
Exchange value	Use value
Gold	Blood
Circulation	Production
Abstraction	Concrete immediacy
Reason	Instinct
Desert	Forest
Intellect	Soul
Zivilisation	*Kultur*
Merchant	Entrepreneur
International socialism and international capitalism	National Socialism

Although Sombart claimed to believe that the Jewish *Geist* and the Jewish people were not synonymous, dichotomies such as the preceding were at one with modern anti-Semitism. As Horkheimer suggested after the war, the destruction of the European Jews certainly drew upon the administration of "the revolt of nature" against abstraction. The dichotomies I have traced in Sombart's works suggest the outlines of an ideology that served as a cultural system by means of which technology was incorporated into such a revolt. Anti-Semitism and antimodernism were always closely connected. But more elements of modernity were part of the anti-Semitic tradition than some previous discussions of the subject would suggest.[99]

Up to now, I have dealt with the problem of how the literary, philosophical, and social scientific intellectuals made their peace with technology. Now it is time to shift focus and examine how German engineers placed technology into the sphere of German *Kultur.*

---

[99] George Mosse has revised his views on this matter. See his preface to *The Crisis of German Ideology* (New York, 1980).

7

Engineers as ideologues

The previous chapters have presented evidence of a cultural shift among right-wing intellectuals, each of whom individually exerted an influence on other literary or academic intellectuals. Now I want to shift the focus from the literati to German engineers. The engineers read and were influenced by one or more of the previously discussed figures. But what is more striking is that, beginning in the last third of the nineteenth century and continuing up through the last years of the Nazi regime, a reactionary modernist tradition with themes similar to those we have discussed in the preceding chapters was developed *inside* the German engineering profession. If the literati sought to win nationalism over to the cause of technological advance, the engineers sought to convince themselves and their skeptical cohorts in law, medicine, the civil service, and the traditional humanistic disciplines that they – the engineers – and the results of their labors – the artifacts of the second industrial revolution – belonged to the *Kulturnation*. Where Jünger et al. were cultural politicians above all, the cultural politics of the engineers also served pragmatic interests: desires for greater political recognition, for prestige and status equal to that of the older professions, especially law, and for more assistance from the state, and, in the last years of the Weimar Republic, for jobs and an end to restrictions on technical advances and rearmament.

There were Germans, such as Walter Rathenau, the director of the largest electrical corporation, the architect Peter Behrens, who organized the German *Werkbund*, and the architects and artists in the Bauhaus, who believed a special synthesis of national traditions and international developments was both possible and necessary. Rathenau's writings in particular combined a technocratic vision of productivity with spiritualized views of technology. There were also engineers who believed *Technik* and *Kultur* should be combined in a way that would avoid the worst consequences of environmental damage and commercial callousness, and who believed this could and ought to be done within a liberal and/or social democratic framework.[1] But the engineering profession in general was not cosmopolitan. On the contrary, the cultural politicians of German engineering began to reconcile technology and culture in a nationalist synthesis long before World War I. And whatever pragmatic interests motivated German engineers, their ideological traditions also opened the door for nazification.

That engineers were drawn to nazism at all does not fit very easily into received sociological wisdom. Thorstein Veblen, for example, expected that engineers would be either completely uninterested in politics, or drawn to "soviets of technicians" contrasting production for use with production for profit.[2] Even an observer as sensitive to the extent of irrationality in the Nazi regime as Franz Neumann found it difficult to accept the idea that engineers could participate in the ideological fanaticism of the Hitler regime. In his now classic work, *Behemoth*, Neumann wrote that there was an acute antagonism between the "magic character" of Nazi propaganda and the rational nature of production processes in industrial society. Because engineers were the practitioners of what Neumann called "the most rational vocation," they would experience this antagonism most intensely, view Nazi ideology as "bunk," and be one of the first social groups to break with the Hitler regime.[3] Neumann was mistaken. If the engineers had misgivings about Hitler's policies on purely technical grounds, with a few important exceptions, they kept such reservations to themselves. There was no revolt of the engineers against the Nazi ideologues and they shared a considerable number of meeting points in both theory and practice.

In his memoirs, Albert Speer claimed that his mistake was that of the artist and architect who remain uninterested in politics, the "apol-

[1] On Rathenau see James Joll, *Three Intellectuals in Politics: Blum, Rathenau, Marinetti* (New York, 1965); Maier, *Recasting Bourgeois Europe: Stabilization in France, Germany and Italy in the Decade after World War I* (Princeton, N.J., 1975); On Behrens and the Bauhaus, see Gay, *Weimar Culture: The Outsider as Insider* (New York, 1968).

[2] Thorstein Veblen, *The Engineers and the Price System* (New York, 1963). On ideology and technology see Daniel Bell, *The End of Ideology* (New York, 1962); and *The Coming of Post-Industrial Society* (New York, 1973); and Alvin Gouldner, *The Dialectic of Ideology and Technology* (New York, 1976). In the 1960s, some observers interpreted engineers as part of a "new working class" that would respond to the gap between technological possibility and capitalist reality with radical politics. See Andre Gorz, *Strategy for Labor* (Boston, 1968).

[3] Franz Neumann, *Behemoth*, p. 471. Also see Gert Schafter's afterword to the first German edition of *Behemoth* (Frankfurt, 1978), "Franz Neumann's *Behemoth* und die heutige Faschismusdiskussion," pp. 665–776.

itical technocrat" who does the work of the devil without asking troubling questions. Hitler's armaments minister from 1942 to 1945, Speer criticized those, like himself, who concern themselves "with [their] own affairs and as little as possible with what was going on outside."[4] The Speer legend, the Eichmann trial and Hannah Arendt's discussions of the "banality of evil," and Weberian visions of the iron cage all lend force to our view of the technocrat and functionary whose ideology is that of smooth functioning and uncritical obedience. Some recent historical work has begun to change this perception. One West German historian, Karl-Heinz Ludwig, has written an exhaustive history of the relation between German engineers and National Socialism, pointing to an "anticapitalism of the technicians" going back to the nineteenth century. Ludwig argues that the incorporation of engineers into large industrial firms brought with it anticapitalist sentiments that the Nazis exploited with great success.[5] The material I will be presenting in this and the following chapter should make clear that the predominant tradition of German engineers was heavily ideological and merged with nazism in important ways. To juxtapose ideologues and engineers underestimates the extent to which the engineers themselves were ideologues. During the crucial years from 1936 on, German engineers opted for the pursuit of ideological goals even when such courses of action flew in the face of functional, means–ends rationality.[6] Understanding the reactionary modernist tradition within the engineering profession helps to account for these commitments and explains how the Nazis shaped their appeals to engineers. Before we turn to the appeal of nazism to engineers in the Weimar Republic or to the administration of the reactionary modernist tradition in Nazi propaganda, we will examine its origins and development in the engineering profession.

The cultural dilemma of Germany's engineers was the following:

[4] Cited in Hortleder, *Das Gesellschaftsbild des Ingenieurs: Zum politischen verhalten du technischen Intelligenz in Deutschland* (Frankfurt, 1970), p. 122. On the intertwining of technocratic and ideological viewpoints in the Nazi regime, see the memoirs of Hans Kehrl, an engineer and minister in the armament ministry: *Krisenmanager im Dritten Reich* (Düsseldorf, 1978), and the afterword by Erwin Viefhaus, "Zwischen Technokraten und Burokraten," pp. 531–46.

[5] Ludwig, *Technik und Ingenieure in Dritten Reich* (Kronigstein, 1979); and Rabinbach's very fine essay on the combination of ideology and technology in Speer's own *Amt Schönheit der Arbeit* (Bureau of the Beauty of Labor), "The Aesthetics of Production in the Third Reich," in *International Facism*, ed. George Mosse (Beverly Hills, Calif., 1979).

[6] It was the nonutilitarian, not the monolithic, nature of the totalitarian regimes that Arendt stressed in *The Origins of Totalitarianism* (Cleveland, 1958), esp. "Totalitarianism in Power," pp. 389–459.

How could technology be integrated into a national culture that lacked strong liberal traditions and that fostered intense romantic and antiindustrial sentiments? Technology would have to be legitimated without succumbing to Enlightenment rationality. Just like the literati, the engineers wanted to demonstrate that technological advance was compatible with German nationalism's revolt against positivism. They also labored to separate technology from the web of liberal rationalism with which it had been associated in Great Britain, France, and the United States. The cultural politics of the engineers created a set of symbols, key words, and emotionally laden metaphors that provided a bridge between the trade union consciousness of the engineers and the more all-inclusive surge of German nationalism.

State-sponsored industrial development in the absence of a strong liberal tradition in both economics and politics was reflected in the central ideas and ideals of German engineers from the 1870s to the 1930s. Ludwig has labeled the traditions of the engineers in this period the "anticapitalism of the technicians," and he stresses four main components. First, technology emanated from the deepest impulses of German *Kultur* and not from the disenchanted materialism of Western *Zivilisation*; second, the cultural, political, and economic crises of modern German society were not due to the machine but to its misuse by private capitalist interests; third, the welfare of the national community could be protected only by a strong state, which ought to predominate over private economic interests; and fourth, engineers had a central role to play in providing the expertise necessary for Germany in an age of technological warfare. Ludwig argues that these ideas expressed a protest against the incorporation of technological production into the system of profit and exchange and that they contributed to the appeal of National Socialism to the engineers.[7] This is certainly plausible. The statist form taken by German anticapitalism was, however, due to the particular combination of capitalist development without a strong liberal tradition.

The cultural politics of German engineers drew on three main sources. The first was a tradition internal to the engineering profession presented in the journals of the national engineering associations and by professors of engineering at Germany's famous technical universities. The mandarins at the technical universities shared with their humanistic counterparts the cultural rejection of the Enlightenment

---

[7] Ludwig, *Technik und Ingenieure*, pp. 15–102. Anticapitalism among the engineers is analogous to romantic anticapitalism among the literary intellectuals in that both denounce capitalist exchange. On the political Right, both traditions in Germany called for statism in place of the market.

and were particularly sensitive to the need to make technology consonant with the idealist culture of the German universities. The second source was essays and books written by engineers and independent polemicists who sought to forge links between the conservative revolution and the German anticapitalism of the engineers. Third, the Nazi party directed propaganda at engineers from the mid-1920s onward. These three sources overlapped. The first two created a cultural climate in which, in the depths of the depression, National Socialism was able to present itself as the force serving to liberate engineers from the distortions of exchange relations in the name of a glorious nationalist future unsullied by crass commercialism.[8] I will now deal with the first two sources and will turn to National Socialist views on technology in the following chapter.

German engineers were organized in two national organizations of particular importance for the forging of a cultural defense of technology. The *Verein Deutscher Ingenieure* (Association of German Engineers, hereafter VDI), founded in 1859, was the largest of the engineering associations.[9] Through its monthly journal *Technik und Wirtschaft* (Technology and the Economy) and through its efforts to enhance the political influence of engineers, the VDI called for "technical labor in the service of the community" (*technische Gemeinschaftsarbeit*). *Technische Gemeinschaftsarbeit* had two implications: first, that there was a unity of interests between engineers and their employers, especially the new large corporations based on chemistry and electricity; and second, that the national welfare required active state intervention in the economy and encouragement of technical progress.[10] The message of the VDI publications was the productivist, technocratic hope that the unity of interest between the state, capital, and technical labor would make class conflicts obsolete.[11] Engineers

---

[8] Ringer, *The Decline of the German Mandarins* (Cambridge, Mass., 1969), pp. 128–30 and 213–27. On the ability of National Socialism to present itself as a movement seeking the liberation of technology from exchange relations, see Ludwig, *Technik und Ingenieure*, p. 90.

[9] See Hortleder, *Das Gesellschaftsbild des Ingenieurs*, pp. 18–71.

[10] Ibid., pp. 51–8. Hortleder stresses control of the VDI by leaders of big industry. His view of the integration of capital, labor, and the state around a rhetoric of common interests beyond class conflict is similar to the view of American developments presented by David Noble in *America by Design: Science, Technology and the Rise of Corporate Capitalism* (New York, 1977); Gabriel Kolko, *The Triumph of Conservatism* (New York, 1963); and James Weinstein, *The Corporate Ideal in the Liberal State* (Boston, 1968). On recent discussions of corporatism in Europe see Suzanne Berger, ed., *Organizing Interests in Western Europe* (New York, 1981).

[11] Maier, *Recasting Bourgeois Europe*; and "Between Taylorism and Technocracy," *Journal of Contemporary History* 5 (1970), pp. 27–51.

were to play a crucial role in what Charles Maier has called the "strategies of bourgeois defense."

Technik und Wirtschaft was not the primary vehicle of the ideologues among the engineers. That vehicle was the monthly journal of the *Verband Deutscher Diplom-Ingenieure* (Union of German Engineers with University Degrees, hereafter VDDI) called *Technik und Kultur* (Technology and Culture).[12] *Technik und Kultur* began publication in 1909 and ceased in 1937, when it was made superfluous by the official Nazi publications. During the Weimar Republic it was the focal point for those engineers who attempted to delineate a cultural mission for technology by focusing attention on works dealing with a "philosophy of technology." A typical issue would include an essay on Nietzsche, Schopenhauer, or Spengler as well as a comment on the cultural contributions made by a recent technical accomplishment – a new train station, airplane, ship, and so on. The technical universities that trained the contributors to *Technik und Kultur* were distinct from the humanistic universities, but the contents of the engineers' essays make it abundantly clear that they felt compelled to legitimate their professional work in terms defined by the mandarin culture of the humanists. Whereas the social sciences in France, England, and the United States were straining for legitimacy on the basis of their scientific claims, in Germany the cultural balance of power between the humanistic and scientific cultures was reversed. Engineers strained for legitimacy with the language of *Kultur*. Militant advocacy of progress through positivism and enlightenment would have been tantamount to identifying with the materialist menace from England, France, or America. Although a "philosophy" of technology sounds slightly ridiculous in the American, French, or British context, in Germany it seemed perfectly appropriate.

The cultural politics of the German engineers reached its apogee during the Weimar Republic. But the tradition on which it was based was by then already half a century old. The first attempt to present a "philosophy of technology" was published in 1877, a time in which thinkers such as Emil du Bois Raymond were attempting to incorporate materialism into the nationalist pantheon. Ernst Kapp's *Grund-*

---

[12] The *Verband Deutscher Diplom-Ingenieure* (VDDI), founded in 1909, was an organization of professors at the technical universities and graduates of those schools. It represented the elite of the engineering profession, whereas the much larger *Verein Deutscher Ingenieure* included technicians without college training. See Ludwig, *Technik und Ingeniewe*, pp. 25–7. From 1909 to 1922, the monthly journal of the VDDI was called *Zeitschrift des verbandes Deutscher Diplom-Ingenieure*. It was published from 1922 to 1937 as *Technik und Kultur*.

linien einer Philosophie der Technik (Foundations of a Philosophy of Technology) advanced the idea that technology followed a logic of "organ projection," or a progressive replacement of human organs by mechanical devices.[13] The hammer replaced the arm; eyeglasses, telescopes, and loud speakers were projections of the eye and ear; the telephone and telegraph were externalizations of the nervous system. Kapp described the machine as the "mirror image of the living," whereas a human being "represents the ideal mechanical system." The effect as well as the intention of such formulations was to "overcome" the dualism that placed technology in the realm of mind and rationality as opposed to that of organic nature. Kapp set a pattern for subsequent authors in placing technical advance in the realm of human anthropology and thus in the sphere of culture as well.

The first of many books to be entitled *Technik und Kultur* was published in 1906.[14] Its author, Edward Mayer, put forward a theme that became common in the subsequent literature: Technology was a manifestation of the "personality" of the engineer and inventor, not the result of the commercial interests who misused technics in the interest of profit. Technology sprang from an "instinct to re-form" (*Umgestaltungstrieb*), a part of "human essence" that seeks to organize and harness nature.[15] It is this organization of nature and her forces that, according to Mayer, was the "essence of technology, the secret of man's victory." The text is replete with references to "creative impulses" (*schöpferischer Drang*) and to a "higher cosmic mission" (*höherer kosmischen Sendung*) that pushes man to subdue a "chaotic nature." Technological mastery over nature combines inwardness (*Innerlichkeit*) and creativity with order and organization.[16] Another work often cited in subsequent statements was Ulrich Wendt's *Die Technik als Kulturmacht* (Technology as a Cultural Force), also published in 1906.[17] In Wendt's view, the history of technology presented a process of "increasing spiritualization" (*steigende Vergeistung*) of labor. Mind or *Geist* was infusing the labor process. The literal translation of *Vergeistung* is "to

---

[13] Ernst Kapp, *Grundlinien einer Philosophie der Technik* (Braunschweig, 1877). Subsequent works on the "philosophy of technology" referred to Kapp as a founder of the tradition. See Eberhard Zschimmer *Deutsche Philosophen der Technik* (Stuttgart, 1937), p. 2; and Friedrich Dessauer, *Philosophie der Technik* (Bonn, 1928).

[14] Edward Mayer, *Technik und Kultur* (Berlin, 1906).

[15] Ibid., pp. 23–4.

[16] Ibid., pp. 50–1.

[17] Ulrich Wendt, *Die Technik als Kulturmacht* (Berlin, 1906). Zschimmer in *Deutsche Philosophen der Technik*, wrote that Wendt's book tore "technology away from the materialism in which the Jew – Marx, in *Capital* – has placed it. In so doing, Wendt planted technology in the soil of German idealism" (p. 62).

make more spiritual" or to "infuse with spirit." Wendt's intention was to associate the language of German idealism with the apparently mundane realm of the engineer and inventor. Technical progress would bring technology and culture, the machine and speculative philosophy, ever closer together, rather than farther apart.

In 1904, Max Eyth, an engineer with poetic inclinations, published *Lebendige Kräfte* (Living Forces), an essay collection in which aggression and resentment toward the "so-called cultivated world" were more evident than in the works by Mayer or Wendt. Eyth claimed that even this so-called cultivated world was beginning to realize that there was more *Geist* in a beautiful locomotive or electric motor than in the most elegant phrases of Cicero or Virgil. Technology, like poetry, domi-nates matter rather than serves it.[18] Most of the cultural politicians of German engineering attempted to legitimate technology with the norms of *Kultur*. But some followed Eyth in asserting that technology was actually more cultural than culture itself.

One of the most cited of the prewar statements of the "anticapitalism of the technicians" was Julius Schenk's *Die Begriffe "Wirtschaft und Technik" und ihre Bedeutung für die Ingeniereausbildung* (The Concepts "Economy and Technology" and Their Importance for Engineering Education), published in 1912.[19] Schenk was a professor at the *technische Hochschule* in Munich and his book was composed of his lectures at the university. The central distinction the work makes is between the profit-oriented "commercial economy" and the "production econ-omy" oriented to engineering and skilled craftsmanship. He claimed that both engineers and visual artists deal with "creative forms and images," that it was time for engineers to give up their inferiority complex concerning the humanities, and that engineering professors should accentuate the "cultural value of construction" (*Bildungswert des Bauens*).[20] Technology should not be equated with the abstract world of "bureaucratism" (*Bureaukratismus*) but should instead be sit-uated in the "world of healthy reality, ... of creative labor."[21] The connection between health and labor, as well as references to engi-neers as industrialized artisans, became commonplace in subsequent literature of the German engineers.

World War I seemed to fulfill some of the prewar hopes of the engineers. Mobilization for technological war underscored the inter-

[18] Max Eyth, *Lebendige Kräfte* (Berlin, 1904), p. 15.
[19] Julius Schenk, *Die Begriffe "Wirtschaft und Technik" und ihre Bedeutung für die Ingenierausbildung* (Breslau, 1912).
[20] Ibid., p. 35.
[21] Ibid., p. 36.

159

dependence of technical knowledge and the politics of a modern nation-state. As they became aware of their importance during the war, engineers increased the volume of protest concerning the insufficiency of cooperation between the state and the engineers in the postwar period. Although the war ended in terrible defeat, the engineers pointed with pride to their wartime accomplishments and were emboldened in their rejection of the antitechnological mood of the pacifist, humanist intellectuals. The cooperation of state, business, labor, and technical expertise during the years of "total mobilization" created a model that the engineers sought to institutionalize on a permanent basis. Whereas Jünger had seen the masculine community of the trenches as a prefiguration of the future, many engineers saw wartime mobilization as a prefiguration of the illiberal, corporatist visions that attracted them during the Weimar Republic.[22]

The problem, as leading officials of both the VDI and VDDI understood, was that the Weimar Republic was not about to reestablish this corporatist relationship. Or rather, as Charles Maier has made clear, reestablishment of corporatist bargaining in the postwar period would have had to accord more political representation to the working class than was acceptable to many industrialists. The Social Democrats remained loyal to the republic and to the Versailles treaty and therefore refused to launch the program of rearmament that the engineering elite desired.[23] From the engineers' standpoint, the Social Democrats, despite their professed enthusiasm for industrial advance, stood for technological stagnation. The anti-Semitic rhetoric of the *völkisch* Right was warmly received among some engineers, but its thoroughgoing antiindustrialism precluded a wide appeal. Neither *völkisch* nature mysticism nor the Social Democrats' pacific cosmopolitanism reduced unemployment among engineers. By 1932, only 20 percent of the graduates of the technical universities found employment as engineers.[24] Obviously, those elements of the political Right who had jettisoned antitechnological outbursts of the *völkisch* tradition and who were eager to rearm the nation could make a powerful political and ideological appeal to engineers. National Socialism promised them

[22] On the meaning of World War I for the social consciousness of the engineers, see Hortleder, *Das Gesellschaftsbild des Ingenieurs*, pp. 79–83.
[23] On the Versailles restrictions on German rearmament, see Karl Dietrich Bracher, *Die Auflösung der Weimarer Republik: Eine Studie zum Problem des Machtverfalls in der Demokratie*, 2d ed. (Stuttgart, 1957), pp. 205–6; and Wolfgang Sauer, *Die Mobilmachung der Gewalt*, vol. III of *Die Nationalsozialistische Machtergreitung* (Frankfurt, 1974), pp. 21–41, 115–65.
[24] Hortleder, *Das Gesellschaftsbild des Ingenieurs*, p. 109; and Ludwig, *Technik und Ingenieure*, pp. 63–73.

the possibility of combining self-interest and service to the *Volksge-meinschaft*. The cultural politicians among the engineers came to believe that National Socialism would silence the critics of technology from the so-called cultivated world and would also wrest technical development from control by commercial interests. Nazism's appeal for the engineers was not an antimodernist attack on technology but a promise to *unleash* modern technology from the constraints the Social Democrats had placed on it.

In the remainder of this chapter, I will examine in more detail the themes elaborated by German engineers during the Weimar Republic and the first years of the Nazi regime. In the following chapter, I will present Nazi propaganda concerning technology to demonstrate that, among other things, the rhetoric of the Third Reich represented an administration of a set of cultural meanings and metaphors that had already been created before 1933. To point to the unoriginal nature of Nazi propaganda is not to dismiss it. On the contrary, it highlights one reason for its success, namely, that it rested on broader popular traditions.

In the previous chapters I focused on intellectuals who were well-known figures in their own right. In this and the following chapters, the focus shifts by and large to contributors to the cultural system of reactionary modernism who were not particularly well known beyond the engineering profession. This broader focus should not be taken to imply that they were less creative or inventive in their cultural politics, but rather that their individual biographies are of less interest to us than their contributions to the consciousness of engineers as a group.[25] The contributors to the journals of the engineering associations and the lecturers at the technical universities fashioned a tradition, a shared set of texts, basic terms, and common metaphors with which they hoped to lift technology from the alien world of *Zivilisation* to the familiar world of *Kultur*. The skeptical student of ideology would not be mistaken to see in their writings a great deal of occupational boosterism laced with some rumblings of fractured class consciousness. But whatever links between social existence and social consciousness their texts manifest, the cultural traditions of the engineers contributed to abandonment of clear perceptions of class interests during the Nazi years. Thus to point to genesis does not deal

[25] On the national traditions of engineers, see Allan Silver, "Nations as Arenas of 'New Class' Formation: The Case of Engineers," paper delivered at American Sociological Association meetings, San Francisco, September 6–10, 1982.

with the problem of meaning, nor does it help us to understand the persistence of tradition when its advocacy contributed to national self-destruction. Although my focus has shifted from individuals to engineers as a group, I remain interested in the problem of myth and unreason.

The following reconstruction of the engineers' cultural traditions draws on a limited number of contributors who, I believe, were representative of the tradition as a whole because they articulated most clearly themes that appeared in many other contemporary books and essays. The authors I will discuss were also important in the sense that they were often cited by other authors or were influential in defining the outlines of the cultural politics of the journals of the German engineering profession. One journal in particular, *Zeitschrift des Verbandes Deutscher Diplom-Ingenieure*, begun in 1909 and published as *Technik und Kultur* from 1922 to 1937, served as a cultural clearinghouse for discussions of technology and politics among graduates of the technical universities. From 1919 to 1934, the journal was particularly active in countering what its contributors depicted as an avalanche of left-wing cultural Luddism. From 1934 to 1937, *Technik und Kultur* continued to publish, but it had clearly succumbed to the effects of the National Socialist *Gleichschaltung* or "coordination" of cultural and institutional life with the demands of the new regime. What often began as an article in *Technik und Kultur* ended as a full-length book. Or sections of books on politics, technology, and culture were printed in the journal, as were reviews of the current and past literature. In this way, the journal helped to establish a tradition internal to the engineering profession and its educational institutions. In 1934, the Nazis launched their own review of cultural politics, *Deutsche Technik*, but the continuity of themes with *Technik und Kultur* only underscored the fact that the latter had been the institutional and intellectual center of the reactionary modernist tradition among German engineers, especially during the years of the Weimar Republic. It was sent to all of the members of the *Verband Deutscher Diplom-Ingenieure*, an organization whose membership grew from 4,000 in 1914 to 10,000 in 1937. To be sure, there must have been many engineers, perhaps even a majority, who remained uninterested in the *Streit um die Technik*, but I think it is fair to say that German engineers – as opposed to English, French, or American engineers, for example – devoted a remarkable amount of time and energy to cultural politics. If he (and the profession was overwhelmingly male) was interested in the relationship between technology and culture, a German engineer would be reading *Technik und Kultur*.[26]

The mixture of cultural despair and fascination with technical advance that I have traced among the literati appeared among the engineers as well. Along with Spengler, Jünger, and others, they excoriated the Weimar Republic as a swamp of political chaos and cultural decay. Eugen Diesel, an engineer and son of the inventor of the diesel engine, expressed such views in *Der Weg durch das Wirrsaal* (The Path through the Confusion) and *Die deutsche Wandlung* (The German Transformation).[27] The first work contained the full complement of cultural despair. Diesel wrote that intellect threatens "our blood and essence" by constructing a world that had become soulless, mechanized, and senseless. The "great crisis" of the present was one in which "living instincts" struggled to survive against the "tyranny of abstract images,...an imperium of abstraction." Not just money but "the world of money" was replacing concrete experience and immediacy. The present was an age of *Entgeistung*, roughly "despiritualization," defined by the "swamp of mammon," big cities, advertising, a crushing division of labor, and *Amerikanismus* (Americanism).[28]

Diesel exempted technology from his indictment of the godforsaken present. It was the product of an innate human instinct for creativity. As such, it served as the basis for new values once it had been separated from "the hell of organization." Diesel complained that technology too often had been confused with *Amerikanismus*, a disease he defined as an "obsession with economics" and instinctual "oppression" linked to mass production and consumption. Americanism plus industrialism did not equal technology. On the contrary, technology carried hints of a "nobler race...of stronger life instincts."[29] In a 1930 work, *Völkerschicksal und Technik* (The Fate of Peoples and Technology), Diesel repeated the motifs of cultural crisis and stressed the threat to Ger-

[26] Ludwig, *Technik und Ingenieure*, pp. 26, 140.
[27] Eugen Diesel, *Der Weg durch das Wirrsaal* (Stuttgart, 1926); *Die deutsche Wandlung* (Stuttgart, 1931).
[28] Diesel, *Der Weg durch das Wirrsaal*, pp. 16, 20, 23, 121.
[29] Ibid., pp. 260–1. The United States aroused both fascination and horror in the German Right. Theodor Luddecke, *Das amerikanische Wirtschaftstempo als Bedrohung Europas* (Leipzig, 1925) praised America's "life energy...demonism and power of action" appropriate for the "dynamism of the machine." Reactions to the United States were also indirect commentaries on German society. See Lethens, *Neue Sachlichkeit: Studien zur Literatur des weissen Sozialismus* (Stuttgart, 1970), and Maier, "Between Taylorism and Technocracy."

many's "old cultural landscape" posed by an international, uniform technology. It was not very clear how Germany would avoid American-style commercialism, but Diesel suggested that the state was the institution to defend the qualities of the German *Volk* in a cosmopolitan era. All paths leading out of the cultural crisis led toward nationalism.[30]

As these passages from Diesel's works show, the language of the literati influenced the traditions of the engineers. Sometimes this influence was even more direct and personal, as was the case with Manfred Schroter, an associate of Spengler's who took it upon himself to disabuse those who thought Spengler's pessimism extended to technological matters. We have already seen that Spengler himself recognized that *Der Untergang des Abendlandes* could foster cultural pessimism conducive to antitechnological sentiments and did what he could to counter them in *Der Mensch und die Technik*. Schroter continued Spengler's efforts within the engineering community.[31]

The contributions to the *Streit um die Technik* have an embattled tone about them. During the postwar years, numerous "defenses" of technology appeared, of which Schroter's *Die Kulturmöglichkeit der Technik als Formproblem der produktiven Arbeit* (The Cultural Possibility of Technology as the Form Problem of Productive Labor) was one of the more eloquent.[32] Few combined productivist and aesthetic categories as elegantly. Schroter pointed out that from a nationalist perspective, German reconstruction after the Great War would be impossible if technology were mistakenly identified with the victorious countries. Like Diesel, he insisted that indigenous, German cultural traditions were conducive to technical advance. Hence anti-Western or anti-American cultural protest ought not be conflated with hostility to technology, for the two were not synonymous.[33]

To be sure, a cultural crisis did exist. It amounted to the domination of "objective culture" (philosophy and natural science) over "subjective

[30] Eugen Diesel, *Völkerschicksal und Technik* (Stuttgart, 1930), p. 74. This work as well as *Die deutsche Wandlung* appeared in a series of works on technology and culture edited by Diesel. The purpose of the series was to develop the self-consciousness of "technical man and to search for a new culture for technology." Other books in the series included Maxmillian Esterer, *Chinas natürliche Ordnung und die Maschine* (Stuttgart, 1929); Siegfried Hartmann, *Technik und Staat* (Stuttgart, 1929); Herman Lufft, *Kulturformung durch Technik und Wirtschaft* (Stuttgart, 1930).
[31] Schroter analyzed the reception of Spengler's work in *Der Streit um Spengler: Kritik seiner Kritiker* (Munich, 1922). After World War II, Schroter issued an expanded edition, *Metaphysik des Untergangs: Eine kulturkritische Studie über Oswald Spengler* (Munich, 1949).
[32] Manfred Schroter, *Die Kulturmöglichkeit der Technik als Formproblem der produktiven Arbeit* (Berlin, 1920).
[33] Ibid., pp. x–xi.

culture" (religion and politics).[34] Schroter depicted this cultural crisis with the aid of a chart. Subjective culture was placed on the right side of a circle, objective culture on the left. The solution or the overcoming of the cultural crisis lay in art and technology, both of which he placed on a vertical line between the two realms. He wrote that technology and art fulfilled a "need for unity" that prevents the pendulum of cultural development from swinging over to the side of either pure objectivism or subjectivism. Schroter believed that Dilthey's *Lebensphilosophie* provided the means to mend the disjuncture between objective and subjective culture. What Schroter found valuable in Dilthey's work was an emphasis on the importance of the will, the "germinal instinct" (*Keimtrieb*) that brings objective and subjective culture together into the "organic synthesis...and deep cultural mission" of technology.[35]

Schroter was uncompromising in his denunciations of the "cultural and spiritual impoverishment and mechanization of life" so threatening to the "enslaved individual."[36] This crisis was a distinctly modern problem. Technology, however, was "not something new or recently emergent," but rather a manifestation of "creative, productive labor for the sake of a life filled with meaning." Thus it could be traced back to the "first step from animal to man, that is, to the origins of human culture."[37] As a derivative of "creative labor," technology was not at all a distinctly modern thing. Creative and productive labor was inseparable from the "creative fire of a permanent and expanding formation of culture,...a path of inwardness [*Weg der Innerlichkeit*] on which economic advance and the life of the soul merge in an inner coherence."[38] The merely "external," though at times "negative," aspects of modern technology should not, Schroter insisted, obscure the role productive labor played in providing a possible cultural foundation for its own "inner, creative possibilities."[39] As we will see, separating the idea of labor from wage labor or commodity relations became an important feature of reactionary modernist rhetoric.

The clever twist in Schroter's appeals to the virtues of creative labor lies in his summoning of the language of inwardness and the German soul in order to stop rather than encourage what he described as a

---

[34] Ibid., p. 39.
[35] Ibid., p. 54.
[36] Ibid., p. 56.
[37] Ibid.
[38] Ibid., p. 69.
[39] Ibid., p. 65.

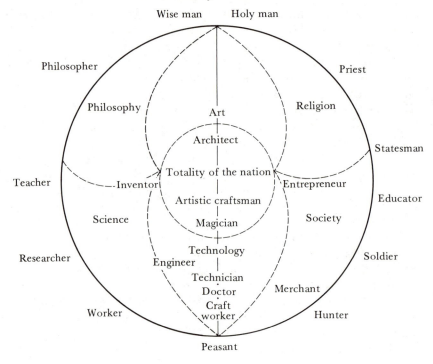

modern "flight from technology."[40] He called for a *Vergeistung* (infusion with spirit) or *Beseelung* (infusion with soul) of technology.[41] There was no contradiction in the idea that the nation of poets and thinkers should also produce great engineers and technicians, because no other nation blended "idealism and exact thinking" as thoroughly as did Germany.[42] These appeals to *Arbeit*, *Geist*, and *Seele* followed a common reactionary modernist strategy of incorporating technology into terms familiar to the Germans in order to accept what was, in fact, unquestionably modern.

In 1934, Schroter published *Die Philosophie der Technik* (The Philosophy of Technology), a work that featured several charts – Schroter called them "structural schemes" – of cultural development. Charts such as the one above offered pictorial illustrations of one variant of reactionary modernism as a cultural system.

[40] Ibid., p. 95.
[41] Ibid., pp. 87–8.
[42] Ibid., p. 95.

166

As with his earlier graphic presentations of cultural crises, this chart places objective culture on the left-hand side and subjective culture on the right. Technology and art again lie on a vertical line separating the two areas. The technician stands in a line of progression preceded by the peasant and skilled worker, and succeeded by the artisan, architect, and artist. Schroter places the engineer and doctor in a cultural sphere that blends technology and art. Not only does this chart present technology as a force of cultural equilibrium serving to balance objective and subjective culture; it also, again through the principle of "creative labor," binds the old and traditional with the new and modern. Symbols of the precapitalist and preindustrial past, such as the peasant and artisan, serve to incorporate technology into an acceptable cultural-political framework. In Schroter's work, "creative labor" emerges as an idea that blends aesthetics and productivity, so that technology appears to be the solution to, and not the cause of, a cultural crisis.

Schroter wrote that the creative labor of technology drew on "all three sides of our inner life – understanding, feeling and will." Research entailed the intellectual assimilation of knowledge from the outer world. Invention required the reworking of such knowledge in "creative fantasy" leading to technical ideas. Realization of fantasy called on an "acting will directing itself outward in formation of works." Together these activities constituted the "fundamental trilogy of technical creation."[43] Schroter's works were strewn with terms such as "joy in creation" (*Schaffensfreude*) or "culture formation" (*Kulturgestaltung*), which endowed engineering with the same cultural aura whose destruction at the hands of civilization drove critics such as Klages and Moeller van den Bruck to despair.

In *Die Philosophie der Technik*, Schroter continued to separate Spenglerian visions of doom from antitechnological sentiment. Rather than emphasize Spengler's occasional criticisms of technology, Schroter stressed his "morphological" perspective, that is, Spengler's view of technology as a form objectified.[44] Along with Spengler, Schroter saw technology as filling the world with clear, distinct forms that comprised a dike against the potential chaos and formlessness of modern liberal politics and culture.[45] In suggesting that technology was inherently authoritarian and illiberal, Schroter echoed a major theme of the views of the right-wing literati as well. He referred specifically to Hans

[43] Manfred Schroter, *Die Philosophie der Technik* (Munich, 1934), p. 26.
[44] Ibid., p. 36.
[45] Ibid., pp. 35, 62. On this see Schumacher, *Die Angst vor dem Chaos* (Paris, 1937; reprint, Frankfurt, 1972).

Freyer when he asserted that the origins of modern technology lay in the common root of the power instinct (*Machttrieb*) and the determination of the will (*Willensbestimmtheit*).[46] And he alluded to Spengler and Max Scheler as well in claiming that the fundamental issue of the crisis of modern culture was whether technology was a culturally neutral system of instruments or, as he himself believed, an integral part of the "life totality of the people of Europe."[47]

Neither liberalism nor Marxism offered acceptable answers to the crisis of modern culture. A third way was imperative: German nationalism. Liberalism amounted to a "mad striving for more and still more money," whereas Marxism advocated a "senseless leveling" of culture and politics to the lowest common materialist denominator.[48] Nationalism contained the possibility of closing the gap between subjective and objective culture in postwar Germany for two reasons. First, both Italian fascism and National Socialism advocated the primacy of politics over economic interests. Such a policy, Schroter believed, was conducive to a renewed "primacy of technology" (*Primat der Technik*) as well.[49] Schroter was vague about what the *Primat der Technik* would mean in practice, but he implied that at the very least it meant breaking with the restrictions on German rearmament imposed by both Versailles and the Weimar Left.

Schroter also stressed what became a central theme among the engineers' cultural politicians in these years, that is, that Germany was the *Kulturnation*, the nation of culture.[50] Like Martin Heidegger, Schroter connected the idea of the *Kulturnation* to Germany's geographical position between East and West. Schroter wrote that Germany's relation to technology must be distinguished from both the "technocratic mechanization" of American liberal democracy and the "forced technical advance" of the Soviet Union's "purely materialist and collectivist system," because in both of those societies, work had been emptied of meaning and cultural significance.[51] For Schroter, Germany, the country in the middle between East and West, rejected the materialism of the Americans and Russians. It was the only modern nation able to create a proper relationship between technology and culture. He interpreted the Nazi seizure of power in this context. National Socialism had once again elevated idealism and the realm of

---

[46] Schroter, *Die Philosophie der Technik*, p. 43.
[47] Ibid., p. 55.
[48] Schroter, *Die Kulturmöglichkeit der Technik*, pp. 92–3.
[49] Schroter, *Die Philosophie der Technik*, pp. 67–8.
[50] Ibid.
[51] Ibid., pp. 64–5.

the spirit over that of materialism and recreated the basis for his longed-for synthesis of "idealism and exact thinking, . . . of technology and spirit."[52] The unification of German *Geist* and German technology finally would occur, dispensing with the depraved and soulless materialist age. Germany's special mission among nations was to create an advanced industrial society in which there was still room for "our life will to search uninterruptedly for redemption."[53]

In his *Deutscher Geist in der Technik* (German Spirit in Technology), published in 1935, Schroter stressed the specifically German contributions to international scientific and technical advance.[54] He argued that German technical advance had occurred because, and not in spite, of the importance of philosophy and art in German culture and society. The Faust legend, for example, prefigured the "demonic technical destiny" that drove German engineers toward expanded domination over nature. Goethe, Luther, Kant, and Hegel passed on traditions of unifying theoretical and empirical work, of "organization and creative performance, . . . an almost titanic leadership will that takes joy in responsibility."[55] Germany's cultural achievements had thus contributed to her technological advances. He was alarmed by the "conceptual exhaustion" and antiintellectualism of the youth movements that fostered hostility to technology. Were such views to become widespread, he feared that Germany would become "hopelessly outdistanced by other peoples."[56]

Schroter's argument can be restated as follows: A precondition for German technological advance was the unification of German idealist philosophy with scientific and technological research and innovation. The development of capitalism and its attendant commercial culture threatened the precapitalist, nonutilitarian traditions of German culture and philosophy, and thus threatened the basis of further technological advance as well. The antimodernist rhetoric of National Socialism promised to preserve this precapitalist culture and paradoxically enhanced further technological development. Schroter implied that societies without feudal pasts (such as the United States) would be unable to fuse technology and culture in the way Germany could. Hence, Germany's illiberal, feudal traditions would enhance technical advance. Of course, the Nazis destroyed, rather than preserved, Kantian or Hegelian legacies, or at least twisted these legacies

---

[52] Ibid., pp. 99, 102.
[53] Ibid., p. 108.
[54] Manfred Schroter, *Deutscher Geist in der Technik* (Cologne, 1935).
[55] Ibid., pp. 23, 59–60.
[56] Ibid., p. 60.

beyond recognition. Schroter's point, however, did not concern Kant's or Hegel's responsibility for National Socialism; he contended rather that a protest against the instrumental reason, the market, and economic individualism served as an ideological support for further technical advance. German modernity and German capitalism were Janus faced indeed.

Although Schroter's work was directed at engineers, he was neither an engineer nor a natural scientist. Friedrich Dessauer, on the other hand, was a physicist from the University of Frankfurt who also made the rhetoric of *Kultur* accessible to his colleagues. From 1907 to 1933, he published over fifteen essays and several books on themes related to the cultural crisis occasioned by technological advance.[57] Dessauer also blamed the excessive influence of the economy for Germany's cultural crisis. In 1921, he urged that a national ministry of technology be created whose purpose would be to correct the misuse of technology at the hands of private commercial interests. The central task of technical thinking, he wrote, was "service to the *Volk* and to humanity," rather than the accumulation of profit envisaged by the "world of finance."[58] He urged his fellow scientists and engineers to end their traditional disinterest in politics. A "breakthrough of technical spirit into public opinion" would bring about a "rebirth of spiritual forces" associated with technical creation as a sphere of activity outside the cash nexus. Along these lines, he wrote that "an automobile is not a heap of iron and wood, but rather, like all machines, it is mathematics that has become form and movement."[59] Dessauer complained that the public had burdened technology with the sins of the economy. Certainly the two were related, but their "essence" was different. Like Spengler, he distinguished between the entrepreneur, the capitalist, and the engineer. The first is a heroic creator of new industries. The second only searches for profit, is uninterested in the common good, and creates large, impersonal, bureaucratized firms. The engineer

---

[57] Friedrich Dessauer, *Streit um die Technik*, 2d ed. (Frankfurt, 1958), pp. 446–57, for a bibliography of his and other contributions from 1900 to 1937. Dessauer's essays were generally published in engineering journals. For example, see "Die Technik bei Wiederaufbau der deutschen Wirtschaft," p.1. *Technik für Alle* (1, 1919); "Weltanschauung und Technik," *Technik Voran* 5 (1925), p. 1. *Bedeutung und Aufgabe der Technik beim Wiederaufbau des deutschen Reiches* (1926) was published as a pamphlet by the *Reichsbund deutscher Technik*, a journal begun in 1918 to promote the interests of engineers through politics.

[58] Dessauer, *Bedeutung und Aufgabe der Technik*, pp. 8–9.

[59] Ibid., pp. 3, 15.

suffers as a result of the predominance of the capitalist over the entrepreneur.

Technology suffered as well. Technology had an "essence," a life of its own that demonstrated "the fulfillment of natural laws."[60] Its philosophy emphasized satisfaction of human needs through "creation of created forms." Technology was inherently linked to the idea of service rather than profit. Dessauer personally took such notions toward the political Center and advocated national economic planning and class compromise in a manner not unlike that of Walter Rathenau. But his idea of service also nourished the previously mentioned anticapitalism of the engineers. For once a reified essence was attributed to technology, anticapitalist rhetoric among the engineers served to defend an essentially feudal social conception of service versus profit. Several historians of engineers and of the German economy have noted that this variant of anticapitalist rhetoric accompanied and may be understood as a reaction to the nature of engineering as a profession born with the modern large corporation. But the engineers did not see themselves as members of a new working class being proletarianized by capitalism. Rather, their self-conception was that of the new middle class, a white-collar group threatened by a vaguer and all-pervasive "economy" and "world of finance." Dessauer left Germany after 1933, but his philosophy of technology surrounded technology with an aura of precapitalist craftsmanship and shifted anticapitalist sentiment into directions in which verbal radicalism was not matched by any real threat to actual property and class relations.

Carl Weihe edited *Technik und Kultur* from 1921 to 1934 and in this capacity played an important role in influencing the political consciousness of the university-trained engineering elite. He endeavored to make the writings of the philosophers and cultural critics accessible to engineers, as well as to foster an autonomous "cultural mission" among his contributors and readers. He not only advocated his own views of the relation between technology and culture, but also self-consciously pointed to the existence of a *tradition* of writing on technology by engineers that countered the antitechnological mood of the humanists. He made abundant use of Nietzsche and Schopenhauer in seeking to establish the harmony of technology with German philosophy and cultural criticism. And having legitimated technics in the court of *Kultur*, he turned to the internal traditions of the German

---

[60] Dessauer, *Die Philosophie der Technik* (Bonn, 1928), pp. 4, 6.

engineers, to Schroter, Dessauer, Kapp, Zschimmer, and others, to give his readership a sense of its own, self-created consciousness.[61]

Earlier, I referred to the embattled quality of the engineers' cultural politics, and this defensive and aggressive tone is apparent in Weihe's criticisms of Spengler. Weihe was not impressed with Spenglerian efforts at reconciliation with technology. What concerned him more was that Spengler's cultural pessimism would foster hostility to technology. He repeatedly rejected Spengler's reference to the "devilish" character of technology and instead stressed the "creative power,...godly spirit and holy causality" that emanated from human beings and that were evident in technical creations. Typically he lashed out at "thinkers and poets" – like Spengler – who knew nothing about technology or its *Geist*, yet felt free to hold it accountable for the irresponsible acts of private economic interests. It was not technology that had created class struggle but rather the nontechnical "outsiders" who had transformed "the machine into a money-making machine, and industry into a stock exchange."[62] It did not seem to bother Weihe that Spengler himself had made exactly the same point.

According to Weihe, Spengler had gone astray in positing a mistaken version of the *Kultur–Zivilisation* dichotomy in which the *Kultur* included "*Geist*, feeling, science, art and religion," and *Zivilisation* encompassed physical artifacts.[63] Presented in this form, the dichotomy belied a lack of appreciation for the synthesis of *Geist* and matter present in human labor. Weihe admitted that postwar German society was suffering from an imbalance between the "labor of the mind, of the soul and of the economy," but he rejected Spengler's "dark prophecies of the twilight of the gods."[64] In fact, Spengler's pessimism probably had the opposite effect of that intended by its author because it forced engineers to figure out how technology could be placed in the

[61] See, for example, Carl Weihe, "Die kulturellen Aufgabe des Ingenieurs," *Technik und Kultur* 15 (1924), p. 45; "Die Technik als Kulturproblem," *Technik und Kultur* 20 (1929), pp. 220–2; "Zur Philosophie der Technik," *Technik und Kultur* 24 (1933), pp. 103–9; "Kultur," I, II, *Technik und Kultur* 25 (2 and 4, 1934), pp. 17–20, 57–113; "Arthur Schopenhauer zum Gedachtnis," *Technik und Kultur* 26 (1935), pp. 165–7. After 1933, Weihe urged engineers to "take a correct position concerning our *Volksgemeinschaft*." Schopenhauer was the decisive philosophical influence on Weihe. On this see "Verwandtschaftliches in der Denkweise des Ingenieurs und Arthur Schopenhauers" (Affinities between the Way of Thinking of Engineers and Arthur Schopenhauer), *Technik und Kultur* 2 (1911), pp. 573–7; and "Anschauliches und begriffliches Denken" (Visualizing and Conceptual Thinking), *Technik und Kultur* 3 (1912), pp. 322–5.
[62] Carl Weihe, "Spengler und die Maschine," *Technik und Kultur* 18 (1927), pp. 37–8.
[63] Weihe, "Kultur, I," p. 18.
[64] Weihe, "Kultur, II," pp. 58, 60.

cultural sphere and thus exempted from the anticivilizational mood of the humanistic cultural critics.[65]

In 1935, Weihe published *Kultur und Technik* (Culture and Technology), a work that summarized his own monthly contributions to the journal *Technik und Kultur*. The bibliography alone was noteworthy, containing as it did over 100 books and essays dealing with the theme of technology and culture written in Germany from 1859 to 1935. Seventy of these had appeared since 1919.[66] Not surprisingly, the book's main point was that technology, that is, what man "makes out of nature with his own devices,...is culture in the broadest and oldest sense of the word."[67] This truth had been championed by Renaissance thinkers such as Leonardo da Vinci yet denied by the idealist and romantic traditions in nineteenth-century Germany. Both had mistakenly restricted culture to the life of the mind and thus fostered antipathy to technology. Marxism and liberalism also widened the *Kulture–Zivilisation* gap because they succumbed to the positivistic spirit of the age and thus failed to grasp technology's cultural contribution.

Weihe then presented a schema of the relation between technology and cultural crises that recalled Schroter's schemes: A harmonious true culture presupposed a balance between "three great major areas,...labor of the mind (*Geistesarbeit*), of the soul (*Seelenarbeit*), and of the economy (*Wirtschaftsarbeit*)." Each of the three forms of labor includes aspects of the others. Intellectual labor includes the natural sciences as well as politics and philosophy; labor of the soul encompasses religion, ethics, and art; labor of the economy includes manual labor, technology, industry, and transportation as well as "landscaping, cattle breeding," and other forms of agriculture.[68] Technology and labor demand a fusion of "spirit and soul" (*Geist und Seele*) that cannot come about if one of the three aspects of labor predominates at the expense of the others. In the chart on page 174 Weihe presents an image of cultural harmony and balance in which the three spheres of mind, soul, and economy are in equilibrium.[69]

---

[65] Carl Weihe, "Oswald Spengler," *Technik und Kultur* 27 (1936), p. 80.
[66] Carl Weihe, *Kultur und Technik* (Frankfurt, 1935), pp. 135–7.
[67] Ibid., p.8.
[68] Ibid., pp. 14–15.
[69] Viewed sociologically, this chart depicts a crisis of rationalization, what Bell has recently called the "disjunction of realms" between culture focused on the self and the social structure rooted in functional rationality and efficiency. See *The Cultural Contradictions of Capitalism* (New York, 1976), pp. 3–33; and *The Coming Post-Industrial Society*, pp. 477–80. As Lowy argued in his work on Lukács the resolution of this cultural crisis could lead to the political Left, Right, or Center. See *Pour une Sociologie des Intellectuelles Revolutionnaires* (Paris, 1976); and Jürgen Habermas, *Legitimation*

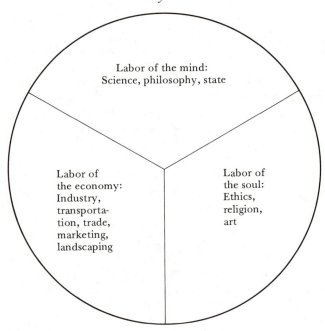

If one sphere predominates over the others, disequilibrium results. For example, Buddhism was a condition in which the soul inclined to world weariness and pastoral escapism won out. At the other extreme, *Amerikanismus* was the result of the domination of the economy over *Geist* and *Seele*. In Europe, it was Marxism and liberalism that had encouraged an "immeasurable overestimation of the intellect." One of the great strengths of National Socialism was that it had created a "spiritual renewal in Germany that awakened understanding for the balance of cultural factors."[70] For Weihe, nazism was a resolution

Crisis (Boston, 1975). Although this kind of cultural crisis is endemic in industrial society, it took particularly intense forms in Germany. On this see Richard Lowenthal, *Gesellschaftswandel und Kulturkrise* (Frankfurt, 1979).

[70] Weihe, *Kultur und Technik*, pp. 20–1. Also see Fritz Schumacher, *Schöpferwille und Mechanisierung* (Creative Will and Mechanization) (Hamburg, 1933). Schumacher took issue with Ludwig Klages's attack on the "soullessness" of technology. "Where, within the mechanizing forces of technology, is there room for an infusion of soul filled with emotion [*gefühlsmässige Beseelung*]? Where, in Klages's words, is there still room for the soul [*Seele*] next to the spirit [*Geist*]? Where is there still space for the creative will alongside mechanization?" (p. 11). Schumacher believed that technology need not be the antagonist of the soul if *Geist* and *Gefühl* (feeling) could be joined. Such a pairing would produce an "infusion of soul" (*Beseelung*) rather than "loss of soul" (*Entseelung*); pp. 16–17. Although Schumacher rejected the "luxury" of "escape

to a cultural crisis brought about by a predominance of the labor of the mind and economy over the labor of the soul that advocated neither Buddhism, *Amerikanismus*, nor European variants of positivism.

All over Europe, the intellectuals drawn to fascism were heirs to and exponents of a tradition of antiintellectualism. The German engineers were no exception. The intimate relationship between modern technology and natural science – especially evident in Germany's electrical and chemical industries – did not stop Weihe and others from expressing open hostility to conceptual thought. It was wrong, he wrote, to claim that technology had been the product of abstract reason. On the contrary, it was the "infusion of spirit into labor power" (*Vergeistung der Arbeitskraft*), and a symbol of the Social Darwinist struggle for existence.[71] Weihe added a Schopenhauerian twist to reactionary modernist rhetoric when he distinguished between "visualizing" and "conceptual" thought. Schopenhauer's thought was "closer than any other" philosopher to that of engineers. His "world-affirming will and high evaluation of visualizing thinking" (*anschauliches Denken*) stood in starkest contrast to conceptualization. It had a close affinity to the world view of engineers, freed as it was from Kant's, and Hegel's "conceptual overrefinement" (*Begriffskünstelei*). Technological advance required an inclination toward fantasy and imagination rather than abstraction.[72]

Weihe expounded on Schopenhauer's importance in his monthly columns in *Technik und Kultur*. Both technology and nature were grounded in the same "final cause," that is, the will.[73] External objects are objectifications of this will, which he described as "blind,...restless,...a never-satisfied insatiable striving." Human beings were merely the instruments through which this will realized its goals. The engineer and the artist were thus "driven and pushed" by an "urge to create" (*Schöpferdrang*) and an "instinct for forming technical objects" (*Trieb zur technischen Gestaltung*). Both the artist and engineer were striving to transform fantasy in tangible, perceptible forms. Both suffered from the commercial world that cared little for their permanent creations and understood less of the "metaphysical foundations of the cultural value of technology."[74]

from technology," he offered no concrete proposals as to how *Geist* and *Gefühl* could be reunited.
[71] Weihe, *Technik und Kultur*, p. 28.
[72] Weihe, "Arthur Schopenhauer zum Gedachtnis," p. 165. Weihe rejected Schopenhauer's pessimism and resignation.
[73] Weihe, *Kultur und Technik*, pp. 67, 76–8.
[74] Ibid., pp. 52–3, 57, 60. The quasi-religious dimensions of the apotheosis of the suprahistorical force animating technology – will, history, nature – are apparent in

Weihe's incorporation of Schopenhauer is a good example of the way the ambiguous legacies of German thought were selectively interpreted to lend support to nazism. In *Kultur and Technik*, he wrote that visual thinking reproduces the external world. It "shows nothing that is not already there or that could not be there." It captures the individual subject in all of its particularity. On the other hand, conceptual thought replaces a sensuous reality with a "formula, a symbol, a so-called concept," the particular and individual object with an "abstract world of concepts that make us alien to the world." Conceptual thinking is the province of the philosopher, theologian, linguist, and jurist. Visualizing and imaginative thought characterizes the doctor, natural scientist, military strategist, painter, and engineer. It is the "foundation of technical labor. Even the simplest technical work demands visual conception of the form (*Gestalt*) of the object to be constructed." The intellectual labor that creates technology, Weihe wrote, "comes almost exclusively from visualizing and imaginative thought."[75] Weihe's arguments went beyond the assertion that engineering involved visualizing as well as conceptualizing kinds of thinking, to the more radical claim that action and aesthetics ought to be completely separated from conceptual work. Statements such as the following make clear that his melange of antiintellectualism, technical boosterism, and Nazi sympathy was more than the practical impatience with theorists one might expect from practically minded engineers. In its philosophical language and thoroughness, there is something of the German *Gründlichkeit* or thoroughness that many observers have seen as one of National Socialism's distinctive features.

Men who come from the *primal* soil of the country, and not from the *writing desk* and bookcase, have leaped into action against the *expanding world of concepts* in one stroke. This world, with its increasingly invisible net, threatens

these passages. The philosopher and cultural critic, Edgar Dacque, offered another example of this reification of technology in *Natur und Erlösung* (Nature and Redemption) (Munich, 1933): "Our knowledge, whether it be mechanistic or magical, perceives and yearns for the eternal idea in things. Even pure technology, such as the construction of a machine, signifies a glimpse into and a realization of the idea of eternity, when we see this technical activity as the physical realization of a primal image through the medium of our own spirit. When we stand in awe and perhaps also in terror of a functioning machine what is it we are seeing other than a true homage to the ideational meaning of iron, that, so to speak, receives life from our spirit and shows us its inner countenance in symbols. It is 'art' in the highest and noblest sense that we see before us. We admire the spirit and powerful manliness that inventors and builders have here represented from within their beings" (p. 53). See Max Horkheimer, "Zum Rationalismusstreit in der gegenwärtigen Philosophie," in *Kristische Theorie der Gesellschaft*, Band I (Frankfurt, 1968), pp. 118–74.
75 Weihe, *Kultur und Technik*, pp. 80, 83.

to completely wrap us and paralyze *healthy* human reason. Man is on the path of *total self-transformation*. The *deed will once again be placed ahead of the work, the fist before the tongue, the vision before the concept,* ... The era of negotiations and compromise, of parliamentary activity and bargaining, is past [emphasis added].[76]

Hitler has emerged from the German people to speak with an "overflowing heart" rather than "clever reasoning." The "flood that was born from conceptual-abstract thought" is giving way to the understanding of "the realities of life," realities that can be understood only with "visualizing-imaginative thought." Engineers and their modern technical products have a duty to "become active in enlightening, lending assistance and serving as examples."[77] The now familiar paradoxes of reactionary modernism are evident in Weihe's celebration of Hitler's rise to power. On the one hand are the praises of *Blut und Boden*, action, deeds, feelings, and visions, and on the other are concepts, parliaments, conceptual-abstract thought. And technology and the engineers belong with the first group evoking all that is old, national, and familiar. The visualizing-imaginative thinker and the artistic engineer were not by definition Nazis. But the notions of such figures did facilitate an embrace of modern technology that did not simultaneously entail the view of human reason we can commonly assume to be linked to it. In a situation of political, economic, and cultural crisis, reactionary modernism as a cultural system made a kind of sense of a bewildering situation. And it did so in a way German engineers could understand.

An important dimension of the peculiarly German qualities of reactionary modernism was a search for a distinctive "philosophy of technology." Although Weihe focused on Schopenhauer, others teaching at the technical universities believed that technology and German idealism were compatible with one another. Eberhard Zschimmer, from Munich's technical university, made an argument along these lines in his 1920 work, *Technik und Idealismus*.[78] Zschimmer added his voice to those bemoaning a modern cultural crisis, the roots of which lay in the historically unprecedented domination of the economy over cultural life – not in technology. "Never," he wrote, had the economy and culture been so much at odds as in the present. The economy raped nature of its beauty, destroyed the people's feeling for culture, undermined national unity, reduced cultural creation to commodity

[76] Ibid., pp. 65–6.
[77] Ibid.
[78] Eberhard Zschimmer, *Technik und Idealismus* (Jena, 1920).

production. "Economic life becomes an end in itself. *Geist* dies."[79]
Along with Schroter, Weihe, and Dessauer, Zschimmer claimed that
the humanist intellectuals had been mistaken in blaming technology
for the sins of the economy. The core of technological activity was
invention, and that, he claimed, was completely unrelated to profit
seeking. On the contrary, its roots were philosophical, namely, the
"freedom to create and form." The "meaning of all technics" was
spiritual freedom. "Technical creation is unconditionally and completely spiritual (*geistiges*) creation." Far from threatening the tradition
of German idealism, technology confirmed one of its basic maxims:
"Spirit is stronger than matter." The engineer's task was to create
permanent and lasting forms that would stand in sharp contrast to
the ephemeral and changing forms thrown up by the market. Zschimmer insisted that such a task was a consummation, rather than a denial,
of German idealism.[80]

Viktor Engelhardt, also a contributor to *Technik und Kultur* and a
professor of engineering, published *Weltanschauung und Technik* (World
View and Technology) in 1922. Engelhardt urged that technology be
separated from any association with materialism, positivism, and even
from the *Geist* of the natural sciences. The latter were the true heirs
of modern conceptual thought and abstraction and were thus removed from the "creative personality" and irrational roots of technology.[81] Engelhardt's attack on modern physics indicated that there
were limits to the reconciliations the reactionary modernists were willing to make with modernity. These limits surfaced in a most specta-
tular fashion in the Nazis' fain efforts to establish an Aryan physics.[82]

The authors just discussed published primarily for other engineers.
There were other engineers who went beyond the tradition internal
to the engineers and tried to bridge the worlds of the conservative
revolutionary literati and their own increasingly politicized and desperate professional colleagues. These personal and intellectual links
added to the internal traditions an external pull toward existing right-

[79] Ibid., pp. 7, 8, 9.
[80] Ibid., pp. 23, 28, 31. Hitler's desire for architectural monuments that would last a
thousand years was one practical result of Zschimmer's plea for the elevation of spirit
over matter and over the constant shifts of the market. On the link between anticapitalist rhetoric and large construction projects in Nazi Germany, see George Mosse,
Nazi Culture (New York, 1966), and *Nationalization of the Masses* (New York, 1970),
esp. pp. 47–72; Robert Taylor, *The Word in Stone: The Architecture of National Socialism*
(Berkeley, 1974); Albert Speer, *Inside the Third Reich* (New York, 1970); and the
discussion of Fritz Todt's views on the *Autobahnen* in the following chapter.
[81] Viktor Engelhardt, *Weltanschauung und Technik* (Leipzig, 1922), pp. 50, 64.
[82] On Aryan physics see Alan D. Beyerchen, *Scientists under Hitler: Politics and the Physics
Community under Hitler* (New Haven, Conn., 1977).

wing political groups and ideas. *Die Tat*, the major journal of right-wing radicalism of the middle classes in Weimar, was the institutional bridge between the conservative revolution and the engineers. Among engineers, Heinrich Hardensett and Marvin Holzer were the most prolific contributors. In 1932 both published books on technology, politics, and culture that summarized the reconciliations between irrationalism and technics made by both the humanist and technical intellectuals of the Weimar Right. After the Nazi seizure of power, both urged their fellow engineers to rally around the new regime.[83]

Die Tat advocated extreme nationalism, denounced Marxism, liberalism, and Weimar parliamentarism, and longed for a strong state to restore the primacy of politics over the economy. The journal had ties to Werner Sombart and popularized his analysis of capitalism and advocacy of German socialism, an idea that its editor, Ferdinand Fried, defined as the revolt of "inner feeling...and blood" against the "abstraction of money."[84] Fried worried that the rationalization of the German economy in the mid-1920s might undermine the spirit of innovation and invention needed for technological progress. What was needed was a spiritual renewal of the nation in which anti-Western and anticapitalist rhetoric would complement expanded state intervention in the economy. According to the circle around *Die Tat*, *Primat der Politik* (the primacy of politics) would revive the now exhausted *Geist der Technik*. In an article entitled "The Tragedy of the German Economy," Holzer bitterly denounced the economic system as being "without essence, idealism or heart."[85] He also attacked the rationalization movement in German industry for having caused growing unemployment. But he rejected antitechnological views and argued instead that technics could be elevated from their present "mechanistic nature" to the level of a "new organism" if the principle of the general welfare were to replace unbridled self-interest in German politics. If such a shift were to take place, "freedom from labor" rather than unemployment would be the consequence of technical advance.[86]

---

[83] On the conservative revolution, the *Tatkreis* and the engineers see Ludwig, *Technik und Ingenieure*, esp. pp. 58–72.
[84] Ferdinand Fried, "Die Auflösung," *Die Tat* 23 (1931/32), cited by Hock in *Deutscher Antikapitalismus* (Frankfurt, 1960), p. 29. Hock's work offers an overview of the economic perspectives of the *Tatkreis*. Also see Fried's *Das Ende des Kapitalismus* (Jena, 1931), and *Autarkie* (Jena, 1932). Fried joined the SS in 1934 in the *Rasse und Siedlungsamt* (Race and Settlement Office). On this see Armin Mohler, *Die konservative Revolution in Deutschland, 1918–1932*, 2d ed. (Darmstadt, 1972), p. 435.
[85] Martin Holzer, "Die Tragodie der deutschen Wirtschaft," *Die Tat* 24 (May 1932/33), pp. 155–66. Martin Holzer was a pen name for Joseph Bader.
[86] Ibid., p. 162.

Holzer expanded on these ideas in a book called *Technik und Kapitalismus*, also published in 1932. He wrote that the connection between technology, on the one hand, and philosophical materialism and capitalist economic organization, on the other, was due merely to a temporal coincidence of nineteenth-century European history rather than to an intrinsic and necessary interdependence.[87] He thought that a "natural rather than mechanistic" technology freed from "capitalist instinct and thing-production fanaticism" (*Sacherzeugungs-fanatismus*) was both desirable and possible. Neither liberalism nor Marxism could bring about such a technology since both were enmeshed in a materialist world view. As for the Nazis, Holzer was less clear, assenting to some of their "individual points" – their nationalism, celebration of the general welfare, anticapitalist rhetoric, promise to restore German military power – while reserving judgment concerning their view of the relationship between technology and capitalism.[88]

Holzer's "natural technology" brought with it an intense nationalism. The rationalization movement was the result of "international technology" and the "Anglo-American spiritual world," which German engineers had uncritically accepted in the wake of the loss of the war. Now German technology was being ruined with "Americanisms,... restless objectification, neutralization, and technicism."[89] Had the war not been lost and had Germans not lost faith in their own traditions, German *Geist* would not have acceded to foreign technocratic views. In 1932, German nationalists faced the danger that in reaction to the previous decade's uncritical absorption of *Amerikanismus*, Germans, especially German youth, would become outwardly hostile to the very technological implements needed to rebuild the power of the German military. Holzer recalled the "human experience" of a sacrificing, national community during World War I as the model of an industrial society that had not succumbed to materialism and civic privatism.[90] Capitalism or technicism meant the United States or Great Britain. As did all of the reactionary modernists, Holzer redirected anticapitalist sentiment away from pastoralism and toward appeals for a "national technology," and he suggested that there was a natural affinity between the authoritarian state and the inherent properties and "autonomous lawfulness" (*Eigensetzlichkeit*) he imputed to technology.[91] Shortly after the Nazi seizure of power, Holzer re-

---

[87] Martin Holzer, *Technik und Kapitalismus* (Jena, 1932), pp. 38–44.
[88] Ibid., pp. 10, 19–20.
[89] Ibid., pp. 65–6.
[90] Ibid., p. 69.
[91] Ibid., p. 73.

solved his doubts about nazism, welcomed the renewed primacy of politics, and urged his fellow engineers to integrate their own creative efforts into the "national revolution."[92]

One of the most prolific and interesting of all the engineers to write on technology and culture was Heinrich Hardensett. From 1925, when his first essay appeared in *Technik und Kultur*, to 1934, when he contributed an essay to a collection published by the Nazis, Hardensett produced a truly remarkable series of essays that combined social theory, right-wing politics, and defense of technology. Like Holzer, he could write for the literati and the engineers. But the subtlety and ingenuity of his writings set him apart. He expressed reactionary modernist themes with remarkable clarity and style. "On the Relationship of Industrial Technology to the Visual Arts," his first essay in *Technik und Kultur*, compared the work of engineers to that of artists and architects. It fulfilled the "great longing of our time for community and form" (*die grossen Sehnsucht unserer Zeit nach Gemeinshaft und Gestalt*).[93] The rationalization movement was encroaching in "grotesque ways on the worker's soul," but the engineer's aesthetic sensibility was manifested in the beautiful and clear forms of bridges, roads, and factories. Now engineers were beginning to understand that their labors were not means to something else, but were themselves filled with cultural value and aesthetic form. Germans were unfortunately accustomed to seeing things with the eyes of "antiquity, the gothic, and the baroque" and hence often accused modern engineering and architecture of impersonality. Hardensett insisted that "pathos" existed in modern functionalism and matter-of-factness (*Sachlichkeit*), as well as in religion and humanistic cultivation of the individual. *Sachlichkeit* did not demand materialism but metaphysical, religious, and aesthetic virtues. It was the "opposite of specialization" and must be differentiated from the "positivistic domination of nature." Hardensett even praised Peter Behrens *Werkbund*, Gropius's Bauhaus, and the expressionists for having made clear that "only in technology does the chaos of our artistic striving find an end point" in forward-, not backward-looking styles.[94]

[92] Martin Holzer, "Freiheit des technischen Fortschritt oder Bindung an die Gemeinwesen" (Freedom of technical progress or connection to the common essence), *Technik Voran* (June 20, 1933), pp. 179–80.
[93] Heinrich Hardensett, "Über das Verhältnis von industrieller Technik zur bildenden Kunst," *Technik und Kultur* 16 (1925), pp. 10–13. This great longing was not a monopoly of the irrationalist Right. On the Bauhaus and its suppression by the Nazis, see Barbara Miller Lane, *Architecture and Politics in Germany, 1918–1945* (Cambridge, Mass., 1968).
[94] Hardensett, "Über das Verhältnis...," pp. 11–13.

One of the things that made Hardensett's work stand out was his knowledge of German sociology, in particular Max Weber and Sombart. For example, in a 1926 essay in *Technik und Kultur*, "Magische Technik" (Magical Technology), he argued that technological advance did not lead to a disenchantment of the world but to a revived understanding of the relation between reason and magic.[95] Technology had a deep religious impulse that persisted despite numerous efforts, beginning with Galileo, to eliminate animism and magic from technics. An irreducible "unmagical magic" remained, evidence of the inseparability of religion and technology.[96] Such essays suggest that Hardensett was intent on placing technology in the context of the dynamic of rationalization and capitalist development that had been a main theme of German social theory. In his 1932 work, *Der kapitalistische und der technische Mensch* (The Capitalistic and the Technical Man), Hardensett did just that, offering one of the clearest and most sophisticated statements to emerge from either the conservative revolutionaries or the engineers' internal traditions. More than any other work of the reactionary modernist tradition, *Der kapitalistische und der technische Mensch* drew effectively from both engineers and literati. Hardensett repeated and refined arguments from Dessauer, Diesel, Schroter, Weihe, and Zschimmer, as well as from such notables of German social science and philosophy as Hans Freyer, Friedrich Gottl-Ottlilienfeld, Max Scheler, Othmar Spann, Sombart, and Weber. The book juxtaposes the capitalist and the technical man as ideal types. In so doing, Hardensett claimed to represent the "standpoint of the engineer" against that of the capitalist who fostered penetration of capitalist exchange relations into the realm of technological production.[97]

Hardensett's capitalist man was an ideal type structured along the lines suggested by Sombart's analysis of capitalism. Capitalist man resided in the sphere of circulation, not production. As an economic actor, he did not view others as fellow men, citizens, community members, or "comrades in production," but as "aliens" beyond "all human bonds." It is hardly surprising that it was the Jews and other transient groups who served as excellent carriers of the capitalist spirit. Capitalist man instrumentalized and depersonalized economic activity and

[95] Heinrich Hardensett, "Magische Technik," *Technik und Kultur* 17 (1926), pp. 173–5.
[96] Ibid., p. 173. Hardensett pursued similar themes in two essays on the poetry of aviation: "Die Flugtechnik in der Dichtung, I and II," in *Technik und Kultur* 19 (5, 6, 1928), pp. 74–7, 89–93.
[97] Heinrich Hardensett, *Der kapitalistische und der technische Mensch* (Munich, 1932), p. 5.

"struggles against all bonds of feeling, blood and spirit."[98] He subjected production to circulation, thereby sacrificing the quality of goods and their "creative formation" to the quantitative considerations of profit maximization. He is a "finance man" at home in a "world of numbers,. . .a colorless, abstract world, an artificial world, a world of money." His pursuit of profit is "one-sided, monomaniacal to the point of pathology."[99]

Hardensett then turned to the impact of capitalist man on technology. It was catastrophic. The rationalization movement of the 1920s, Taylorism, and time and motion studies were indicative of a "soulless demonism of labor" that eliminated from the workplace all "comradely playful transcendence, all joyful, plastic sensuality." Capitalist man was repeatedly robbing "great technical deeds" of their "humanitarian, liberating, buoyant or cheerful content," because the beauties of production remained "incomprehensible to the mentality of exchange."[100] The capitalist's mentality is typically "mechanistic, positivistic, but not that of the machine," because it is wholly lacking in any appreciation for the active "teleology" of the will infusing technology. In short, because capitalist man is oriented to "commodity production" (*Warenerzeugung*) and exchange, he is unable to grasp technology's activistic metaphysic.[101]

Hardensett's ideal-typical technical man was no less an amalgam of factual and evaluative statements than his ideal-typical capitalist. Unlike the capitalist oriented to commodity production, technical man focused on "object production" (*Sacherzeugung*), something that has an inherent "service value" (*Dienstwert*).[102] In fact, the distinction between production of commodities and production of objects constituted the essential difference between the capitalist and the technical economy. Technical man was imbued with the "ethic of the master builder" and thus stressed the creation of objective works on the basis of noneconomic, purely aesthetic considerations.[103] Capitalist man created a world of ephemeral, abstract values, whereas technical man sought to create permanent, concrete objects that are "cosmic, eternal and godly."[104] He strives to "transcend time and space through creation of form. . .and to transform variable incompleteness into eternal

[98] Ibid., p. 25.
[99] Ibid., pp. 29, 34, 51. Hardensett's view of capitalism drew heavily on Sombart's *Das Wirtschaftsleben im Zeitalter des Hochkapitalismus* (Munich, 1927).
[100] Hardensett, *Der Kapitalistische und der technische Mensch*, pp. 30–1, 33.
[101] Ibid., p. 40.
[102] Ibid., pp. 65–6.
[103] Ibid., pp. 67, 81.
[104] Ibid., p. 128.

duration." Instead of the ceaseless striving of the market, the technical man desires "the utopian redemption of eternal, completed permanence, and the eternal present instead of the infinite future. He is a classicist and not a romantic, a man of measures and laws."[105] Capitalist circulation produces chaos and anarchy; the engineers produce enduring order in the classic forms of streets, bridges, canals, and dams. Their sheer solidity and endurance are evidence of an implicitly anticapitalist nature. Like all of the reactionary modernists, Hardensett attributed an autonomous will to technology. A turbine, for example, combined the "lawfulness of spirit and the timeless functional relationships of nature" with the "circles of immaterial cosmic energy and steel's inner order of tension."[106]

Hardensett's methodology was radically subjectivist. Social practices, institutions, and relationships were the outcome of particular kinds of individuals. He identified the merchant with the circulation sphere, whereas the master builder was at home in production. The former was driven by crass self-interest, the latter by "joy in creation."[107] Unlike Sombart, Hardensett did not explicitly distinguish German productivity from Jewish parasitism. But this methodological approach did not preclude such a translation of social categories into racial stereotypes.

What Hardensett's book again made clear was that the surface archaism of this ideological tradition coexisted with a fundamental reconciliation with modern technology. His work is filled with references to communities and comrades of production and creation. *Produktionskameraden* and *Leistungsgemeinschaft* are terms that associate feudal and preindustrial terminology with modern industrial production.[108] The community, a powerful will, clear form, dazzling experience, beautiful creation – all of these things exist now in the labor of engineers. The "fundamental principle of technical production" is communal labor, not self–interest; its "decisive locus" is the workshop, not the market; its "decisive value" is "service value, not exchange value"; and it forms communities based on performance, not self-interest.[109]

---

[105] Ibid.
[106] Ibid., p. 102. Like the nineteenth-century romantics, Hardensett spoke of a "tragedy of completion" (*Vollendung*) and of powerful forces working beneath the surface of reality. But his image of the end of the romantic journey was far less complex. On this see M. H. Abrams, *Natural Supernaturalism* (New York, 1973), esp. his discussion of the "romantic spiral" in Goethe, Hegel, Hölderlin, Novalis, and Schlegel, pp. 197–252.
[107] Hardensett, *Der kapitalistische und der technische Mensch*, p. 94.
[108] Ibid., pp. 95–7.
[109] Ibid., pp. 116–17.

This was anticapitalism, but a German anticapitalism, and an anti-capitalism of the Right. The appeal to community was made by the Left as well. Reactionary modernists such as Hardensett were no less sincere in their revulsion at the market than were the cultural radicals of the Left. But the effect, if not also the intention, of their writing, was to stabilize rather than challenge existing class relationships. German engineers may have protested against commercial perversions of their efforts but they never suggested expropriating the expropriators.

In 1933, Hardensett published an essay on technical ethics in the United States and the Soviet Union, which presented the familiar juxtaposition of Europe and the East and West.[110] As Diesel and Schroter, among the engineers, and Heidegger, among the philosophers, had done, Hardensett disparaged the United States as a country made for the capitalist and merchant, not the engineer. American pragmatism saw in technology nothing more than a means to some other end. The Soviets were no better. They idealized some of the worst aspects of American capitalism (Taylorism, for example), established an officially sponsored materialism, and, like the Americans, lacked appreciation for the deeper cultural meanings of technology. Europe was the real home of the ethos of the master builder, which was unable to root in American or Russian soil. Europe, especially Germany, was the place to combine *Geist* and *Technik*.[111]

Whether Hardensett set out to defend capitalism is a secondary matter. What is important is that here is another example of a set of ideas and images that, as we will soon see, were politically effective because they drew on important themes in German cultural traditions. With an obsessive repetitiveness, engineers such as Hardensett asserted that technology was German, spiritual, cosmic, complete, whole, permanent, formed, and orderly, and as such had about it something pre- and/or noncapitalistic. It had escaped from and was an alternative to the exchange society and cosmopolitanism. Technology and technical man were the natural forces. They stood for irrational and instinctual forces that fought the good fight against the "unhealthy, nonsensuous life form" of modern capitalism. We return to Mann's insights in *Doctor Faustus*. To say that nazism was a logical fulfillment of German culture makes no more sense than to say it was a complete

[110] Heinrich Hardensett, "Technische Gesittung in USA und USSR," *Blätter für deutsche Philosophie* 7 (16, 1933/34), pp. 479–503.
[111] Ibid., pp. 482, 495–6. For another elaboration of this Heideggerian theme, see Enno Heidebroek, *Das Weltbild der Naturwissenschaften* (The World View of the Natural Sciences) (Stuttgart, 1931).

betrayal of it. To understand why nazism took place in Germany, it is necessary to see how some of the most creative elements of German culture made this possible – how, in Mann's words, the cunning of the devil could turn what was best in German culture into what was worst. Hardensett's advocacy of engineering and technology is indicative of this larger process through which nazism built on and transformed Germany's traditions. In combining nationalism and socialism, the Nazis claimed goals compatible with those the engineers had been advocating for half a century.

The merger of nazism and the indigenous traditions of the engineers was evident in an essay collection published in 1934 by the *Verein Deutscher Ingenieure* called *Die Sendung des Ingenieure im neuen Staat* (The Mission of the Engineers in the New State). The essays present a mixture of self-interest and ideological commitment, as well as a belief that the Nazis had abandoned the antiindustrial themes of *völkisch* thought. As the editor of the collection, Rudolf Heiss, put it, Hitler's goals of rearmament and full employment required that "technics be placed in the service of the totality of our *Volk*."[112] Hence practical politics and ideological traditions could reinforce one another.

Heinrich Hardensett contributed an essay on "technical-creative individuals," in which he repeated the arguments of *Der Kapitalistische und der technische Mensch*.[113] The main difference was that here Hardensett claimed that the National Socialist "revolution" had consigned the "liberal-capitalist era" to the past. In differentiating the engineer from the capitalist, he referred to "creative" (*schaffende*) versus "parasitic" (*raffende*) capital, the terms Gottfried Feder had popularized. In Hardensett's view, the "new state" possessed the "technical idealism" that German engineers had been seeking for the previous half-century.[114]

Heiss offered another example of the confluence of the engineers and the Nazis. His first contribution was an affirmative answer to the question, Will National Socialism Solve the Cultural Crisis of Technology?[115] He claimed that the "spirit of the front soldier" (*Frontkämpfergeist*) was intrinsic to technology and that this spirit could not be held accountable "for the sins of capitalist man." In place of pessimism, National Socialism offered a way of embracing modern tech-

[112] *Die Sendung des Ingenieure im neuen Staat*, ed. Rudolf Heiss (Berlin, 1934), p. 152.
[113] Heinrich Hardensett, "Vom technischen-schöpferischen Menschen," in *Die Sendung des Ingenieure*, pp. 12–18.
[114] Ibid., p. 18.
[115] Rudolf Heiss, "Wird der Nationalsozialismus die technische Kulturkrise lösen?" in *Die Sendung des Ingenieure*, pp. 1–11.

nology while rejecting materialism at the same time. He referred to Hardensett's ideal-typical "technical-creative individual" and argued that the Nazis were coming to his aid in his battle with capitalist man. National Socialism, he continued, would not only end "hopelessness" over finding a solution to the cultural crisis of technology. It would also make engineers the "officer corps" in the battle to place technics in the service of the whole nation and thereby give them the positions of responsibility and power they had yearned for since the beginning of German industrialization.[116]

In a second essay, "Volk und gestaltende Arbeit" (The People and Forming Labor), Heiss stressed the relation between technical form and the health of the nation. The forming of matter was a "measure of health" that released "powers of the soul." One of the greatest attributes of the Germans was their "ability to form, to master matter through the power of spirit." In the new regime, "the people and technology... and the makers of forms" have become one.[117] No longer need engineers suffer from a feeling that their work was alien to the nation. On the contrary, they were among "the millions who are called to battle against the misuse of our creations." Now engineers must give up their past indifference to politics and "revolt and place the power of *Geist* over the power of gold." For the central ideal of National Socialism, the primacy of the common interest over self-interest, was inherent in technology as well.[118] Hitler's seizure of power was a sign that at last the "hour of freedom for the technical-creative individual" had arrived.[119] The Nazi regime posed no threat to engineers. On the contrary, it was the agency of deliverance from years of political powerlessness and low social status in comparison to the other middle-class professions. The ascendancy of the creative individual over the calculating capitalist was also a time of tremendous opportunity for engineers, who would now find jobs in Hitler's rearmament and public works programs.

As we will see in the following chapter, the residues of irrationalism in the reactionary modernist synthesis took their toll on the capacity of the Nazi regime to either coordinate its research and development policies, or to think strategically about the relation between ends and means in politics. But reconciliations did allow for an uneasy part-

---

[116] Ibid., pp. 10–11.
[117] Rudolf Heiss, "Volk und gestaltende Arbeit," in *Die Sendung des Ingenieure*, pp. 26–30.
[118] Ibid., pp. 29–30.
[119] Rudolf Heiss, "Die Erziehung des Ingenieurs zur Totalität," in *Die Sendung des Ingenieure*, pp. 125–34.

nership between technics and unreason. The conflict between Nazi ideology and modern science was far sharper, as the ill-fated effort to establish an "Aryan physics" to replace "Jewish physics" demonstrates.[120] Heiss's essay was a fascinating example of hostility to natural science combined with enthusiasm for technology. He wrote that the natural sciences existed in a world of laws, regularities, and impractical abstractions, rather than in the creative and heroic immediacy of the inventor and engineer.[121] Engineers produced "beautiful forms"; natural scientists produced "dead knowledge." Theory "not aimed at the soul," that remains on the surface rather than probing "the depths, remains more or less useless knowledge."[122] The reactionary modernists celebrated the accomplishments of the first and second industrial revolutions, not those of modern physics. It remained "theory not aimed at the soul."

This simultaneous reconciliation with technology and rejection of natural science was as bizarre as their efforts to seal off a pristine sphere of German productivity from a parasitic realm of Jewish circulation. German physics had been too closely associated with the Jews – whom the anti-Semites called a people of reason and not emotion – to incorporate it easily into exclusively German national traditions. It was their enduring hostility to abstractions and intellect, rather than emotion, immediacy, and the self, that explains the relative ease with which the reactionary modernists could incorporate technology into German *Kultur* while leaving modern physics in the wasteland of Western *Zivilisation*. Despite the many paradoxes of this ideological tradition, it was institutionalized and persisted up to the end of the Nazi regime.

---

[120] See Beyerchen, *Scientists under Hitler*. Beyerchen's study tends to equate hostility to technology with hostility to science. However, his claim that the major impact of World War II was to affirm utilitarian rather than ideological values insofar as the effort to establish an Aryan physics is concerned should not be extended to the technological field. Although the Nazis certainly wanted new technical innovations during the war, their ideological views remained in the way of coordinated efforts at research and development. On research and development under Hitler, and technology during the war, see Ludwig, *Technik und Ingenieure*, pp. 210–300, and pp. 403–73.

[121] Heiss, "Die Erziehung des Ingenieurs," p. 132.

[122] Ibid.

8

Reactionary modernism in the Third Reich

I have documented the claim that the reactionary modernist tradition was an important component of modern German nationalism, that it was pervasive within the conservative revolution in Weimar and in the cultural politics of German engineering from the 1870s to the collapse of the Weimar Republic. Before 1933, the Nazis were aware of the tradition and contributors to it. But what happened after the seizure of power? In this chapter I will present evidence suggesting that the reactionary modernist tradition continued up through the very end of the Nazi regime. It did not give way to rural nostalgia or postideological technocratic world views. This is not to say that Luddites and technocrats did not exist in the Hitler regime. Rather, the continuity of reactionary modernist ideology after 1933 was both more pervasive than these other views and more important in accounting for the primacy of ideological politics during the Hitler years. The irrationalist embrace of technology articulated by the reactionary modernists contributed to the mixture of deficient technical innovation and strategic miscalculation that characterized the Third Reich.

Development of a distinctive National Socialist view of technology began well before the seizure of power. At the center of all Nazi views on the subject stood a mythic historical construction of a racial battle between Aryan and Jew, blood and gold. Like the reactionary modernists we have examined so far, the Nazis combined anti-Semitism with approval of technological advance, which is important to note given the frequency with which anti-Semitism and generalized rejections of industrial society have been associated with one another. In the years immediately following World War I, Gottfried Feder, himself an engineer, dominated discussion on the subject in the Nazi party. In the early 1920s, his pamphlet, *Das Manifest zur Brechung der Zinsknechtschaft des Geldes* (The Manifesto on Breaking the Interest Slavery of Money) was, along with Hitler's *Mein Kampf* and Alfred

Rosenberg's *Mythos der 20. Jahrhundert* (Myth of the 20th Century), one of the party's most important tracts.[1] Feder distinguished between "Jewish finance capital" and "national capital," thereby encouraging anticapitalist rhetoric that left actual property relations intact. "Creative labor" and industrial capital would have to be liberated from the tentacles of international Jewish power.

His works borrowed from Marxist vocabulary, speaking of the "liberation of productive labor" and calling on the peoples of all nations to unite against the force of international finance.[2] In his 1923 pamphlet, *Der deutsche Staat auf nationaler und sozialer Grundlage* (The German State on National and Social Foundations), Feder insisted that "the Jew" had remained remote from productive labor and was the bearer of a parasitic spirit. But at the same time he claimed that German big industry – Krupp, Mannesmann, Thyssen – and its property were "not at all in conflict with the interest of the totality. The fundamental recognition of private property is deeply anchored in the clear awareness of the Aryan spiritual structure."[3] Feder summarized his "theoretical" contribution to National Socialism in the formula, "creative versus parasitic capital" (*schaffendes gegen raffendes Kapital*), which appeared in his 1933 work, *Kampf gegen Hochfinanz.*[4] Creative capital was a source of utility, employment, and technological advance, whereas parasitic capital drained national resources for the benefit of a smaller number of international financiers. Feder's conspiratorial outlook served to shift the conflict between capital and labor into a nationalist idiom. Describing capital as "creative" banished any talk of class conflicts arising from the labor process, blamed the banks for the problems of the whole economic system, and carried hints of the aestheticization of the labor process that the Nazis made so much of in the Bureau of the Beauty of Labor (*Amt Schönheit der Arbeit*).[5] Moreover, the associations in Feder's slogan between beauty and pro-

[1] Gottfried Feder, *Das Manifest zur Brechung der Zinsknechtschaft des Geldes* (Munich, 1919).
[2] Feder, *Das Manifest*, p. 62. On Nazi economic theories see Werner Krause, *Wirtschaftstheorie unter dem Hakenkreuz* (Berlin, 1962).
[3] Gottfried Feder, *Der deutsche Staat auf nationaler und sozialer Grundlage* (Munich, 1923), p. 21.
[4] Gottfried Feder, *Kampf gegen Hochfinanz* (Munich, 1933).
[5] On the Bureau of the Beauty of Labor, see Rabinbach, "The Aesthetics of Production in the Third Reich," in *International Facism*, ed. George Mosse (Beverly Hills, Calif., 1979).

ductivity with the German racial character and ugliness and parasitism with the Jews were standard fare in German anti-Semitism.[6]

In 1926, Hitler selected Feder as the final arbiter of disputes arising from formulation of the party's twenty-five-point program.[7] Feder used this position to publish a series of pamphlets, the "National Socialist Library," which set forth a Nazi "theory" on economic organization and technology. Feder's anticapitalist rhetoric fell out of favor with Hitler after Hitler developed closer ties to some German industrialists in the last years of the Weimar Republic, but his distinction between creative and parasitic capital accorded with the anticapitalism of the engineers that had developed outside the Nazi party.[8] In July 1933, *Technik und Kultur* published a speech by Feder in which he claimed that National Socialism was compatible with the internal tradition of the engineers and with their desires to elevate "service" to the nation above individual profit.[9] In his view, National Socialism would fulfill the engineers' demands for greater social recognition and more state intervention to unleash technology. He admitted that technology posed dangers, for example, undue dependence on foreign raw materials, an unhealthy urban atmosphere, and an excessive division of labor that might destroy the German "feeling for home" (*Heimatgefühl*). But all of these problems could be surmounted

[6] George Mosse elaborates on the distinction between Aryan beauty and productivity vs. Jewish ugliness and parasitism in *Towards the Final Solution* (New York, 1978); and *The Crisis of German Ideology*, (New York, 1964).

[7] See Neumann, *Behemoth: The Structure and Practice of National Socialism* (New York, 1944), pp. 228–9; Ludwig, *Technik und Ingenieure im Dritten Reich* (Königstein, 1979), p. 76. Hitler referred to Feder's *Der deutsche Staat auf nationaler und sozialer Grundlage* as the "catechism of our movement"; Neumann, p. 229.

[8] David Schoenbaum, in *Hitler's Social Revolution* (New York, 1966), refers to the "rural, racist, anti-industrial pole around Feder" (p. 22) that survived only as "characteristic folklore" (p. 46) with "the option for industrial rearmament in 1933 and against Feder in 1934. ...This was an option against the new aristocracy of *Blut und Boden* and in favor of the long-term dynamics of industrial society as they had been working in Germany and all other industrial societies since the beginning of the nineteenth century" (p. 240). Charisma and faith replaced ideology. First, nothing in Feder's distinctions between productive and parasitic capital conflicted with industrial rearmament. Feder was a racist but not a Luddite. Second, Schoenbaum's claim that ideology was replaced by faith assumes a highly rationalistic conception of ideology. But both before and after 1933, Nazi ideology was deeply emotional and antirationalist. The distinction between faith and ideology simply does not apply, especially when dealing with totalitarian politics.

[9] Gottfried Feder, "Die Aufgaben der Technik beim Wiederaufbau der Deutschen Wirtschaft" (The Tasks of Technology in the Reconstruction of the German Economy), *Technik und Kultur* 24 (1933), pp. 93–100. The essay was originally delivered as a speech to the *Kampfbund Deutscher Architekten und Ingenieure*, a Nazi organization of architects and engineers.

if technology were placed in the service of the national "totality." In practical terms, this meant job programs, highway construction, and production of synthetic fuels to reduce German dependence on imported oil.[10]

Feder's National Socialist Library was the vehicle for the first "official" Nazi statement on modern technology, which appeared in 1930. *Nationalsozialismus und Technik: Die Geistigkeit der nationalsozialistischen Bewegung* (National Socialism and Technology: The Spirituality of the National Socialist Movement) was written by Peter Schwerber, a philosophically adept engineer who, four years earlier, had written that right-wing politics and Christian ethics were the path of salvation from the depravity of modern industrialism.[11] *Nationalsozialismus und Technik* was the earliest effort to synthesize Nazi ideology with the indigenous traditions of German engineers. Schwerber made reference to Dessauer, Zschimmer, and Spengler as well as to Feder and Hitler. His pamphlet rested on one obsessively repeated idea, namely, that racism was the logical end point of Germany's reconciliation with modern technology.[12]

As we will soon see, Schwerber's argument became a familiar one in Germany after 1933: Far from being antitechnological, National Socialism was dedicated to liberating technology from the "domination of money" and the "fetters" of Jewish materialism. "Jewish abstraction" was alien to the "autonomous life element of the German *Volk*," whereas technology was not only in tune with the *Volk* but was something around which a whole world view could and ought to be constructed.[13] Schwerber wrote that technology was more than a material foundation of Nazism. It was an "independent factor" of a new, postliberal, postmaterialist culture. It was the generation that survived the *Fronterlebnis* that really grasped the idea of freedom inherent in technology. National Socialism was the product of this generation. But the idea of freedom – from physical labor and for free time – remained unrealized due to the "domination of a power alien to the

---

[10] Ibid., pp. 98–100.

[11] Peter Schwerber, *Nationalsozialismus und Technik: Die Geistigkeit der nationalsozialistischen Bewegung* (Munich, 1930).

[12] Ibid., p. 72. Schwerber also made favorable reference to Henry Ford, whose biography was also published in the National Socialist Library. The Nazis praised Ford for his anti-Semitic views and for being what they saw as an ideal-typical "technical man" who excluded all "merchant" activity or dependence on finance capital by creating a self-financing industrial corporation. Other works from the engineers' own tradition cited by Schwerber included Viktor Engelhardt, *Weltanschauung und Technik* (Leipzig, 1922); Richard Coudenhove-Kalergi, *Apologie der Technik* (Leipzig-Vienna, 1922); Robert Weyrauch, *Die Technik* (Stuttgart, 1922).

[13] Schwerber, *Nationalsozialismus und Technik*, p. 3.

essence of technology, that is, the power of money...the Jewish-materialist suffocating embrace [*Umklammerung*] of our life elements."[14]

The really decisive contribution of National Socialism, Schwerber continued, lay not only in recognizing the "major cause of our misfortune," but also, and more importantly, in moving to the level of the "decisive deed...the act of liberation."[15] Only "blood" and action would prevail against "the titanic power of money."[16] National Socialism was more than a collection of protests against materialism and the Jews. Schwerber attributed to both technology and National Socialism a "primal life instinct." Both would join forces against "Jewish-materialist restrictions."[17] Like the engineering professors at the technical universities, Schwerber saw technology as a natural force, at once demonic and passionate, which sought a victory of "spirit over matter."[18] But Schwerber and the Nazis after him introduced a new twist: Whereas the Jews destroyed and misused technology, the Nordic race was ideally suited to it. Technical *Geist* and the Nazi racial myth would form a common front against Jewish materialism.

National Socialism was dedicated to emancipating technology from capitalist exchange, a goal that bore striking similarities – at least on a rhetorical level – to the engineers' own anticapitalist language. Schwerber's protest was against insufficient rather than excessive technological progress. If we substitute "relations of production" for "Jews" and "technology" for "forces of production," Schwerber's rendition of Nazi ideology amounts to an appeal to liberate a will or telos said to be inherent in the forces of production from restrictions imposed by the existing bourgeois social relations of production. Destruction of the Socialist and Communist parties and the trade unions, abolition of parliament, and breaking the Versailles restrictions on German rearmament were the practical meaning of such a program. This conception of the "primacy of politics" was simultaneously a plan for political reaction and technological modernization presented as a cultural revolution from the Right.

At the center of Nazi Germany stood the figure of Adolf Hitler and his ideas. The view, first expressed by Hermann Rauschning, that Hitler was an opportunist without scruple, has, in my opinion, been effectively laid to rest by scholars such as Eberhard Jäckel and Joachim Fest. Hitler's *Weltanschauung* was both fanatically coherent and polit-

[14] Ibid., p. 6.
[15] Ibid., p. 6.
[16] Ibid., p. 21.
[17] Ibid., p. 23.
[18] Ibid., p. 37.

ically decisive. At no time did he join in the hostility to technology found in *völkisch* ideology. For Hitler, the decisive element remained the ideology of the will to power. If life and politics were essentially a struggle in which the strongest won, then in politics among nations the technologically weak would deserve to be defeated. He insisted that the Germans must succeed in the battle against nature in order to win in the battle among nations and races. As early as 1919, in a speech advocating German rearmament and abrogation of the Versailles treaty, Hitler said that "the misery of Germany must be broken by Germany's steel. That time must come."[19]

In *Mein Kampf*, he divided humankind into three categories: founders, bearers, and destroyers of culture, and assigned these historical roles to the Aryans, the Japanese, and the Jews, respectively. He went so far as to define Aryan culture as a synthesis of "the Greek spirit and Germanic technology."[20] He also acknowledged his debt to Gottfried Feder's ideas on "breaking interest slavery." This notion was "a theoretical truth which would inevitably be of immense importance for the future of the German people. The sharp separation of stock exchange capital from the national economy offered the possibility of opposing the internationalization of the German economy without at the same time menacing the foundations of an independent national self-maintenance by a struggle against capital."[21] This selective anticapitalism had been common in the *völkisch* tradition. But where Sombart's anticapitalism attacked Jewish *Geist*, Hitler turned this cultural revolution into a biological revolt.

Hitler did not write extensively on the subject of technology. Albert Speer reports listening to Hitler's theory of "ruin value," according to which the purpose of Nazi architecture and technological advance should be to create ruins that would last a thousand years and thereby overcome the transience of the market.[22] (As we saw in the previous chapter, the juxtaposition of permanent technology and evanescent capitalism was an important theme among the reactionary modernists.) Hitler was the first political leader of the twentieth century to use the airplane extensively. The radio spread his voice and fast cars

[19] Adolf Hitler, *Mein Kampf* (Boston, 1939), p. 318. Cited in Eberhard Jäckel, *Hitler's World View: A Blueprint for Power*, trans. Herbert Arnold (Middletown, Conn., 1972), p. 90.
[20] Cited in Jäckel, p. 28.
[21] Hitler, *Mein Kampf*, p. 213. Also see Iring Fetscher, "Die industrielle Gesellschaft und die Ideologie der Nationalsozialisten," *Gesellschaft, Staat und Erziehung* 7 (1962), pp. 6–23.
[22] Albert Speer, *Inside the Third Reich*, trans. Richard Winston and Clara Winston (New York, 1970), pp. 93–4.

sped him over the *Autobahnen*. His conversations with associates, published as the "table talks," reveal a man fascinated with the details of military technology.[23] His embrace of modern technology as an expression of Aryan will was fully consonant with rejection of the Enlightenment and the social consequences of the French and industrial revolutions. Given his outlook, Hitler never feared that a rearmed Germany would be a soulless Germany.

Hitler's propaganda minister, Joseph Goebbels, devoted a great deal of effort to convincing the Germans that their souls were compatible with modern technology. Goebbels's speeches on the subject are interesting because they were directed to the general public as well as to engineers, and thus combined elements of the conservative revolution, romanticism, and *völkisch* ideology with a cult of technological modernism. For example, in a speech in 1932, Goebbels echoed Hitler's view that the true politician was an artist whose task was to give form to the "raw material" of the masses. In the century of mass politics, the political leader must avail himself of the most modern means of propaganda, such as the radio, to encourage "spiritual mobilization" (*geistige Mobilmachung*). In March 1933, he assured his audience that he was not "an unmodern man who is inwardly opposed to the radio . . . but a passionate lover of the press . . . theater . . . radio." In his view, the radio should not be used to create an illusory objectivity but to assist in the spiritual mobilization the National Socialist regime was fostering. The Germans, he argued, must learn the primary lesson of World War I: Germany was defeated by deficiencies of the spirit rather than by material deficiencies. "We did not lose the war because our cannons failed, but rather because our spiritual weapons didn't fire." The radio gave National Socialism unprecedented means for reaching the masses with this message of spiritual revolution.[24]

From his earliest broadcasts to his last, Goebbels returned to a theme that reflected reactionary modernism. In November 1933, he first celebrated a "steely romanticism" (*stahlernde Romantik*) that had "made German life worth living again." This new romanticism did not hide from the "hardness of being" or dream of escape into the past. Instead it "heroically" faced up to the problems of modern times.[25] Goebbels often discussed the meaning of *stählernde Romantik* and his speeches were reprinted in *Deutsche Technik* (German Technology), a monthly journal published from 1933 to 1942. One particularly graphic ex-

[23] See *Hitler's Table Talk*, ed. H. R. Trevor-Roper (London, 1953).
[24] Joseph Goebbels, *Reden* (March 25, 1933).
[25] Joseph Goebbels, *Reden* (March 15, 1933).

ample appeared in the February 1939 issue of this journal. The cover shows Goebbels delivering a speech, a Volkswagen on one side, Hitler on the other. The following passage indicates Goebbels's skill at administering a cultural tradition – what Horkheimer later called the bureaucratic dispensation of the revolt of nature:

We live in an era of technology. The racing tempo of our century affects all areas of our life. There is scarcely an endeavor that can escape its powerful influence. Therefore, the danger unquestionably arises that modern technology will make men soulless. National Socialism never rejected or struggled against technology. Rather, one of its main tasks was to consciously affirm it, *to fill it inwardly with soul*, to discipline it and to place it in the service of our people and their cultural level. National Socialist public statements used to refer to the steely romanticism of our century. Today this phrase has attained its full meaning. We live in an age that is both romantic and steellike, that has not lost its depth of feeling. On the contrary, it has *discovered a new romanticism in the results of modern inventions and technology*. While bourgeois reaction was alien to and filled with incomprehension, if not outright hostility to technology, and while modern skeptics believed the deepest roots of the collapse of European culture lay in it, *National Socialism understood how to take the soulless framework of technology and fill it with the rhythm and hot impulses of our time* [emphasis added].[26]

This is a remarkable condensation of reactionary modernist themes. Over and over again, Goebbels claimed that the cultural crisis German conservatism had feared had been "overcome" by National Socialism. Filling technology with soul was a practical matter as well. The Volkswagen meant that now modern technology was accessible to the masses and accessible in a way that spread the "rhythm and hot impulses of our time."

During the war years, Goebbels continued to boast that National Socialism had developed a "new ideal of cultivation" freed from the "false and saccharine romanticism" of the past.[27] In Heidelberg in July 1943, Goebbels elaborated on the theme of the kind of romanticism peculiar to National Socialism.

Every time has its romanticism, its poetic presentation of life... Ours does as well. It is harder and crueler than a previous romanticism, but it remains romantic. The steely romanticism of our time manifests itself in actions and deeds in service of a great national goal, in a feeling of duty raised to the level of an unbreachable principle. *We are all more or less romantics of a new German mood.* The Reich of droning motors, grandiose industrial creations, an almost unlimited and unenclosed space which we must populate to preserve

[26] Joseph Goebbels, *Deutsche Technik* (March 1939), pp. 105–6 (speech at the opening of the Berlin Auto Show, February 17, 1939).
[27] Joseph Goebbels, *Reden* (Berlin Sportpalast, June 5, 1943).

the best qualities of our *Volk* – is the Reich of *our* romanticism [emphasis added].[28]

For Goebbels, the war years were a period "overflowing with deeds," in sharp contrast to the "exaggerated intellectualism" of Weimar politics and culture. German victories were possible only because German engineers and scientists approached their work with the "same fanaticism and wild determination" as did German soldiers, workers, and peasants. In the last year of the war, Goebbels again turned to *stählernde Romantik*. The *geistige Mobilmachung* must again turn for assistance to the "German genius for invention" (*deutsche Erfindungsgenie*) to avoid impending defeat. In July 1944, Goebbels promised that Hitler's leadership, the spirit of the *Volk*, and the V-1 and V-2 rockets would combine to snatch victory from the jaws of defeat.[29]

There are two points to be made about these passages. First, Goebbels spoke with slogans and stock formulas. He was, in other words, an administrator of political meanings. But however administered these meanings were, they were not arbitrary. On the contrary, Goebbels spoke a language familiar to German engineers (among others), one stemming from traditions that really did, as he put it, "grow from the *Volk*." Without this cultural resonance, he would not have been the successful propagandist he was. Second, it is difficult to determine the degree of cynicism or belief Goebbels aroused in his listeners, but we certainly ought not to rule out the possibility that he actually believed what he was saying. Sociology has devoted much effort to measuring public opinion, but less thought has been given to the effect of political propaganda on the political elites that express it. It is – and was – obvious to anyone with minimally unclouded vision that "fanaticism and wild determination" would do little to turn the tide of the war in 1944. The point about Goebbels's steely romanticism was that it most certainly had obscured his vision. Although Nazi ideology may not have drugged the entire German people, it certainly acted as an opiate of the Nazi political elite, one that made them oblivious to the catastrophic consequences of Germany's ideology, technical deficiencies, and totalitarian leadership.

Hitler was an enthusiast of technical advance. The reception of nazism among German engineers also appears to have been enthusiastic, but less so than that of the legal and medical professions, as indicated by the results of student elections at German technical universities in 1933. About 41 percent of the 10,000 students at the

[28] Joseph Goebbels, *Reden* (Heidelberg Stadthalle, July 7, 1943).
[29] Joseph Goebbels, *Reden* (July 26, 1944).

technical universities voted for the Nazis in student elections compared 48 percent of the 37,000 students at the nontechnical universities. Beyond the campuses, approximately 300,000 people were classified as engineers in 1933, including Germany's 36,000 architects and 31,000 chemists. Of this total, around 7,000 belonged to the Nazi party. In January 1933, party membership stood at 720,000 (of a population of 32 million). Hence, about the same proportion of German engineers was drawn to membership in the Nazi party as German citizens generally, but less so than white-collar workers and independent professionals. After 1933, the number of engineers in the Nazi party doubled but the increase in the other middle-class professions was even greater (about 230 percent). Only 13.1 percent of the leadership positions in the mid-1930s were held by engineers, compared to 56 percent for lawyers, and 15.5 percent for doctors.[30]

Since their inception, the national engineering associations in Germany had bemoaned their lack of political influence and social prestige relative to the nontechnical middle-class professions. Both the *Verein Deutscher Ingenieure* (Association of German Engineers, VDI) and the cultural politicians publishing *Technik und Kultur* called for a national office of planning for technical development, a *Staatstechnik*, which would coordinate state, industry, and engineering in the interests of the national community.

The overall leadership of the new regime's efforts at "coordination" (*Gleichschaltung*) lay with Robert Ley, the director of the German Labor Front, whereas Feder directed the activities of the *Reichsbund deutscher Techniker* (RDT). Feder wanted to replace the existing technical associations – *Fachvereines* – with Nazi organizations focused on his version of German anticapitalism; Ley sought to integrate the existing engineering organizations into the German Labor Front. The RDT had been founded in 1918 to foster the interests of engineers in national politics. Although Feder envisaged a *Front der Technik* under leadership of the RDT, by the end of 1933 it had collapsed. Some of its functionaries turned to the *Deutsche technokratische Gesellschaft* (DTG), founded in 1932 as an international *Weltbund* organized around slogans of a technocratic socialism. Although Feder saw the greatest opportunity for technocratic ascendancy in private or state capitalism, those who took seriously the goal of production for human needs over the needs of profit became increasingly uncomfortable with the Nazi regime, especially after the announcement of the four-year plan directed at rearmament. The DTG, whose Veblenian socialism of the

---

[30] See Ludwig, *Technik und Ingenieure*, pp. 105–8.

technicians was utterly removed from the goals of the regime, ceased to exist in 1937.[31]

The *Gleichschaltung* process of the engineers is a chapter in the story of the underestimation of Hitler by the conservative elites of German society. Initially it entailed a trade-off between the regime and the engineering organizations. In exchange for accepting and assisting the new regime, the engineers sustained a semblance of organizational independence, which, however, was gradually whittled down to insignificance. The leadership of the VDI (which now had about 30,000 members) informed the new government that it was ready to help deal with the problems of unemployment, energy, and rearmament and to work with the Nazis' own organization of engineers, the *Kampfbund deutscher Architekten und Ingenieure* (KDAI). In April 1933, the KDAI membership included only 3 percent of Germany's engineers, a fact that led Rudolf Hess and Todt to urge integration rather than destruction of existing organizations. The leadership of the VDI viewed Feder as an economic crackpot and was more interested in placing the engineers' technical skills at the service of the new regime through combining the energies of industry, engineers, and the state. Hitler also regarded Feder's anticapitalist rhetoric as unhelpful when the regime was intent on convincing the existing organizations that their interests were best served by adapting to the program of the new regime.

Although not enamored of Feder's ideological pronouncements, the leaders of the VDI opted for political accommodation rather than resistance. In exchange for offering their services to the new regime in a spirit of objective functionality – *objektive Sachlichkeit* – the engineering associations were able to survive as organizations, although the leadership positions were controlled either by members of the Nazi party or sympathizers.[32]

The executor of the political coexistence of regime and the preexisting engineering organizations was Fritz Todt. In 1934, Hitler designated him as his representative for "all questions" concerning the organization and development of technology. Todt, a party member since 1923, had strong and enduring ties to the engineering profession and to its political and cultural traditions. Rudolf Hess and Alfred Rosenberg also sang the praises of technology in National Socialist terms, but it was Todt, more than any other leading figure of the

[31] Ibid., pp. 123–4.
[32] Ibid., p. 111. Ludwig's is the definitive account of the process of *Gleichschaltung* or "coordination" process of the Nazi regime as it concerned engineers.

regime, who could truthfully claim roots in both the Nazi party and in the engineer's cultural politics. Following initial bureaucratic struggles with Feder, Todt assumed leadership of the *Amt der Technik*, the office charged with coordinating Hitler's goals and the aspirations of the engineers. Whereas Ley viewed the *Amt der Technik* primarily as a tool for political control, Todt hoped to present this new political control as itself the outcome of the engineer's own traditions. To this end, he linked practical issues of raw material resources, new energy sources, and decreasing German dependence on raw materials with the ideological traditions that German engineers had themselves developed. Todt urged his fellow engineers to consider political as well as technical issues and to favor both "revolution and tradition." In 1934, under the umbrella of the German Labor Front, Todt assumed leadership of the *Amt der Technik*, which in turn administered the *Nationalsozialistischen Bund deutscher Techniker* (NSBDT). Members of the NSBDT were also members of the Nazi party whereas most engineers were also required to join a broader front organization, the *Reichsgemeinschaft Technischewissenschaftlichen Arbeit* (RTA), and to pay dues to the all-encompassing Labor Front.[33]

Thus Feder's political demise did not mean that Nazi ideology had given way to the solvent of industrial rationality. His eclipse was accompanied by Todt's ascendancy and Todt was by no means an apolitical technocrat. On the contrary, he understood that the price of formal autonomous existence for the *Vereines* was not a high price for the regime to pay for their political submission. As part of this strategy of politicization, Todt used his office to publish the "technopolitical journal," *Deutsche Technik*, from 1933 to 1941, a magazine of essays and photographs that sought to convince its approximately 80,000 readers that Nazi ideology was compatible with modern technology. *Deutsche Technik* thus supplanted *Technik und Kultur*, some of whose contributors were more taken with Feder's anticapitalism than with Todt's emphasis on *Staatstechnik*. By 1937, Todt announced with great pride that the "new ordering of German technology was complete" and that the Nazi party and regime had completely integrated the organizations of German engineers that predated 1933.[34] The number of engineering organizations had been reduced from eighty to sixteen, and in 1937 these were placed under the control of a central government office called the *Hauptamt für Technik* (Central Office for

---

[33] Fritz Todt, "Tradition undReaction," *Zeitschrift des Vereines des deutschen Ingenieure* 78 (1934), p. 1,047.
[34] Fritz Todt, "Die Neuordnung der deutschen Technik," *Deutsche Technik*, 5 (1937), p. 204.

Technology). About 81,000 of Germany's 300,000 engineers participated in the schools and in propaganda efforts and received journals published by the *Hauptamt für Technik*. In 1939, Todt was elected chairman of the VDI.[35]

By 1936, when Hitler announced a four-year plan of economic development, rationalization of industry, expanded development of synthetic energy substitutes, and rearmament, the *Hauptamt für Technik* and the NSBDT gave the Nazis an organizational monopoly over the technical instruments necessary for rearmament. If up to 1936 the focus of Nazi economic policy had been recovery from the depression, the four-year plan contained the additional goal of reducing German dependence on the world economy through technical innovation. Fundamentalist slogans of national economic autarky went hand in hand with technical advances. Nazi publicists presented the plan as yet another act of liberation of technical workers from the tentacles of Jewish finance, and the leaders of the engineering associations extolled the ideal of placing their skills in the service of the *Volk*.[36]

Pragmatic, rationalizing themes existed alongside traditional Nazi ideology. The propaganda of Todt's office of technology insisted that there simply was no contradiction between developing new energy sources, building the *Autobahnen*, and rearmament, on the one hand, and serving the "general interest," on the other. Whereas the Nazis claimed that *völkisch* ideology and technical advance went hand in hand with Hitler's ideology of the will, the engineers drawn to the regime believed that their sober commitments to technical rationality would finally be placed in the service of the state. They also realized that their own power and importance would grow as the demands for armaments production expanded. This history of organizational survival through political acquiescence reminds us that many German engineers remained outside the ideological disputes over the relation between technology and Germany's soul. The most that can be said on the basis of the evidence presented here is that in this period, when and if German engineers turned their attention to the connection between technology and Germany's national identity, the terms of discussion were dominated by the cultural tradition of reactionary modernism.

The Nazis were more successful at preserving their ideological souls than the engineers were at imposing pragmatism on the German

[35] Ludwig, *Technik und Ingenieure*, p. 172.
[36] For example, Fritz Nonnenbruch, *Die dynamische Wirtschaft* (Munich, 1936).

dictatorship. The examples of lack of coordination of political ends with technical requirements are impressive. The most spectacular, of course, was the damage done to German nuclear physics by the doctrine of "Aryan physics." But German technical advance was hindered in less visible ways as well. The combination of appointments based on ideological rather than scientific and technical criteria with bureaucratic conflicts over jurisdiction hindered technical innovation and research. For instance, the number of patents actually declined from the levels at the end of the Weimar Republic. This was the case even in chemistry, in which twice as many patents were awarded in 1932 as in any of the years from 1933 to 1937. Todt's program of highway construction along with the advances associated with the four-year plan were based on research that took place before 1933. Hitler's view that innovation was the outcome of the creative forces slumbering within the German soul was hardly conducive to the requirements of scientific and technical research. The Nazis accumulated a large number of weapons, but their qualitative technical backwardness in such crucial areas as torpedoes, radar, communications, air defense, and airplane design became apparent during World War II.[37]

Even if German engineers had not been hindered by ideological criteria, fewer of them were being trained in the late 1930s to design Hitler's weapons of war. Although the VDI estimated in 1936 that Germany needed 4,000 more engineers, the number of students at the technical universities fell from 17,745 in 1933 to 10,747 in 1936 and rose to 12,287 in 1939 only to fall steadily to 7,866 in 1940 and 6,675 in 1943. At the same time, study length was cut from eight to seven semesters. By comparison, in 1940 enrollments at technical universities in the Soviet Union were three times what they were in 1928.[38] In 1937, several months before he left his position as minister of economics, Helmar Schacht warned that National Socialism's preference for political-ideological training at the expense of technical education threatened Germany's technical superiority over other nations, a decline that had grave consequences both because of the importance of exports for the German economy and for military purposes.[39] Schacht's understanding of the relation between science and technology was not widely shared in the regime. Nazi propaganda focused on the accomplishments of individual inventors and on the immediate, practical benefits of technical advances. In weighing the

[37] Ludwig, *Technik und Ingenieure*, p. 255.
[38] Ibid., pp. 275–7; and Kendall Bailes, *Technology and Society under Lenin and Stalin: Origins of the Soviet Technical Intelligentsia, 1917–1941* (Princeton, N.J., 1978), p. 221.
[39] Ludwig, *Technik und Ingenieure*, p. 284.

causes of German technical backwardness, political terror and persecution must be placed alongside the generally antiintellectual and antiscientific ideology of the Nazi regime. Many people in positions of responsibility – Speer, Himmler, Ley, Bormann, and Hitler – simply lacked the background to grasp the implications of scientific advances for technical advances.

At the outset of the war, Germany's technology was both quantitatively and qualitatively inferior to that of its enemies. In 1939, Germany was producing 27 million tons of steel a year, in contrast to over 100 million tons produced by the Great Britain, the Soviet Union, and the United States. By 1941, Germany had not yet developed a tank that was a match for the Soviet T-34. By 1943, when the Germans finally produced a new model, the Russians had advanced still further. Perhaps most striking were the enormous quantitative inferiorities of German compared to Russian tank production. From 1941 to 1944, the Soviet advantage ranged from 1.5:1 to 4:1. The actual production figures in these years were 6,590 Soviet to 3,796 German tanks in 1941, 24,719 to 6,189 in 1942, 30,000 to 10,757 in 1943, and 30,000 to 18,284 in 1944. Although the Nazis made much of their love of airplanes, by 1943 Germany's airplane production had fallen to about 20 percent of that of the Allies.[40] In short, the German dictatorship simply lacked the technical means to win the war, except, of course, its war against the European Jews.

Ironically, it was Fritz Todt who confronted Hitler with the contradiction between his ideological goals and German technical capabilities. By December of 1941, it was clear that the invasion of the Soviet Union in the previous June had not resulted in the quick, decisive victory Hitler expected. Just before the Japanese attack on Pearl Harbor and the American entry into the war, Todt urged Hitler to sue for peace with the Russians. Speaking as an engineer, Todt argued that time was on the side of the enemy; a long war would mean a German defeat. But Todt himself had entered into the pact with the devil. By 1941 it was too late for rational, strategic calculations to sway Hitler from his goals. His ideological politics triumphed over considerations of traditional power politics. The very same ideological frame of mind that had prevented Germany from developing its scientific and technical potential now contributed to overestimation of German capacities, underestimation of the capabilities of the Allies, and refusal to face the consequences of Germany's technical shortcomings. The constant of Hitler's ideology of the will was a refusal

[40] Ibid., pp. 440–1.

to match political ends with existing means. Todt's confrontation with Hitler in December was the exception that proved the rule: German engineers, including Todt up to this point, subordinated their knowledge of technical realities to the demands of Nazi ideology.

In the first issue of *Deutsche Technik*, published in September 1933, Todt wrote that the new "technopolitical journal" would make "German technology into a pillar of the total state" and place technology's "cultural and spiritual outlook on the foundation of a pure National Socialist world view."[41] Todt was able to speak in terms similar to the aesthetic and philosophical themes of the engineers' traditions. For example, the construction of the national highway system would be based on a unified plan, in sharp contrast to the alleged "chaos" of the Weimar "system." It flowed from a unified *Geist* and represented an artistic effort to give proper form to the German landscape. Germany's highways were to be far more than an engineering feat; they must be "an expression of the German essence." Todt argued that the "decisive" fact of the era for German engineers was that National Socialism was liberating technology from the "material bonds" that had restricted it for the last half century. Here were both an opportunity and a necessity for "total engagement" by engineers in the nationalist revival.

During the first years of the dictatorship, Todt pointed with pride to the construction of the *Autobahnen* as evidence that the Nazis had rescued technology from an era that had treated it as an object without soul or spirit. Like Freyer and Schmitt, Todt argued that now politics, not economics, was in command. Aesthetic criteria were displacing the profit motive, and the Nazis were demonstrating that technology did not consist of dead matter, but of "soulful cultural works" that grew organically from the *Volk*. Todt even claimed that there was a specifically National Socialist conception of technology that elevated creativity over materialist considerations. During these years, *Deutsche Technik* was filled with photographs of the highways gracefully weaving through valleys, mountains, and farmland. These roads demonstrated that, as Todt put it, "the artistic and technical powers of invention and formation live together in the creative engineer." The following passage is typical of Todt's view of technology as an art form:

The following are the features that make a road as a totality into an artwork that brings the environment joy through its intrinsic beauty and harmony

---

[41] Fritz Todt, "Mein Auftrag," *Die Strasse* (15, 1933), reprinted in *Deutsche Technik* (August-September, 1941), p. 2.

with the environment: The direction of lines is bound to the land [*land-schaftsverbundene Linineführung*]. Construction remains true to natural forms [*naturformgetruere Erdbau*]. Workmanship is based on the craftsman's principles of building and implantation in the earth [*bodenstände Bepflanzung*].[42]

If this was what highway construction was about, it hardly conflicted with the cultural revolution promised by National Socialism. Building the "highways bound to the land" (*landschaftsverbundene Strassen*) and saving the German soul were mutually reinforcing projects. Todt's message was clear: The new highways posed no threat to the German *Volk*. On the contrary, they promised to restore the nation's lost unity. As Albert Speer later put it, Todt did not see "brutal and loveless images of iron and cement" when he looked at highways, but rather deliverance and redemption from a fragmented, materialist era.[43] As one of the official eulogies for Todt in 1941 put it, the Nazis had learned to lift technology out of the web of "bureaucratism" and had taught German engineers that "the language of technical works must rest...on the grammar of nature."[44]

Deutsche Technik is a striking document of the continuity of the reactionary modernist tradition after 1933. The *Zeitschrift des Vereins deutscher Ingenieure* continued to appear in these years, but it was primarily devoted to technical discussions combined with promptings for loyalty to the führer. *Deutsche Technik* proceeded to adapt many of the themes that first appeared in *Technik und Kultur*. Unlike Albert Speer's Bureau of the Beauty of Labor, *Deutsche Technik* did not replace *völkisch* pastoralism with technocratic aesthetics but, as Todt urged, incorporated technology into the National Socialist *Weltanschauung*. Articles were short, usually no more than three pages long, and repetitive. Little was new or original. The message of the journal

---

[42] Fritz Todt, *Leistung und Schönheit: Der Technik im Dritten Reich: Bild-Beilage zur Zeitschrift 'Deutsche Technik'* (July, 1939), p. 2. As the title indicates, *Leistung und Schönheit* was a photo magazine that complemented *Deutsche Technik*, providing space for reproductions and photos from exhibitions organized by the *Amt der Technik*, usually on the theme of art and technology.

[43] Albert Speer, "Der Baumeister Fritz Todt," *Deutsch Technik* (April 1942), p. 128.

[44] *Münchner Neueste Nachrichten*, "Deutschlands erster Ingenieure" (February 9, 1942), reprinted in a special issue of *Deutsche Technik* (March 1942), entitled *Dr.-Ing. Fritz Todt: Schöpferischer Techniker – Vorbildlicher Kamerad – grosser Deutscher* (Dr.-Eng. Fritz Todt: Creative Engineer – Visionary Comrade – Great German). This is a very interesting collection of remarkably similar-sounding eulogies, including Hitler's oration at Todt's funeral ("I have lost one of my most loyal colleagues and friends."); Alfred Rosenberg ("Todt had never abandoned the old sense of struggle born of deeply rooted agreement on a *Weltanschauung*); and numerous statements from the press and engineering journals.

was straightforward: Whatever had been posed as a problem before 1933 had now been solved.

At the *Haus der deutschen Technik* in Munich, the Nazis presented annual exhibitions on the theme of art and technology. *Deutsche Technik* reproduced many of these paintings as well as photographs of cars, planes, trains, and roads. Typical of the commentary was a 1942 essay asserting that National Socialism understood that art infuses technical processes with *Geist*. As a result of this understanding, German artists were "no longer out of step" with technology, but saw in it instead "the essential and necessary principle of our being," which established law over arbitrariness, duty over selfishness. Now that technology had become part of the *Volksgemeinschaft*, it had assumed clear and beautiful forms.[45] Technical advance under the Nazis was a cultural revolution that gave new meaning to cold steel. Among the accomplishments of nazism regarding technology were a "victory over the elementary," "overcoming" the threat of Americanization, balancing city and country, and bringing to the surface a uniquely German "surrender" to technology.[46]

Deutsche Technik elaborated the engineer's view that there was a specifically German technology. As contributors to *Technik und Kultur* had done before them, the writers for *Deutsche Technik* traced technology back to famous figures of preindustrial Europe, such as Leonardo da Vinci, who were stylized as models of the not-yet-divided engineer-artist or scientist-soldier.[47] The point of these generally fatuous accounts of the past was to stress links between the very old and the very new and to root technology in precapitalist and preindustrial traditions.[48] A great deal was made of "Goethe the technologist." One author, for example, claimed that Goethe's *Faust* was a fundamental text for understanding the secrets of the technological *Geist* in electricity, central heating, and photography.[49]

But the central message of *Deutsche Technik* was that National So-

[45] Fritz Nimitz, "Vor einen neuen Syntheses von Kunst und Technik," *Deutsche Technik* (September 1942), pp. 367–71.
[46] Heinrich Doll, "Die geistigen Verantwortung der Technik," *Deutsche Technik* (September 1942), pp. 284–5.
[47] Essays on these themes included the following: Heinrich Doll, "Die geistigen Verantwortung der Technik"; *Deutsche Technik* (September 1942), pp. 284–5; and Richard Grun, "Der Geist der Technik," *Deutsche Technik*, (June 1940), pp. 5–6.
[48] Joseph Bader, "Der Deutsche und das Wesen der abendlandischen Technik," *Deutsche Technik* (November 1940), pp. 475–8; a catalogue of German contributions to technical advance is presented by Dr.-Ing. L. Erhard in "Zur Technikgeschichte des Reichsprotektorate," *Deutsche Technik* (September 1940), pp. 211–14.
[49] Kurt Schuder, "Der Techniker Goethe," *Deutsche Technik* (August-September 1941), pp. 417–18.

cialism had indeed overcome the conflict between technology and culture. An essay published in February 1943, "NS-Technik," surveyed the first ten years of technology under Hitler. Its argument was as follows: Before 1933, Germany and German technology had suffered from capitalist misuse, the Jewish financial "plutocracy," American "desouling" (*Entseelung*), and the threat of enslavement by the Bolsheviks. National Socialism had made clear that it was the Germans who were the truly chosen people and had helped them construct a new German landscape saved from the "filth of civilization" and the "American-Jewish destruction of German nature." Ferdinand Fried, editor of *Die Tat* in the Weimar years, presented such views in several essays. Although Germany's "racial soul" was in tune with technical advances, technology had been "raped" by the Jewish *Ungeist*. Under the Nazis, the German soul was reasserting itself.[50] The Volkswagen, the *Autobahnen*, the air force, and Speer's Bureau of the Beauty of Labor were all examples of a new *NS-Technik*. Fried claimed that envy and resentment of Germany's liberation from "the chains of Jewish money" were the real motivations of the Reich's enemies.[51] The danger of dehumanization at the hands of the machine or of destruction of the German landscape had been averted. National Socialism meant deliverance from a wasteland.

Deliverance from the past only highlighted present dangers. Like the reactionary modernists, the Nazi propagandists transformed Germany's geographical location into a cultural-political identity. Germany, they said, as the country between East and West, was the only one to really grasp the "essence of technical creation." The *Deutsche Technik* authors repeated the complaints about American and British materialism and Soviet-style dialectical materialism. Only the Germans had synthesized technics and nature. By the time Hitler's armies dominated Europe from the Soviet Union to the Atlantic, such ideas were developed into a *Grossraum Technik*, a unified, integrated technological system in Europe, with Germany as its center.[52]

---

[50] Ferdinand Fried, "Die Soziale Revolution: Der Pakt mit der Technik – Die industrielle Revolution," *Deutsche Technik* (October 1942), pp. 410–13.

[51] Walter Ostwald, "NS-Technik: Was die nationalsozialistischen Revolution aus der deutschen Technik gemacht hat," *Deutsche Technik* (February 1943), pp. 48–50. Ostwald's essay was in an issue devoted to "the first ten years" of "national socialist technology after Adolf Hitler's assumption of power." Ostwald celebrated the *Autobahnen* in word and photos in "Vom Wesen der Reichsautobahn," *Deutsche Technik* (October 1939), pp. 396–401.

[52] Kurt Wagner, "Grossraum Technik," *Deutsche Technik* (April 1942). Wagner published a book by the same title: *Grossraum Technik: Die Technik im neuen Europa* (Berlin 1944).

The reader will recognize the familiar themes of reactionary modernism in these ideas. As I put it earlier, the Nazi propagandists were administrators of already existing traditions. But they were distinct within the panoply of German nationalism for the emphasis they placed on anti-Semitism and the biological foundations they gave to German technological advance. They wrote that the Nordic race had peculiar technical and scientific abilities. Had Germany only been a nation of poets, philosophers, and artists, it would be defenseless. Fortunately for the Germans, the Nordic race had a distinctive urge to dominate nature. One contributor referred to the electric motor as the "great symbol of German technology," a technology whose roots lay in the Nordic soul. Unlike the Americans, or the Jewish-Bolsheviks, who introduced technology with murder and forced labor, the Nazis built on German racial foundations to ward off the threats from both capitalism and socialism.[53] As one frequent contributor, Richard Grun, put it, "In this ruthless world, a nation of poets is defeated, a nation of philosophers hungers, a nation of aesthetes is subject to ridicule. Only a people able to produce arms, weapons, commodities, machines and knowledge is able to survive."[54] Grun argued that Germany must compensate for its numerical disadvantages in relation to its enemies with its technical capabilities and with efforts to increase the birth rate among the scientifically and technically talented.

Deutsche Technik, like *Technik und Kultur* earlier, published excerpts from books or from essays that later were expanded into books published in editions of about twenty to twenty-five thousand. The continuities with reactionary modernist ideology are striking. In 1936, for example, Fritz Nonnenbruch's *Die dynamische Wirtschaft* (The Dynamic Economy) was published by the Nazis. He wrote that National Socialism had overcome the abstract economic laws of a capitalism bereft of "ties to the *Volk*." The primacy of politics, not class conflict, had led to "the actual overcoming of capitalism." Nonnenbruch periodized the history of German capitalism in terms of predominance of either the Jewish or the Nordic spirit. Whereas pre-1933 capitalism had been dominated by the spirit of the merchant and financier, he argued that after 1933 it was dominated by the spirit of the "Nordic peoples" and was therefore productive and favorable to the interests of German engineers.[55] Economic crises had been brought about by

---

[53] Joseph Bader, "Das Deutsche und das Wesen des abendlandischen Technik."
[54] Richard Grun, "Sterbende Technik?" *Deutsche Technik* (September 1942), p. 282.
[55] Fritz Nonnenbruch, *Die dynamische Wirtschaft* (Munich, 1936), pp. 8, 124–5.

production for the market rather than for the needs of the nation. But the economic recovery after 1933 was evidence of the affinity between "the *Geist* of technics and the *Geist* of the race."[56]

In a manner reminiscent of Ernst Jünger, Nonnenbruch recalled the soldier formed by the *Fronterlebnis* as a "master of technology." The war had shown a generation of young Germans that technology need not be soulless and impersonal, but could be "great, manly, dangerous, free and wild...The will of the race speaks in highway construction."[57] Like many other contributors to *Deutsche Technik*, Nonnenbruch argued that the Nazis' great accomplishment was to have restored a dynamic to capitalism without also restoring bourgeois rationalism. Placing economics at the center of attention would have been a purely "intellectual exercise." But surrendering to the "will of the race for technology" would be a matter of the spirit and the soul, which are "superior to the intellect." "Where the race speaks, the intellect can offer no resistance. Appeals to the intellect bring disharmony. Appeals to the will of the race bring unity, harmony and creation."[58]

Nonnenbruch's brand of irrationalism lies within the reactionary modernist tradition, indicating its continuity after 1933. Nonnenbruch picked up on Goebbels's efforts to recast romanticism for a technological age, thereby linking National Socialism to another German tradition:

Technology is romantic but in a way that is totally different from any other kind of romanticism. It is not a flight from reality but a flaming illumination of reality. Flying in an airplane, driving in a car, the thunder of the elevated railway, the various landscapes of the battlefield, the glowing stream of flowing iron in the ghostly night filled with steel ovens – all of these thing are incomparably more romantic than anything previous romantics could imagine.[59]

Both Goebbels's steellike romanticism and Nonnenbruch's new romanticism were directed against those elements of the romantic tradition that supported a reconciliation with or return to nature. There were only two alternatives for the reactionary modernists: effeminate and cowardly escape into the Asian or pastoral past, or masculine and

---

[56] Ibid., p. 125.

[57] Ibid., pp. 142–3.

[58] Ibid., p. 151. The idea that National Socialism had "overcome" the cultural crisis occasioned by technological advance was common in *Deutsche Technik*. As early as 1934, K. F. Steinmetz, who had just been appointed the new editor of *Technik und Kultur*, wrote that technology was no longer a problem now that liberalism had been overcome and engineers had been reintegrated into the nation. See K. F. Steinmetz, "Die Technik ist kein Problem," *Technik und Kultur* 26 (1935), pp. 97–99.

[59] Nonnenbruch, *Die dynamische Wirtschaft*, p. 153.

courageous flight into the German future.[60] In one of the last issues of *Technik und Kultur*, Paul Ernst's criticisms of the dehumanizing impact of the division of labor were rejected in favor of a Jüngerian celebration of the *Gestalt* of the worker. Ernst was charged with escapism, having a merely "external" view of technology, and failing to recognize that technology was essential to the nation and grew out of the "inner necessity of our being."[61] The process of selectively borrowing from past cultural traditions, in this case romanticism, is again apparent in these statements. The reactionary modernists took those metaphors and symbols they found useful and rejected those they did not. However selective they were, the reactionary modernist tradition would have been inconceivable without romantic legacies.

Nonnenbruch's second book-length propaganda effort, *Technik, Politik und Geist*, repeated many of the themes he had developed in *Die dynamische Wirtschaft*. The immediate purpose of the book was to depict the four-year plan, in particular the achievements of the German chemical industry, as examples of a will-to-freedom present in the German nation. Development of synthetic fuels would free Germany from foreign sources of raw materials, and state direction of the economy abolished restrictions on growth due to commercial greed. In Nonnenbruch's account, National Socialism was attempting to reverse the results of World War I by "unleashing" technology. In so doing, the Nazis demonstrated that technology expressed the will of the *Volk* rather than the will of "international capitalism hostile to the *Volk*."[62] The synthesis of energy and organization in the four-year plan had been prefigured by the *Fronterlebnis* of World War I.

Like all of the Nazi propaganda concerning technology, *Technik, Politik, und Geist* was neither creative nor original. Its effectiveness rested on an obsessive repetition of the now familiar and stale metaphors and associations with which technology was presented in the language of National Socialism – *Geist, Gemeinschaft, Schicksal* (destiny), *Heldentum* (heroism), *Opferbereitschaft* (readiness for sacrifice), will, freedom, and race. In this cultural perspective, rationalization of in-

[60] See R. N. Coudenhove-Kalergi, *Revolution durch Technik* (Leipzig, 1932). Coudenhove-Kalergi juxtaposed European man – energetic, active, goal oriented, romantic, heroic, Dionysian, and manly – and Asian man – harmonious, rooted and settled, static, classical, idyllic, Apollonian, and effeminate. The European character is oriented to the domination of nature; the Asian character is oriented to self-control. Coudenhove-Kalergi saw the former as well suited for technology, whereas the latter was inclined to reject it. See pp. 25–9.
[61] Eberhard Ter-Nedden, "Paul Ernsts Stellung zur Technik," *Technik und Kultur* 28 (1937), pp. 82–4.
[62] Fritz Nonnenbruch, *Technik, Politik und Geist* (Munich, 1939), pp. 53–4.

dustry and preparation for aggression appear as a momentous cultural revolt against the now obsolete and historically bypassed liberal era. *Politik, Technik, und Geist* is evidence of the reactionary modernist effort to preserve the charismatic experience of World War I on the eve of the next war, and of the persistence of reactionary modernism after the first several years of the Hitler regime.

In 1937, Wilhelm Stortz, a professor of engineering at the technical university in Stuttgart, presented a National Socialist version of technological development in modern Germany, *Der Weg der deutschen Technik*. His reconstruction was as follows: Nineteenth-century Germany was spared the full brunt of the soulless materialism that engulfed England, France, and the United States because its industrialization process was guided by the state under Bismarck, Germany's "first National Socialist."[63] But by the turn of the century, "production of useful goods" (*Gebrauchs gutererzeugung*) was replaced by "commodity production" (*Warenerzeugung*), with a resultant decline both in the quality of goods and in the skills of the labor force, as well as growing unemployment. The years preceding World War I were characterized by the increasing predominance of "capitalist market calculation" over "technical quality."[64] But the war reversed this trend by wrenching technology out of the control of exchange relations and placing it in the service of the nation.

For Stortz, the tragedy of German technology was that at the very moment the generation formed by the war experience became aware of the value of technology for German nationalism, the Treaty of Versailles blocked German technical expansion. The Weimar system once again established the primacy of "economic thinking" over that of technical idealism. No wonder Spengler's pessimism found an echo. Stortz saw in National Socialism a political movement that presented resistance to cultural pessimism and that averted the "escape from technology which threatened to strangle us before 1933."[65] Stortz credited the Nazis with having successfully incorporated technological advance into the spiritual renewal of a victorious national revolution. As with so many of the reactionary modernists who preceded him, Stortz saw in war and nationalism the ideological and political alternative to the culture and politics of the market.

Book-length expositions of reactionary modernist themes continued to appear during the war years. Several works published from

[63] Wilhelm Stortz, *Der Weg der deutschen Technik* (Stuttgart, 1937), p. 8.
[64] Ibid., p. 12.
[65] Ibid., p. 39.

1940 to 1943 deserve mention: Alexander Friedrich's *Die unsichtbare Armee: Das Buch der Energie* (The Invisible Army: The Book of Energy), Richard Grun's *Wir und die Technik*, and Anton Zischka's *Erfinder brechen die Blockade* (Inventors Break the Blockade), and *Seig der Arbeit: Geschichte der fünftausendjährigen Kampfes gegen Unwissenheit und Sklaverei* (Victory of Labor: The History of the 5000-year-long Struggle against Ignorance and Slavery). All three authors continued to protest that no, technology is not a threat to the German soul, and to insist that yes, it is an expression of the heroic virtues of a united *Volksgemeinschaft*. All of them attacked intellectuals and artists who have shown no appreciation for technics and no understanding that "from Gutenberg and Luther through Hitler," the Germans have used technology to advance national unity.[66] And all of them attacked those remaining humanist Luddites who, they believed, were incapable of grasping the higher laws working in technical processes. These laws were not social or economic laws but determinations grounded in Germany's racial soul. True, for years German technology had suffered from the unproductive *jüdische Geist*, but those days of depraved commercialism were over. The Germans were bound to win the war because Germany's productivity would prevail over Jewish parasitism.[67]

Grun in particular stressed the masculine nature of technology. The proper order of things suggested that men built technological artifacts while women remained in the home. Further, he distinguished between tradition, which was good because it offered ties to the past and hope for the future, and reaction, which was bad because it stubbornly clung to obsolete methods of production and could thus harm the nation. The Nazis had addressed the engineers' need for tradition by integrating technology into the traditions of the whole nation. The calling of engineers demanded that they be innovators and revolutionaries, but this did not mean that they would be separated from the *Volk*. Recalling Todt's words on nature and technical form, Grun celebrated the synthesis of a German feeling for nature with a no less German drive for technical progress.

Finally, Grun wrote that National Socialism demonstrated that So-

[66] Richard Grun, *Wir und die Technik* (Berlin, 1942); Alexander Friedrich, *Die unsichtbare Armee: Das Buch der Energie* (Berlin, 1942); Anton Zischka, *Erfinder brechen die Blockade* (Berlin, 1940); and *Sieg der Arbeit: Geschichte der fünftausendjährigen Kampfes gegen Unwissenheit und Sklaverei* (Leipzig, 1941). Also see Ulrich Troitzsch, "Technikgeschichte in der Forschung und in der Sachbüchliteratur während des Nationalsozialismus," in *Naturwissenschaft, Technik und NS-Ideologie: Beiträge zur Wissenschaftsgeschichte des Dritten Reiches*, ed Herbert Mehrtene and Steffen Richter (Frankfurt, 1980), pp. 215–42.

[67] Richard Grun, *Wir und die Technik*, pp. 36, 60, 126.

cial Darwinism, the laws of nature, and the laws of technological advance were compatible. If the survival of the fittest was an unavoidable requirement of life, restricting technical progress would conflict with biological laws and make possible the triumph of those less racially fit. The real Nazi achievement was to have seen that technology was a biological rather than an economic phenomenon. To have succumbed to the antitechnological currents within German nationalism would have meant rejecting National Socialism's racial theory of history.

Zischka and Friedrich also attacked Jewish influence on German technology, praised Hitler for restoring technical progress in Germany, and advocated further development of synthetic fuels to overcome Germany's paucity of natural resources. Both Friedrich and Zischka emphasized the importance of scientific and technical discoveries for Germany's independence. As Zischka put it, Germany was strong because "invention lies in our blood," unlike the British, whose technical skills were merely "external" and lacking in the inner depths that continued to push German technological progress forward.[68] Now that the power of the Jews over German energy and technology had been broken, a bright future of national independence, technical advances, and authoritarian politics promised to sustain the *Volksgemeinschaft* indefinitely.[69] Germany's enemies – the United States, Britain, and the Soviet Union – still labored under the burden of the Jews and thus would fall behind the Nazis' technical capabilities.

In view of the balance of military and industrial power between Germany and her enemies, these statements were complete delusions. Earlier I recalled Todt's famous 1941 meeting with Hitler in which he urged that a respect for strategic realities be given equal weight with ideological goals. When Albert Speer took over the position of armaments minister after Todt's death in a plane crash following his meeting with Hitler, he remained loyal to Hitler almost to the very end, despite the fact that he had the same information about the relative strengths of the German and Allied military-industrial capabilities as Todt. There was no revolt of the technocrats against the ideologues.

The reactionary modernist tradition reached its end point in the SS. In the last years of the war, Hitler's ideological convictions remained unshaken, as did his faith in technological breakthroughs that would

[68] Anton Zischka, *Erfinder brechen die Blockade*, pp. 94–5. Cited in Ulrich Troitzsch, "Technikgeschichte in der Forschung," pp. 28–9.
[69] See Friedrich, *Die unsichtbare Armee*, p. 54. See Ulrich Troitzsch, "Technikgeschichte in der Forschung," pp. 225–33.

bring about a dramatic reversal of the course of events. Hitler became both an advocate of the omnipotence of the will and a seeker after a technological fix – the wonder-weapons such as the V-1 and V-2 rockets that would win the war. In 1942, Goebbels opened an office for weapons propaganda, presented visions of a European technology of the future, and, above all, spoke more and more about a new *Waffenmythos* as the course of the war went from bad to worse. Goebbels's hopes were grotesque in view of the imbalances between Germany and the Allies. In 1944, German war production amounted to 4 percent of American war production alone. In 1945, the Germans did not even have a wind tunnel in which to test airplanes.[70]

In this hopeless situation, it was only fitting that the ideological fanatics in the regime should be the major proponents of the technological fix. By 1944, the SS had 900,000 men under arms in thirty-eight divisions. It conducted research leading to innovations in machine guns, flame throwers, tanks, air defenses, and airplanes. Himmler also supported research into high-frequency electronics at Dachau. (One of the most fortunate ironies of modern German history was that the Nazis' anti-Semitism sent much of the physics community into exile, thereby hindering the development of the real "wonder-weapon," the atom bomb.) But the most important of the SS projects was the rocket program at Peenemünde, where the V-1 and V-2 were developed and tested. These were to be the wonder-weapons that would reverse the course of the war and demonstrate that the German racial soul could compensate for quantitative (and in many cases qualitative) inferiorities. They were also the fitting culmination of the reactionary modernist tradition. However destructive they may have been, placing hopes in them at that date was indicative of the contempt for strategic thinking, that is, for relating means to ends, that had permeated the Nazi regime.[71] Reactionary modernist views of technology must be given credit for this remarkable instance of nonutilitarian flight into ideological politics up to the very end.

German engineers, along with the conservative economic, military, foreign policy, and civil service elites of German society allied with Hitler to serve their own particular ends. Like these other elites, the engineers were convinced that Hitler was devoted above all to the

---

[70] For a thorough discussion of German weapons technology in 1944–5, see Ludwig, *Technik und Ingenieure*, pp. 451–73.
[71] On the role of the SS in the German armament program see Ludwig, *Technik und Ingenieure*, pp. 473–514. On the forced emigration of the German Jewish physicists and its impact on physics under the Nazis, see Beyerchen, *Scientists Under Hitler: Politics and the Physics Community under Hitler* (New Haven, Conn., 1977).

preservation of the existing order, albeit in its most reactionary form. But among the engineers, just as among these other elites, there were currents of ideas, partly indigenous and partly fanned by the Nazis, that pointed to a cultural and political revolution centered around a racial utopia. This utopia flew in the face of the logic of capitalist profit, Prussian military tradition, traditional German foreign policy, and the engineers' technical reason. But none of these groups had been sufficiently wedded to liberal values to see the point of resisting Hitler before it was too late. And each could draw on traditions similar to reactionary modernism that dispirited those who questioned the regime and gave heart to others who believed Hitler really was speaking for Germany.[72]

In this chapter, I have presented evidence that the reactionary modernist tradition by no means faded away under the pressures of political rule and the conduct of war. On the contrary, the Nazis gave to the tradition both institutional and propagandistic expression. They borrowed from its language and metaphor to assert that their rejection of the Enlightenment was compatible with technology, but that very same rejection became a barrier to technical innovation as well as to matching technical capacities with strategic realities. The German soul and will proved tenacious but woefully inadequate when confronted with the Allied arsenal. Hitler's defeat reminds us that National Socialism was not only a monstrous evil. It was also self-destructive, a self-destructiveness due in part to the tradition this book has documented. Had the Nazis been committed Luddites, they would not have been able to start World War II. Had they been cynical, calculating technocrats, they might have won a more limited victory or, at the very least, avoided catastrophic defeat. The reactionary modernist tradition was politically consequential in three fundamental ways. First, it contributed to the technological strength that made the war conceivable, if not winnable; second, by preserving an antiscientific and antirational ethos it created a barrier to technical innovations that could compare with efforts in Russia, Great Britain, and the United

---

[72] On Hitler and the Reichswehr see Michael Geyer's *Aufrüstung oder Sicherheit: Die Reichswehr in der Krise der Machtpolitik, 1924–1936* (Wiesbaden, 1980). Geyer concludes that despite its intensive rearmament, the Third Reich was not in a position to conduct a war based on the strategic coordination of means and ends characteristic of Bismarckian military tradition. The parallel to German engineers is striking: The politicization of the military in the Third Reich pointed to a war unguided by technical or strategic rationality. For the generals to have resisted would have demanded a defense of their professional best judgment, yet that resort to expertise was ruled out with the politicization of the military elites. See pp. 489–505.

States; and third, it was part of the ideological fanaticism that convinced the Nazis they could win even though they lacked the means to attain victory and replaced strategic coordination of ends and available means with political gambles based on the language of the will.

9

Conclusion

In this study I have stressed three broad themes concerning sociology, technology and society, and totalitarianism in power under Hitler. First, both the form in which modernity arrived and the cultural responses to it, one of which was reactionary modernism, were deeply shaped by the peculiarities of modern German history and society. Reactionary modernism was a specifically German response to a universal dilemma of societies facing the consequences of the industrial and French revolutions: How can national traditions be reconciled with modern culture, modern technology, and modern political and economic institutions? I view this study as an exercise in interpretive historical sociology that sets forth universal dilemmas confronting modernizing societies, examines how different social actors respond to these dilemmas with complexes of meaning that form the basis of their social and political action, and finally, traces the impact of these responses on the course of historical and political events. Within the ongoing debate over the nature of the Nazi regime, this study lends support to the "intentionalists," that is, those observers who insist that Nazi ideology, however base, was politically decisive.

Political sociology that is interpretive and historical is necessarily a pluralistic undertaking. Events cannot be reduced to any single variable or factor. This study has focused on politics, culture, and ideology. No monocausality is thereby intended. The question of why ideas such as these arose, and then why their adherents were able to seize dictatorial powers, returns us again to the conventional issues of sociological and structural analysis: the social basis of Nazi support, the predominance of the state over society, the failure of the bourgeois revolution and the weakness of liberalism in Germany, the identification of German nationalism with antidemocratic, authoritarian institutions, the tension between charisma and bureaucracy within the Hitler regime, and the cooperation and conflict between conservative

217

elites and the Nazis. All of these factors must be taken into account to explain the political outcomes of the Third Reich. In my view, in the last decade, structural analysis has too often come to be a code word for neglect of the cultural and ideological dimensions of political and historical sociology. In seeking to give ideas their due, I am hoping to right a methodological imbalance, rather than put forth a new and equally unconvincing single factor to which everything can be reduced "in the last analysis." But I do believe that analyses that slight the role of ideas offer at best the necessary, but insufficient, conditions to account for the political consequences of the German dictatorship.

Second, in discussions of the relation between technology and society, this study is intended to offer a sober warning about the seemingly irresistible temptation to derive political, economic, or cultural imperatives from technology. The literary, philosophical, and sociological contributors to the reactionary modernist tradition knew precious little about technology, and the engineers' understanding of the social world was equally primitive. Not surprisingly, their political views on how to respond to the challenges of the second industrial revolution were disastrous.

Third, these ideas contributed to political disaster because their institutionalization in the Nazi regime did not require routinization of ideological politics. Reactionary modernism was an important part of totalitarian dictatorship in power in several senses: It offered a comprehensive explanation of a supposed nonpolitical phenomenon, thus demonstrating the capacity of nazism to provide answers to all of life's dilemmas; it gave the Nazis a political language of movement and dynamism that helped to counter a waning of the emotional force of Nazi ideology after the seizure of power; and most important, it surmounted the ideological conflict between technical advances and Nazi ideology.

In discussions of technology and society in Germany, two ideas have continued to appear. The first is that the conservative *Kulturkritik* of the Weimar years was exclusively and predominantly antitechnological. The second is that technology was responsible for war and the various discontents of modern life.[1] This study of the reactionary

[1] See Helga Grebing, *Linksradikalismus gleich Rechtsradikalismus: Eine falsche Gleichung* (Stuttgart, 1969), esp. chap. 3, "Antiindustriegesellschaftliche Kultur-, Zivilisation-, und Kapitalismuskritik," pp. 37–50; Helmut Schelsky, *Sozialistische Lebenshaltung* (Leipzig, 1934), and his *Der Mensch in der wissenschaftlichen Zivilisation* (Cologne, 1961); René König, "Zur Soziologie der Zwanziger Jahre: oder ein Epilog zu zwei Revolu-

modernist tradition suggests that the first claim is historically inaccurate and that the second is the result of an inadequate understanding of the connection between technology and politics, economics and social relationships. There is a similarity between these varieties of cultural pessimism and it lies in the reification of technology, that is, in talk of its "imperatives" or "autonomy." Such concepts displace responsibility for the shaping of events from political leaders onto impersonal forces and obscure the fact that although technical innovations in themselves do follow the demands of efficiency and means–ends rationality, the social, cultural, and political responses to technical innovation vary widely in different national contexts. Reactionary modernist arguments were made by individuals in England (Wyndham Lewis), Italy (Marinetti), and the United States (Henry Ford), but nowhere else did such a tradition become a constitutive part of the national identity as in Germany.[2] The reconciliations of technics and irrationalism that this book has documented were not and are not inherent in modernity, capitalism, or the Enlightenment, but rather in a peculiarly authoritarian, illiberal, and unenlightened national variant of them. When these cultural patterns have appeared in places other than Germany, it is because Germany's path to modernity has been reproduced outside Europe.

The starting points of this study were the following questions: How did the ideologists of the German Right, heirs to an irrationalist tradition, reconcile themselves to modern industrial technology? When did these cultural reconciliations occur? What emerged as the main themes and metaphors of the ideology as a cultural system? What impact did they have on the ideology and practice of National Socialism before and after 1933? I posed these questions to confront difficulties in presenting Nazi ideology as primarily antiindustrial or backward looking, on the one hand, or as technocratic, on the other. The Hitler regime never pursued antiindustrialism, but neither did it behave as technocratic reason would suggest it should. To describe the Nazis as *völkisch* ideologues or as cynical technocrats suggests that they regarded their own world view as a tool of mass manipulation that was incompatible with ruling an industrial society. Both of these

tionen, die niemals stattgefunden haben, und was daraus für unser Gegenwart resultiert," in *Die Zeit ohne Eigenschaften: Eine Bilanz der Zwanziger Jahre*, ed. L. Rheinisch (Stuttgart, 1961), pp. 82–118. (Berkeley, 1975), pp. 82–3.
[2] On Lewis, See Frederic Jameson, *Fables of Aggression. Wyndham Lewis: The Modernist as Fascist* (Berkeley: University of California Press, 1979); on Ezra Pound, see Miriam Hansen, *Ezra Pounds frühe Poetik und Kulturkritik zwischen Aufklärung und Avantgarde* (Stuttgart, 1979); on Marinetti, see Joll, *Three Intellectuals in Politics: Blum, Rathenau, Marinetti* (New York, 1965).

implications appeared to me to be wrong in view of the combination of advanced technology and political irrationality, what Goebbels so aptly called "steellike romanticism," that characterized the Third Reich, especially in the years of war and genocide. As Arendt pointed out in her still indispensable study of totalitarianism, what perplexed contemporaries and subsequent commentators about totalitarian rule was its antiutilitarian commitment to ideological absolutes.[3] That nazism was a monstrous evil is obvious. What Arendt understood so well was that added to evil was its self-destructive, means–ends irrationality in regard to any of the conventional institutions it was supposed to be protecting, such as capitalism or the nation. It subordinated these interests to fulfillment of a racial utopia grounded in a totally irrational, biologically based Nazi ideology.

I have tried to show that the paradoxical combination of irrationalism and technics was fundamental to Hitler's ideology and practices and to National Socialism. This tradition began in Germany's technical universities in the late nineteenth century, was nurtured by the national engineering associations, given new life by Weimar's conservative revolutionaries, and became a constituent component of Nazi ideology from the early 1920s up to 1945. This synthesis of political reaction with an affirmative stance toward technological progress emerged well before 1933 and contributed to the ongoing ideological dynamism of the regime after 1933. The rise of the Nazis to positions of economic and political power did not, as Schonbaum and Dahrendorf suggested, require the decline of Nazi ideology. And although, as Rabinbach has pointed out, there was a shift in Speer's Bureau of the Beauty of Labor in the 1930s from *völkisch* ideology to technocratic aesthetics, this Nazi *Sachlichkeit* existed alongside a more pervasive and widespread irrationalist continuum evident in the propaganda efforts of Todt and Goebbels. The institutionalization of the reactionary modernist tradition did not entail its domestication or routinization. By the time the four-year plan was initiated in 1936, both the Nazis and the conservative elites had broken with the more pronounced pastoral and antitechnological resentments that had previously characterized German nationalism. Fulfillment of Nazi ideology and industrial advance reinforced one another until the former brought about the destruction and self-destruction of German society. Reactionary modernism contributed to the terrible consistency of Nazi ideology and practice, the core of which was anti-Semitism, not the

---

[3] Arendt, *The Origins of Totalitarianism* (Cleveland, 1958), esp. the chapters on totalitarianism in power and ideology and terror.

traditional conservative animus against industrialism. As Thomas Mann understood, the unity of Nazi ideology and practice was partly due to the peculiarly German synthesis of "dreams of the past" with visions of a "robust modernity."[4]

The discussion of Sombart, Jünger, Freyer, Schmitt, Heidegger, and Sombart suggests that we revise our view of Weimar's conservative revolution to incorporate their affirmations of modern technology.[5] But it also suggests that there were as many bridges as chasms between the "two cultures," literary-humanistic and scientific-technological, on the German Right in this period. The work of the right-wing philosophers, social scientists, and essayists possesses its own fascination. But what strikes us as perhaps even more unusual is to come across a tradition of cultural politics within the German engineering profession. According to the cultural politicians of German engineering from the 1870s up through Weimar, there were two main threats to German engineers. The first was German cultural pessimism and misguided romanticism, which assumed that technology would destroy the German soul. The second was the industrial capitalist system itself, which failed to grasp that the engineer was a modern artist and instead treated him and his work merely as a source of commercial advantage. This anticapitalism of the engineers shared with the literary-philosophical intellectuals a disdain for the expansion of exchange relations into the sphere of culture, in this case technical culture. The Nazis were fully aware of this tradition and sought to present themselves to engineers as a movement dedicated to emancipating technology from its misuse by market interests and then to placing it in the service of the state. The tradition of the engineers is predominantly one of cultural nationalism. But the Nazis had little difficulty using the reactionary modernist tradition to present a biological-racial version of German technology struggling for its freedom.[6]

The contributors to *Technik und Kultur* insisted that technology was part of the *Kulturnation*. The contributors to *Deutsche Technik* claimed that Hitler was fulfilling the engineers' own goals: Technology had been unleashed; the degenerate materialist era was a thing of the past; technology now served the general welfare. It might be said that, after all, relatively few engineers bothered themselves with these disputes. But of the 300,000 engineers in Weimar Germany, about 10,000 re-

[4] Mann, "Deutschland und die Deutschen," *Thomas Mann: Essays*, Band 2, *Politik*, ed. H. Kunzke (Frankfurt, 1977).
[5] See Norr, "German Social Theory and the Hidden Face of Technology," *European Journal of Sociology* XV (1974), pp. 312–36.
[6] Ludwig, *Technik und Ingenieure im Dritten Reich* (Königstein, 1979), pp. 18–102.

ceived *Technik und Kultur*, and about 80,000 received *Deutsche Technik* during the Hitler years. These numbers are considerable in themselves. Moreover, these engineers were the graduates of Germany's elite technical universities and they assumed leading positions within the profession and then within the Nazi regime. And most important, to the extent German engineers thought about the problem of technology and culture, they did so in the terms defined by reactionary modernism. Technocracy remained a feeble impulse. Leaders of the national engineering organizations who were less interested in cultural politics responded to Hitler's promise to restore national honor and end unemployment. They did not wage a battle of ideas with the Nazis for the souls of their members. There was no other tradition of German nationalism to compete with it or to offer an alternative interpretation of technology, society, and culture in modern Germany.

Nazi propaganda was not created out of thin air. If it had been it would not have been effective. Nazi propaganda concerning technology is simply incomprehensible without seeing its background in the reactionary modernist tradition. And this propaganda produced important political effects. First, it contributed to the nazification of German engineering. The fact of engaging in "the most rational vocation," as Neumann put it, did not mean that engineers were immune from the Nazis' "magic propaganda." It is not surprising that engineers would favor technological advance. What is interesting is that they did so in the vocabulary of German *Innerlichkeit*. There were thousands of engineers for whom the distinction between ideologue and technocrat simply did not exist. Second, we often forget that propaganda has an effect on its advocates as well as on those at whom it is directed. In a totalitarian system lacking in free public discussion, ideology need not test itself against reality or at least opposing interpretations of reality. If leading members of the Nazi regime actually came to believe that German technology was in fact the expression of an Aryan racial soul or that the will to power was pulsing through and over the *Autobahnen*, then there would be no limit to the strategic miscalculations they could make. Their antiintellectualism caught up with them. The price to be paid for the reactionary modernist synthesis was severe: declining enrollments, reduced study time, and a glaring deficit of understanding at the highest levels of the Nazi regime concerning the relationship between developments in modern science and technical innovation. The number and quality of German arms were simply insufficient to match those of nazism's enemies. In this sense, the reconciliations of reactionary modernism came up against the limits imposed by its rejection of the Enlightenment. Reactionary

Conclusion

modernism had taught them to neglect strategy for ideology. Neumann was quite right that the sobriety of technical reason demanded a break with Hitler's two-front war and the Holocaust. The break never came. Opportunism, fear, and cynicism played a role in the loyalty of the engineers. But they do in any regime, authoritarian or democratic. Reactionary modernism in the form of Nazi ideology was a powerful contributing factor in the subordination of technical rationality by Nazi engineers to the claims of Nazi ideology.

I believe this argument is reinforced when we compare the German and Russian experiences, a comparison facilitated by Kendall Bailes's recent study of technology and society under Lenin and Stalin.[7] In both regimes, engineers and politicians took as their model for the future the coalition of industry, government, and technology forged in World War I; new political elites monopolized political power and advanced technical programs requiring the knowledge of engineers; and relations between government and engineers were marked by cooperation stemming from mutual desires for technical advance as well as conflict caused by political ideology. But these similarities are less important than the differences.

First, both Lenin and subsequently Marxism-Leninism were highly enthusiastic about science and technology without the residue of philosophical irrationalism that burdened National Socialism. In cultural terms, Marxism-Leninism was far less hostile to the *Geist* of capitalism than was the cultural revolution of the Right that nourished Hitlerism. Lenin's enthusiasm for Taylorism is only one manifestation of the Marxist-Leninist view that communism comes about as the unfolding of the scientific and technological trends within capitalism. Whereas the whole ethos of the German dictatorship was directed against the Enlightenment, the Soviet leaders believed they were in possession of a science of history and society. It is no wonder that the Nazis sought to separate technology from soulless *Amerikanismus* while the Soviets strained to catch up with and overtake the latest capitalist developments. As we have seen in the previous chapter, German romanticism proved a far greater barrier to technical advance than did Russian scientism. While engineers in the Soviet Union were attacked for being class enemies or for having too much knowledge in a society professing egalitarianism as a goal, German engineers existed in a climate in

[7] Bailes, *Technology and Society under Lenin and Stalin: Origins of the Soviet Technical Intelligentsia* (Princeton, N.J., 1978). Also see Martin J. Wiener's fine study, *English Culture and the Decline of the Industrial Spirit, 1850–1980* (New York, 1981). Wiener documents the antipathy toward technical and industrial advance and argues that the decline of the industrial spirit has been a major factor in British economic decline.

which the dominant political ideology persistently challenged the kinds of knowledge needed for technical innovation. *Deutsche Technik* referred primarily to advances that predated 1933. Marxism-Leninism proved a far more effective suppressant of antiscientific currents in Russian culture than reactionary modernism was in Germany. Both dictatorships established barriers to technical innovation, but those of the Nazi regime were more in keeping with the fundamental world view of its political leadership. Viewed comparatively, the reactionary modernist reconciliations of technology and unreason were still so filled with antiintellectualism and dread of the Enlightenment that it is no wonder the Nazis' scientific and technical advances – with the important exception of the SS-guided rocket program – were meager compared to those of the Allies.

This said, the accomplishments of the reactionary modernists were considerable. They removed technology from the world of Enlightenment reason, that is, of *Zivilisation*, and placed it into the language of German nationalism, that is, of *Kultur*. They claimed that technology could be described with the jargon of authenticity, that is, slogans celebrating immediacy, experience, the self, soul, feeling, blood, permanence, will, instinct, and finally the race, rather than what they viewed as the lifeless abstractions of intellect, analysis, mind, concepts, money, and the Jews. By identifying technology with form, production, use value, creative (German or Aryan) labor, and German romanticism, rather than with formlessness, circulation, exchange value, and parasitic (Jewish) finance capital, they incorporated technology into the "anticapitalistic yearnings" that National Socialism exploited. To oppose or defend the Enlightenment and industrial progress together is straightforward enough. The paradox of reactionary modernism is that it rejected reason but embraced technology, reconciled *Innerlichkeit* with technical modernity.

The main themes of the reactionary modernist tradition were as follows. First, it presented an aesthetic view of technology as comprising new, stable forms that constituted beautiful alternatives to a flabby and chaotic bourgeois order. The reactionary modernists celebrated beauty and form as ethical ideals in themselves. In so doing they shared affinities with the modernism of the avant-garde as well as with technical innovators. As Benjamin perceived at the time, the politicization of this ideal of beauty served authoritarian purposes. Second, reactionary modernism put forth the belief that technology was an externalization of the will to power. This Nietzschean motif celebrated the domination of nature with Social Darwinist overtones and excoriated antitechnological romanticism as effeminate and escapist. The reactionary modernists also drew on *Lebensphilosophie* in describing technological artifacts as external expressions of an inner, mysterious soul. Thus they could view technology as the physical embodiment of inner qualities, rather than as the product of positivism. Third, reactionary modernism claimed technology was indispensable to a renewed primacy of politics. The state, not the economy, would dominate society. This new Caesarism would break the dictatorship of money and create a new mastery of blood. Fourth, after World War I, reactionary modernism associated technology with the masculine community of the *Fronterlebnis*. This community was the alternative to bourgeois decadence but it was anything but pastoral or backward looking. As Jünger put it, the war showed the conservative revolutionaries that nationalism and modern life were compatible with one another. Fifth, reactionary modernism claimed that technology was a uniquely German product and must not be confused with the financial swindles of the Jews. Both the conservative revolutionary intellectuals and the engineers presented anticapitalist rhetoric that easily slipped into anti-Semitism. It was the Jews who were responsible for the misuse of technology; Germans were, by contrast, a productive people. Sombart's translations of social and economic categories into racial categories were further taken up by the Nazis. National Socialism would liberate technology from Jewish materialism. As Postone put it, anti-Semitism in Germany was a kind of "fetishized anti-capitalism" transformed into a biological juxtaposition of the abstract Jew and the concrete German. "Auschwitz, not [the seizure of power in] 1933 was the real 'German Revolution.' "[8] Once the Jews were equated with capitalism and communism, their destruction would eliminate the major evils of the modern world and bring about a National Socialist revolution. And finally, reactionary modernism maintained that Germany, as the country located between East and West, had a unique mission. It alone was able to combine technology and soul. Where the Americans and the Soviets were lost in materialism, Germany would become technically advanced but remain a community. By articulating these themes, the reactionary modernists helped to define German national identity.

There were, of course, eminently practical reasons for German nationalism to distance itself from its antitechnological aspects. As Spengler put it, "conservatism of means" in the era of modern war was a recipe for national defeat. He and the other contributors to

---

[8] Postone, "Anti-Semitism and National Socialism: Notes on the German Reaction to 'Holocaust,' " *New German Critique* 19 (Winter 1980), pp. 97–115.

reactionary modernist ideology made a virtue of necessity. Whereas German conservatives had argued that too much technical advance would destroy the German soul, the reactionary modernists claimed that too little would destroy the nation and without it the German soul would be lost. It is true that many of the reactionary modernists were not the biological racists the Nazis were. But by the time those who cared realized that differences existed, it was too late. Goebbels's "steellike romanticism" or Todt's "highways bound to the landscape" referred to familiar traditions. The Nazis appeared to be fulfilling the fondest dreams of the reactionary modernists. The engineers' own traditions were sufficiently irrationalist that they were unable to reflect on the wildly impractical and antinational nature of the ultimate goals of the Hitler regime. The incorporation of technology into modern German nationalism brought a set of apparently discordant meanings together in a coherent and compelling ideology. This ideology is presented in the following list of conceptual opposites comprising a cultural system.

Kultur and Technik (culture and technology)	*Zivilisation und Wirtschaft* (civilization and economy)
Concrete immediacy	Abstraction
Experience	Analysis
Soul	Mind
Feeling	Intellect
Visualizing thinking	Conceptual thinking
Blood	Intellect and/or money
Life	Death
Community	Society
Form	Chaos-formlessness
Order	Chaos-formlessness
Gestalt	Chaos-formlessness
Will	Passivity
Will toward form	Parliamentary confusion
Beauty	Ugliness
Permanence	Transience
Ruin value	Exchange value
Productivity	Parasitism
Production	Circulation
Entrepreneur	Merchant
German	Jew
Germany the *Kulturnation*	America and Russia
Creative labor	Finance capital

Worker-soldier	Citizen
Anticapitalism	Capitalism
German socialism	International socialism
General welfare	Private selfish interest
Production for use	Production for profit
Primacy of politics	Primacy of the economy
Use value	Exchange value
Quality	Quantity
Masculine domination over nature	Feminine reconciliation with nature
Sacrifice	Self-interest

This chart summarizes the cultural incorporation of technology into German nationalism and subsequently into Nazi ideology. The reactionary modernists believed that modern technology could be made compatible with particularity, immediacy, and experience rather than with analysis, intellect, and abstraction; with life, soul, and feeling, rather than with deadly concepts and formulas; with blood rather than with money; with the permanence of form over the transience of the chaotic market; with the beauty of authoritarian politics rather than with the confusion and lack of clarity of parliamentary discussion; with production and use value over circulation, parasitism, and exchange value; with masculine will rather than with effeminate reconciliation with nature; with the primacy of nationalist politics rather than with the selfish economic interests; with the racial *Volk* rather than with the Jews. In the technology of the first and second industrial revolutions, that is, in cars, trucks, airplanes, tanks, battleships, steam engines, electric motors, machine guns, radios, telephones, highways, and bridges, the reactionary modernists saw objects that were external manifestations of *Kultur* rather than of *Zivilisation*.

There were limits to their selective embrace of modernity. Reactionary modernism remained too provincial to embrace modern physics, a science that could not claim to be an exclusively Aryan creation. Neither was reactionary modernism a fully technocratic ideology, one that encouraged long-range planning or strategic thinking in Germany in the 1930s. On the contrary, the more the glaring deficiencies of the Nazi war preparations came to light, the more Goebbels turned to the ideology of the will. Although the reactionary modernists helped Germans overcome their famous distaste for modern technology, they did not teach them how to balance means and ends. If technology was to be filled with *Geist* and *Seele*, what difference did it make if the

Russians produced twice or three times as many tanks? This was, as Hitler put it, merely a technical problem; the will would triumph.

That it did not was not due to lack of effort. This fact was obvious in the immediate postwar years but has been forgotten in much of the social scientific literature on the subject. There are different reasons for this forgetting. Marxists kept trying to fit the facts into a theoretical framework that viewed National Socialism as a variant of capitalism and that, "in the last analysis," viewed politics and ideas as subordinate to class interests. Theorists of modernization paid more attention to the role of ideology as an autonomous force but their dichotomous thinking prevented them from understanding that Germany could be both modernizing and irrationalist.[9]

"I am unutterably thankful," wrote one British general soon after the end of the war, "that the lunatic devotion of the madman's judgment pervaded every aspect of German activity. Never before has the truth of the old saying been so conclusively borne out, 'Whom the gods wish to destroy they first make mad.' "[10] Despite years of criticism, the great merit of Hannah Arendt's analysis of totalitarianism was her understanding that National Socialism was driven by a set of ideological absolutes that were antiutilitarian in the extreme. The great drawback of the Marxist analyses, of which Neumann's remains the most impressive, is that they simply could not account for the direction of the Hitler regime by referring to capitalism or imperialism. To focus on capitalism simply begged the question, for it left open the issue of what was unique about Germany that led to National Socialism, while the economic crises of the 1930s had such different outcomes in other capitalist societies.[11] In the last decade, a vogue for "structural" explanations of political events has entered Anglo-American sociology, thus adding a bias against looking at the subjective meanings actors attach to political actions. As Max Weber argued, historical and political sociology requires attention to, rather than

---

[9] See discussion in chap. 1.

[10] Lord Tedder, Foreword to H. R. Trevor-Roper, *The Last Days of Hitler* (New York, 1979), p. 14.

[11] In addition to Arendt's analyses of totalitarianism, see Karl Bracher, "The Role of Hitler: Perspectives of Interpretation," in *Fascism: A Reader's Guide*, ed. Walter Laqueur, (Berkeley, 1976), pp. 211–25; Erich Goldhagen, "Weltanschauung und Endlösung," *Vierteljahresheft für Zeitgeschichte* (October 1976), pp. 379–405; and Andreas Hillgruber, *Hitlers Strategie: Politik und Kriegführung 1940–1941* (Frankfurt, 1965), and "Die 'Endlösung' und das deutsche Ostimperium als Kernstück des rassenideologischen Programms des Nationalsozialismus" (The Final Solution and the German Empire in the East as the Cornerstone of National Socialism's Racial-Ideological Program), *Vierteljahresheft für Zeitgeschichte* (April 1972), pp. 133–53; and Norman Rich, *Hitler's War Aims* (New York, 1973).

neglect of, intentions, culture, and ideas in politics. I hope this book demonstrates the merit of Weber's contention.[12]

The underestimation of the importance of Nazi ideology by scholars studying it after the fact only mirrored the underestimation of Hitler and Nazi ideology by his contemporaries. Neither Germany's conservative elites nor Hitler's opponents on the Communist Left took his ideas very seriously. The former believed they could use him as a tool to destroy the Weimar Republic, smash the organizations of the working class, rearm – and then dismiss him. The latter deluded themselves into believing that, as the Communist slogan went, "After Hitler, comes us."[13] In the history of diplomatic appeasement, this underestimation was repeated in the realm of foreign affairs. The generation that witnessed these events and their consequences learned that neither common sense nor interest group politics triumphed over ideological absolutes. Hitler's racial ideology undermined calculations based on traditional Prussian concepts of power politics. In Weber's terms, nazism represented the ascendancy of an ethic of ultimate (racial) ends over the politics of (nationalist or capitalist) responsibility. Hitler's racial ideology went far beyond the point at which it served as a useful mechanism of social integration by projecting discontents onto a scapegoat.[14] The utopia of a biologically superior master race, not the defense of German capitalism, was the core of Hitler's world view. And his world view was both coherent and politically consequential.[15] Both at the time and since, "sophisticated" insight into the real purposes behind Hitler's ideology has relied basically on a nineteenth-century utilitarianism unwilling or unable to come to terms with twentieth-century totalitarian politics. The analysis of reactionary modernism presented in this book is an effort to right the balance and give cultural and ideological traditions their due.

That said, it is only fair to inform the reader that this study had its origin in a theoretical perspective whose interpretation of National Socialism now appears to me to have been profoundly mistaken. Unlike most of the liberal and Marxist contemporaries of the Nazis, the

[12] Max Weber, *The Theory of Social and Economic Organization*, trans. Talcott Parsons (New York, 1964), pp. 88–100. Recently, Anthony Giddens has argued for bringing together the philosophical discussion on intentionality and motives in social action with analyses of politics and social structure. See his *Central Problems in Social Theory* (London, 1979).

[13] Bracher, "The Role of Hitler: Perspectives of Interpretation."

[14] Klaus Hildebrand, *The Foreign Policy of the Third Reich*, trans. Anthony Fothergill (Berkeley, 1973), pp. 106–7.

[15] A point well made by Eberhard Jäckel in *Hitler's World View: A Blueprint for Power*, trans. Herbert Arnold (Middletown, Conn., 1972).

critical theorists of the Frankfurt school clearly perceived the cultural paradoxes, the syntheses of reason and myth, which this book documents in greater detail. They devoted more attention to culture than Marxists ordinarily did while as dialectical thinkers they did not shy away from paradoxes for the safer havens of dichotomous thinking. Before making my criticisms explicit, my extensive intellectual debts to them must be made clear.

The concept of reification is important for placing technology in the social and political contexts of its introduction and development. Lukács discussed the issue in his analysis of Soviet Marxism. Adorno, Benjamin, Horkheimer, and Marcuse also noticed that the German right-wing intellectuals separated technology from its social context. Benjamin was the first social theorist and cultural critic to discuss the connection between the European avant-garde, the cult of technics, German romanticism, and the post-war Right in Germany. Contemporary discussions of Nazi aesthetics derive from his comments on the right-wing celebration of war's beauty. Horkheimer's discussions of the revolt of nature and of the anti-Semitic separation of circulation and production blended Marx and Weber into a preliminary statement of the synthesis of reason, myth, and domination that he and Adorno elaborated most fully in the *Dialectic of Enlightenment*, a work that will remain one of the classics of twentieth-century social theory. Ernst Bloch, though not a member of the Frankfurt school circle, was one of the very few Marxists to notice that nazism was able to blend technical modernity and German romanticism. Bloch was so perceptive that he actually took the trouble to write several very insightful essays on the unlikely topic of the mixture of mysticism and technical reason in the writings of German engineers in the Weimar Republic.[16]

Contemporary epigones of the critical Marxists have also influenced the development of this work. The concept of romantic anticapitalism, when applied to German intellectual life, does more than offer a materialist analysis of cultural revolt. It suggests the different paths anticapitalist cultural revolutions may take. Whereas the far Left saw the future community in the workers' councils and soviets, the far Right saw that community in the *Fronterlebnis*. Here was the "lost treasure" that would be regained and made permanent by right-wing politics. This lost treasure did not lie in the distant past, nor was it agrarian or antiindustrial. The war and German nationalism were fully modern alternatives to capitalist exchange and bourgeois society. This analysis of romantic anticapitalism qualifies not only the equa-

---

[16] On the contributions of the critical Marxists, see chap. 1.

tion of antimodernity and Nazi ideology but also that of of antimodernity and anti-Semitism. Identifying the Jews with circulation and finance meant that anti-Semitism would leave untouched existing class and property relations in the production sphere. This simple distinction facilitated the incorporation of a romantic anticapitalist rhetoric into nationalist appeals. Here the selective nature of anticapitalist protest, rather than a blanket condemnation of modernity, must be kept in mind. Once the Nazis had identified the Jews specifically with finance, there was no reason why anti-Semitism should imply rejection of modern industry.

Reactionary modernism, especially the nazified versions of the tradition, identified the Jews with capitalism in a more all-encompassing sense than that implied by the distinction between production and circulation. It viewed the Jews as the symbol of the Enlightenment as a whole, of the rationalization of society, and of capitalism's effort to reduce life to economic categories. Modern anti-Semitism translated this cultural protest against capitalism into racial-biological categories. If the Jews were the physical embodiment of abstraction or rationalization, then their elimination would be synonymous with the victory of a cultural revolution that restored feeling and immediacy to a world threatened by soulless rationality. The Holocaust was one outcome of this cultural revolution. The idealism and élan of the SS could draw sustenance from the belief that destruction of the European Jews would eliminate the spirit of capitalism from Europe.[17]

Reification, romantic anticapitalism, fascist aesthetics, the dialectic of Enlightenment, anti-Semitism as cultural revolution – all of these notions contribute to understanding reactionary modernism, yet none addresses the question of the relationship between German society and culture and National Socialism. The ideologists I have examined drew selectively on Germany's past and then refashioned this material in light of their own interests and experiences. When Ernst and Friedrich Jünger referred to the *Blutgemeinschaft* of the First World War, they associated *Gemeinschaft* with technical advances. After the war, *Gemeinschaft* was as likely to connote images of technology unleashed amid manly camaraderie as of bucolic villages. When they heard the word *Volksgemeinschaft*, not all Germans assumed that appeals to will and blood required right-wing Luddism. Timothy Mason has rightly

---

[17] On the missionary zeal with which the Nazis pursued the war against the Jews, see Arendt, *The Origins of Totalitarianism*; Bracher, *The German Dictatorship* (New York, 1970); Norman Cohn, *Warrant for Genocide* (London, 1967); Lucy Dawidowicz, *The War Against the Jews, 1933–1945* (New York, 1975); and Postone, "Anti-Semitism and National Socialism."

pointed out that archaic-sounding rhetoric may change its meaning in different contexts. Jünger and Schmitt called themselves romantics, but insisted that they meant something quite different by this than what they criticized as the escapist doctrines of the nineteenth century. They were masculine and active, rather than effeminate and passive. Many of the reactionary modernists prided themselves on being Nietzschean advocates of the will to power and aestheticized politics, but they omitted Nietzsche's criticisms of nationalism, anti-Semitism, and idolatry of the state.

But the fact remains that however selective the reactionary modernists were toward German cultural traditions, there was very fertile soil in which their ideas could grow. From the romantics through the *völkisch* ideologues, Nietzsche, Wagner, *Lebensphilosophie*, the youth movements before World War I, and the conservative revolution afterward, Germany produced a series of thinkers who celebrated nonrational values on a scale simply not matched anywhere else in Europe. However much the terms may have changed to accommodate the industrial landscape, German *Innerlichkeit* remained a tradition hostile to liberalism, which insisted that politics was either beneath contempt or the place where souls were saved, often toyed with violence as a value in itself, and dreamed of apocalyptic visions of total community erasing a wholly degenerate age. As Mann put it, there was only one Germany and it placed its highest values in the service of evil. Although Heidegger and Mann did not agree about much of what was fundamental in the Third Reich, they both understood that Hitler had seized on an important aspect of Germany's national identity in bringing into existence a "highly technological romanticism."

Finally, we should recall that historical and sociological observers of modern Germany agree on the following peculiarities of Germany's path to modernity. Compared to England and France, industrialization in Germany was late, quick, and thorough. Economic units were large, and the intervention of the state was direct and extensive. No laissez-faire traditions gained acceptance in the propertied classes. Most important, capitalist industrialization took place without a successful bourgeois revolution. The bourgeoisie, political liberalism, and the Enlightenment remained weak. Nowhere else in Europe did rapid industrialization confront feudal structures so rapidly and harshly as in Germany. No other European society became capitalist and industrial to such an extent without a single successful bourgeois revolt or strong liberal political tradition. On the contrary, in Germany the liberal principle remained weak. Although aesthetic modernity and the cult of technics existed elsewhere in Europe and in the United

States, nowhere did modernity and tradition meet in such unmitigated confrontation as in Germany. Nowhere else did the reconciliation of romanticism and modern technology become a matter of national identity. It was this – in Lukács's term – "Prussian path" that constituted the historical and social background for the language of romanticism and then reactionary modernism and that insured that the values of the Enlightenment would remain weak in German ideology. It was the Enlightenment's weakness, not its strength, that made reactionary modernism a force of political significance in Germany, while elsewhere cults of technology similar in some respects remained the harmless preoccupations of literary intellectuals. Without a strong liberal tradition to balance the traditions of the engineers and right-wing intelligentsia, German society could not mount a successful resistance to the romantic obfuscation of the nature of technology and its relation to society that culminated in Goebbels's speeches, Todt's highways, Speer's war machine, and Hitler's final solution.

However critical the Frankfurt theorists were of developing Soviet orthodoxy, their analysis of National Socialism, even after World War II, was imprisoned in the limits of Marxist theory. Probably the most peculiar and bizarre analysis of nazism was Marcuse's view that liberalism and fascism were intertwined. He mistook the weakness of German liberalism, its failure to have effectively confronted the authoritarian forces in German society, for the essence of liberalism. Benjamin's analysis of fascist aesthetics was particularly insightful in grasping the appeal of fascism for the intellectials in France and Italy as well as in Germany. But again, Benjamin generalized a phenomenon that was most widespread and pervasive in Germany into the problem of fascism as a European phenomenon. Franz Neumann's *Behemoth* was embarrassingly wrong about the Holocaust because he could not believe that the Nazis would do something so irrational as to kill the scapegoats that allegedly held their rule together. He, too, interpreted National Socialism as a German variant of a crisis generally inherent in advanced monopoly capitalism.

But the most important work on National Socialism written by the critical theorists was the *Dialectic of Enlightenment*. Let us recall its first sentence: "The fully enlightened world radiates disaster triumphant."[18] Adorno and Horkheimer went on to argue that implicit in the beginnings of the Enlightenment, in Rousseau, Kant, and Hegel, was the synthesis of reason, domination, and myth that was revealed in all its truth in de Sade's orgies and Nietzsche's aphorisms, and then

[18] Horkheimer and Adorno, *Dialectic of Enlightenment* (New York, 1972), p. 3.

put into practice in Auschwitz. Auschwitz was the Enlightenment's truth: reason as total domination. What is striking in rereading this now-classic work is how little, if any, space is allotted to the Enlightenment as a contributor to the liberal political tradition – political pluralism, parliaments, public discussion, the defense of individual liberty against the state – and how much the book focuses on scientific reason undermining universal normative claims to the good life. The book is also striking in how little it has to say about the fate of the Enlightenment in Germany, discussing it instead as if it were a uniform development throughout Europe and America. Its authors' clear intention was to suggest that Auschwitz presented the possible fate of the modern world as a whole. Modernity in general, not only German modernity, combined myth and reason. Enchantment and disenchantment exist side by side. Auschwitz, not the proletariat, is the specter that haunts the modern world.[19]

Because they viewed modernity through the prism of Auschwitz, and because they were accustomed to laying bare the antinomies and inner tensions within bourgeois thought and society, Horkheimer and Adorno saw paradoxes the Marxists and modernization theorists missed. But they mistakenly attributed to the Enlightenment what was in fact the product of Germany's particular misery. Germany did not suffer from too much reason, too much liberalism, too much Enlightenment, but rather from not enough of any of them. De Sade's orgies and Nietzsche's aphorisms were warnings of the possibilities of rationalized domination in the absence of liberal freedoms. Horkheimer and Adorno misinterpreted modern German history so badly because they remained too loyal to a version of Marxist orthodoxy that failed to reflect enough on the weakness of liberalism in the German national context. It is ironic that two theorists so devoted to salvaging the particular and unique should have attempted to interpret National Socialism in the context of an overgeneral theory of modernity. It was not the "fully enlightened world" that radiated disaster. Hitler's Germany was never more than partly and woefully inadequately enlightened. Auschwitz remains a monument to the deficit and not the excess of reason in Hitler's Reich.

This is not to say that reactionary modernism as a set of ideas existed only in Germany. The appeal of fascism to intellectuals all over Europe after World War I included this very combination of irrationalism and technical advance. Reactionary modernism also deserves to be

---

[19] Theodor Adorno develops this point at greater length in *Negative Dialectic*, trans. E. B. Ashton (New York, 1973), pp. 361–5.

described as an aspect of cultural modernism, as Bell and Habermas have described it. Goebbels's steellike romanticism partook of the legend of the creative individual at war with the bourgeoisie. Todt's celebrations of the *Autobahnen* are both kitsch and an example of aesthetic standards replacing normative or utilitarian ones. All of the reactionary modernists were fascinated by the new. They believed technology opened up infinite opportunities for self-expression without limits. There was a disjunction of the technical and cultural realms in Germany. Like the Italian futurists, the reactionary modernists in Germany placed cultural rebellion in the service of technology.[20]

The twentieth century has witnessed a depressing number of occasions on which political leaders have done precisely what they said they were going to do, even though such actions contradicted common sense. Equally sobering is the realization that such leaders have been able to count on a supporting cast to aid them in their follies. National Socialism did not lack for opportunists without scruple, but in the end, it was the ideologues who made the difference. One reason they could remain steadfast in their actions in the last six years of the Nazi regime was that their *Weltanschauung* had offered them answers to cope with the contradictory matter of industrializing a society while denouncing reason. Whether they recalled their professors' prewar lectures on the beauty of German technology as opposed to English commercialism, the masculine community of the *Fronterlebnis*, the hope of a new national identity fusing technology and the soul, or a community freed from racial enemies, the reactionary modernists helped to prevent an end to ideology after the Nazi seizure of power in 1933.

The will did triumph over the mundane facts of international politics. In learning to speak the language of *Kultur*, will, authenticity, and the soul, the reactionary modernists contributed to the victory of totalitarian ideology over traditional power politics. Nazi ideology was by no means an unambiguous rejection of modernity.

The solutions offered by the reactionary modernists were incomparably worse than the political, economic, and social problems that gave use to them. The challenges created by the second industrial revolution were not to be mastered by philosophical speculation on technology and the soul.

---

[20] Bloch, *Erbschaft dieser Zeit* (Frankfurt, 1962); and Fest, *Hitler*, trans. Richard Winston and Clara Winston (New York, 1974).

Bibliographical essay

Bibliographical essay

PRIMARY SOURCES

The periodical literature of the conservative revolution offers much material on the right-wing cultural integration of technology. Armin Mohler's *Die konservative Revolution in Deutschland, 1918–1932*, 2d ed. (Darmstadt: Wissenschaftliche Buchgesellchaft, 1972) offers a comprehensive compilation of journals and groups. Hans Peter des Coudres's *Bibliographie der Werke Ernst Jünger* (Stuttgart: Klett, 1970) is essential.

For bibliographical sources on the political views, professional organizations, and attraction to National Socialism by German engineers see Karl-Heinz Ludwig's important study *Technik und Ingenieure im Dritten Reich* (Königstein, Ts./Düsseldorf: Athenaeum/Droste, 1979). Gert Hortleder's *Das Gesellschaftsbild des Ingenieurs: Zum politischen Verhalten der technischen Intelligenz in Deutschland (Frankfurt: Suhrkamp, 1970)* and a collection of essays by Herbert Mehrtens and Steffen Ricther, *Naturwissenschaft, Technik und NS-Ideologie: Beiträge zur Wissenschaftsgeschichte des Dritten Reiches* (Frankfurt: Suhrkamp, 1980) discuss the relation between German engineers and big industry and the ideological material of the 1940s, respectively.

SECONDARY LITERATURE

This book introduces new material while reinterpreting the problem of modernity and National Socialism. Chapters 1 and 2 contain extended discussions of the classic sociological and historical background works on National Socialism. The analysis of National Socialism as an ideological and cultural rejection of the modern world was presented in its most compelling manner in the works of Karl Dietrich Bracher (*The German Dictatorship*, trans. Jean Steinberg [New York: Praeger, 1970]), Georg Lukács (*Die Zerstörung der Vernunft* [Darmstadt: Luchterhand, 1962]), George Mosse (*The Crisis of German Ideology* [New York: Grosset and Dunlap, 1964]), Talcott Parsons ("Democracy and Social Structure in Pre-Nazi Germany," in *Essays in Sociological Theory*, rev. ed. [New York: Free Press, 1964]), Helmut Plessner (*Die verspätete Nation* [Frankfurt: Suhrkamp, 1974]), and Fritz Stern (*The Politics of Cultural Despair*

[New York: Anchor Books, 1965]), and has been recently and succinctly summarized by Henry J. Turner in "Fascism and Modernization," in *Reappraisals of Fascism* (New York: New Viewpoints, 1975).

Ralf Dahrendorf's *Society and Democracy in Germany* (New York: Doubleday [Anchor Books], 1966), Franz Neumann's *Behemoth: The Structure and Practice of National Socialism* (New York: Oxford University Press, 1944), and David Schoenbaum's *Hitler's Social Revolution* (New York: Doubleday [Anchor Books], 1967) argued that industrial society in Germany was a solvent that dissolved the power of ideology, a conclusion Barrington Moore, Jr., also drew in *The Social Origins of Dictatorship and Democracy* (Boston: Beacon Press, 1966). Neumann in particular drew out the implications of an analysis that suggests that ideology declined in significance. It was precisely against such utilitarian notions that Hannah Arendt argued in *The Origins of Totalitarianism* (Cleveland: Meridian Books, 1958).

Most of the Marxist literature on "fascism" avoids the complexities of the problem of modernity by viewing the Hitler regime as a variant of capitalism. The cultural Marxism of Ernst Bloch and the Frankfurt school was a welcome effort to stretch radical categories to their limit. Bloch's *Erbschaft dieser Zeit* (Frankfurt: Suhrkamp, 1962), and his essays on the cultural politics of conservative engineers in the Weimar Republic in *Verfremdungen* I (Frankfurt: Suhrkamp, 1962) are especially rewarding. The idea that myth and modernity were inseparable was, of course, the central notion of Max Horkheimer and Theodor Adorno's *Dialectic of Enlightenment* (New York: Herder and Herder, 1972). Horkheimer discussed the link between irrationalism and technology in "Zum Rationalismusstreit in der gegenwärtigen Philosophie," in *Kritische Theorie der Gesellschaft* (Frankfurt: Suhrkamp, 1968), and in *The Eclipse of Reason* (New York: Seabury Press, 1974). For the first and still one of the more penetrating applications of the concept of reification to right-wing views of technology in the immediate post-war years see Walter Benjamin's "Theorien des deutschen Faschismus," in *Walter Benjamin: Gesammelte Schriften*, vol. 3 (Frankfurt: Suhrkamp, 1977), pp. 238–50.

A small number of sociologists have rejected the dichotomies of tradition and modernity, or progress and reaction, and have tried to relate cultural developments to social-economic structures. Daniel Bell's *The Coming of Post-Industrial Society* (New York: Basic Books, 1973) and *The Cultural Contradictions of Capitalism* (New York: Basic Books, 1976) taken together contain abundant insights into political and economic ramifications of technical change, and the tension between modernist culture and technical rationality. Bell's discussion of the political vicissitudes of the modernist ideal of the self-infinitizing self are particularly trenchant. Anthony Giddens argues for a synthesis of analyses of meaning and of power in *Central Problems in Social Theory* (London: Heinemann, 1979); his essay "Classical Social Theory and the Origins of Modern Sociology," *American Journal of Sociology* 81 (1976), pp. 703–29 is a powerful critique of the dichotomous habits of much sociological theorizing. Jürgen Habermas also offers interesting comments on modernism and politics in "Modernity vs. Post-modernity," *New German Critique* 22 (Winter 1981), pp. 3–14, and in his essay collections *Kultur und Kritik* (Frankfurt:Suhrkamp, 1973), and *Philosophische-politische Profile* (Frankfurt: Suhrkamp, 1971). Reinhard Bendix argues against the schematic use of sociological categories in "Tradition and Modernity Reconsidered," *Comparative Studies in Society and History* 9 (1967), pp. 292–346.

The idea that the front experience of World War I served as a model of a forward-looking community suggests the importance of sociological analysis of the intelligentsia. Tocqueville and Max Weber are the starting point for analysis of intellectuals who turn to politics to save their souls. Karl Mannheim's *Ideology and Utopia*, trans. Louis Wirth and Edward Shils (New York: Harcourt, Brace, World, 1936) contains further insight into the utopian, as well as irrationalist, currents of central Europe after World War I. After World War II, revulsion with totalitarian politics of the Right and the Left once again led to sociological reflection on the intellectuals. In addition to Arendt's *Origins of Totalitarianism*, Albert Camus's *The Rebel* (New York: Random House [Vintage Books], 1956), essays by Edward Shils in *The Intellectuals, the Powers and Other Essays* (Chicago: University of Chicago Press, 1972), and Raymond Aron's *The Opium of the Intellectuals* (New York: Norton, 1962) shed light on the dangers of the search for *Gemeinschaft* and justification by history in politics.

Phillip Rieff's collection *On Intellectuals* (New York: Doubleday [Anchor Books], 1961), and George Mosse's *Germans and Jews: The Right, the Left and the Search for a "Third Force" in Pre-Nazi Germany* (New York: Fertig, 1970) shed light on the extrapolitical dimensions of politics. Paul Hollander's *Political Pilgrims* (New York: Oxford University Press, 1981) helps to revive sociological analysis of political intellectuals by combining an excellent theoretical integration of the classic analyses with telling empirical examination of American radicalism in the 1960s.

Any sociologist interested in the relation between culture and politics will benefit from reading Clifford Geertz's arguments concerning the importance of a literary sensibility for analysis of ideology in *The Interpretation of Cultures* (New York: Basic Books, 1973). J. P. Stern's *Hitler: The Führer and the People* (Berkeley: University of California Press, 1975) is an excellent analysis of Hitler's incorporation of the language of the authentic self, complementing and adding considerably to Kenneth Burke's early perceptive comments on Hitler in *The Philosophy of Literary Form* (Baton Rouge: University of Louisiana Press, 1941). George Steiner comments on the connection between culture and barbarism in *Language and Silence (New York: Oxford University Press, 1967)*, and rather more speculatively in *In Bluebeard's Castle* (New Haven, Conn.: Yale University Press, 1979).

The idea that literature preserves insights that social science neglects or forgets is given striking confirmation in Thomas Mann's understanding of the synthesis of romanticism and a cult of technology in National Socialism. Of central importance are *Doctor Faustus*, trans. H. T. Lowe-Porter (London: Martine Secker and Warburg, 1949), and his wartime essay on romanticism and National Socialism, "Deutschland und die Deutschen," in *Thomas Mann: Essays*, Band 2, *Politik*, ed. Herman Kunzke (Frankfurt: Fischer, 1977). Among general treatments of National Socialism, Joachim Fest's *Hitler*, trans. Richard Winston and Clara Winston (New York: Random House [Vintage Books], 1974) does a superb job of incorporating insights from Benjamin, Bloch, Adorno and Horkheimer, and Mann into a subtle analysis of the mixture of "Biedermeier and modernity" in the Nazi regime.

Several studies of European romanticism of the nineteenth century help to clarify the issue of the romantic dimensions of twentieth-century politics. Especially useful are Jacques Barzun's *Classic, Romantic and Modern* (Chicago: University of Chicago Press, 1934), which challenges the equation of romanticism and the Right alone, and Meyer Abrams, *Natural Supernaturalism* (New York: Norton, 1973). Alvin Gouldner's essay "Romanticism and Classicism: Deep Structures in Social Science," in *For Sociology* (Middlesex, 1973), is one of the first efforts to trace the links between romanticism in literature and debates in social theory.

The case of Georg Lukács is paradigmatic of the relation between political romanticism and the appeal of despotic visions of community on the Right and the Left after World War I. In the last decade a number of works have appeared that are most helpful for understanding the vicissitudes of cultural revolution in Central Europe. In particular see Andrew Arato and Paul Breines's study of the links between romanticism and Lukács's critique of reification in *The Young Lukacs and the Origins of Western Marxism* (New York: Seabury Press, 1979); Lee Congdon's excellent study of the link between Lukács's search for community and the appeal of despotism, *The Young Lukacs* (Chapel Hill: University of North Carolina Press, 1983), appeared too late to be adequately integrated into the present study; Ferenc Feher brilliantly reconstructs the significance of World War I as "the turning point of romantic anticapitalism" in "Am Scheideweg des romantischen Antikapitalismus: Typologie und Beitrag zu deutschen Ideologiegeschichte gelegentlich des Briefwechsels zwischen Paul Ernst und Georg Lukacs," in Agnes Heller et al.; *Die Seele und das Leben: Studien zum frühen Lukács* (Frankfurt: Suhrkamp, 1972); and Michael Lowy uses the notion of romantic anticapitalism to offer a suggestive, if slightly schematic, interpretation of cultural politics across Weimar's entire political spectrum in *Pour une Sociologie des Intellectuelles Revolutionnaires* (Paris: Presses Universitaires Française, 1976). Lukács's own *Die Zerstörung der Vernunft* (Darmstadt: Luchterhand, 1962) combines dogmatic and unfair renditions of former teachers with quite useful discussions of right-wing figures.

Debates spawned by the new Left in the 1960s concerning the similarities and differences in the view of industrial society between the far Left and far Right were another starting point. John Norr's essay, "German Social Theory and the Hidden Face of Technology," *European Journal of Sociology* XV (1974), pp. 312–36, exaggerates the Frankfurt school's indebtedness to conservative culture criticism and the fascist fascination with technology but is nevertheless a thoughtful discussion of the right-wing cult of the machine. A balanced and thorough account of antiindustrial, cultural radicalism in Weimar appears in René Konig's "Zur Soziologie der Zwanziger Jahre...," in *Die Zeit Ohne Eigenschaften: Eine Bilanz der Zwanziger Jahre*, ed. Leonard Rheinisch (Stuttgart: Kohlhammer, 1961). Claus Offe also stresses the links between Marcuse's analysis of one dimensionality and conservative cultural criticism in "Technik und Eindemensionalitat: Eine Version der Technokratie-these?" *Antworten auf Herbert Marcuse*, ed. Jürgen Habermas (Frankfurt: Suhrkamp, 1968).

Schoenbaum's *Hitler's Social Revolution* (New York: Doubleday [Anchor Books, 1966]) remains very useful as one of the first attempts to examine the tensions between National Socialism and industrial society. Charles S. Maier offers a reliable guide to the social and economic background of right-wing modernism in *Recasting Bourgeois Europe: Stabilization in France, Germany and Italy in the Decade After World War I* (Princeton, N.J.: Princeton University Press, 1975), and "Between Taylorism and Technocracy: Eurpean Ideologies and the Vision of Productivity in the 1920s," *Journal of Contemporary History* 5 (1970), pp. 27–51. Timothy Mason focuses on the appeal of the wartime experience as a community transcending class conflicts and a warning of possible future working-class revolts in his *Sozialpolitik im Dritten Reich: Arbeiterklasse und Volksgemeinschaft* (Opladen: Westdeutscher Verlag, 1978). For a suggestive analysis of the mixture of modern and antimodern themes in Nazi labor legislations see Mason's essay "Zur Entstehung des Gesetzes zur Ordnung der nationalen Arbeit, vom 20 Januar 1934: Ein Versuch über das Verhältnis 'archaischer' und 'moderner' Momente in der neuesten deutschen Geschichte," in *Industrielles System und politische Entwicklung in der Weimarer Republik*, ed. Hans Mommsen, Dieter, Petzina, and Bernd Weisbrod (Düsseldorf: Droste, 1974). Eike Hennig's *Bürgerliche Gesellschaft und Faschismus in Deutschland: Ein Forschungsbericht* (Frankfurt: Suhrkamp, 1977) offers a thorough overview of the American, British, and West German literature on "fascism" and presents criticisms of modernization theories that also raise the issue of the mixture of modern and antimodern themes in the Nazi regime. David Abraham's *The Collapse of the Weimar Republic* (Princeton, N.J.: Princeton University Press, 1981) stresses the disunity of German capitalists to account for the failure of parliamentary democracy.

There are a number of excellent general accounts of the history of Weimar politics and culture including Karl Dietrich Bracher, *Die Auflösung der Weimarer Republik: Eine Studie zum Problem des Machtverfalls in der Demokratie*, 2d ed. (Stuttgart: Athenaeum/Droste 1978); and *The German Dictatorship*, pp. 124–227; Gordon Craig, *Germany: 1866–1945* (New York: Cambridge University Press, 1980), pp. 396–568; Peter Gay, *Weimar Culture: The Outsider as Insider* (New York, 1968); and Walter Laqueur, *Weimar: A Cultural History, 1918–1933* (New York: Putnam, 1974). The best overview of the ideas of the Weimar's conservative revolution is Kurt Sontheimer's *Antidemokratisches Denken in der Weimarer Republik* (Munich: Nymphenburger Verlagsbuchhandlung, 1968). Other works placing the right-wing intellectuals in the context of Weimar politics include Bracher's *The German Dictatorship*; Gordon Craig, *Germany: 1866–1945*; Klemens von Klemperer, *Germany's New Conservatism* (Princeton, N.J.: Princeton University Press, 1957); Herman Lebovics, *Social Conservatism and the Middle Classes in Germany* (Princeton, N.J.: Princeton University Press, 1969); Laqueur's *Weimar: A Cultural History, 1918–1933* (New York: Capricorn Books, 1976), and Walter Struve, *Elites Against Democracy* (Princeton; N.J.: Princeton University Press, 1973). On National Bolshevism, see Ernst Otto von Schuddekopf *Linke Leute von Rechts: National Bolschewismus in Deutschland, 1918–1933* (Frankfurt: Ullstein, 1972), which has interesting material on the fascination of Russian authoritarianism for the German Right.

Several studies of the impact of World War I on the postwar cultural politics of the Right proved helpful. From the large literature on the conservative revolution, Karl Prumm's *Die Literatur des soldatischen Nationalismus der 20er Jahre: 1918–1933*, 2 vols. (Kronberg: Scriptor, 1974) presents the most exhaustive analysis of Junger's extensive corpus of books and essays dealing with the *Fronterlebnisse*. Also helpful on this issue are Paul Fussell's *The Great War and Modern Memory* (New York: Oxford University Press, 1975); Eric Leeds, *No Man's Land* (Cambridge: Cambridge University Press, 1979); and Robert Wohl, *The Generation of 1914* (Cambridge, Mass.: Harvard University Press, 1979). Hannah Arendt's *The Origins of Totalitarianism* and "The Revolutionary Tradition and Its Lost Treasure," in *On Revolution* (New York: Viking Press, 1965), contain insightful comments on the links between the mythic presentation of the war and the emergence of totalitarian politics.

I am skeptical of the uses of psychoanalytic interpretations of history and politics, largely because they are done without the benefit of the conversation between analyst and patient. Klaus Theweleit's psychoanalytic, feminist study of the diaries and essays of members of the Free Corps, *Männerphantasien*, 2 vols. (Frankfurt: Roter Stern Verlag, 1978–9) shares this shortcoming but creatively presents much material on the emotional dimensions of right-wing fascination with the machine.

For Ernst Jünger, Karl Prumm's aforementioned study raises the issue of *Versöhnung* or reconciliation of irrationalism and modern war very persuasively. The best study of the relation between aesthetics of the avant-garde and right-wing politics in Jünger's work is Karl-Heinz Bohrer's *Die Ästhetic des Schreckens: Die pessimistische Romantik und Ernst Jüngers Frühwerk* (Munich: Hanser, 1978). Other important works of analysis and exposition on Jünger are Christian Graf von Krockow's *Die Entscheidung: Eine Untersuchung über Ernst Jünger, Carl Schmitt, Martin Heidegger* (Stuttgart: Enke, 1958); Gerhard Loose, *Ernst Jünger: Gestalt und Werk* (Frankfurt: Klosterman, 1957); Hans-Peter Schwarz, *Die konservative Anarchist: Politik und Zeitkritik Ernst Jüngers* (Freiburg: Verlag Rombach, 1962); and J. P. Stern *Ernst Jünger: A Writer of Our Time* (Cambridge: Cambridge University Press, 1953).

On Oswald Spengler, see H. Stuart Hughes, *Oswald Spengler: A Critical Estimate* (Cambridge, Mass.: Harvard University Press, 1953) and the appropriate sections of the works by Klemperer, Mohler, and Struve. On Heidegger's views of technology and their relation to his attraction to National Socialism see the excellent study by Winfried Franzen, *Von der Existenzialontologie zur Seinsgeschichte: Eine Untersuchung über die Entwicklung der Philosophie Martin Heideggers* (Meisenheim am Glan: Verlag Anton Hain, 1975), as well as Theodor Adorno's influential critique, *The Jargon of Authenticity*, trans. Knut Tarnowski and Frederick Will (Evanston, Ill.: Northwestern University Press, 1973). George Steiner's *Heidegger* (Harmondsworth: Penguin Books, 1979) is a useful introduction. The aforementioned book by Krockow discusses the relation between subjectivity and Heidegger's political resignation, and the previously mentioned essay by John Norr comments on Heidegger's views on technology. For Carl Schmitt and Hans Freyer, one can consult the works on the Weimar Right by Bracher, Craig, Krockow, Sontheimer, and Norr. Joseph Bendersky's essay, "The Expendable *Kronjurist*: Carl Schmitt and National Socialism," *Journal of Contemporary History* 14 (1979), pp. 309–28, has recently been supplemented by a full-length study. Jerry Muller's dissertation on Hans Freyer in progress at Columbia University should help to fill the gap left by the absence of a full study of this intriguing and troubling figure.

The literature on Werner Sombart is more extensive. Wolfgang Hock's perceptive study, *Deutscher Antikapitalismus* (Frankfurt: Knapp, 1960), places Sombart's anticapitalism in the context of German nationalism and traces his links to the circle around *Die Tat*. Talcott Parson's *The Structure of Social Action* (New York: Free Press, 1968) stresses his analysis of capitalism and the entrepreneurial spirit. Arthur Mitzman's *Sociology and Estrangement* (New York: Knopf, 1973) is very good on the evolution of Sombart's anticapitalism toward the Right against the background of an unchanging commitment to a Nietzschean stress on the will. Herman Lebovics's *Social Conservatism and the Middle Classes in Germany, 1914–1933* (Princeton; N.J.: Princeton University Press, 1969) presents Sombart as one of the most articulate spokesmen of the middle class caught between capital and labor. Werner Krause's *Werner Sombarts Weg vom Kathedersozialismus zum Faschismus* (East Berlin: Akademie Verlag, 1962) stresses Sombart's contributions to National Socialism from a Marxist-Leninist viewpoint. The *Leo Baeck Yearbook* has published some excellent essays on Sombart by Toni Oelsner (1962), David Landes (1974), Paul Mendes-Flohr (1976), and Werner Mosse (1979) that document the centrality of anti-Semitism in Sombart's view of capitalist development. Julius Carlebach's excellent study, *Karl Marx and the Radical Critique of Judaism* (London: Routledge & Kegan Paul, 1978), compares Sombart's views on capitalism and the Jews to those of Max Weber and Max Horkheimer. Horkheimer's views on anti-Semitism are most fully developed in the *Dialectic of Enlightenment*, trans. John Cumming (New York: Herder & Herder, 1972), and *Autoritärer Staat* (Amsterdam: Verlag de Munter, 1967).

The best discussion of the treatment of anti-Semitism in the historical literature on National Socialism is Lucy Dawidowicz's *The Holocaust and the Historians* (Cambridge, Mass.: Harvard University Press, 1981). The issue of anti-Semitism and modernity receives extensive treatment in issues 19 to 21 of the journal *New German Critique*. In particular see the essays by Ferenc Feher, Martin Jay, Jeffrey Herf, and Anson Rabinbach, and Moishe Postone.

A number of excellent studies exist on the role of Hitler and the formation of his foreign policy. On his world view, see Eberhard Jäckel's *Hitler's World View: A Blueprint for Power*, trans. Herbert Arnold (Middletown, Conn: Wesleyan University Press, 1972), and Joachim Fest's biography. Andreas Hillgruber's *Hitler's Strategie: Politik und Kriegführung, 1940–1941* (Frankfurt: Bernard and Graefe, 1965) demonstrates the centrality of the final solution in Hitler's planning. On this also see Norman Rich, *Hitler's War Aims* (New York: Norton, 1973), and Erich Goldhagen, "Weltanschauung und Endlösung," in *Vierteljahresheft für Zeitgeschichte* (October 1976), pp. 379–405. Klaus Hildebrand's *The Foreign Policy of the Third Reich*, trans. Anthony Fothergill (Berkeley, University of California Press, 1973) is an extremely lucid discussion of the elements of continuity and discontinuity between Nazi and traditional Prussian-German foreign policy goals. Gerhard Weinberg's *The Foreign Policy of Hitler's Germany* covers the period from 1933 to 1939 and is the definitive study of the subject. See volume one, *Diplomatic Revolution in Europe: 1933–36* (Chicago: University of Chicago Press, 1970); and volume two, *Starting World War II, 1937–1939* (Chicago: University of Chicago Press, 1980).

A considerable literature on "fascist aesthetics" has developed in the last two decades, which through emphasis and sins of omission might lead the reader to think National Socialism was primarily a well-financed art exhibition. However, some works of this genre do not lose sight of the forest for the trees. The discussion of fascist aesthetics begins in the work of Walter Benjamin, which is analyzed and interpreted very effectively by Ansgar Hillach in "Die Ästhetisierung des politischen Lebens," in *Links hatte noch alles sich zu enträtseln: Walter Benjamin im Kontext*, ed. Walter Burkhardt (Frankfurt: Syndikat Verlag, 1978). George Mosse's *The Nationalization of the Masses* (New York: New American Library, 1975) and *Masses and Man* (New York: Howard Fertig, 1980) stress the role of form in the creation of national symbols. Anson Rabinbach's "The Aesthetics of Production in the Third Reich," in *International Fascism*, ed. George Mosse (Beverly Hills, Calif.: Sage, 1979), fruitfully combines reflection on Nazi aesthetics with an study of Nazi modernism in Albert Speer's Office of the Beauty of Labor. Helmut Lethens's *Neue Sachlichkeit: Studien zur Literatur des weissen Sozialismus* (Stuttgart: Metzlersche Verlagsbuchhandlung, 1970) contains much material on the right-wing cult of technology in Weimar presented as the ideological buttress of capitalism. For the relation between aesthetics and politics in Germany to that of the European avant-garde in general see Bohrer's *Die Ästhetik des Schreckens*, Ernst Nolte's now classic *Three Faces of Fascism*, trans. Leila Vennewitz (New York: Holt, Rinehart and Winston, 1966), Miriam Hansen's *Ezra Pound's frühe Poetik und Kulturkritik zwischen Aufklärung und Avantgarde* (Stuttgart: Metzlersche Verlagsbuchhandlung, 1979), and Frederick Jameson's *Fables of Aggression. Wyndham Lewis: The Fascist as Modernist* (Berkeley: University of California Press, 1979). Gillian Rose' fine study of Theodor Adorno, *The Melancholy Science* (New York: Columbia University Press, 1978), presents cogent analyses of the modernism dispute involving Lukács, Benjamin, Brecht, Adorno, and Bloch. J. P. Stern and Joachim Fest, in their respective studies of Hitler, offer insightful comments on the nineteenth-century German legacy that fostered the celebration of amoral aestheticism in twentieth-century German politics. Susan Sontag's *Under the Sign of Saturn* (New York: Random House [Vintage Books], 1981) and *On Photography* (New York: Dell [Delta], 1978) also contain material on fascist aesthetics.

Several studies of engineers and politics in other societies deserve mention. Kendall Bailes's *Technology and Society under Lenin and Stalin: Origins of the Soviet Technical Intelligentsia, 1917–1941* (Princeton; N.J.: Princeton University Press, 1978) skillfully combines ideological and institutional history. In *British Culture and the Decline of the Industrial Spirit, 1850–1980* (Cambridge: Cambridge University Press, 1981), Martin J. Wiener presents the antiindustrial views of the British political and cultural elites and argues that they have contributed to British economic decline. David Noble's *America by Design: Science, Technology and the Rise of Corporate Capitalism* (New York: Knopf, 1977) stresses the links between engineers, business, government, and the universities. Alan Silver, of the Columbia University Department of Sociology, compares national traditions of engineers in his unpublished essay, "Nations as Arenas of 'New Class' Formation: The Case of Engineers." David Landes's definitive study, *The Unbound Prometheus* (Cambridge: Cambridge University Press, 1969), documents and interprets the interaction of economic, political, social, and cultural forces as they influenced and were influenced by technological change throughout Europe during the first and second industrial revolutions.

Working on this book has deepened my skepticism about the value of philosophical speculation on "the relation between technology and society." Readers whose goal is an understanding of fashions among intellectuals can profitably consult Manfred Stanley's comprehensive *The Technological Conscience* (New York: Free Press, 1978), Otto Ulrich's *Technik und Herrschaft* (Frankfurt: Suhrkamp, 1977), a book that reflects the post-Marxist radicalism of West Germany's ecologists, and Langdon Winner's *Autonomous Technology: Technics-out-of-Control as a Theme in Political Thought* (Cambridge, Mass.: MIT Press, 1977), which covers the terrain from the story of Frankenstein to the industrial society theorists of the 1960s.

One conclusion to be drawn from this review of the scholarly literature on National Socialism and modernity is that by the mid-1980s, we have progressed forward to Thomas Mann's insights of the 1940s, a sobering reminder of the importance of historically oriented examinations of society, politics, and culture. Progress often occurs as a remembrance of past insights.

Index

Abrams, Meyer, 12n, 26n, 65n, 184n
Adorno, Theodor W.: on anti-Semitism, 130–2, 233–4; on the dialectic of enlightenment, 9, 47, 233–4; on jargon of authenticity, 13; on *Lebensphilosophie*, 26–7; on reification and technology, 230; on Oswald Spengler, 53
aestheticism, 10, 78, 103
aesthetics, 29, 30, 129, 132, 141
Americanism, 19, 35, 87, 163, 174, 206, 233
anti-Americanism, 42
anticapitalism, 9, 51, 60, 126–7, 129, 143, 150; technicians, 154
antimodernism, 5, 11, 23, 49, 130–1, 151
anti-Semitism, 9, 11, 35, 46, 130–1, 151, 189, 191, 208, 231–2
Arendt, Hannah, 23, 220
Aryan physics, 188, 202
authenticity, 12; jargon of, 224
Autobahnen, 3, 13, 201, 207

Bailes, Kendall, 223
Baudelaire, Charles, 29
Behrens, Peter, 152
Bein, Alex, 59n
Benjamin, Walter: on aesthetics and politics, 8, 92, 95, 224, 230, 233; on aesthetics and technology, 30–4; on German romanticism and idealism, 121; on *Lebensphilosophie*, 34
Benn, Gottfried, 12
Bloch, Ernst: on *Neue Sachlichkeit*, 41; on technology and engineers, 54n, 73n; on technology and romanticism, 230; on tragic consciousness, 88–9; on *Ungleichzeitigkeit*, 8, 22–3; on war as concrete utopia, 70

Bohrer, Karl-Heinz: on aesthetics and politics, 29–30; on Ernst Jünger, 10, 99
Bormann, Martin, 203
bourgeois revolution, 5, 48
Bracher, Karl Dietrich, 4n, 20
Breines, Paul, 14n
Broszat, Martin, 8n
Bruck, Moeller van den, 23, 25–6, 35, 37–8, 40, 49, 58, 80
Buber, Martin, 29
Bukharin, Nikolai, 32, 122
Burckhardt, Jacob, 125
Burke, Kenneth, 16n

capitalism, 7, 10, 35, 45, 133, 135, 140–1, 180, 225, 231
Carlebach, Julius, 9n
Catonist imagery: Barrington Moore, Jr. on, 6
Céline, Louis-Ferdinand, 77
Christianity, 39
class, 7–8
communism, 12, 225
Communist Party, 41
Communists, 20, 41
Comte, Auguste, 123
conservatism, 21, 124
conservative revolution, 3, 21, 23, 35–9, 45, 48, 59, 189, 195, 221, 231; public sphere of, 24–5; social basis of, 21–2
conservative revolutionaries, 11, 26, 29, 35, 38, 50, 70, 220, 225, 232
Coudenhove-Kalergi, R.N., 210
cultural crisis, 32, 50, 67, 166, 196
cultural pessimism, 18, 67, 120, 124, 172, 211, 221
cultural revolution, 112, 130, 194, 231
Curtius, Ernst Robert, 31n

Index

Dacque, Edgar, 176n
Dahrendorf, Ralf, x, 6–7, 220
D'Annunzio, Gabriele, 77
Darwin, Charles, 65
decisionism, 118
Dessauer, Friedrich, 170, 172, 178, 182, 192
Deutsche Technik, 200, 204–9, 221–2, 224
dialectic of enlightenment, 9–10, 47, 131
Diesel, Eugen, 163–4, 182, 185
Doblin, Alexander, 41
Drieu la Rochelle, 47
Durkheim, Emile, 33

Engelhardt, Viktor, 178
engineers, 16, 62, 146, 152, 170, 178, 201, 208, 212, 222, 226; aesthetic views of, 181; anticapitalism of, 154, 221; and cultural politicians among, 161; cultural politics of, 155, 200; cultural revolution, 215; and cultural tradition, 162, 186; and Hitler, 214; and National Socialism, 153, 177, 197–9; political and economic goals of, 155, 187, 198; as students in technical universities in 1930s, 202; views on World War I of, 159–160
England, 5, 6, 12, 15, 28, 46, 47, 50–1, 58, 144, 148
Enlightenment: antagonism in Germany toward, 3, 5, 16, 18, 24, 26, 29, 34, 38, 42, 46–8, 56, 105, 195, 222–3; dialectic of, 9, 131, 231, 234; and reactionary modernism, 224, separation from German nationalism, 10
Ernst, Paul, 39–40, 210
expressionists, 181
Eyth, Max, 159

fascism, 18, 31, 33; and capitalism, 10; Italian, 168, 233–4
fascist aesthetics, 31, 231
fascist intellectuals, 12
Feder, Gottfried: 3, 41, 186–92, 198–9, 200
Feher, Ferenc, 13, 14n, 95n
Fest, Joachim, 193
Fichte, Johann G., 122, 144
Ford, Henry, 41
Fordism, 19, 41, 150
Frankfurt School, 8, 34, 230, 233
Freikorps, 10, 24, 71
French Revolution, 1, 195, 217
Freud, Sigmund, 33, 72, 74n

Freyer, Hans: and conservative revolution, 3, 36, 42–4, 46; 204, 221; on German romanticism and idealism, 121–3; on liberalism and Marxism, 127–9; on modern technology, 127; on nationalism and technology, 125–6; on primacy of politics, 128, 204; on revolution from the right, 128; on subjective vs. objective spirit, 123; on the *Volk* and industrial society, 128
Fried, Ferdinand, 179, 207
Friedrich, Alexander, 212–3
Fronterlebnis, 15, 18, 70, 81, 104, 192, 209–10, 225, 230, 235
Fussel, Paul, 68n, 85n
Futurism, 5, 235

Geertz, Clifford, 16
Gemeinschaft, 30, 36, 71, 84, 113, 136
genocide, 7
German anticapitalism, 185
German idealism, 32, 144
German nationalism, 6, 7, 10, 14, 19, 48–9, 85, 137, 189, 208, 211, 213, 220, 227; as alternative to bourgeois society, 230
German romanticism, 9, 13–5
Geyer, Michael, 215n
Giddens, Anthony, 2n, 229n
Gide, Andre, 12
Giese, Fritz, 42
Goebbels, Joseph, 3, 12, 47, 195–7, 209, 214, 220, 226, 235
Goethe, Johann Wolfgang, 122, 144, 169
Goldhagen, Erich, 7n
Gouldner, Alvin, 13n, 116n
Gropius, Walter, 40, 181
Grun, Richard, 208, 212
Grundel, Gunther, 80
Gunther, Albrecht Erich, 92n

Habermas, Jurgen, 24n, 78n, 235
Hardensett, Heinrich, 179, 181–7; on capitalist vs. technical man, 182; on rationalization, 182
Hegel, G. W. F., 9, 33, 61, 122, 123, 144, 169, 175, 233
Heidegger, Martin, 3, 43, 108, 113, 232; and dislike for modern technology, 109; on Germany between East and West, 113–14, 168, 185; on Germany's cultural mission, 109; and National Socialism, 110–14
Heiss, Rudolf, 186, 188

246

Index

Hennig, Eike, 10
Hess, Rudolf, 199
Hildebrand, Klaus: on Hitler's ideology and foreign policy, 8n
Hillach, Ansgar, on fascism, technology and aesthetics, 8n, 32n, 55n
Hitler, Adolf, 44, 113–14, 177, 200, 207; assault on Weimar Republic, 20; and conservative elites, 214–15; and conservative revolution, 21; as cultural revolutionary, 12; 213–14, 228, 232; and foreign policy, 203; four-year plan of, 201; ideology and practice of, 7; and reactionary modernists, 46–7; on technology and the Jews, 194–5; underestimation of, 199, 229
Hitler regime, 2, 8, 107, 153, 218
Hölderlin, Friedrich, 57, 231
Holocaust, 7, 223
Holzer, Martin, 179–80
Horkheimer, Max: on anti-Semitism, 130–2; on dialectic of enlightenment, 9, 47, 233–4; on myth and rationalization 9–10, 13, 33–5; on National Socialism as a revolt of nature, 33–5, 196, 230
Hortleder, Gerd, 38n
Husserl, Edmund, 111

ideology, 1, 6, 8, 35, 161; of the will, 203
individualism, 119
industrialization, 48, 232
industrial revolution, 1, 152, 195, 217
industrial society, 6
Innerlichkeit, 2, 15, 30, 68, 222
intellectuals, 14, 20, 48, 53, 89, 113; antiintellectualism of, 28, 56, 75; and Enlightenment; right-wing, 30–1, 34, 42, 70, 152
interpretive sociology, 4
irrationalism, 1, 22, 24, 40, 46, 235
Italy, 12, 41, 46–7, 233

Jaeckel, Eberhard, on Hitler's world view, 193
"Jewish circulation," 188
"Jewish finance," 3, 41
"Jewish *Geist*" 130, 135, 137, 139, 142–3, 148–9, 151
"Jewish materialism," 22, 192
"Jewish physics," 188
Jews, 5, 11, 21; and association with capitalism and modernity, 45, 47, 50, 59, 61, 71, 132–3, 139–41, 143, 145, 149;

circulation sphere and, 9, 150, 231; collective psychology and capitalism of, 138–41; and misuse of technology, 193–4, 225; and transition from feudalism to capitalism, 136–7
Judaism, 138
Jünger, Ernst, 3, 10, 112, 115–16, 120–2, 130, 209, 221, 231–2; on aesthetics and technology, 77–80, 103, 106; and Americanism, 87; on cities and German nationalism, 85–6; and conservative revolution, 3, 42–3; and eclipse of individual, 87; and *Fronterlebnis*, 70, 81, 104; on *Gestalt* of worker-soldier, 101–2, 104, 107; on Italian fascism, 91; magical realism of, 83–5, 97; as modernist, 12, 47; 83–5; and National Socialism, 43, 46, 106; on nationalism and technology, 82, 85, 89–90; on Nietzsche, 29; nihilism of, 74, 83; on overcoming "tragic consciousness," 89; on pain, 107–8; on photography, 99–100; and reification of war and technology, 73; on romanticism, 15, 30–1, 33–6, 45, 78, 81, 89; on selectivity of antimodernism, 87; on the Soviet Union, 91; on technology and military strategy, 97; on total mobilization, 92–6, 105; on wartime *Gemeinschaft*, 24–5, 75–6; on will, 72, 77; on World War I, 68–9, 73–5, 91

Kaiser, George, 40
Kant, Immanuel, 9, 123, 169, 175, 233
Kapp, Ernst, 157, 172
Kastner, Erich: 41
Kehrl, Hans, 154n
Klages, Ludwig, 39, 58, 99, 167
König, René, 44n
Kracauer, Siegfried, 41
Krockow, Christian Graf von, 78
Kultur, 1, 35, 43, 45, 50, 54, 58, 68, 84, 87, 124–5, 130, 155, 157, 161, 172, 173, 188, 227, 235; *see also Zivilisation*
Kulturnation, 15, 29, 35, 129, 168, 221

Lagarde, Paul de, 26
Landauer, Gustav, 29
Landes, David S., 135
Langbehn, Julius, 26
Laqueur, Walter, 4n
Lebensphilosophie, 26, 29, 34, 51, 73, 165, 225, 232
Lebovics, Herman, 147n

Index

Lenin, V.I., 66, 223
Lethens, Helmut, 40n
Lewis, Wyndham, 12, 47
Ley Robert, 38n, 198, 200, 203
liberalism: attacked, 5, 21, 25, 27, 28, 35, 39, 47, 89, 119, 124, 168, 173–4, 179–80; loss of its revolutionary élan, 127; separated from technology, 87; weakness in Germany, 6
Lifton, Robert J., 100n
Lukács, George, 32, 70, 88, 89, 95, 104, 121–3, 139; on Germany's "Prussian path," 233; on irrationalism, 4; on *Lebensphilosphie*, 26n; theory of reification, 31, 34, 230

macro- vs. micro-sociology, 4
"magical realism," 83
Maier, Charles, 20, 41, 160
Malraux, André, 12
Mann, Thomas, 2, 13, 15, 23, 95, 232
Mannheim, Karl, 4, 23
Marcuse, Herbert: on aggression in industrial society, 78; on a different technology, 115n; on reification of technology, 230; on technological rationality, 34
Marinetti, Filippo Tommaso, 12, 47
Marx, Karl, 11, 33, 50, 60, 90, 123, 132, 139n
Marxism, 5, 7, 12, 27, 34, 37, 39, 45, 47, 50–1, 87, 89, 90, 123, 141, 147, 168, 174, 180
Marxism-Leninism, 223–4, 51
Marxist analysis of fascism, 22, 26
Marxists, 7, 8, 9, 23, 101, 228
Mason, Timothy, 10, 24n, 36, 231
materialism, 2, 22, 35, 72, 207
Maurras, Charles, 47
Mayer, Edward, 158
Mayer, Hans, 68n
means-ends rationality, 141
Mendes-Flohr, Paul, 136, 137n
Mittlestand, 22
Mitzman, Arthur, 134–5
modernism, 12, 47, 101
modernity, 11, 15, 25, 35, 40, 230; Germany's path to, 5–6; and National Socialism, 4–10; selective embrace of, 30, 217
modernization theory, 5, 26
Moore, Jr., Barrington, on Catonist imagery, 6
Mosse, George, 5, 37n, 125; on *völkish* ideology, 5

Mosse, Werner, 142n
Muller, Adam, 116, 123
Mussolini, Benito, 68

national Bolsheviks, 37
nationalism, 86, 89, 90, 126, 225; after World War I, 86, 89; alternative to Marxism, 90; antiindustrial themes in, 18; and conservative revolution, 179; contrast of *Kultur* and *Zivilisation* in, 35; as cultural system, 2; and modern life, 126, 225; as secular religion, 148; separated from the Enlightenment, 10; and technology, 125, 168; as third force, 12
National Socialism: appeal to Carl Schmitt, 45; appeal to engineers, 191; and capitalism, 224, 228; and conservative revolution, 21, 23, 37; vs. cultural pessimism, 211; as cultural revolution, 205–6; and dialectic of enlightenment, 9–10, 233, 229; and engineers, 153; Heidegger and, 110–15; impact of World War I on, 18; importance of Hitler to, 3; and industrial society, 6; and modernity, 4–5; as revolt of nature, 132; and romanticism, 15; self-destructiveness of, 215; *see also* Third Reich
Nazi ideology, 1, 6–8, 16, 220; and engineers, 153; persistence of after 1933, 2
Nazi propaganda, 6, 18
Nazi regime, 6, 33
nazism, 11, 13, 23, 44
Neue Sachlichkeit, 41
Neumann, Franz, 7, 16, 153, 221, 223
Niekisch, Ernst, 37, 39–40, 100
Nietzsche, Friedrich, 12, 29–30, 46, 51, 65, 80, 144, 157, 171, 232, 233
Nonnenbruch, Fritz, 208–10
Norr, John, 2n, 37n, 90n, 115
Novalis, 116, 123

Parsons, Talcott, on National Socialism, 5
pastoralism, 2
Peenemünde, 3, 214
phenomenologists, 4
Plessner, Helmut, 5, 131
political romanticism, 14, 151
positivism, 27, 46, 120, 123, 155
Postone, Moishe, on anti-Semitism and National Socialism, 11, 132, 138, 225

248

Index

Pound, Ezra, 47
primacy of politics, 16, 22, 24, 36, 179, 229
production, sphere of, 9
Protestant ethic, 138
Proudhon, Pierre Joseph, 131, 139
Prussia, 6, 51

Rabinbach, Anson, 10, 23n, 64n, 220
racial utopia, 7
Rathenau, Walter, 143, 152, 171
rationality, 28-9, 33
rationalization, 1, 5, 9-10, 33, 55, 64, 132, 138, 141, 182-3
Rauschning, Hermann, 7
Raymond, Emil du Bois, 137, 154
reactionary modernism, aesthetics of, 224; and anti-Semitism, 45, 150, 231; as a cultural system, 177; and fascism, 234; and German nationalism, 48; and German engineers, 222; as German response to modernity, 217, 233; irrationalism of, 40; and National Socialism, 215, 220; paradox of, 10; and romanticism, 30; and science, 227; and the will to power, 224
reactionary modernist ideology: as a cultural system, 226; continuities from Weimar to the Third Reich, 208
reactionary modernist tradition: aesthetics of technology in 224; after 1933, 189; and conservative revolution, 11, 21, 45, endpoint in SS, 213-14; and German engineers, 152, 154; Heidegger's relation to, 109; Hitler as practitioner of, 47; main themes of, 224-7; and Nazi propaganda, 222; persistence of after 1933, 205, 208, 214, 220; political consequences of, 215-16, 218, 223; reconciliation of technology and irrationalism in, 1, 2, 46, 224; and revolution from the right, 2, 121, 127, 129; and romanticism, 210; Sombart's contribution to, 130
reactionary modernists, 13; accomplishment of, 16, 29, 40, 46, 109, 184, 224-6; and conservative revolution, 38; distinctions between science and technology, 188; as nationalists, 2, 180, 232; work of selective tradition, 210
reification, 31, 60, 73, 122
Remarque, Erich Maria, 72
Ricardo, David, 124

romantic anticapitalism, 2, 13, 24, 139, 230-1
romanticism: and conservative revolution, 27; criticism of passive and effeminate aspects, 30, 45, 118-21; defined, 15; and German industrialization, 18; and National Socialism, 3, 230; reconciled to modern technology, 50, 78; and technical progress, 233; and völkisch ideology, 87; and World War I, 33
Rosenberg, Alfred, 189-90, 199
Rousseau, Jean-Jacques, 233
Russia, 215

Sade, Marquis de, 9, 233
Saint-Simon, 119, 123
Sartre, J.P., 131n
Sauer, Wolfgang, 43n
Schacht, Helmar, 202
Scheler, Max, 57n, 168, 182
Schelling, 116
Schenk, Julius, 159
Schiller, Friedrich, 122-3, 144
Schmitt, Carl: and conservative revolution, 3, 15, 27, 30, 42, 44-6; political romanticism of, 116, 118; and primacy of politics, 108
Schoenbaum, David, 6, 7, 191n, 220, 221, 232
Schopenhauer, Arthur, 157, 171, 175-7
Schumacher, Joachim, 55
Schwerber, Peter, 192-3
science, 5, 27, 39
scientism, 3, 14
second industrial revolution, 109, 152, 160, 188
Simmel, Georg, 61, 88, 123, 126, 134
Smith, Adam, 124
Social Democrats, 19-20, 23, 41
Sohn-Rethel, Alfred, 56
Sombart, Werner, 88; antimodernism of, 130; on capitalism and the Jews, 130, 135, 136-9, 142, 149, 151, 184, 225; compared to Max Weber, 141, 144; and conservative revolution, 3, 42, 45-6, 221; on German anticapitalism, 129, 130, 143; on Jewish psychology, 138-9, 142; on Judaism, 138; on technology and modern capitalism, 133, 145-6, 182; on transition from feudalism to capitalism, 136
Sontheimer, Kurt, 13n, 37
Sorel, Georges, 73
Soviet Marxism, 230

249

Index

Spann, Othmar, 182
Speer, Albert: 10, 153–4, 203–4, 214
Spengler, Oswald, 101, 112, 115; on circulation sphere, 150, 160; and conservative revolution, 3, 11, 23, 25, 35, 42–3, 163; on cultural pessimism and technology, 38, 80; on entrepreneurs and engineers, 62, 170; on Germany and the "third way," 37; on Jews, 60–1; *Lebensphilosophie* and, 54; on Marx, 50; and National Socialism, 46; morphological perspective of, 52; on Nietzsche, 30, 134; on overcoming cultural crisis, 84; on primacy of politics, 57; on production vs. parasitism, 55–9; and reactionary modernist tradition, 48; on technology and cultural crisis, 67; on technology and form, 53, 167–8, 226; on technology and German nationalism, 64–5, 68, 130; on techology and materialism, 66; on the will to power, 51; and work of selective tradition, 122
stählernde Romantik, 3, 47, 195–6, 220
Stalin, Joseph, 223
Stern, Fritz, 5, 26, 37n
Stern, J.P., 72n, 93n
Stortz, Wilhelm, 211
Stresemann, Gustav, 20
structuralists, 4
Struve, Walter, 49n

Die Tat, 179
Taylorism, 42, 87, 150, 183, 185
technical rationality, 1, 17
technical universities, 2, 197–8, 202
Technik und Kultur, 157, 171, 173, 175, 178, 200, 205, 208, 210, 220, 221
Technik und Wirtschaft, 156–7
technocrats, 189
technology: aesthetics of, 34, 78, 106, 188; as alternative to capitalism, 185; circulation sphere and, 150; conservative antagonism to, 34–41; "creative labor" and, 159, 165, 224; cultural crisis of, 165, 187; and culture, 2, 16, 18, 19, 67, 106, 166; debate about, 18, 48; distinguished from Americanism, 163, 180; distinguished from commercial interests, 128; distinguished from materialism, 2, 66, 168; and eclipse of individual, 87; essence of, 158, 171; fascist intellectuals and, 10, 46; Faustian nature of, 61, 67; *Geist* of, 120–1; German nationalism and, 2, 63, 168;

German soul and, 19, 47, 61–2, 65, 126–7, 173, 201, 212, 235; inherent authoritarianism of, 105; inherent metaphysics of, 120; *Innerlichkeit* and, 2, 16; irrationalist embrace of, 30, 189; and "jargon of authenticity," 76; "liberation" of, 32; military strategy and, 96; National Socialism and, 6–7, 94, 187; and productivity or productive sphere, 43, 59; rationalization and, 182; reification of, 31, 44; and sacrifice, 84; and science, 188; unleashed, 221; and use/value, 224
Theweleit, Klaus, 10, 68n, 71, 74n, 78
Third Reich, 1, 11; primacy of politics in, 161; and youth, 49; *see also* National Socialism
Todt, Fritz, 3, 199–204, 212–13, 20
Toller, Ernst, 40, 72
totalitarian ideology, 2, 17
totalitarianism, 217, 220, 228
total mobilization, 92–5, 105; *see also* Ernst Jünger
Troeltsch, Ernst, 120
Turner, Henry, J., 5

Ulrich, Otto, 44n, 122n
Ungleichzeitigkeit, 8, 22–3; *see also* Ernst Bloch
United States, 100, 185, 203, 211, 216

V1 and V2, 3, 197, 214
Veblen, Thorstein, 153
Verband Deutscher Diplom-Ingenieure (VDDI), 157, 162
Verein Deutscher Ingenieure, 156, 186, 202
Volk, 6, 35, 112, 113, 127–8, 148, 170, 205, 210, 212
völkisch antimodernism, 80, 85
völkisch ideology, 5, 15, 29, 131, 160, 201, 220, 227

Weber, Alfred, 88
Weber, Max, 4, 13–4, 27, 45, 54n, 61, 66, 88, 103, 123, 182; compared to Sombart, 144; on cultural pessimism, 120; on ethic of ultimate ends, 14, 27, 118; on interpretive sociology, 228–9; on modern capitalism, 141; on parliamentary institutions, 57; on romanticism and politics, 76
Weihe, Carl, 38n, 171–8, 182
Weimar Republic, 1, 13, 20–1, 35, 70, 129, 157, 191, 202
Wendt, Ulrich, 158

Werkbund, 152, 181
Wiener, Martin, J., 223n
Wilde, Oscar, 30
will: ideology of, 227; in technology, 13,
    46, 51, 77, 134, 216, 224, 228, 235
Williams, Raymond, on work of selective
    tradition, 28.
Winner, Langdon, 61n
Wohl, Robert, 68n
working class, 22
World War I, 13, 15, 18, 21, 51, 68,
    135, 159, 210–11, 225; as lost treasure
    of reactionary tradition, 75–6; mascu-
line *Gemeinschaft* of the trenches in,
    225; as natural catastrophe, 92; as
    turning point of romantic anticapital-
    ism, 13

Yeats, William Butler, 12

Zischka, Anton, 212–13
Zivilisation, 1, 6, 15–16, 35, 43, 45, 49–
    50, 55, 58, 60, 122, 148, 155, 161,
    172, 188
Zschimmer, Eberhard, 172, 177–8, 182